———— ⚚ Truth's Fool ————

Truth's Fool

Derek Freeman and the War over Cultural Anthropology

Peter Hempenstall

The University of Wisconsin Press

The University of Wisconsin Press
1930 Monroe Street, 3rd Floor
Madison, Wisconsin 53711-2059
uwpress.wisc.edu

3 Henrietta Street, Covent Garden
London WC2E 8LU, United Kingdom
eurospanbookstore.com

Printed in the United States of America

This book may be available in a digital edition.

Library of Congress Cataloging-in-Publication Data

Names: Hempenstall, Peter J., author.
Title: Truth's fool: Derek Freeman and the War over cultural anthropology / Peter Hempenstall.
Description: Madison, Wisconsin: The University of Wisconsin Press, [2017] | Includes bibliographical references and index.
Identifiers: LCCN 2017010440 | ISBN 9780299314507 (cloth: alk. paper)
Subjects: LCSH: Freeman, Derek. | Mead, Margaret, 1901-1978. | Anthropologists—New Zealand—Biography.
Classification: LCC GN21.F67 H46 2017 | DDC 306.092 [B]—dc23
LC record available at https://lccn.loc.gov/2017010440

For

Don Tuzin,
who shared the danger

Man is a noble animal,
splendid in ashes,
and pompous in the grave.
Sir Thomas Browne, 1605–82

Contents

List of Illustrations   ix
Preface   x

Introduction: The Freeman Show   3

Part I. A Heretical Life

1   The Man-Most-Likely-To   17
2   Preparing for a Heretical Life   27
3   Mr. Southeast Asia or Mr. Pacific?   43
4   "My Kierkegaardian Earthquake"   58
5   Remaking Himself   79
6   Face-to-Face with the Incubus   96
7   "The Trouble with Derek Is . . ."   111
8   On the Edge   131

Part II. The Mead Thing

9   A Not-So-Simple Journey   157
10   The Banquet of Consequences   172
11   Hunting Heretics   198
12   "We Are Kin to All That Lives"   226

Conclusion: Truth's Fool?   247

Contents

Notes	261
Bibliography	293
Index	309

Illustrations

Following page 142

Elsie (Did) and John Freeman with Derek and his sister, Margaret, 1920s
Mount Evans location where Freeman and two companions fell,
    January 1938
Freeman's long-standing passion for truth
Young Derek, 1939
Map of Western Samoa, with Saʻanapu on the south coast of Upolu
Freeman in Western Samoa on the horse he rode to Saʻanapu, 1941
Lauvī Vainuʻu
Off to war, 1943
Freeman and Monica waste no time getting to work among the Iban
Derek and Monica with their Iban family, 1950
Saʻanapu village center, 1967
The Freemans with Saʻanapu villagers, 1967
Freeman is remembered in Dunedin, 9 February 1983
Freeman working at home
"Me, on an outing with the Saʻanapu *ʻaumaga*"
Map of the Samoan islands, 1889
Freeman in thoughtful profile
Freeman at peace in his garden
Freeman, photographed for an article in *Good Weekend: The Sydney
    Morning Herald Magazine*, 1996

Preface

For anthropologists, as for philosophers, "what does it mean to be human?" is the fundamental question that the discipline has wrestled with for more than a century. In January 1983 Harvard University Press published a book that resonated with the deep echo of this question and sparked a controversy that became the longest-running dispute within anthropology during the twentieth century. The book was Derek Freeman's *Margaret Mead and Samoa: The Making and Unmaking of an Anthropological Myth*, and it was a refutation of Margaret Mead's little study from the 1920s, *Coming of Age in Samoa*. Mead's book had exercised a powerful, energizing influence on American social sciences and culture with its message of how the cultural environment shaped the way humans developed through the phase of adolescence. Freeman's book and his subsequent battles to defend a portrait of Samoa that was diametrically opposed to Mead's—and to argue for a more behavioral and biological approach to the study of culture—provoked tremors across anthropology, particularly in the United States, where Freeman was vilified and dismissed as a dangerous heretic.

The disruptive figure of Derek Freeman is the subject of this book. Who was this antipodean anthropologist who had such an unsettling effect on anthropologists in North America? Why did he attack the seminal work of Margaret Mead, celebrated advocate of progressive social reform and the public face of anthropology in the United States? The repudiation of Mead's arguments and the statements Freeman made in support of a new kind of anthropology that took behavior and biological drivers seriously in the evolution of human cultures threw up dangerous questions about the nature of human beings. For American scholars, Freeman seemed to invoke the threat of racial theories once more invading the social sciences.

The last two decades of the twentieth century were full of rancorous dispute that had the character of rolling warfare between Freeman and the serried ranks of American anthropologists. Freeman spent the last twenty years of his life defending his arguments, expending his energy in a vain attempt to convince his adversaries about Mead and to herald the new anthropology. Echoes of the confrontations find their way into the literature even today, and Freeman's name still has the power to arouse emotion.

Though there are several books about the Mead controversy and any number of journal and magazine articles, this is the first book by a historian to analyze the ideas, motivations, and personal and professional intentions that underlay Derek Freeman's various quests. It is part biography, part intellectual history, and partly a historian's appraisal of the controversy that swirled around Freeman's view of Mead and that consumed so much professional energy on the part of anthropologists, particularly in North America, from the 1980s into the new century.

Truth's Fool takes a biographer's perspective and the historian's tools to excavate the muddy waters of the Freeman–Mead debates. Its exploration of Derek Freeman as an individual firmly anchored in a particular disciplinary regime offers us a way to reenter the past of anthropology. By probing the interior intellectual and emotional life of Freeman, it sets out to understand what he was trying to do within a field of study that seemingly would concede little or nothing to his arguments. The book also sets Freeman's "war" with anthropology within the changing historical contexts of the discipline and sketches into place the personal and institutional forces that influenced the dynamics of the arguments between Freeman and his adversaries over a thirty-year period. *Truth's Fool* is part of what Adam Kuper, the historian of the British tradition of anthropology (Freeman's original tradition), would call the "ethnohistory" of anthropology itself, indeed of the interlocked subdisciplines of Pacific anthropology and history, of which I myself as author am a part.

I make no apology for emphasizing the book's biographical approach. For too long the motives and arguments of Freeman have been overshadowed by snap judgments about his personality in the pages of books and journals, the "truth" about Derek Freeman captured in a few essential brushstrokes, as in an impressionist still life. This is a particular irony in a discipline where the detailed observation of lives set within contexts of community, ritual, and symbolism has been the bedrock of ethnographic practice since the days of Bronisław Malinowski and Franz Boas. That Derek Freeman was a nonconformist oddity in a discipline known for strong, intellectually driven individuals cries out for the pursuit of a biographical and historical rendering in depth and detail. That is what *Truth's Fool* seeks to fulfill.

The book's title— *Truth's Fool*—comes from Freeman's frequent summation of his own persona, both as one who spoke truth to power and as the devotee of Karl Popper's philosophical approach to "truth" as the continuing elimination of error; it also plays on the negative reputation Freeman had in many anthropologists' minds. Freeman's interpretation of truth, his dogged pursuit of an objective world ruled by scientistic principles, and the debates among those who thought differently about truth in the social sciences all have a peculiar relevance for readers across many fields as we enter an era that is being dubbed "the age of post-truth," when objective facts are less influential in shaping opinion than appeals to emotion and personal belief. Derek Freeman and his war with anthropology offer us lessons as the world learns to deal with this new-old definition of its existential reality.

This book has taken an unconscionably long time to complete for reasons that will become apparent in the introduction. I have to thank the Freeman family, especially the late Monica Freeman for her patient answers to my questions and for allowing access to her husband's papers kept at home. Derek Freeman's daughters, Jennifer and Hilary, have been the soul of patience and cooperation, without interfering in any way in the manner with which I have prosecuted this project. I am wholly responsible for the portrait of their father that emerges in these pages. I hope I have treated him with dignity.

Don Tuzin invited me in to share the project. I owe him everything, for originally Derek Freeman was only going to be the subject of an essay I was preparing for another book. Since his death, Beverly, Don's wife, has been equally supportive, allowing me access to Don's papers.

Three institutions have been the bedrock of academic support. The University of Canterbury, Christchurch, New Zealand, is where I began the enterprise, and my department and the Marsden Fund of the Royal Society of New Zealand provided funds for the first stage of record gathering. Newcastle University in Australia, where I am now based since the Christchurch earthquake destroyed our home, continued the funding and infrastructural support. I thank particularly Philip Dwyer and Catherine Coleborne for their optimism and occasional goading to test my ideas. I enjoyed three summers at the University of California, San Diego, working with Don Tuzin and researching Freeman's papers, kept immaculately in the Mandeville Special Collections and tended with complete professionalism by their director, Lynda Claassen. Lynda facilitated financial support for the research and tracked down images, which Matthew Peters provided. Kathy Creely of the Melanesian Archive, an old friend from Pacific history conferences, was a stalwart of goodwill and support.

Other institutions to which I am grateful are the New Zealand National Archives, the Alexander Turnbull Library, the National Library of Australia, and the archives of the Australian National University; Maggie Shapley, archivist, reminded me why historians so value archivists and librarians by nursing me through some complicated records management.

The list of individuals to whom one owes gratitude is traditionally lengthy, especially over such a long period of incubation. Let me acknowledge the most important for this project: Russell McDougall, professor of English at the University of New England, Australia, sparked the initial interest in writing something about Freeman. Historian Doug Munro acted as a kind of pro bono research assistant and cheerleader, feeding me odd documents I did not know about, snippets of advice on biographical writing, and continual cheerful encouragement in the midst of his own research and writing. I owe him a great deal. So too the anthropologist Geoff Gray, who got me access to overseas papers I could not otherwise find. Both of them read portions of the manuscript as it wobbled its way forward. Philippa Sandall, Freeman's agent in Australia at the end of his life, let me keep a box of papers belonging to her late husband, Roger Sandall, that turned up mysteriously in a rented house in Sydney and contained some real gems from Freeman's correspondence and hard-to-get publications.

The list of people I interviewed about Freeman and anthropology and to whom I say a heartfelt thank you is contained in the bibliography. Monica Freeman and Don Tuzin were the most important, but I must mention anthropologist Penelope Schoeffel for the time she gave me and for her candor and insights. Other individuals like George Appell and Anton Ploeg supplied documents from their private papers while the late Anthony Low generously allowed me access to a section of his papers on Freeman. David Williamson, the playwright, let me badger him with questions and was graciously forthcoming. Wayne Harrison, theater director, wrote a marvelous memoir of Freeman's participation in the preparations for the play *Heretic*. Donald Denoon, first among a bevy of storytellers about Freeman, supplied a typically picaresque story. I thank everyone—individuals, families, and next of kin—who readily gave permission to quote from materials over which they hold copyright control. I have acknowledged them through proper attribution in the notes to each chapter.

Several institutions were crucial in getting the materials onto paper, and I am grateful to them for their cooperation and permission: the archives of the Australian National University, especially archivist Maggie Shapley; the National Library of Australia; the office of the deputy vice chancellor (registrar) of the University of Sydney; the National Archives and the Turnbull Library of New Zealand; the Mandeville Special Collections in the Geisel Library at the University of California, San Diego; and the Association for Social Anthropology in Oceania.

Toward the end of the writing, a group of readers helped scrutinize and critique my arguments. Peter Brandon, schoolteacher with a no-nonsense feeling for syntax and grammar, was the first. Penelope Schoeffel, Geoff Gray, Karen Nero, and Serge Tcherkézoff continued the lessons. Klaus Neumann gave the manuscript a thorough going-over, querying my arguments and improving the structure immeasurably. Ebony Hutchin brought the manuscript's punctuation into line with the University of Wisconsin Press's requirements. Finally, my wife, Jacquie Monti, did the proofreading with a more ruthless eye than mine, and our children cheered on from the sidelines with eyebrows raised every time I promised them the book was finished. I thank each and every one, including the individual anthropologists and others who appear in these pages arguing with Derek Freeman and with each other and with whom I have argued. The book would have no flesh, no substance, without their ideas and robust opinions. Of course, I accept responsibility for the representations of them I have made and for the case I have argued.

Finally, I owe a great debt of gratitude to the staff of the University of Wisconsin Press, especially to editors Gwen Walker and Sheila McMahon, to Sarah Kapp, Sheila Leary, and Anna Muenchrath for manifold acts of assistance; to my copyeditor, Mary Hill, who made my text look brighter than I ever could; and to production staff Terry Emmrich and Patrick Flynn for their faith in what the book might add to their powerful list of works on the world of ideas in anthropology. I salute their professionalism and patience in the face of my pedantic questions and for the choices they helped me make. In Scotland, Jim Henderson did a sterling job organizing the index.

 Truth's Fool

Introduction

The Freeman Show

When Derek Freeman died in Canberra, Australia, on July 6, 2001, fulsome obituaries in international dailies and Australian and New Zealand newspapers remembered him mostly for one big thing. In 1983 he demolished the book that had launched the career of Margaret Mead, America's "Mother to the World," cosmopolitan public intellectual, and confidante of presidents. Freeman's book, *Margaret Mead and Samoa: The Making and Unmaking of an Anthropological Myth*, pointedly challenged the portrayal of Samoan society that Mead had painted and her conclusions about the malleability of human nature.

Mead's little book, *Coming of Age in Samoa*, was published in 1928. Written in an engaging tone that captured both popular and professional attention, *Coming of Age* became enormously influential in American social science and educational circles. Mead painted a picture of idyllic life among the coconut groves and taro patches of the Samoan islands in the western Pacific, where, according to Mead and unlike the United States, the period of adolescence for girls especially was a time of sexual freedom and minimal discipline. This was a society and a Polynesian culture that seemed to know how life should be lived. Mead's book was aimed quite explicitly at preaching an educational lesson to Americans: phases of human and social growth were culturally conditioned, not a universal feature of human nature, and American child-rearing practices, if carefully engineered, could release the potential of each generation. Here was proof from one society to another that the right sort of upbringing, not some universal, unreconstructed human nature, was the foundation for human cultural improvement. Over the years, with a raft of authoritative works on other Pacific societies and aspects of cultural evolution, Margaret Mead became the public face and popularizer of anthropology in the United States and an international figure as a progressive social and cultural commentator.

Where Mead found a relaxed, sexually free environment for adolescents, Freeman found a tightly constrained, highly regulated sexual atmosphere for young people, with significant competitiveness and sexual violence. Mead had got Samoa entirely wrong. *Margaret Mead and Samoa* also questioned Mead's methods in gathering her evidence, and its author criticized the agenda with which she arrived in the American half of the Samoan archipelago. This agenda was, Freeman said, to test an idea her teacher and mentor, the "father" of American anthropology, Franz Boas, had proposed: Was the storm and stress associated with growing up in the West a universal feature of human nature, or was a person's experience of adolescence conditioned by the culture in which one grew up? The answer for Boas and Mead, said Freeman, lay in culture, and Freeman set about disputing what he saw as American anthropology's ideological commitment to culture as the driving impulse of human evolution.

Margaret Mead and Samoa prompted an extraordinary, highly public explosion of arguments and venom among North American anthropologists, and Derek Freeman spent the last twenty years of his life responding relentlessly to every opponent of his views. He followed up in 1999 with a sequel, *The Fateful Hoaxing of Margaret Mead*, an absorbing account of Mead's time in Samoa that, Freeman argued, showed Mead was duped into her beliefs about sexual freedom in Samoa by the jokes of her female Samoan companions.

Derek Freeman was born in 1916 in Wellington, New Zealand, where he grew up, attended university, and trained to be a teacher. In 1940 he sailed to New Zealand's colony of Western Samoa to teach at local schools. In Samoa, Freeman caught the ethnographer's bug. After war service with the navy in England and Southeast Asia, Freeman began training in London and Cambridge to be an anthropologist. He met and married an English woman, Monica Maitland, and together in 1949 they went out to do research for Derek's doctorate among the Iban, the river Dayaks of Sarawak, Borneo. After a brief stint in his homeland in a humble post at the Otago Museum in Dunedin, Freeman was invited in 1954 to join the staff of Siegfried Nadel's new Department of Anthropology at the Australian National University in Canberra, Australia. He and Monica spent the rest of their lives there.

4

Freeman was disillusioned with the anthropology of his day. In the 1960s he had turned away from his British training in the structures of social systems and become absorbed in psychology, evolutionary biology, and the study of animal behavior. Mead and Boas were, Freeman decided, the pivot around which turned an anthropology that saw culture and environment as determining every aspect of human behavior. Freeman instead promoted what he called an "interactionist paradigm" for his discipline in which anthropology's study of culture would include human nature's biologically evolved capacity for choice and the consequences of such choices for the diversity of human cultures. His 1983 book was a formal refutation of Mead's methods and conclusions about Samoan society, but it was also a prelude to this new kind of program in anthropology.

Freeman's books on Mead made him a scandal to some and a hero to others. He became a "protagonist in the longest, most acrimonious controversy in the history of cultural anthropology," a controversy that brought more public attention to anthropology than any other in the twentieth century.[1] In his attack on the early career findings of Mead, and in his passionate rejection of cultural determinism and relativism, Freeman opened fresh wounds in the century-long disagreements over nature versus nurture.

He was also a polarizing figure. The style with which he asserted his views, the vehemence of his replies to opponents, and the unyielding quality of his mission to prove Mead wrong alienated many anthropologists. Such fervor had its roots deep in his own past and personality, but his aggression also had to do with the way many anthropologists dealt with his unorthodox ideas and behavior. The profession seemed to round as one on Freeman in two decades of vituperative debate over his books and articles. Few were prepared to come to his defense.

According to his fiercest critics, especially in America, his books about Margaret Mead were driven by personal venom, and, his critics claimed, he deliberately waited till she was dead before launching his attacks. This Freeman was a crude sociobiologist in his constant bluster about "interactionism" in anthropology. To many professional believers in the ability of humans to reshape their destinies according to their environment, Freeman became a figure of loathing, an antipodean Antichrist, a dangerous heretic. The Australian playwright David Williamson added fuel to the fire in the 1990s when he wrote a play, *Heretic*, revolving around Freeman's relationship with Mead, his wife, and his hostile anthropologist colleagues. It played to packed houses in both Australia and New Zealand.

Even after Freeman's death in 2001 at the age of eighty-four, the campaign to whittle him down to size and reverse his strictures against Margaret Mead continued in journal articles and books. They were spurred on partly by the centenary of Margaret Mead's birth the same year Freeman died.

In the last decades of his life, Freeman proudly boasted he was "Truth's Fool," by which he meant that, like the medieval fool at a royal court, he had the temerity to prick the illusions of his master; he also could not help himself in his striving for the truth of any matter by attacking and eliminating error. After his death, the obituaries and memorial addresses to Freeman portrayed a man of huge intellectual power and integrity, an avid mountain climber during his youth in his native New Zealand who continued to climb new intellectual peaks into old age. But darker stories also circulated, then and for years afterward. These told of a difficult, eccentric, even incendiary character given to strange turns, notorious for his skewering of opponents during university debates or in public exchanges and in his correspondence with opponents. Derek Freeman was, it was said, a bully, a disruptive influence among his colleagues, a thorn in the side of university authorities, alienating people across a wide spectrum. He was even said to have thrown blood, or threatened to, over an Aztec image donated to the Australian National University by the Mexican government. These kinds of stories have been the object of Chinese whispers ever since in university corridors and among anthropologists from Canberra to Chicago; at conference dinners the profession passes lurid "Derek stories" back and forth, even before the drinks have arrived. Clearly, the shadow of Derek Freeman has loomed large over sections of anthropology in the years since his death.

His fame or notoriety within anthropology rests most prominently on "the Mead thing," as his former student and surrogate son, the American anthropologist Don Tuzin, dubbed it. Tuzin likened the Mead thing to a black hole into which every sensible judgment disappeared and was crushed out of reasonable recognition.[2] The Mead debates and their history are therefore at the center of *Truth's Fool*: no one, before now, has fully laid out the historical sequence of the labyrinthine twists and turns of the arguments that raged during the 1980s and 1990s and continued into the twenty-first century. This book does so.

Truth's Fool also seeks to enlarge the narrow world in which anthropologists have confined Freeman. He is known, especially to anthropologists, almost as a cartoon cutout figure whose asperities define his character. "Our whole normal intercourse is made up of conjectures about others," says a character in one of A. S. Byatt's novels. "And if misinterpreted, we drag a grotesque shadow."[3] *Truth's Fool* is a study of the whole man behind the Mead thing. It seeks to peel back the grotesqueries lurking in Derek Freeman's shadow by explaining his historical background, how his particular personality and career agendas emerged, and what personal and professional intentions underlay his Mead quest.

The series of combustible events surrounding Freeman's Mead books also throws light on the ways the anthropological fraternity dealt with one of its own. There are those anthropologists who argue that Freeman's refutation of Mead and his subsequent work contributed nothing to the field and the man is not worth a book. But anthropologists in teaching the subject to their own students use the war of text and words that has swirled around him. In the years after his 1983 book, the popular consensus was that Freeman had a point—indeed several points—about Mead's shortcomings. But that consensus seems to be shifting in recent years, perhaps as Margaret Mead's reputation is being rehabilitated. The *New World Encyclopedia*'s present online entry on Margaret Mead concentrates far more on the criticisms of Freeman's position than on a critique of Mead.[4] In light of these considerations, Freeman's defenses of himself at least deserve a decent coverage, though a tension continues to exist between the narrative arc Freeman propagated about his Mead campaign and the dominant "war stories" that anthropologists tell. The "third way" narrative of biography, events, and ideas that *Truth's Fool* represents hopefully will resolve some of that tension.

The book also argues that the Mead thing is but one frame through which to look at Freeman's impact on anthropologists. His reputation as a master ethnographer, with classic works of observation and analysis on the Iban people of Borneo, remains largely unsullied. How Freeman got to Mead through Borneo is part of a complicated trajectory and a fascinating tale. So too is the second and indispensable part of Freeman's Mead campaign: his battery of arguments about the evolution of humans as sentient beings and higher primates and the relation between their genetically predisposed behavior and the *creation* of their cultures. Freeman's refutation of Margaret Mead was originally intended as the prelude to a future of anthropological promise, as his professional colleagues would learn to absorb neuroscientists' discoveries about brain functions and their evolution and apply them to the study of behavior in culture. *Truth's Fool* explores Freeman's own journey from British social anthropology toward this vision of a new anthropology that was neither simply cultural nor biological. Along the way, it investigates how Freeman's claims (and those of his supporters) that he was onto something new were refracted through the Mead debates.

The most extreme reach of retribution against Freeman lies in the open or disguised claims after his death that Freeman was "mentally unstable" or just plain mad. "Barking mad" was how a columnist of the *Canberra Times* described Freeman.[5] One of Freeman's erstwhile collaborators turned critic, the political scientist Hiram Caton of Griffith University in Australia, even published his own diagnosis of Freeman as suffering from "narcissist personality disorder."[6]

Beyond the question, therefore, of whether Derek Freeman is a significant figure in anthropology's own history is the puzzle of who Derek Freeman was as a person. A question mark hangs over Freeman's lifelong state of mind, which this book will also probe. *Truth's Fool* does not set out to defend Freeman or his arguments, but it does proceed from the conviction that he is not to be defined simply by the cult of hostility and the regular ritual denunciations that seem to have grown around him. There is a historical personality beyond the gargoyle and a series of mental and intellectual journeys that pose important questions about the value of his ideas within anthropology and the complexity of a personality that highly intelligent people found difficult to fathom. This is a book that sets out to peer behind Freeman's international notoriety and the influence he has had on others for good or ill, to make sense of Freeman's world, and to understand how Freeman himself made sense of it. In so doing, the tale acknowledges frailties on all sides.

The structure of *Truth's Fool* reflects these manifold objectives. Part I provides what is usually missing from the literature on the Mead controversy and Freeman's role in it: a proper historical account of Freeman's intellectual life as background to and explanation for the mission that drove him. Freeman's motivations, the accusations about his state of mind, and the quality of his relationships with colleagues, friends, and enemies are all tested against the voluminous historical evidence of his professional life. Part II then zeroes in on the Mead thing, examining Freeman's attempts to draw Mead out, the volcanic shock of his book upon American media, and the blows and counterblows of the controversy both during Freeman's life and after his death. *Truth's Fool* rests on a history that traces Freeman's evolutionary climb as person and anthropologist while explaining the nature of his conflict with cultural anthropology.

My own involvement with the Derek Freeman story is curiously both logical and accidental. Moving across the Tasman Sea from Australia to New Zealand in 1998—while Freeman, though elderly, was still doing battle with anthropologists—I had become fascinated by the relationship between my old and my new country. Both were Anglo-Celtic settler societies symbiotically connected in a myriad of ways yet enduringly cynical of each other's place in the world; they were like siblings who constantly fought with each other but then united if someone bigger threatened their patch. With colleagues I launched into a project to study the nature of the cultural connections between the two societies. Designed to overcome the shallow quality of each country's knowledge about the other and to enliven historians' appreciation of the connections, the project focused on the hidden histories of engagement between the two countries.[7] And in that engagement I found Derek Freeman, the New Zealand–born anthropologist then living in Australia. He seemed a likely subject for exploring the why and the how of "Kiwi" influence upon Australian intellectual life.

Of course, I already knew about Derek Freeman. I was a historian of European colonialism in the Pacific, especially in the Samoan islands, and Derek Freeman's work dating back to the 1940s was a familiar reference. His reputation, both scholarly and personal, had penetrated wherever students of Samoa gathered. Pretending an admirable independence of spirit but really out of cowardice because of his allegedly difficult personality, I avoided conferring with Freeman about my researches into Samoan history, even during a period in the 1970s when I enjoyed a fellowship at his university in Canberra and lived for eighteen months just along the corridor from his office. I seemed to escape censure, and I pursued a career that took me occasionally to Samoa without any hint of a summons from Derek. Nevertheless, I read and used Freeman's historical studies on Samoan Christianity, as well as Margaret Mead's *Coming of Age*, and for teaching and research consumed the literature on the Mead debate from the 1980s onward, though always at a distance and without ever contacting Freeman.

In 2000 I sent Freeman a letter requesting permission to do something biographical on him as part of our trans-Tasman project. Shaming my decades of avoidance, he readily agreed, but he died before I could begin. However, his wife, Monica, generously allowed me to interview her, made available some of Derek's papers, and put me in touch with anthropologist Don Tuzin, who was in the early stages of research for a full-scale intellectual biography. Tuzin was convinced Freeman had sensible things to say to his discipline that it would not hear. He believed that, working together as anthropologist and historian, we could add necessary, rounded dimensions to an understanding of Freeman's harsh intellectualism and eccentric personality.

Tuzin's generosity in taking me on board was perhaps part of his own working out of his relationship with Derek. Chicago-born Tuzin came to be one of Freeman's students in 1969, ironically through Margaret Mead's recommendation. Tuzin wanted to study Papua New Guinea societies, and Mead, whom he met in 1968, advised him that the best place for Melanesianists was Canberra. Don arrived at the Australian National University after spending time in London, where he met the Australian anthropologist Phyllis Kaberry, who stoked his interest in the Sepik area of Papua New Guinea. He was also tutored in Arapesh language by Reo Fortune, Mead's former husband.[8] As a young student, Don was dismayed at the dismissal of Mead by his American professors. She had worked among the Mountain Arapesh and visited Tuzin in 1971 when he was in the field in the East Sepik. Mead was, on Tuzin's own admission, "like a grandmother to me."[9]

If Mead was Tuzin's "grandmother," then Derek Freeman became his surrogate father. Freeman, who loomed over others like a Polynesian chief, did not loom over Tuzin. When the six-foot-four-inch Tuzin met Freeman, they connected, two self-assured and unafraid individuals who knew how to massage authority and submission between them. Freeman became Tuzin's supervisor for his PhD, sending detailed, encouraging responses to Tuzin's fieldwork reports and books for leisure reading on mountaineering, conquering the Antarctic, and other outdoor adventures. The relationship lasted the rest of both their lives, and the two were closer than anyone but Freeman's immediate family.

Freeman had a strong influence on Tuzin's developing method and ideas, especially the vision of an anthropology informed by evolutionary genetics. But more intimately, Tuzin came to recognize a level of existential pain running through Freeman's campaigns against others and himself. He saw Freeman as a prisoner of the debates around Mead, endlessly provoking his jailers. Tuzin was also contemptuous—no, "contemptuous" is too strong a word: he was suspicious of those who thought Derek Freeman's personality was easy to capture and could be reduced to a formulaic pathology. He wanted to show people that Freeman possessed inner complexities and redemptive qualities that deserved illumination.[10]

Don Tuzin died in April 2007 at the age of sixty-one. He died from the complications of pulmonary hypertension, partly the result of scarring of his lungs after radium therapy for Hodgkin's lymphoma, a disease he developed thirty years earlier while he was a student in Australia. He spent the last of his strength, during a sabbatical year, reading Freeman's diaries and taking notes for our project. The last of the bons mots Tuzin was wont to send me was Oscar Wilde's warning: "Every great man nowadays has his disciples, and it's always Judas who writes the biography."

The theme of betrayal of one's subject is a constant among biographers writing about biography—"the dirty little secret of biography," one historian has called it.[11] But Tuzin's final aim, as is mine, was to understand how Derek Freeman understood himself—empathy, not betrayal. That is the mission of *Truth's Fool*, which I have written alone now: to do Freeman justice, but not, in the process, to gild the lily. Justice for Derek Freeman might well mean describing a very different flower altogether, something closer to the Venus flytrap.

A Note on Sources

Derek Freeman was an inveterate record keeper. He wrote down in tiny spiral notebooks everything he heard and read that warranted a response. He kept a copy of everything he wrote and of the replies to his exhaustive correspondence. There is a trace of monumentalism about this, as though his past should be memorialized in a future that must not be allowed to forget who he was. Of other people's views of him there is a mountain of evidence; of self-insight, relatively little outside a set of diaries (more on these later). His voluminous papers are kept in meticulous order in the Mandeville Special Collections of the Geisel Library at the University of California at San Diego (UCSD). Interestingly, Theodor Geisel's Dr. Seuss stories are not a thousand miles distant from the fabulistic life story of Derek Freeman. Roughly two hundred archive boxes, each holding an abundance of alphabetically ordered folders, contain the evidence of his intellectual life and interests. One must work hard to prevent the archive overwhelming the psychic reality embedded in these boxes. Freeman is in good company. I have held in my hand the solid gold Nobel Prize Medal for Physics awarded to Maria Mayer, one of only two women to be awarded the prize in that discipline. UCSD has two Nobel medals in its vaults, and the university has seven Nobel laureates to its credit or on its campus and nearby, including Francis Crick of DNA fame.

Don Tuzin was instrumental in UCSD's acquiring the Freeman papers. Some few remain in Australia. The archives of the Australian National

University (ANU) hold papers relating to Freeman's career within that institution, especially records belonging to his Department of Anthropology. It is curious, given the fame or notoriety Freeman brought to the university in the 1980s and the colorful nature of the anecdotes about him, that he gets no treatment in the 1996 official history of ANU. On the other hand, Freeman is the barely disguised elephant in the room in the published book of reminiscences about the Coombs Building, where Freeman worked.

Several interviews with him exist. Don Tuzin carried out an extensive series with Freeman twelve months before he died, talking him through the great professional crises of the past decades, which had also been personal crises for Freeman; a copy of those interviews is in the Melanesian Archive at UCSD. A more formal interview with Australian filmmaker Frank Heimans is in the collection of the National Library of Australia. I possess a copy of an interview of Freeman by Pacific historian Doug Munro in 1999. Hiram Caton, professor of politics and history at Griffith University in Australia, also carried out an interview and produced a manuscript, copies of which are held in several libraries. Each is characterized by subtle variations in light and shade, but they all provide strong evidence of Freeman's personality and his views. Of course, I also interviewed or corresponded with many of his contemporaries, colleagues, friends, and enemies so that I could hear their sides of the story.

Monica Freeman was a valuable informant before her death a decade after Derek's. Her life is integral to the story of Derek Freeman, and her diaries on their time among the Iban from 1949 to 1951 are not only a mine of information but also a prestigious addition to a scholarly field.

One set of original documents that was significant in Freeman's life I have not been able to access, which is one reason why *Truth's Fool* does not set out to be a comprehensive biography. This is the set of diaries Freeman kept for forty years starting in the 1960s, written up each day in large, stern, black notebooks. The diaries were both an aide-mémoire and Freeman's muse. Leaving aside the monumentalism already referred to, they are evidence of an extraordinary objectification and self-study of Freeman's life, day by day. The family has decided to wall off this emotional site, which is so close to their own life experiences. Although that is understandable, the pity is that Freeman's private self is therefore obscured from view, and in that shadow the determined views of others have often prevailed, or at least gained ground that is difficult to reclaim.

This impediment has been offset to some extent because Don Tuzin, as Freeman's original biographer, was allowed to read these "commonplace books," as Freeman described them.[12] When I came on board, Tuzin began preparing excerpts from them, along with his notes and views, to share with me for our joint book. These excerpts stretch from 1963 to 1990, the last year Tuzin was able to complete before he died. The family has kindly let me use these excerpts. They are not necessarily verbatim extracts from the diaries (though many are), and they contain Tuzin's summaries, insights, and sometimes his own surmises about Freeman's frame of mind and pen from the moment Freeman really began to think about his Mead quest to the beginning of his final decade of life. Tuzin makes it clear the diaries describe a life intensely lived, with considerable self-analysis, recrimination, pondering, and planning: "Derek lived his life as if he were always in the ethnographic field."[13] No mere collection of the most favorable of Freeman's thoughts, the excerpts crackle with Tuzin's wonder and frustration that Freeman could be so obtuse, stubborn, naïve, or unforgiving, but they also reveal Freeman flaying himself for repeated misadventures. Because of their secondhand quality, I have used the excerpts with a discretion the reader will have to take on trust. But I believe Tuzin has presented a representative selection designed to underpin a no-nonsense, objective appraisal of Freeman the man and anthropologist.

There is no autobiography outside the diaries, and only one rather uncritical Festschrift appreciation by George Appell and T. N. Madan was published in 1988. Freeman, however, maintained an immense circle of correspondents, not always willing or flattered participants, it is true, but among them a roll call of some eminent anthropologists and thinkers of the twentieth century—Margaret Mead, Raymond Firth, Meyer Fortes, Edmund Leach, Karl Popper, Niko Tinbergen, E. O. Wilson, and Jonas Salk, among many others. A vapor trail of stories and impressions about Freeman continues to drift across internet websites and correspondence lists. As always with a historian's project, one has to know when to stop researching and start writing.

Part I

A Heretical Life

1

The Man-Most-Likely-To

The landscape of stories about Derek Freeman shifts according to whether one is an anthropologist or not and whether one supports his views or is hostile to them. But while he was alive, Freeman made sure he himself controlled the perspectives from which his life story should be seen. A Festschrift volume of papers dedicated to Freeman that was edited by two of his students, George Appell and T. N. Madan, and published in 1988 sets out an approved version of the educational track that led Freeman to his life's missions; Freeman reinforced this foundational tale in lectures and interviews. In 1998 Freeman gave a public lecture at Victoria University in Wellington, New Zealand, that reconstructed a heroic history of his time as an activist student there during the 1930s. A year before his death, he and Don Tuzin spent a week going over his life in a series of relaxed talks at his home in Canberra. Then, eight months later and barely five months before his death, Freeman sat down with the filmmaker Frank Heimans to record an interview about his life for the National Library of Australia's oral history collection on significant Australians.[1]

In all these self-reports, one figure dominates Freeman's earliest years: his mother. Born in Western Australia in 1886, her father was an English immigrant to the gold rushes in the eastern Australian colonies and then to New Zealand. Elsie May Adair, or "Did," as she was known, was of strong, fervent Presbyterian stock; one uncle had a theology degree from Yale. The family was prominent in New Zealand's small, national life. Another uncle, George Adair, introduced the American summer camp idea to New Zealand; he was awarded an OBE by the British government.

Did was the dominant force in Freeman's early life, a cultured woman of character whose force could not but impress itself upon her eldest child. "She hadn't been to university," Freeman told Heimans, "but she would have finished up there, I'm sure, had there been a university available. She had a formidable collection of literature . . . and she was quite good at playing the piano and had a bust of Beethoven up there and used to sing Beethoven songs and so on."[2] Did told Derek she had turned down a proposal of marriage from the man who became chief justice of New Zealand. She could have been a Margaret Thatcher, Freeman believed.[3]

Instead she married a handsome barber, John Henry Freeman, who had a stylish salon in the center of Wellington. Derek was inordinately ashamed of this high-class establishment, with its padded leather chairs and massive mirrors, given over to "gentlemen's hairdressing."[4] He was even more ashamed of his father. John Henry was feckless, according to his son, "sort of the fault-free man, you know. He lived his life and he read the newspaper from beginning to end. But here was a house with a very good collection of literature in it, and he never touched it. He never looked at it."[5]

Derek, on the other hand, was let loose among his mother's books and had to perform for her friends, reciting the twenty-third psalm on request from a very early age. Did equally expected him to exploit his talents on the sports field, buying him a pair of spiked running shoes when his father refused so that he could win athletics medals. She had high hopes for Derek: she had given him back to God, and he was going to be a missionary, with the task of saving the world. Though enjoying her encouragement, Derek also felt oppressed by her constant, judgmental gaze, even as a university student. The pressure made itself felt in a lifelong interrogation of his feelings about both his parents.

The good but dominating mother and the ineffectual father: they are perhaps clichés, but they signify Freeman's lifetime struggle against domination by others. Freeman conceded in later life that Did was the force that turned him against his inoffensive father. Memories of one's youth drawn up in old age, however, are notoriously untrustworthy. The relationship with one's mother and father is an element of those unfinished dramas of childhood that are forever replayed in adult life. As we shall see, Derek spent some decades of introspection attempting to plumb the eccentricities of his personality. He had one sibling, a sister, Margaret, younger than he, who remembered the spell their mother in particular cast on their upbringing and how dramatic life within the family could be: "What a frightened little girl I was—always hating the rows there were with you and your dirty football knees! You were always so strong and argumentative. . . . You always were going to be a 'Great Man.' I am sure Mother would be so proud of you, as I am—though I was always scared as well."[6]

The Great Man's growing up to be an anthropologist is, in his telling of it, a mission fulfilled through a series of epiphanies and opportunities that the depression years of the 1930s threw in his way. Wellington, as the country's first major planned settlement for British immigrants and gradually its financial hub, became the fledgling colony's capital city. Its history was infused with the migration tracks, conquests, and stories of its indigenous Polynesian people, the Māori. They had largely retreated from the city's center but remained a living, if troubled, force in the growing population of the region and the country. Wellington, squeezed between the southern coast of the North Island and the Rimutaka and Tararua Ranges, was a compact city of 115,000 people in the 1930s. It lay in the path of the Roaring Forties, whose winds regularly buffeted the green, bushy hills surrounding its harbor. The city's center occupied a short ribbon of harbor-side land, with quirky weatherboard houses jostling up and down the forested hills behind, its university college clinging to the slopes overlooking the solemn mortar and brick buildings of government. Wellington was—and remains—prone to earthquakes, which made for regular tremors and occasional severe shakings, a not imperfect setting for John Derek Freeman.

Wellington escaped the worst of the Great Depression through the government's utilization of public relief works for the unemployed. The city and country were on the cusp of an economic boom that was symbolized at the end of the decade by the New Zealand Centennial Exhibition, which drew millions of citizens to the capital to celebrate a hundred years of nationhood. In 1934 Freeman became an undergraduate at Victoria University College, one of the four colleges of the University of New Zealand. According to his account, he spent much of the 1930s as a leading activist student within a lively student body. He studied psychology and philosophy and courses in education; if anthropology had been offered, Freeman claimed, he certainly would have taken it. He also attended Wellington Teachers' Training College during 1936–37 and gained his certificate.

In 1938 Freeman became a member of Ernest Beaglehole's graduate seminar in psychology, and it was here that the seed of an idea to become an anthropologist was sown. Freeman undertook studies in the socialization of children, convinced by and impressed with the power of cultural conditioning. Margaret Mead's study of Samoan culture was in the air, and the students in Beaglehole's classes absorbed her ideas. From 1938 on,

Freeman was very much an advocate of cultural determinism, and with the prospect of doing some anthropological field research in Polynesia, he leapt at the opportunity in 1939 to travel to the Samoan islands—Mead's old stomping ground—as a trained teacher. And so, with his rapid-fire learning of the Samoan language and certification by government examination, Derek Freeman was launched upon the Great Mission of his life.[7]

This was the approved tale. In reality his route to becoming an anthropologist was rather less destined and more fraught. At primary school he fell foul of a particular teacher, Miss Van Stavaren, who demanded feats of spelling Derek was unable to perform. Too much was expected of him, he later felt. For the rest of his life there were words he (deliberately?) misspelled. He missed getting accepted to the school of his mother's choice at age twelve. Instead, he had to go to Wellington Technical College, where he failed the proficiency tests and had to matriculate to the university via an alternative route. A small seed of self-doubt sprouted at that point. It stayed with Freeman in later life even while he was proclaiming his triumphs.

When he enrolled at Victoria University College, his father agreed to pay full-time fees for only one year; John Freeman wanted his son to join him in hairdressing, or at least to get "real" employment. Derek instead got a job on the local Wellington newspaper and went part-time to university in the evenings.[8] The college was small, with no more than seven hundred to one thousand students during the 1930s, and it suffered from the financial sacrifices forced on all educational institutions by the depression. Nonetheless, it grew stronger during the decade as young academics in psychology, history, literature, and education replaced a tiring, older professoriate. "This was the decade of the Fellow Traveller and the Popular Front, of documentary film, the proletarian novel, social realism and socialist realism, of the Left Book Club and Mass Observation," says the university's historian.[9] This was also the age of the burgeoning social sciences. Two Beagleholes were at the center of the renaissance: John as a lecturer in history, later the preeminent biographer and editor of explorer James Cook's journals; and his younger brother, Ernest, in psychology, student of Morris Ginsburg in London and Edward Sapir at Yale and a researcher alongside Peter Buck at the Bishop Museum in Hawai'i. Ernest Beaglehole eventually rose to the chair of psychology and produced anthropological studies as well.[10]

The 1930s crisis of capitalism, the rise of Fascism, socialist resistance by Communists throughout Europe, and the slide toward another world war had their bitter impacts on New Zealand, on Wellington, and on its university college. John Beaglehole would become a champion of academic freedom much criticized by university authorities, who were suspicious of academics showing left-wing, socialist, and pacifist tendencies.[11]

Derek Freeman shared the liberal disquiet about the direction world events were taking. He was drawn into vigorous activity with the student body reputed to be the most radical in New Zealand.[12] Freeman was secretary of the antiwar movement, on the committee of the left-wing Cooperative Society Bookshop, and part of a Marxist studies group (though he always rejected collectivism). He ran the Free Discussions Club, produced and acted in plays, and from 1936 helped turn out the students' annual magazine, *Spike*. He was also literary editor and then editor of the weekly students' newspaper, *Salient*, whose title he created.

"I was a firebrand at university," Freeman told Frank Heimans, even though he claimed he was a pacifist and took part in antiwar marches in the streets of Wellington.[13] His poems railed against the martial spirit building during the decade.

Nursery Rhyme

Go on playing little boys
With your leaden soldier toys
Marshal them in companies
Call some Huns and others Tommies,
Shoot them over one by one
With bullets from your tiny gun,
Put them in your Hornby train
And bomb them from your aeroplane.
Yes,
Practice youngster while you play
How to bomb and shoot and slay
And perchance
One day
You may
Become
Our
Next
Unknown Soldier.[14]

In 1937 Freeman was a prominent figure when the German consul, Dr. Walter Hellenthal, came to talk to the Free Discussions Club. After a lengthy attempt by Hellenthal to praise the accomplishments of Hitler while glossing over questions of rearmament and persecution of the Jews, Freeman challenged him about the evidence of Nazi violence. Quoting a British report that documented 447 murders committed by the Nazis, Freeman tried to press on the consul photographs of people displaying injuries from severe beatings. Hellenthal walked out, declaring himself insulted.[15]

The Spanish Civil War aroused singular passion in Freeman. He won an award for best speaker arguing against Franco's cause in a debate in July 1938. In the year of Munich and appeasement, Derek entered an oratory competition called the Plunket Medal. His speech on the great-grandson of Charles Darwin, poet John Cornford, who was killed in Spain, did not win (the judges considered it propaganda), but the student newspaper praised his "fierce harangue" in defense of the Spanish people: "There may never be a more fitting tribute to [Cornford's] memory than that, a thousand miles from Spain, another man, scarcely more than a boy, a poet and a student, should move an audience with ideals that they both shared."[16] It was an act of Freemanesque intensity, the likes of which, a generation later, anthropologists would witness with more hostility than appreciation.

Late in his life Freeman told Don Tuzin that the Spanish Civil War seemed to him the end of civilization, impelling him to "get out" of the increasingly tight social and moral atmosphere of New Zealand; he even considered journeying to Europe and joining the International Brigade. Looking back in a talk at his old university in 1998, Freeman summed up "the mood of desperation and derring-do" of the time by quoting W. H. Auden's 1937 poem "Danse Macabre." In a world gone mad, it did not seem right to Freeman to be settling down to academic work.[17]

A growing sense of disillusionment with his own country showed up prominently in his poem "(love)ution," which appeared in *Spike* in 1937:

> ONCE I would have said—
> "There is nothing of confining here
> no hemming in
> between the deliberate dissonance of walls
> naught but the full quick-flowing beauty
> of water curving round a stone."
> AND NOW "Empty—
> Empty are the ways of this land,
> As empty as a Lord Mayor's laugh.

Empty—yes and bitter
—bitter as the unvintageable sea."[18]

That same year, he took first prize in *Spike*'s literary competition with three poems that were judged "intricate and difficult."[19] He also wrote a small prose piece, "Paranoia," in which the protagonist calmly cuts off his left ear because his enemy's words grate on him—a macabre presentiment of Freeman's old-age crusade against his critics.

As if to feed his sense of alienation, Freeman literally fell off a mountain in January 1938. He was a keen mountaineer, "rampaging all over the Tararuas" and climbing several untouched peaks in the Southern Alps. He and two companions, Norman Dowling and Stan Davis, made only the second successful ascent of Mount Evans in the South Island and were on their way down roped together when they fell two hundred feet down the icy slope of a glacier. Dowling hit a jutting rock ledge and was killed, and in growing darkness Freeman had to carry Davis off the mountain, leaving Dowling's body behind.[20] Freeman's lifelong fascination with mountains was forever clouded by this youthful trauma.

In 1939 another force added to Freeman's growing desire to break away from New Zealand and the conventionalities of Wellington life. He became a disciple of the Indian divine Jiddu Krishnamurti, who preached a radical skepticism about all dogmas. According to his later accounts, Freeman, at the age of sixteen, threw over his Christian religious beliefs after reading Charles Darwin, T. H. Huxley, and the rationalist philosophers. (After long arguments, his mother followed him out of Presbyterianism, leaving Derek's father as the sole church attender.) Krishnamurti, whom Freeman took leave from his work to interview when the sage visited New Zealand, planted in the young student a seed of belief that worldly enlightenment was possible through "the primacy of the individual."[21] The truly free individual did not run with the crowd but relied on himself, living with vulnerability and psychologically apart from society to escape the conformity, the social conditioning, that was the security blanket of most social beings.[22]

Freeman had set out to debunk Krishnamurti for his student newspaper. Instead, meeting him was an epiphanal moment that produced a new element in Freeman's thinking and strengthened his questioning, though he never entered fully into Krishnamurti's mystical world. In place of Freeman's father, who appeared to show little interest in his son as an individual, the great antiguru Krishnamurti now became the figure whose influence radiated through Freeman's life story. His name and importance recur again and again throughout Freeman's Promethean struggle, beginning in his youth, to understand himself and separate that self from those around him.

At the time of his encounter with Krishnamurti, Freeman had not finished his university degree. When his parents could not, or would not, pay his fees any longer, he went to Wellington Teachers' College for two years, with a probationary period in the classroom. Freeman was older than the other students but found no trouble fitting in and rising to the top: "I ran that place too."[23] He also found he had a gift for teaching small children. One of his former pupils, Heather Morrison, who as a ten-year-old encountered Freeman at Ridgeway School in Wellington, remembered how his teaching style was different, emphasizing drama, free expression, and the making of puppets. He turned the worst class in the school into the best and pointed many students toward later learning. Morrison's memory had lingered for fifty years on the small bag of cherries that Freeman gave each child on the last day of school.[24]

Freeman kept up his literary and social activities at Victoria while he was at Teachers' College. More importantly, despite poor results in his university papers (perhaps because of the competing pressure of his teacher training), Freeman was allowed in 1938 to join Ernest Beaglehole's graduate seminar in psychology. He had studied some psychology—to level III, he claimed—under Sir Thomas Hunter, an experimental psychologist who taught courses that linked a biological understanding of humans with an appreciation of cultural formation. Both Hunter and Beaglehole were friends of Margaret Mead, and Freeman later admitted he was fed a diet of Mead during these years, imbibing a general sense of the dominance of culture as social formation. The book that introduced him to Mead was *The Making of Man: An Outline of Anthropology*, edited by V. F. Calverton. Ernest Beaglehole was also president of the Wellington Cooperative Book Society, whose committee members included Freeman and Barter Fortune, brother of Reo, Margaret Mead's second husband. Reo was in New Zealand in 1937, and Barter was a frequent correspondent with Margaret Mead. The diet of Mead that Freeman was fed may well have included conversations with Barter. At the very least, the stars were aligning for Freeman's future relationship with Mead.[25]

Also in 1938—nine months before his encounter with Krishnamurti—Freeman wrote for *Salient* an article titled "Anatomy of Mind" in which he declared that the social environment determined the aims and desires that set patterns of human behavior. Freeman in old age remembered standing on a street corner in Wellington watching the flow of humankind and wondering "what it was all about." He accepted then that culture was the driver of human behavior.[26] From Beaglehole Freeman also learned about Freud and psychoanalysis, and he carried out some psychological research on the superego in young children in several Wellington schools.[27]

All these connections and opportunities made Derek Freeman the man-most-likely-to, a talented all-rounder who could have been anything he chose. But a cloudiness of purpose, reflected in a failure to complete his degree, afflicted him. Failing to accomplish his Great Missions became a motif of Freeman's career and one of the criticisms later held against him. It suggests a blockage in his approach to life that he was never able fully to overcome. In the late 1930s, as his disillusionment with New Zealand grew, he decided to seek a way out of his surroundings. Along with Krishnamurti's encouragement to strike out as a liberated individual, a combination of circumstances propelled Freeman to undertake some form of social observation in the Pacific islands.

Ernest Beaglehole had published a paper in *American Anthropologist* in 1937, "Polynesian Anthropology Today," in which he suggested that Mead's findings for Manuʻa in American Samoa needed checking for Western Samoa, New Zealand's colony (in the expectation the west would complement the east). In 1939 he also reviewed Mead's book on the Mountain Arapesh in the *Journal of the Polynesian Society*. These articles, Freeman later remembered, added to the ferment of his studies with Beaglehole, who was promoting the islands at the same moment the New Zealand Education Department was advertising for teachers.[28]

One of Derek's tramping companions (and fellow activist at Victoria College) added to Freeman's restlessness. Wolfgang Rosenberg, a young German and a socialist who had left Germany to escape the Nazi regime, had seen the film *Moana* in Germany and hoped some day to visit Samoa. Rosenberg never did get to the islands. In old age he remembered Freeman as possessing "a great hierarchical personality—a *mana* that distanced him from people." He was single-minded rather than obsessive, said Rosenberg, and without the abrasiveness that dogs the memory of those who dealt with him professionally in later life. Both Rosenberg and Freeman fondly remembered sitting together on Mount Hector in the Tararua Range behind Wellington in 1939, with Freeman wondering whether to go to Western Samoa as a teacher. Rosenberg both encouraged him and corrected his pronunciation of *fale*.[29] Add to this Freeman's prosaic desire to escape his mother and the pressures she represented, and the pull toward the Pacific was well-nigh irresistible.

In February 1940 the New Zealand Education Department advertised for a male assistant teacher for Leifiifi school in the only large town and "capital" of the colony, Apia, to take the place of a teacher about to join the armed forces; the war in Europe and Britain's plight were beginning to drain off available staff. The conditions were not particularly inviting. A state education was not compulsory for Samoans, and pupils tended to come and go in an arbitrary fashion during a school week that comprised just sixteen hours. Class sizes were large—around seventy to each room. Teaching resources were scarce, especially materials printed in Samoan, libraries nonexistent, and the buildings and furniture in a poor state.[30] Pastor or mission schools dominated the villages, though the administration also ran village schools staffed by Samoan teachers. Leifiifi was the government school in Apia, with six hundred pupils, mainly part Samoan, part European children. Most staff were also of mixed ethnic descent, though the senior staff were New Zealanders. The salary structure was poorer than in New Zealand, and housing was not provided; a "tropical allowance" was meant to compensate.

Though he did not have a full degree, Freeman was at least a trained teacher, and he had strong support from the schools in which he had taught and good references from the education department. The inspector for schools described him as a young man with "any amount of ideas, very thoughtful and intelligent, with a great capacity for work and [he] has no difficulty in maintaining discipline."[31] Wellington-trained teachers had the reputation of being more adult and assured than the students of other colleges.[32] On 5 April Freeman was appointed assistant master at Leifiifi school.

2

Preparing for a Heretical Life

Freeman arrived in Apia on board a banana boat, the *Maui Pomare*. Western Samoa, a colony of imperial Germany from 1899, had fallen into New Zealand's hands on the outbreak of the Great War. A small naval force had forced the surrender of the German governor and his officials and proceeded to install a military regime that became a civilian administration with the issue of a League of Nations mandate in 1920. New Zealand's administration of the islands was not a happy experience during the interwar years. Under the Germans, Samoan factions had stirred up political turmoil; a resistance movement based on the island of Savai'i was put down with a mixture of threats and deportations. New Zealand's military regime experienced some economic resistance, but it was the flu pandemic of 1919 that caused major resentment. The disease carried off 20 percent of the population after a failure in the quarantine imposed by New Zealand, decimating the ranks of older, experienced chiefs. The 1920s was a period of escalating tension, culminating in a violent confrontation in Apia on 28 December 1929 between marching Samoans and New Zealand police; eleven Samoans and a New Zealand policeman died, among them Samoa's highest ranking chief, Tupua Tamasese.[1]

By the outbreak of World War II, Western Samoa was much quieter. The Samoan resistance movement, the Mau, a protonationalist movement that not all major families nor all churches supported, had been harassed into sullen, passive resistance. But the election of a less conservative, Labour Party government in New Zealand in 1935 heralded some reconciliation if not outright cooperation. All sides marked time during the war until peace returned and a new future might be constructed under different conditions.

New Zealand's administration met face-to-face not with ordinary Samoans but only with chosen individuals among the Samoan chiefly hierarchy.[2] Government and the rule of law were concentrated in Apia, located on the north coast of Upolu. White prestige and a deliberate distance from all but a few elite "natives" were taken for granted among civil servants. Samoans were still largely dispersed among their many villages, which were strung along the coasts of both Upolu and Savai'i. The greater the distance from Apia, the less were villagers touched by New Zealand's policies or by the European war.

Freeman had come to observe Samoan society, to become an "anthropologist," if his later comments are to be believed. But other than retrospective accounts of his life's work in texts and interviews and the story of his experience on that street corner in Wellington, there is precious little evidence that this is precisely what he had in mind. Freeman's was an undetermined life at this point, though anthropology, or some sense of its mysteries, had been an influence from his student days. Ernest Beaglehole and his works in psychology and ethnography were crucial factors— anthropology held the key to understanding humans and solving human problems. Perhaps the conviction was also growing in Freeman that here was a field and method of study where the kind of missionary zeal his mother and his student days had prepared in him could find some fulfillment. Anthropology matched Freeman's intensity and individualism and gave shape to an unfinished youth.

Forty years later, when Freeman became the nemesis of Margaret Mead and her North American supporters, he claimed that his war against Meadian error began in wartime Samoa. Time and again, accounts of his earlier life declare that he breathed an air saturated with claims, based on Mead's researches in Samoa, that social conditioning accounted for every expression of human culture. So taken with this concept was he, Freeman told a Wellington audience in 1998, that he had gone to Samoa with Beaglehole's encouragement "so [that] there I might investigate at first hand, the cultural determination of human behavior." By the time he left the islands in November 1943, it had become apparent to him that "Mead's depiction of Samoa was gravely defective in numerous ways, and her account of the sexual mores of the Samoans in outright error."[3]

Again, the direct evidence for Freeman's claim is sparse and was made by inference much later; it was not demonstrable in anything he did while he was in Samoa in the 1940s. There is no evidence in his correspondence or in his published papers at the time, or in his notes on Samoan village culture, of the kind of cognitive revelation Freeman himself later famously invoked to explain his sudden mental switch in direction. His realization of Mead's errors and his personal sense of disillusionment with her were in fact a more drawn out and cumulative process.

What is true is that Freeman fell immediately in love with the Samoan islands. Like Robert Louis Stevenson and Rupert Brooke before him, he found Samoa's lushness, its handsome people, and the romance of the islands' past arresting and galvanizing. This was the release he was seeking.

Freeman fitted quickly into Leifiifi, teaching primary school children up to the fifth grade. "I loved these children," he reminisced later. They called him *vae tulī*—"heron legs"—because of the thin, straight legs sticking out of his Bombay shorts.[4] He employed unusual methods, and the children responded, the boys even visiting him in the evenings to join him in making things. So good was he that the local superintendent of schools made Freeman temporary head of the teachers' training institute for four months, which occasioned protests from rivals.[5] But the relaxed teaching regime, which stretched from 8:00 a.m. till midday, afforded Freeman plenty of time to pursue his own interests. He quickly picked up Samoan (he had a gift for languages), studied it formally, and sat the government exam to prove his proficiency; it added a welcome twenty-five pounds a year to his salary and became a matter of consistent pride in his wrestling with later opponents.

With his restless curiosity, he also began archaeological explorations of caves and earth mounds that he was told about on Upolu. He took precise measurements of the Falemaunga Caves five miles inland from Malie on the north coast and researched the history of their discovery by German planters. On one occasion in 1943, Freeman took seventeen Samoans from the teachers' training school to clear the site around a large megalithic circle of stone columns, which the New Zealand collector John Macmillan Brown had in earlier days likened to Stonehenge and which Samoans believed was of godly origin. Freeman searched for grave sites, collected traditions from local chiefs, and read all the authorities he could find on Samoan myths, including Margaret Mead. He concluded that the blocks were natural and that the site's meaning for Samoans shifted through their history. His first academic pieces were a series of articles on these findings for the *Journal of the Polynesian Society*, based in New Zealand.[6] In breaking with older European opinions about these places and exploring with local people the meaning of traditions surrounding them, Freeman began his oppositional stance on things Samoan. "That was my first refutation," he told Don Tuzin. He saw it as the start of his reputation as a "heretic."[7]

The exploration of Seuao Cave in Safata on the south coast netted Freeman his first stone adze, which was still hanging in his Canberra home in 2000, sixty years later. It also led Freeman to the village of Saʻanapu.[8] This was a moment of great significance in Freeman's professional and personal life. His finding of Saʻanapu and the shape of his relationships and work there are the centerpiece of Freeman's Samoan testament, the personal narrative that underpins the seriousness of his knowledge about Samoan society in the face of unbelievers. Saʻanapu captured his heart, and, rather like Margaret Mead for the eastern Samoan islands, he did not stray from his understanding of this corner of Samoa and its culture-bearing institutions for the rest of his life.

The village lay on a small isthmus facing the sea, and to get there one had to walk or ride for more than four hours across Upolu from Apia, climbing dense, mountainous country to three thousand feet before dropping down to the south coast. Saʻanapu became the location for the remainder of Freeman's investigations of Samoan culture and the kernel of his emotional relations with the people. This is where Freeman claimed he began to see through Margaret Mead.[9] Freeman became friendly during his visits to the Seuao Cave with a senior talking chief and village mayor, Lauvī Vainuʻu. Having decided to make Saʻanapu the base for his first ethnographic observations alongside his teaching tasks, Freeman discovered that Vainuʻu regarded him as reparation for the death barely a month before of his youngest son, Faʻimoto, also known as Loani, or John. John Derek Freeman now became Loani, the adopted son of Lauvī Vainuʻu, a privileged position that granted him access to the family circle.

His good fortune increased when the assembled chiefs conferred on him the title *logona-i-taga* (heard at the tree felling), a title belonging to the *manaia* (son) of the leading chief of the lineage ʻAnapu and thus the leader of the *ʻaumaga*, the young untitled men of the village. Freeman was enabled to attend all *fono* (village councils), and, with his fluent Samoan, he was able to understand their oratory and observe at first hand the conduct of chiefs and their expectations of village behavior. Of equal if not more importance (because Freeman's exposure to "ordinary" Samoans was a bone of contention among his later detractors), he heard the stories told among the *ʻaumaga* and spent time with the *aualuma*, the group of unmarried women and widows of the local district, listening to their ribald joking.[10]

Freeman spent some five months living and working in Sa'anapu during 1942–43, maintaining his work as a teacher in Apia and visiting the area on weekends. Sa'anapu people also visited him in town, the chiefs sometimes staying as his guests. In all, Freeman had the village and its surroundings under fairly close scrutiny for nineteen months.[11] He was now living opposite the hospital in the comfortable home of an Austrian doctor, a refugee from Nazi Germany, Hans Neumann, who had traveled with Freeman from New Zealand. Neumann was an important agent of instruction to Derek with his experience of Europe and his wit and intelligence. They sailed together, played chess, and had countless long discussions about the world and ideas, becoming firm friends for life.[12]

Freeman's other serious friendship, which deepened his emotional attachment to Samoa, was with a Samoan nurse, Sisi, who treated him in the hospital after a fall from his horse. An ardent romantic affair developed, but Sisi would not allow sexual intercourse, for she informed Derek that Samoan culture required her to guard her virginity until after marriage. Characteristically, in the direct manner that became his habit, Freeman checked Sisi's explanation with other nurses. He later argued that this revelation, along with his experience in Sa'anapu of witnessing an *ifoga*, or ceremonial abasement by a titled chief (*matai*) because of the rape of a fifteen-year-old girl, and other similar incidents persuaded him that Mead had Samoan adolescent sexual behavior totally wrong.[13] This revelation is difficult to prove, but given his developing ethnographic skills, it is likely that Freeman's increasingly intense relationship with Samoan culture was moving him to ponder more closely Mead's picture of a society of uninhibited sexual relations.

His growing engagement with Samoa was partly the reason Freeman's relations with the New Zealand administration turned sour. This had nothing to do with official suspicion of interfering amateur anthropologists and everything to do with Freeman's refusal to join the local defense militia. On the eve of the Japanese entry into the war, the acting administrator in Samoa, A. C. Turnbull, argued to Wellington that Freeman should be sent home because he would not assist the war effort either by joining the local force or by volunteering for overseas service: "He is a man of peculiar ideas (and undoubtedly a pacifist)."[14] His peculiarities as an expatriate New Zealander who often spent time with "natives" did not help: "When I openly associated with Samoans I received frequent expressions of disapproval, and when I persisted, was ostracized by the ruling establishment."[15]

31

Freeman's pacifism was based on a complex mixture of feelings. Antiwar sentiments had been part of the education of the children of the Great War, Freeman's generation. John Mulgan's novel *Man Alone* gives a sweeping view of men who returned to New Zealand from another world in 1919, too tired to speak of what they had been through.[16] Wariness and disillusionment seeped down into school textbooks and journals. By the early 1930s it had become almost conventional to speak skeptically of modern warfare and its toll on lives and ideals. A religiously inspired pacifism (to which Freeman was susceptible despite giving up Presbyterianism) was undoubtedly part of the mix, but it was not the only reason to resist state pressure to march off to war again. Freeman's antimilitarism was partly driven by the kind of disenchantment manifested in the antiwar novels of the 1920s and 1930s, stiffened by his experiences at university and his absorption of Krishnamurti's views. Once war broke out in 1939, uncertainty over war aims and the terms of any postwar peace led to opposition to war in all its forms in New Zealand.[17]

The Japanese attack on Pearl Harbor, the shelling of Pago Pago in American Samoa by a submarine, and the dire implications for the defense of the South Pacific jolted Freeman. Since 1938 the New Zealand Labour government had been aware that the country would be, to all intents and purposes, on its own for an indefinite period if Japan attacked the United States or Southeast Asia and Britain were caught in a European conflict. At the Pacific Defense Conference in Wellington in April 1939, New Zealand took the lead in agreeing to defend Fiji against Japanese aggression, but it left other islands in the southwest Pacific, including Samoa, to be defended by local militia. With the Pearl Harbor attack, conscription was also extended into civilian life and industry.[18]

Western Samoa suddenly found itself transformed. From a sleepy backwater with a small local defense force and the site of an occasional fund-raiser to buy a Spitfire airplane for Britain, the islands became a staging base for the tens of thousands of American soldiers, sailors, and airmen who began arriving in March 1942. Upolu was turned into a garrison and training area. Villagers were made to move from Satapuala so an airstrip could be built. Troops were dispersed along the coastal fringe of Upolu and Savai'i; there may have been as many as thirty thousand troops during 1943–44, and segregation was impossible.[19]

Western Samoans were not asked to make the war their war, but they experienced enormously accelerated activity compared to the slow pace of interwar life. Economic prosperity extended down to the village level from the increase in laboring jobs, and there was much closer contact with Europeans, at least on the north coast of the main island. Relative fortunes were made in laundering soldiers' clothing and supplying fresh fruit and vegetables. A rush to learn English meant school classrooms were even more crowded. The Apia beachfront saw a rash of new restaurants and hamburger joints.

According to the anthropologist Bill Stanner, who paid a rushed visit to Western Samoa after the war, government reports showed "a deterioration of morals" and "a great deal of sexual promiscuity."[20] Derek Freeman in his writings says nothing about any of this for the period of war when he was moving back and forth between Apia and Sa'anapu. That absence has been held against him by his Mead opponents for reasons we shall explore later (see chapter 10).

But Freeman finally abandoned his pacifism after the Japanese attack on Pearl Harbor, enlisting the next day in the Royal New Zealand Volunteer Reserve. He took part in patrolling the islands, reaching parts of the group he had never visited. His term as a teacher was due to expire on 9 April 1943, and Freeman initially indicated he was prepared to stay for another term with the Education Department.[21] But in November 1942 while on furlough, he decided to return to New Zealand and join the navy. Freeman was a keen yachtsman and had been secretary of the local sailing club in Western Samoa. He volunteered for Scheme B, a specialist classification system for members of the Royal New Zealand Naval Volunteer Reserve who had the potential to become officers after training in Britain.[22]

The only thing we know about Freeman's return to his homeland in 1943 was his claim to Frank Heimans nearly sixty years later that he visited Ernest Beaglehole in Wellington and informed him that he thought Margaret Mead had made an error in her conclusions about Samoan society. Beaglehole "sort of just laughed."[23] If this was a declaration of hostilities on Freeman's part, then it was soft enough, and any further combativeness would have to wait, for a larger and more existential war claimed his attention for the next two years. Shortly after this meeting, in company with other new sailors, Freeman boarded a battered tramp steamer, the *Themistocles*, and sailed for England.

Like the Freeman–Mead stories that circulated decades later, Freeman's war-time escapades after he joined the navy in 1943 became the plaything of others long after the events. Among the young New Zealanders who sailed with Freeman was the future academic historian and enfant terrible of New Zealand letters, Keith Sinclair. Sinclair's published views on Freeman, who was older than the men he sailed with, present a singular figure from the beginning: "a big man, with a big voice. He was an intellectual extremist or fanatic."[24] (Freeman disputed Sinclair's description of him as a fanatic, though he conceded that he was "a heretic, yes."[25]) Donald Denoon, a later colleague of Freeman's in Canberra as professor of Pacific history, remembers Sinclair at the end of a long party, "when he and Freeman were vying for the last word," drawing Denoon aside to tell him the secret to understanding Derek:

> In 1941 Freeman was a militant pacifist in Samoa. As the war came closer, he changed his mind and became a militant militarist. In that capacity he joined the navy, where he distinguished himself by complaining about his superior officers to their superior officers. When he graduated, they took revenge by making him commander of a landing craft, with a life expectancy of seven days.
>
> And on the sixth day, the first atomic bomb was dropped, since when [concluded Sinclair triumphantly] Derek was convinced he'd been spared for a Great Purpose. Though the purposes changed, they were always Great.[26]

This is a good story retailed in turn by two master storytellers, and it has all the hallmarks of anecdotes handed down about Freeman through the years. It represents in a few lines the typical shorthand history of Freeman the eccentric, which the world around him came to embrace as though it were documented truth.

The historical reality was more prosaic, if colored by aspects of Freeman's personality. The New Zealanders sailed west to Europe via Australia, the Indian Ocean, and South Africa. In Melbourne the "intellectuals," Freeman and Sinclair, headed for Melbourne University library, Freeman to follow up translations of Samoan songs. Both were cynically unimpressed with the well-heeled students they met who claimed to be members of a political club devoted to working-class interests. After a stopover in a very hot Perth, in Western Australia, the *Themistocles* limped across the Indian Ocean to Durban, keeping well to the south to avoid Japanese submarines. They spent a month in South Africa observing at close quarters the tightening tentacles of the embryonic apartheid state. The bitter divide on racial and class lines, together with a noticeable degree of anti-Semitism, struck Sinclair and Freeman head-on. One night Freeman stole a South African flag with other sailors and slept on the flag in a gutter. This is a story in line with Freeman's reputation as an earnest student radical prepared to make a public protest. Freeman and Sinclair, with their intellectual pursuits and political commitments, were unlike most of the sailors they traveled with. Both preferred to stay sober and make local acquaintances (and observations) rather than spend their shore leaves carousing.

Once the men were in England in September 1944, their time was taken up with training in signals, weapons, officer leadership, navigation, and sailing; Freeman also played rugby. There were personality tests, for one of which the men had to write about themselves from the standpoint of a severe critic. Freeman recognized in himself the stern disciplinarian (Keith Sinclair admitted that his problem was talking too much). And once or twice the moral righteousness that Freeman had learned at his mother's knee (and that later Mead combatants found distasteful) flared up: when married men in his unit took off their wedding rings at local dances, Freeman would surreptitiously let their favored women know the men were married so the women would not be "hoodwinked."[27] But he had his own emotional memories. Samoa kept breaking into his drab British world through Sisi, who wrote often to him, always ending her letters affectionately. While drilling at HMS *Raleigh* near Plymouth in 1945, Freeman received a letter informing him that Sisi had died of yellow fever. He had a little weep.[28]

The officer trainees underwent regular interviews by boards of officers, they were tested in sea conditions, and they had to sit exams. Freeman and Sinclair stood out for their unusual verbal and literary skills but were weak at mechanical things. Nevertheless, at the end of the classes, the drilling, the training on small ships, and the induction into rigid Royal Navy protocols, Freeman placed third and Sinclair fourth, and both were commissioned as temporary sublieutenants. Many sailors fell by the wayside; only eleven of fifty Kiwis passed, four from the original draft, along with a handful of Englishmen.[29]

The war against the Axis powers was only one of Derek Freeman's campaigns while he was in England. He was also making preparations against the day when the war was over and he could think about a different kind of professional training. He was setting up networks and making contacts with scholars in the field that he had decided he wanted to enter formally: anthropology, or at least ethnographic observation of the kind his mentor, Ernest Beaglehole, had undertaken.

The trainee officers had ample leave during their courses, and London was the center of attention for people like Freeman and Sinclair, though they still had to dodge German V1 and V2 rockets when they traveled up from Plymouth. While Sinclair went off to the theater and concerts, Freeman used his time to approach Raymond Firth, himself a New Zealander and the successor to Bronisław Malinowski as professor of anthropology at the London School of Economics (LSE) within the University of London; Firth was working in signals intelligence during the war and was secretary to the Colonial Social Science Research Council, a key career enabler for the ambitious young scientist. Freeman sent Firth testimonials about his studies in both New Zealand and Samoa (and later claimed he told Firth at their first meeting of his intention one day to write a book about Margaret Mead and Samoa).[30] He hoped to be allowed to register for a PhD under Firth, which Firth encouraged, setting his sights on Freeman working back in the Pacific after the war in either the Gilbert and Ellice Islands or the Solomon Islands. Firth put the case to the higher-degree committee of his university and approached the Rehabilitation Board in New Zealand on Freeman's behalf. In May 1945, as the European war was ending, they hit a snag. The University of London regulations would not allow a student to register for a PhD who had not completed his bachelor's degree; Freeman was one unit shy. The university would not budge, despite Firth's willingness to take Freeman on, citing his ability and the research work Freeman had already carried out in Samoa.[31]

These matters were literally academic while the war against Japan ground on. After graduation as an officer, Freeman applied to Naval Intelligence and was sent to study the Japanese language in London at the School of Oriental and African Studies as a prelude to the invasion of Japan. Keith Sinclair's version of the cocky maverick who was punished after going over the heads of his superior officers—published in 1993 a decade after the first wave of assaults in the Mead campaign—is the kind of half truth that dogged Freeman during his war with anthropologists and continued after his death.[32] The Freemanesque half of what actually happened was that he became impatient at the prospect of months spent studying a new language and approached the professor of Japanese, a New Zealander, successfully persuading her that he was unsuited to the course, which she duly reported to the navy. Freeman was assigned to a far more hazardous undertaking a long way from London: as watch officer on board a landing ship tank (LST) joining the Eastern Fleet, later the British Pacific Fleet, to participate in the last stages of the advance against Japan.[33]

Freeman never reached Japan. When the atomic bomb was dropped on Hiroshima, he and his crew were in Ceylon. "Without the atomic bomb I probably wouldn't be here," Freeman told Don Tuzin, "because I had to stand up in the forecastle of the ship, you know, and give the sign when the doors were to be opened, and [I] would have been a sitting duck."[34] Instead, he and his crew were dispatched to Hong Kong and thence to Borneo to take the Japanese surrender. Japanese troops on the coasts of Brunei, Sarawak, and Dutch West Borneo were shipped into camps at Kuching. "All in all it's been a rather novel and exciting period," he told his new London mentor, Raymond Firth. "Our cargo at present consists of 200 war criminals who have been brought to Labuan for trial."[35] According to Sinclair's memoir, Freeman also accumulated an impressive collection of Japanese officers' swords. (This may have been a metaphorical allusion by the notoriously tongue-in-cheek Sinclair to Freeman's warlike encounters with anthropologists in later years.) More tellingly for his later life as anthropologist, Freeman had his first encounter with the Iban, an imperious proto-Malay people, head hunters, who lived in large family groups in riverside long houses. Long after, Freeman remembered his first sight of them: "When I was on this LST we were beached at the mouth of a river and these Iban tribesmen came swaggering on. They wear little loincloths and had long hair and spears in their hands and they walked straight into the captain's cabin, you know, as if they owned the place. I was enormously impressed by these people, the first really wild people I had seen."[36]

If meeting the Iban was a moment of recognition, its consequences were delayed some years, for Freeman was now transferred back to Dominion Forces in New Zealand. However, he was in regular correspondence with Raymond Firth, determined to devote his energies to some kind of anthropological work in the western Pacific (though, perhaps taking a page from George Orwell, who in the 1920s spent time in Burma as a policeman, he applied for a job in the Burma Frontier Service as a backup). With a PhD seemingly out of reach for the present, Freeman suggested that he study instead for the diploma in anthropology at the LSE. Freeman was prepared to expend all his limited resources and borrow money if necessary to get back to London, even if the New Zealand Rehabilitation Board was reluctant to admit New Zealand had need of trained anthropologists.[37]

Samoa was really the focus of Freeman's attention, and he was already proposing to submit his Sa'anapu research for the diploma. Convalescing in Sydney from tropical sores, Freeman took the opportunity to refresh

and enhance his historical research on the islands. He examined manuscripts on Samoan folklore and early missionary records in the Mitchell
Library and did the same when he reached the Turnbull Library in Wellington. In 1946, still technically in the navy though demobilized, Freeman
returned briefly to Western Samoa to act as research assistant for the Irish
travel writer and illustrator Robert Gibbings, who was on a sojourn through
New Zealand and Polynesia,[38] and to renew his impressions and contacts
(he had been writing to Sa'anapu villagers while in Britain during the war).
In a foretaste of the peerless orderliness of his research and his confidence
in its outcome, Freeman told Firth he was making typewritten notes on
everything "relevant to the problem of culture contact" in the Samoan
islands: "Each note is fixed in time and place, and indexed. I plan to build
up a card index covering all cross-references. I consider that when this task
is finished it will furnish an exact and detailed account of cultural changes
over the past 150 years."[39] Freeman already perceived himself as "kind of
an academic," so it was just as well the Rehabilitation Board finally agreed
to support his study overseas.[40] By 1947, now released from reserve naval
duties, he was back in London on a bursary, enrolled with Firth.

Freeman arrived in London with an immense amount of information
garnered from archives: more than two thousand pages of material on Samoa
"hitherto untouched by anthropologist and historian alike," hundreds of
pages on folklore, hundreds of suggested books to follow up, Samoan language word lists, and of course his Sa'anapu notes and drawings.[41] He even
carried one hundred typewritten pages of notes on Peruvian slave raids into
the Pacific. (These, with much else besides, he turned over in their entirety
years later to a historian colleague in Canberra, Harry Maude, so that Maude
might finish off his own life's work.)

Freeman was already displaying great self-confidence in his methods
and future achievements. He had got hold of a copy of the first grammar
and dictionary of the Samoan language, compiled by missionary George
Pratt and published in Samoa in 1862, extracting all the terms of interest to
an anthropologist and classifying them under headings. His folklore material, he told Firth, "would form the basis of several papers," while his
coming study of Samoan society "has not, to my knowledge, been before
attempted," giving perhaps the clearest sign that he had as yet no serious
knowledge of Margaret Mead's *Social Organization of Manu'a*, published in
1930. Freeman was nothing if not energetic and ambitious, collecting sources
that extended his data on historical origins, populations, and religion across
several other Polynesian islands. This was to be a fully fledged campaign in

which exhaustive ethnographic observations and historical archives would wrestle for his attention as he attempted to explain cultural change in Samoa and the evolution of Christianity in those islands. The amassing of historical documents, the learning how to take notes, and the drawing up of regiments of lists were his way of learning the arts of ethnography.

Freeman was also collecting and negotiating. Peter Buck of the Bishop Museum in Hawai'i paid him to travel to Dublin to study the Polynesian collection at Trinity College and arrange for photographs and copies of reports by Captain Cook's officers held there. He spent time in Monmouthshire classifying the Pacific papers of A. M. Hocart for transfer to the Turnbull Library in New Zealand. And he was always on the lookout for Polynesian artifacts to buy for the Otago museum, whose director was H. D. "Harry" Skinner, a student of A. C. Haddon and New Zealand's first teacher of anthropology. Skinner was a father figure to Freeman and, from Freeman's student days, an enthusiast for his leaning toward ethnography. Freeman seemed destined for a career made out of Polynesian offerings. His eager collecting eye even settled on Raymond Firth's wastepaper basket, into which Firth was throwing the detritus from Malinowski's old study. When Firth wasn't looking, Freeman found Malinowski's ivory cigarette holder, astonished that Firth would discard a thing that had been in the great man's mouth. Many years later Freeman presented it to Malinowski's biographer Michael Young.[42]

The authorized introduction to Freeman's late-life Festschrift by George Appell and T. N. Madan makes Freeman's passage through British anthropology of the 1940s appear a straightforward, busy round of courses and challenging seminars that set him up for his professional life.[43] These were certainly "heady days" in British social anthropology as Freeman, looking back at the end of his life, saw them. But they were far from settled days. Nor was anthropology guaranteed a prosperous future as a discipline. While Derek was struggling to find his identity in 1930s New Zealand, British social anthropology was endeavoring to fashion an academic identity for itself and gain an institutional presence in British universities. These "new theoreticians of social form and function" were not yet themselves fully formed. The war had interfered with research and career opportunities, and a fierce rivalry over patronage, funding, and intellectual approaches underpinned the relationship between the dynamic LSE, with Malinowski its talismanic spearhead, and the more genteel, conservative atmosphere of Oxford under Alfred Radcliffe-Brown.[44] Freeman was part of the bulge that occurred in British social anthropology after the war and was drawn to the LSE because of his compatriot, Raymond Firth, Malinowski's successor, and the research-led postgraduate teaching they established there. Intellectual currents flowed differently through each institution, muddied by the distinct administrative arrangements and possibilities in the two universities. But the LSE was perfectly suited to an outsider like Freeman, as it was to Malinowski and to the philosopher Karl Popper, Freeman's hero of the future.

Freeman spoke to Frank Heimans in the last year of his life as though he had already been aware of the great differences of approach and style between London and Oxford and had been able to negotiate his way quietly through the contention. Whether he had really been able to do so during this period of inchoate growth is highly uncertain. But he was already showing signs of a radical individualism, *pace* Krishnamurti, beholden to no dogma and free of the colonial cringing that prompted many of his fellow antipodeans to flee to the mother city of the empire. Freeman was animated more by the sentiment his mother inscribed in a copy of mountaineer Eric Shipton's book *Upon That Mountain*, given to him in 1944: "Our own souls must become our disciplined ally."[45]

Perhaps Freeman's first inkling of the dissonances in the discipline came from a seminar he gave in Oxford during 1947. It has become part of his story about himself as anthropologist arrivé, repeated at strategic points throughout his life.[46] "Exceedingly brilliant" was how Meyer Fortes, according to Freeman, described the paper, which was on Samoan social structure. When Freeman presented the paper again the next day in London, Firth described it disgustedly as "pretentious" and "nonsense," "structure *ad nauseam.*" A fellow graduate student, Maurice Freedman, dismissed it as "mere phantasy." Freeman's later opponent Paul Shankman presents this opposition to the paper alongside a typically secondhand story about Freeman, hollow-eyed and unshaven, missing for days and finally found in the bowels of a library, poring over the back copies of an anthropology journal.[47] Both "incidents" are designed to render for the reader a picture of weirdness and intensity in Freeman, already at odds with the establishment in British social anthropology, a puzzle to his contemporaries and a sign of things to come.

There is no doubt Freeman was upset with the London anthropologists' reaction to his paper, at their impatience with his endeavor to show that the Samoans had clearly formulated notions about their own social structure; he said as much to Fortes, whom he wrote to, thanking him for his support.[48] Freeman's supervisor, Raymond Firth, was not known for highly theoretical works; he was more interested in the description of social behavior by anthropologists, its "narrative coherence" as part of a humane literature—the genre that had grown out of Malinowski's practice.[49] Freeman was more drawn to the Oxford anthropologists and their formal studies of social structure, especially kinship, which fitted with his growing scientistic tendencies. Ernest Beaglehole had been advising him to hitch his wagon to whichever star would advance his career; Beaglehole imagined that star was Firth and London and a career oriented to Polynesia.[50] But it was Fortes whose star was on the rise; he would soon move to Cambridge as a professor. Meyer Fortes was a South African who had come to England to do a PhD in psychology, but he joined a formidable trio with system-structural interests in Oxford: Radcliffe-Brown, Max Gluckman, and E. E. Evans-Pritchard. Freeman began meeting Fortes for "secret" tutorials in London. He also defied Firth by taking extra courses in areas Firth disapproved of—physical and early biological anthropology under Nigel Barnicott, archaeology with V. Gordon Childe: "I tramped through the snow to the Institute of Archaeology in Regent's Park. I was so keen."[51] And he was learning from Siegfried Nadel, the Austrian who trained under psychologist Karl Bühler in Vienna and was an enthusiastic advocate of psychology in studies of human society.

Some forty years later, Freeman implied that the seed of his disillusionment with the theoretical schools in which he was trained was planted in his disagreements with Firth and the clashes over his seminar paper.[52] But he was embedded within a web of interlocked patronage systems, with their competing ideologies, that as a young, aspiring anthropologist he could not sidestep, no matter how mature he was in years. He told Anna Freud as much in a letter in 1962: "It is difficult to transcend the orthodoxy of an academic discipline, particularly when it is also the orthodoxy of one's teachers and examiners."[53] He may have had his uncertainties, inspired by his stubborn individualism, his living among Samoans, and the contradictions between the theories of culture he learned in New Zealand and the conditions he experienced in Sa'anapu. But for now the key acts in his professional development—and his movement toward a new paradigm for anthropological thinking—lay in exposure to the "mandarins" of Malinowski's LSE, Firth, Fortes, and Nadel and the wide diversity of ideas and disciplines he was enabled to explore in that still-developing intellectual environment.[54]

First he had to submit his diploma thesis, which he did in June 1947. "The Social Structure of a Samoan Village Community" was examined successfully by Max Gluckman, and the diploma was awarded in 1948. The work is a structural analysis of Sa'anapu's village formation, its social groupings, and its leadership. Lists, tables, and charts covering demographic information, age categories of title holders, and lines of succession underpin the study, parts of which read like a protoquantitative survey of aspects of Sa'anapu daily life. The data attest to the disciplined collection of materials that Freeman accrued during his wartime stay in the islands and to the precise measurement of social phenomena that became his "calling card," according to one anthropologist.[55] But the thesis is much more than a dry, abstract study within the conventional frame of the day. There is none of the later self-reflectiveness of the ethnographer musing upon his positioning in the process, yet Freeman showed himself to be a fine, even romantic storyteller, and the work brims with life and color. People are at its heart, chiefs especially. Freeman lucidly recounts stories about individual title holders within lineages—the *matai*—and describes their encounters with neighbors, controversies among villagers, and the deceptions they practiced. His admiration for their culture is clear. In an irony neither Freeman nor any of his later enemies seemed to notice, his opening chapter has a Margaret Mead–like quality in its description of the Samoan landscape and Sa'anapu village resting on its tiny tongue of land beside the sea, dominated by the tides. Freeman's own line drawings enliven the text.[56]

Yet there is no engagement with Mead's Samoan work, a fact his enemies would use against him in the future. If any tone of dispute is evident, it lies in Freeman's strike against the Radcliffe-Brownian argument that social structure was an abstraction, given flesh as a structural explanation by the anthropologist's observations in the field. Freeman was convinced that Samoans themselves were perfectly clear about the living nature of their social structure, which was demonstrated in every village council meeting and the disciplined rigor of the *fa'alupega*—the recitation of honorific phrases connected to each lineage of note, rooted in that lineage's history and precedence within the village. His small thesis showed that Samoan society, exemplified in Sa'anapu, operated as a dynamic matrix of relationships in which chiefs played the leading roles but that extended to embrace all person-to-person relationships. Freeman's ability to harness history to anthropological description, crudely realized though it was at this stage in his career, foreshadowed later jousts over the historical accuracy of others' portrayals of Samoan society and enabled him to produce his final book, a persuasive historical study of Mead's time in Samoa of the 1920s.[57]

3

Mr. Southeast Asia or
Mr. Pacific?

In the master story of Derek Freeman's life and career, the phase of his life after finishing his studies in London is a curiously understated interlude. Yet this next phase made Freeman into a consummate ethnographer. This transformation came by way of fieldwork among the Iban of Borneo, the production of seminal reports about their culture and developmental needs, and the levering of this masterful knowledge into a doctorate at Cambridge. Freeman became the foremost expert on the Iban, an indispensable guide to swidden agriculture in Southeast Asia, and "a paradigm for those working in Borneo and elsewhere."[1]

Freeman also saw his Iban phase as being part of that "slow fuse" that burned off his roots in the structural and functional anthropology of his mentors, Raymond Firth and Meyer Fortes. It exploded in his mind the enterprise of a new genetically based and evolution-centered approach to human behavior and culture. "I would have become Mr. Southeast Asia, and I would have just been an ordinary social anthropologist," was Freeman's guileless reflection on his life if he had remained the great expert on the Iban.[2]

Freeman came among the Iban courtesy of that network of patronage rapidly coalescing in British postwar anthropology. The Colonial Social Science Research Council (CSSRC) was an outgrowth of the Colonial Office's concern with the trajectory of development in the postwar empire. The grants for research into a multitude of land, economic, and social conditions—with Firth, as secretary, a crucial instrument—played a vital role in securing the career fortunes of social anthropologists, Freeman among them. He was unlikely to be directly aware at the time, but tensions were at work in the council between academics interested in wide-ranging research agendas and bureaucrats focused on colonial social problems, and between the LSE and the University of Oxford, whose anthropologists believed London academics were swallowing all the funds and orienting the research work in the direction of their intellectual interests.[3]

Most of the work was done in Africa and the Caribbean, but in 1947 Edmund Leach, an anthropologist with whom Freeman's life and work would converge at various moments, was invited by the government of Sarawak to make recommendations for a series of "sociological" projects in the then newly constituted Crown Colony in Borneo. Leach began his academic studies in mathematics and engineering. He worked in China, studied under Malinowski, and then when war broke out joined the army and served in Burma. He did fieldwork in Borneo for his PhD and joined the staff of anthropology at the LSE; in 1953 he moved to Cambridge, where he later served as professor and provost of King's College and was knighted. An eminence of the discipline and a shaper of modern British anthropological thought, he became noted as a key interpreter of Claude Lévi-Strauss's structuralism to the English-language world.[4]

Derek Freeman later became grumpily at odds with Leach's purist, structuralist approach, but in 1948 Leach became one of the hinges on which Freeman's career prospects hung. Leach had come out of Sarawak convinced that a disproportionate amount was known about the inland peoples, while the coastal Iban, the Land Dayak, and the Melanau had been ignored as too sophisticated and detribalized to be of ethnographic interest. He recommended some eight projects to the colonial government, four of them of the highest priority, including the Iban. The mandarins of the CSSRC worried about the lack of experience in colonial conditions of the young men (and the rare woman) passing through the portals of anthropology training in Britain. Derek Freeman was older, had already earned his fieldwork spurs in colonial Samoa, and, importantly, had met the Iban in that striking end-of-war encounter. To clinch matters, when he heard that the projects were up for assignment, Freeman hastened to Saint Augustine's College in Canterbury, which housed a rare Iban dictionary. He set about learning the language—he had already demonstrated in Samoa that he had a gift for languages, and Iban was an Austronesian language of similar structure—so that when the meeting took place to divide up the projects Freeman announced he already had a familiarity with Iban. Among his competitors this provoked a frisson of emotion, a not infrequent accompaniment to Freeman's later life, but Leach appreciated his verve and dash, and Freeman was given the Iban project.[5]

Derek's life swung upon another hinge that summer. After submitting his thesis on Sa'anapu, Freeman set off to climb the Matterhorn. On the train to Switzerland, carrying his climbing gear, he ran into a young woman whom he had once met in the company of her fiancé. Her name was Monica Maitland. Monica grew up in Cheshire, England. Her father was a doctor who studied in Paris and became medical superintendent of the Cunard Lines and a founder of industrial medicine. Her mother, Gwen, was a nurse who, unusual for the day, rode a motorbike and was one of the first women pilots in England. Monica Maitland had a modest blue-blood background through her mother's link to the family line of the Queen Mother.

Her parents sent Monica to interesting, progressive schools—she remembered being in class with Bertrand Russell's daughter and Lucien Freud—but she had a tendency to shyness and isolation. Her father eventually helped her into a career as a radiographer, which she did not much like, preferring nursing or a medical degree, both hard to enter after the war. Monica's passion was drawing and painting, which would become her vocation in ways she did not anticipate in 1948.

Though she was engaged to be married to a young colonial officer setting out for the Pacific, Monica did not much like that prospect either. By chance she happened upon Derek Freeman at Victoria station while looking for a spare seat on her own trip to Switzerland, and they began a comfortable journey together that became a lifelong love affair. Monica Maitland became the person between Freeman and the world whom he could always count on to grant forgiveness for his failings and show a bemused tolerance. They married three months after their train ride together as Freeman was readying himself to leave for Borneo. Their best man was James "Jim" Wightman Davidson, another New Zealander and a friend and kindred spirit about Samoa who was fashioning a career as a historian at Cambridge. Davidson became a close colleague as a professor of Pacific history later in Australia. Monica, now Freeman, cut her hair into a bob, packed her bags, and boarded a tramp steamer for Singapore, arranging to meet Derek once he had set up camp in deepest Borneo.[6]

Freeman's mission was to complete a study of a traditional, stable Iban community practicing shifting dry rice cultivation in the mountainous jungles inland from Sibu in the Third Division of colonial Sarawak. He arrived in January 1949 and would not leave again until June 1951. Freeman negotiated a base camp among the Iban at Rumah Nyala, a long-house upstream from Kapit, and made his ethnographic observations over a wide area of the Baleh region. In his report to the government of Sarawak, published in 1955 as *Iban Agriculture* (which Leach, with unalloyed admiration, called "this excellent book"), Freeman described a dynamic people, short in stature, black haired and cinnamon colored, speaking a dialect of the widespread Malay language and comprising 34 percent of the more than half a million people of Sarawak. They were scattered over most of the interior zone of Sarawak as a result of aggressive agricultural expansion and headhunting raids on hapless neighbors who had been only recently brought under control. Some Iban communities on the coast led a profoundly modified way of life following the establishment of colonial rule, but Freeman's Iban lived fifty to one hundred miles from the coast in hilly country drained by fast-flowing and fickle rivers.

In *Iban Agriculture* and in his fuller account, *Report on the Iban*, published the same year,[7] Freeman gives a description of the Iban long-house that would be his and Monica's home for over two years. It is classic Freemanesque prose, pellucid, evocative, with a sting in its tail:

> Anyone who has travelled in the interior of Borneo is familiar with the conspicuous shape of a long-house: an attenuated structure supported on numerous hard-wood posts, it stretches for a hundred yards or more along the terraced bank of a river, its roof forming an unbroken expanse. Superficially viewed the Iban long-house has the appearance of being a single structural unit, and many casual observers have made the facile inference that the long-house is therefore the outcome of some sort of communal or group organization and ownership. For the Iban, at least, this inference is the very reverse of true. Among the various families that make up a long-house community there does exist a network of kinship ties, but the Iban long-house is primarily an aggregation of independently owned family apartments. The fact that these long-houses are joined one to the other so as to produce a long-house detracts little from their essential autonomy. Indeed, the unbroken expanse of roof tends to reveal the fact that the Iban long-house is fundamentally a series of discrete entities: the independent family units of a competitive and egalitarian society.

Monica joined Derek in June 1949 at Rumah Nyala, where he had built their apartment (or *bilek*) onto the long, open verandah of the twenty-one apartments in their long-house. She came not as mere helpmeet but as paid assistant, for Freeman soon realized that her drawing skills relieved him from the ethnographic illustrating that was a vital part of his work; Monica produced hundreds of line drawings, portraits, and sketches, which still filled their home in Canberra on the day of a memorial service in her honor in 2012.

Monica also began a diary that saved Freeman the added task of logging every moment of every day. Published finally in 2009, Monica Freeman's diary is for the historian a unique document, bearing witness to the rhythms of their life among the Iban for over two years. It registers the daily grind of observing, collecting, measuring, and writing up, as well as describing the illnesses and pain they both suffered and recording the Iban's charm-laden response to the Freemans' vulnerability. The diary is particularly effective in imparting the Iban of Rumah Nyala's sense of themselves and rendering that confident swagger that had so impressed Freeman when he first encountered Iban in 1945.

The Freemans lived among the people, with rice bins in the lofts above their heads and trophy heads hanging over the fireplace. Derek and Monica were looked after by a young woman, Gering, with her two children. They also had an interpreter, Patrick, who cooked for them. They were caught up in family quarrels and the existential crises of the long-house, but from the moment she arrived Monica regarded their surroundings above the river Sut as a paradise. She records in her diary the heavy work done by the men clearing the jungle-covered slopes for firing and planting or hewing canoes from wood, while the women wove the clothes and the indispensable ikat weavings used in rituals. These ikat weavings were the women's equivalent of trophy heads, and Monica too had to learn the techniques for creating them. Children had great standing and were much tolerated, if they survived the harrowing birthing rituals to which their mothers were subjected. Each long-house had its headman and its experts on augury, as well as perhaps a noted shaman who possessed the capacity to call wayward souls back to a troubled body.

The *bilek* was a field of spirits, charms employed at every turn to cure illnesses and ward off dangerous forces; if an omen bird sounded, the men would not go out to the fields. Freeman was performing up to fifteen offerings in the course of a day's work to keep the spirits on his side. At one point he jokingly presented a strip of his own skin, peeled from his swollen hand after a bout of sunburn, as a charm; the piece was promptly buried, and an incantation was recited to make the rice grow.[8] Writing one night in September 1949 as torrential rain threatened plantings and anxious Iban banged gongs, Monica noted: "These people put so much into fighting these elements they don't understand, and most of the night they went out to try and disperse the clouds and the rain's downpour increased."[9]

47

Eloquent storytellers and dreamers was how Monica Freeman described the Iban, who were brilliant at poetic invocations performed in lengthy chants during rites and festivals. But they were gossipers too who got Freeman into trouble when he sat in on a meeting during which a head-man expressed anger at the district leader. More than once Freeman had to journey to interview the district officer, on one occasion even going to the governor-general of the Federation of Malaya, to satisfy these men that he had not fomented unrest or cast aspersions on the local administration.[10]

Much of his time—and Monica's too—was spent on the subsidiary farms, or *dampa*, tucked away in the ranges, Freeman taking notes, asking questions, and measuring everything in sight. The Iban's hackles were raised when Freeman suggested he should survey the farmland using the equip-ment he had brought from England. Once before surveyors had visited the region, he was told, and in the ensuing years there had been disastrously bad harvests, the spirits of the fields disturbed by the brusque manner of the surveyors. Freeman used every argument he could think of—his research would help the Iban, he would perform the proper sacrificial rites at every step—but his audience was adamant. When Freeman resorted to a sterner tone, arguing that the Iban must trust the government, he only provoked a more fierce reaction: "His eyes flaming and his voice suffused with emotion, Nyala—the *tuai rumah* [long-house headman]—averred that the Govern-ment could shoot them and burn down their long-houses, but they would not submit to having their *padi* farms surveyed. The others present sprang to his support, and for several minutes there was a babble of disturbed voices. If I were not to jeopardize the whole of my research, retreat was imperative; I was compelled to disavow my plans, and apologize for my effrontery." Freeman reports this encounter in candid detail in his *Iban Agriculture*.[11] He was finding his way around Iban society by trial and error and soon learned that the Iban, when convinced he was seriously interested in their methods, would invite him to many more field rituals than he had time to attend. Nonetheless, he was not beyond seeking a way around this impasse, surreptitiously using twine and a prismatic compass and pacing noncha-lantly between points to make his survey of some hill farms. He reported this too, though not as a boast, more as a rather glib, indeed naïve comment on his inventiveness.

Life on the *dampa* was much less private and peaceful than in the main long-house, but Derek and Monica enjoyed it all, trekking arduously up and down the steep valleys to observe the planting and harvesting, Freeman singing operatic songs and emitting deafening battle cries.[12] Monica was the first white woman ever to visit these places and was feted by the women while she sat and sketched.

Traveling down the rivers in Freeman's boat was a more hazardous occupation. Shooting the rapids always presented the danger that the boat might capsize, trapping them under its awning. But the rise and fall of the rivers with the tropical downpours meant that the Freemans spent most of their time strenuously poling the boat around banks and rocks. As time lost significance, only Sundays were distinguishable, for on Sundays the Freemans rested and read the few newspapers or magazines that Monica's mother sent from England. Occasionally, they would go downriver to Kapit to fetch supplies at the bazaar, eat a morale-boosting meal, see a film, or visit the local British official or missionary. These visits eased the malaise that came over them after weeks in the jungle.

In the long-house the Freemans entertained themselves and the Iban by playing records on their gramophone, the Freemans' tastes conventionally classical, the Iban's running more to Danny Kaye singing "Bloop, Bleep," played so many times that the record wore out. There were serious moments when groups of men would gather with Derek on the open verandah and ask him about the shape of the world and its elements. He would amuse the neighbors with conjuring tricks that he had learned for school teaching or do a Samoan dance to reciprocate the Iban's own. The Iban mimicked Freeman's incessant note taking and camera shots to accompanying shouts of laughter. A cat and a gibbon, purchased in Kapit, completed their domestic family in these first two years of marriage. The gibbon, a source of endless amusement and frustration at its antics, became the center of attention and the bane of their life; it would accompany them back to London.[13]

While they both entered into the Iban world of feasting and offerings to the spirits, Derek and Monica experienced a succession of small and large crises along the way. Boats would be lost in the floods, or the roof would leak while they were away and damage their few belongings. Their best tinned food was once stolen; worse still, someone made off with the Benedictine liqueur they kept for special occasions. They were subjected to constant trial by insect—ants, mosquitoes, sandflies—and endured leeches, scorpions, and snakes. Small illnesses and dental pain dogged their days; both struggled with malaria and amoebic dysentery. The worst trial, and perilous in its effects, was Monica's attack of paratyphoid in the last six months of their stay. Derek had to carry her downriver to the hospital in Sibu—they covered 120 miles in eight hours—where she lay for two weeks, barely saved from death.[14]

What can we glean from Monica's diary about Derek Freeman's temperament during the first two years of married life? The jungles of Sarawak were an unusual start to a life together, to say the least, and one in which they were thrown upon one another's company twenty-four hours a day, seven days a week wherever they were. Monica was familiarizing herself with Derek's personality, but her comments are few and only hint at features that she discerned. He was a fanatically hard worker, operating at his best when the Iban were around, "deeply disturbed" if the long-house were empty; at the same time, he was put out by interruptions. Occasionally, he was withdrawn and depressed, but no more, it seems, than Monica herself. Freeman could spend long periods alone meditating or ruminating upon his work. But he was capable of relaxing and lounging with Monica in their *bilek*—if it were a Sunday. When Monica was ill Derek was tender and all-caring; he could weep.[15]

Clues to more rigid edges of Freeman's personality also surfaced. He had a tendency to lecture the Iban about ways to improve their lives and could fly into a temper when crises hit, once even losing his self-control with the pet gibbon and getting bitten during his outburst; the gibbon was apparently terrified of Derek.[16] Among the Iban he had a reputation for sternness, especially with Gering, their housekeeper. All this is to be expected, living as closely as the Freemans did with the local people and always expected to provide extra resources. The couple enjoyed a generally harmonious relationship with the Iban throughout their stay, and Monica's diaries testify to the affection they both felt for the people of the long-houses they visited. As for their relationship, Monica found she got a lecture when Derek was impatient. Toward the end of their time in Sarawak, she wrote to her mother that Derek seemed to expect her to provide the same sort of thoughts and advice as his own mother. "I couldn't be very much different!" she exclaimed. "As you know 'Did' is rather a high standard to live up to."[17]

Derek piled up information while Monica grew her collection of sketches and weavings. In their first year Derek was unsure where he would end up with his materials. He seems to have flirted with the idea of Manchester University under Max Gluckman, but there was no anthropology department there. By March 1950 he had firmed up with Raymond Firth a plan to go to Oxford and write up both Borneo and Samoa. Now he regretted his impetuous willfulness in not finishing his degree in New Zealand. At the time, a degree may not have mattered as much, but in the postwar world he would have to do his bachelor of science before going on to a doctorate; Monica would go back to part-time radiography to make ends meet. They made plans for the autumn term of 1951, and Derek sent off an application, hoping for a bursary.

His ambitions were clear and confident now. Monica told her mother their plans: "One or two years there [Oxford] would be ideal. Then perhaps a year's fieldwork again, and then settle down to lectureship and with an Oxford degree, we hope, professorship. That of course may be anywhere! Canberra, Otago, Honolulu, Florida. . . . That is, if there is no good post in England available."[18] So Derek was confident of reaching the peak of the profession quickly with the Oxford tag to his name; he would be no mere journeyman anthropologist. And Canberra was clearly one of the pearls Firth was dangling before him.

A month later a letter arrived from Meyer Fortes. He was transferring to Cambridge and wanted to take Freeman with him. Suddenly Derek and Monica spied hidden obstacles in the other place: "Oxford is a tight little group who have all dealt with Africa and have little knowledge of Polynesia. Also are all Roman Catholics (this sometimes makes progress difficult)."[19] Monica was excited by the prospect of studying Iban weavings for her own diploma and was imagining a settled life for the future with infants to follow. By December 1950 Freeman had been accepted by Cambridge.

But first, Derek was granted an extension of his time in Sarawak to survey Iban cultures in the Second Division farther south and to compare these more acculturated people, investigating infant mortality rates, birthing methods, and the rate of social change. From November 1950 to April 1951 the Freemans toured settlements by boat and ancient truck. Along the way they ran into "Derek's deadly rival," W. R. "Bill" Geddes, another of Leach's anthropological students investigating the Land Dayak.[20] After reading the literature on the places they visited, they expected to find "a broken-down, hopeless, spiritless, dirty and diseased people," according to Monica, but were pleasantly surprised by the industrious activity, the neatly con-structed houses, and the well-built, healthy populations. In other places closer to the coast, however, constant farming had degraded the land, and the people were described by Monica as decadent, "quiet, spiritless and [they] have no talk," unlike the Iban farther north, who "enjoyed life enor-mously and found utter satisfaction in their beliefs, religion and activities."

The Freemans encountered British colonial officials who were often inefficient and mostly uninterested in the people they governed. Monica and Derek confronted one portent of future days in the form of Tom Harrisson, director of the Sarawak Museum in Kuching, which they found poorly arranged, with misleading information on odd objects. Harrisson, noted Monica, looked "very sinister and cynical" when they met at a social evening.[21] That was the only hint of a malign force that would stalk Freeman's mind a decade later.

On 6 June 1951, after a succession of tearful farewells and gift givings to their Iban family, Derek and Monica boarded the tramp steamer *Ulysses* for their passage home to London—another bungle by colonial officials, for the Freemans had expected to be rewarded with more comfort. They made the most of a cramped journey among a relaxed crew, visiting Singapore, Ceylon, and Red Sea ports on a meandering voyage. Freeman could not avoid a moment of deep depression—this was the first time he had stopped to truly rest in two and a half years of unremitting activity amid the babel of Iban voices. They reached Avonmouth in the Bristol Channel in July and made their way to London.

Derek Freeman was returning to a British social anthropology that was experiencing a transformative era as a new "field of competence."[22] Built on the back of commissioned work for colonial regimes, anthropology was progressively disconnecting itself from its status as the handmaid of colonial empire and from the "practical men" who had hitherto carried out observation of indigenous societies. (Tom Harrisson of Borneo was the very model of the practical man.) The prewar functionalist approach to the study of culture by Malinowski and the more abstract structural-functionalist approach and search for integrating mechanisms endorsed by Radcliffe-Brown were now institutionalized in London and Oxford. Funding from bodies like the CSSRC had enhanced the status of anthropologists and eased more of them into the growing number of university positions. Cambridge, once the refuge of armchair physical anthropologists, was becoming noted for innovation and, with the arrival of Fortes and then Leach, as a center for radical approaches to structuralism; students oriented themselves to one or the other of the two leaders. Kinship studies, with their analytical potential as the engine of social structure, were the new focus, emblem of the new scientism of the discipline.

Where did Freeman fit as a student returning from his first "professional" bout of fieldwork? His practice in the field had sharpened to a new pitch; the publications that follow the Sarawak years show that his skill as an anthropologist had developed significantly. He was drawn to Fortes's kind of structuralism and its scientific aspirations. Freeman's confidence in his future as an anthropologist was not built on unreal expectations. He was going up to Cambridge with all the materials he needed for his PhD, as well as for his voluminous *Report on the Iban*, delivered to the Sarawak government in 1953.

He also went with singular endorsements ringing in his ears. Fortes was moving mountains to get Freeman into Fortes's own college, Kings. Both he and Firth wanted Freeman as a future lecturer there, according to Leach, who, with fulsome praise, told Freeman that his was "probably the greatest Far East fieldwork done for 20 years."[23] Leach regarded Freeman as having advantages not afforded his "deadly rivals" in Borneo. He had been in the field longest (with his Samoan experience to bank as well). He had Monica by his side as field assistant, artist, and diarist—she was being encouraged to study anthropology at Cambridge too. And "Derek's Iban" proved to be unusually congenial and cooperative. To top it off, the CSSRC received a comprehensive, original, and elegantly written report on agriculture.

But a strain of resistance lay in Freeman, not unlike that which he displayed against Firth's academic restrictions when studying for his diploma. He recognized that in himself. "Often in the past I must have appeared uncompromising, recalcitrant and wayward to you," he admitted remorsefully to the ever patient Firth as he prepared to enter the Borneo jungle in 1949;[24] indeed, there was a lot of Firth's own methodological individualism surfacing in Freeman. It is interesting that among the few books he took to Sarawak and strove to preserve from tropical decay were a handbook of psychiatry and the work of Geoffrey Gorer, a social anthropologist known for his application of psychoanalytic techniques to anthropology.[25] That may have been the cumulative influence of Ernest Beaglehole in New Zealand and Siegfried Nadel in London; Nadel would become Freeman's mentor in the years to come. Fortes, too, was aware of and interested in the role of psychology and emotion in social life. But these aspects of mind and behavior were of more intrinsic interest to Freeman and nagged away at his growing discomfort with the strict analysis of structure and function in British social anthropology. He also continued to regard himself as a Polynesianist with a Pacific future, despite his sojourn among the Iban.

Any idyllic vision of life on the banks of the Cam in Cambridge had to wait, for Monica was still very ill on arrival in London and was hospitalized for six weeks; she was diagnosed as suffering from five different strains of dysentery. Freeman was busy with the Colonial Office bureaucracy and preparations for his reports and PhD writing. The gibbon that had traveled all the way with them became an exotic attraction as it crossed the street or frolicked in Hyde Park. According to Freeman, there was even a move in Cambridge to have it made an honorary fellow of Kings! But its profligate toilet habits soon had the gibbon banished from the Freemans' digs in London, and they gave the animal to the London zoo, where it would go through a special ritual for them every time they visited.

As he had with his Samoa research, Freeman the indefatigable collector and measurer had thousands of pages of notes and drawings, ten times more than he needed for his thesis but an invaluable investment in his future career. He wrote his dissertation and produced his reports for the CSSRC in two years, traveling between London and Cambridge, where he stayed with Jim Davidson. Davidson was on his own gradual journey away from Cambridge and Britain toward the new national university in Australia, where he would become Freeman's early patron, although later Davidson became Freeman's competitor as a Samoa expert. Two luminaries, Leach and Firth, examined Freeman's PhD dissertation, "Family and Kin among the Iban of Sarawak." Any lingering self-doubt was erased, Freeman claiming the examination a triumph. "I was looked on as the coming force in anthropology," he told Frank Heimans as he looked back on his life in 2001. "That was a structuralist's thesis, that, and I was thought to be one of the two or three leading people in the whole discipline." That may have been Edmund Leach talking. Freeman's other examiner, Raymond Firth, while complimentary about the great mass of data Derek and Monica had collected in conditions of considerable hardship, quibbled about Freeman's rather labored treatment of his methods, the fine distinctions he made about Iban kinship structure, and the paucity of comparative references on kinship theory. But he agreed that the study was "a very important contribution to the regional ethnography of Borneo" and a revelation about a hitherto unknown social structure.[26]

Freeman could probably have stayed in England if he and Monica had wanted to. Despite Firth's quibbles he recognized Freeman's talent, maturity, and value to the burgeoning discipline of anthropology. Freeman had been sounded out about a temporary lectureship at the LSE (which he declined) while he was still in Borneo. Meyer Fortes also seems to have tried to get Freeman a fellowship at King's College in Cambridge. But Freeman was bonded to New Zealand under the terms of his postwar rehabilitation grant. Moreover, his mother, that dominant force in his formation, had died in Wellington in 1951 after he and Monica had returned to London. At first stoical, Freeman was overwhelmed by pent-up grief on a visit to Westminster Abbey. He had not been home for eight years, and the urge to be back in his land of mountains and bush was strong in that moment, and it stayed with him throughout his life. He felt compelled to return. Serendipitously, he received in early 1953 a letter from the vice chancellor of Otago University in Dunedin, asking if he would accept a visiting lectureship in anthropology for 1954. This would enable him to fulfill his obligation to the New Zealand government, as well as reconnect him to one of his early New Zealand patrons, Harry Skinner, at the Otago museum.[27]

Skinner, already retired from the Otago museum and university, had great plans for Freeman. He had secured him an honorary curatorship as a reward for Freeman's collecting work in Samoa and the United Kingdom on behalf of the museum. Freeman was being groomed to take over as curator of the ethnological collections, with a permanent lectureship in anthropology at the university as tantalizing bait for the future. Freeman's Pacific seemed but a hop, step, and jump away.

But more powerful patrons had other plans. The Freemans made landfall in New Zealand in late January 1954, Derek brimming over with pleasure: "How good it was, in the gusty dawn, to smell again the warm, sweet smell of the tussock, and to see again the sharp outlines of familiar hills," he wrote to Jim Davidson.[28] Dunedin was New Zealand's largest city in the far south of the South Island, a relaxed, hilly, cold place still carrying much of its Victorian-era architecture. Hardly settled at all into the museum, with the family living outside the city on the beautiful but windswept Otago peninsula, Monica pregnant with their first child and feeling rather isolated, Derek Freeman received a letter from Raymond Firth in London. A readership in Southeast Asian anthropology was about to be advertised at the School of Oriental and African Studies (SOAS) at London University. Would Freeman be interested? Did he feel his obligation to New Zealand was sufficiently discharged?

Freeman had traveled a good distance from his earlier romantic cleaving to his home soil. He replied hastily to Firth that he would definitely be clear of his obligations to Otago and New Zealand by the end of 1954.[29] Though conditions in Dunedin were "most congenial," it was not the place to follow up his real interest in social and cultural anthropology. Freeman had discovered "a great and almost unbridgeable gulf between my own outlook and that of Dr. Skinner, who is really an archaeologist with predominant interests in the pre-historic material culture of Murihiku." Besides, he and

Monica had decided, even before Firth's letter, that sooner or later they would return to England ("after great societies like London and Cambridge we find Dunedin excessively parochial"). Suddenly Freeman's interests were firmly tied to Southeast Asia rather than the Pacific: "It is there that my heart lies." He wanted to push ahead with publishing his Iban material, especially his "wonderfully rich data on religion," and gradually extend his research to Indonesia and the region—to become, in effect, Mr. Southeast Asia.

All these statements may have been for the private consumption of Firth and the mandarins who would decide the fate of the readership. Barely six weeks later, Freeman replied in very different terms to Jim Davidson, who had now forsaken Cambridge for Canberra, ensconced as the world's first professor of Pacific history at the Australian National University (ANU). Davidson, an energetic, no-holds-barred activist historian of empire, had been engaged by the New Zealand government to work on—some said to meddle in—the constitutional negotiations between New Zealand and Western Samoa for the latter's eventual independence.[30] He and Freeman, the two Kiwis from Wellington, remained close friends and had been swapping notes for years, particularly about Samoan matters; Davidson was using Derek's Sa'anapu thesis in his government work. He knew the same Samoans and their foibles, shared Derek's distaste for the narrow-minded insularity of the New Zealand civil officials, and even notified Freeman while he was still in Borneo of Margaret Mead's new book, *Male and Female*, in which Samoa was one of the societies studied (without any suggestion from Davidson that anything about her work was suspect).[31]

In late March 1954 Davidson sounded out Freeman about an appointment as a senior research fellow under Siegfried Nadel at ANU. Nadel, Freeman's old teacher in London, wanted him, but Nadel's (overly) strict sense of protocol forbade him from approaching Freeman directly. It would become a permanent job, with a gentleman's agreement that Freeman would be promoted to senior fellow or reader once his stream of publications began to flow. Derek would look after graduate students studying Southeast Asia or Polynesia and teach theory. Nadel was prepared to wait for him.

Freeman crafted another swift reply. He told Davidson about the London option but agreed that, on balance, Canberra offered the greater advantages, for there he could straddle both his Iban and his Samoa interests. Mr. Southeast Asia could be Mr. Pacific as well. Freeman's disillusionment with Otago had deepened, for the university had led him to expect a full, permanent university appointment in anthropology, with a curatorship at the museum on the side. Now university officials were proposing the reverse, with Freeman's position tied to the uncertain local government finances of the museum. He would have none of it. "I have no intention of becoming a museum mole, and slowly to dessicate [*sic*] amid glass cases. . . . Besides, weighed down with artefacts of stone and bone that another had collected, I should soon become the loneliest and most morose *social* anthropologist in all the world. Even before your letter arrived I had decided Dunedin was not for me. For better or for worse social anthropology has become my *ignis fatuus*, and follow it I must."[32]

Nadel, needless to say, was delighted and followed up with a flattering letter expressing his desire to have Freeman in a senior post.[33] Thus were careers forged in the flush of growth in Australia's postwar national university. Freeman possessed the qualities ANU was searching for and had earned his spurs. His academic supporters in England sent glowing references ahead of him. Leach thought Freeman "the most able student with whom I have had dealings during the past eight years of academic teaching in anthropology," his Iban work "one of the very finest pieces of anthropological research carried out during the present generation." Meyer Fortes named him "one of the two or three outstanding social anthropologists not yet in professorial positions in the British Commonwealth."[34] These acts of academic patronage boosted Freeman's ego and strengthened his intellectual self-assurance.

So, with only the melancholy and embarrassing task of explaining to benefactors on both sides of the globe why he was turning down their offers, Derek and Monica prepared for life in Australia. He had been a successful teacher, and his students presented him with a book of Pieter Bruegel's artwork; Freeman still had it in his library at the end of his life. The "warm, sweet smell of the tussock" gave way to a new desire: to sit atop Ayers Rock (Uluru) in the central Australian desert in the glare of the colors and shapes of softer, very different hills. He polished off his Iban publication for the Colonial Office and turned toward the Pacific: "At odd moments I've been taking down my Samoan notes and turning them over lovingly, in anticipation of Canberra." He planned to get back there, his heart set on two studies: "a definitive account of Samoan social structure and an agnostic's analysis of the coming of Christianity—and its aftermath."[35] He expressed no concern about the state of social anthropology or unhappiness with the route down which his studies were taking him. No word either of Margaret Mead, though her specter would materialize eventually in Canberra.

4

"My Kierkegaardian Earthquake"

New Zealanders and Australians had been crisscrossing "the ditch" of the Tasman Sea for a century when the Freemans set out from Dunedin. Australia was a kind of metropole for Kiwis on their way to England, the mother country, though Melbourne or Sydney was their preferred stopover, not Canberra. "That dreary place on a cold plateau" was how Otago University's vice chancellor described Canberra to John Passmore, a philosopher who was himself going there about the same time as Freeman, surrendering his professorship at Otago for a readership at the new national university.[1] Passmore and Freeman were joining Australia's most daring experiment in educational organization to that time. The town they were moving to (it could hardly yet be called a city) squatted astride the Australian Capital Territory, a region bigger in size than Ireland and a world apart from the rest of the nation, let alone the rest of the globe. Canberra, the national capital, founded in 1913, was a garden city in the making, designed by American architects Walter Burley Griffin and his wife, Marion Mahony Griffin. It lay beneath the soaring blue walls of the Brindabella Range, a place of blond plains surrounding geometric patterns of roads and parks, of electric, clear air, and of sharp winters that made the adrenaline flow. Jim Davidson made a point of emphasizing to Freeman the autumn beauty of the place, with its lavish, scarlet colors.

Coming to Canberra from any other place was a shock in the 1950s. It had grown beyond its reputation among country folk as "a good sheep station spoiled," but the early postwar years saw much of the public service population still living in boardinghouses, hostels, barracks, and camps. The shackles were finally coming off as the Freemans made their move with the rapid influx of new people into government departments and the university and a host of new, if temporary, buildings. But housing was still critically short, the transport and communication systems were basic, and the "city" had an amiable but semiprovincial air.

The Australian National University shared many of these growing pains, though senior appointees received preferential building leases as an incentive to join the new venture. ANU was to be a research university of international stature, an Elysium for advanced research straddling the sciences, both physical and social, and the humanities led, it was hoped, by eminent expatriate academics enticed back to Australia.[2]

Until the postwar years, Australian anthropology's center of activity was the University of Sydney, where Radcliffe-Brown was the inaugural professor in 1925 and oriented courses toward the British tradition of the structure of social relations. He was succeeded by Peter Elkin, an Anglican priest and self-made anthropologist who dedicated his department to be the clearinghouse for research among Australia's Aboriginal populations. Elkin acquired a reputation as the controlling figure in early national anthropology, gathering funds and influence at government level in the cause of understanding the ancient culture of Aborigines and encouraging their assimilation into European settler society. Until ANU formed, with other universities following from the 1960s, this was Australian anthropology in substance and style: practical, empirical understandings of precolonial Aboriginal social order, with little or no theoretical and methodological cast, and political avoidance of a variety of contemporary Aboriginal problems.[3]

The Australian National University was designed to be different and was where the unities and the discordances of Freeman's professional life were to be found from that point on. He was joining an elite team occupying a privileged place, though most of the new academic staff were of middling standard, with stellar exceptions tucked here and there into the new research schools. There were four of these, Freeman joining the Research School of Pacific Studies, signaling the broader and more flexible approach of the new institution. The planners of ANU were looking for creative people, including designers, organizers, and research leaders, though they fretted about the lack of theoretical unity in studies of the Pacific region in particular and about the dictatorial potential of the directors of the schools.[4]

Freeman's new home in the Department of Anthropology and Sociology reflected this mix of talent and high tension. Siegfried Nadel was without a doubt the star, a genuine world figure. Peter Worsley, the British sociologist who was a doctoral student in anthropology and otherwise thought Canberra "a dump," recognized the intellectual brilliance that Nadel brought to the fledgling department. But Nadel was a martinet whose "restless quest for power and status (and disdain for anyone below the rank of professor)" alienated colleagues to such an extent that they would not entertain the idea of his becoming director of the Research School of Pacific Studies, a position he coveted.[5] Another colleague Freeman found on his arrival was W. H. "Bill" Stanner, who had worked as an anthropologist in East Africa and Papua New Guinea and toward the end of the war found himself as a civil affairs officer in British North Borneo, close to Freeman's future field site. Two decades and more later, Stanner would become the prophet of a new national consciousness about the miseries visited upon the country's indigenous populations over a period of two hundred years. But in the 1950s he acquired a reputation as a conservative critic of liberal postwar development philosophies, a restrained, Colonel Blimp–type character who seemed unwilling to take up the responsibilities of the senior positions he clearly craved.[6] Stanner was to become Freeman's bête noire in Canberra, among others, and their relationship played out in a theater of petty confrontations as the years wore on.

The rest of Freeman's colleagues in the Research School of Pacific Studies were by one account a "rabble" of individualists. Freeman's friend Jim Davidson agreed they were a curious and at times uneasy lot—Nadel always on the make; Oscar Spate, the professor of geography, with "a scholar's liking for anarchism"; and Davidson himself, "with my tendency to become the demagogic leader of 'the people.'" The year before Freeman arrived, Davidson was caught up in a controversial political protest statement over the coming war in Indochina, which had him and two other idiosyncratic ANU professors, Charles Manning Clark, the Australian historian, and C. P. Fitzgerald, professor of Far Eastern history, named in Parliament along with the local Anglican bishop as Communist sympathizers.[7]

A vibrant, close-knit community of strong individuals and powerful intellects thrown together in a collection of narrow wooden huts while the campus was built alongside the expanding town center: this, then, was the Canberra where Freeman and Monica—and new baby Jennifer—made their home in February 1955. Freeman was bringing his own idiosyncrasies, among them an intensity that Raymond Firth characterized as a "defect": "His intense concentration on a problem, and enthusiastic application of a particular point of view, sometimes makes it hard for him to appreciate alternative viewpoints."[8] Despite this tendency, Firth recommended that

ANU should hire Freeman while warning them, presciently, that he was interested in more than social anthropology. Firth calculated that this would be an asset for the university and thought Freeman would follow his "other" interests through museum materials and cultural details.

Hindsight might deem that a miscalculation on Firth's part, but there is no doubt that Freeman's early Canberra years were his salad days. He and Monica delighted in the ravishing autumn colors of the high country; they reminded Monica of her school days in Switzerland. They bought a small car, had furniture made by a team of German joiners they found, and contentedly set about making home and office comfortable. Derek was not the clubbable kind who would frequent the beer garden of University House with friends, but he played tennis with Jim Davidson and others, and his fascination with mountains had him exploring the Brindabellas and nearby hills, a routine that became a lifelong habit. He and Monica were among the lucky ones to secure a plot of land in the suburb of Deakin, like most of Canberra a primitive work in progress but a front-runner in the prestige stakes, for the home of Australian prime ministers, The Lodge, was virtually at the end of the street across a small park. Derek and Monica got ANU's architect to design them an L-shaped bungalow of brick and wood, with a verandah facing inward to the yard. Here they lived for the rest of their lives, a sanctuary with an almost Japanese aesthetic, low, peaceful, their "one steadfast piece of earth" surrounded by plants and trees from New Zealand stock, only the vivid, noisy birdlife breaking the academic silence.[9] Their two daughters, Jennifer, born in 1955, and Hilary, born in 1958, grew up in Deakin amid the noise of their father's career.

That career accelerated in conventional ways for the first few years. The same year he became an Australian citizen, 1955, Freeman's two major works on the Iban were published: the report for the government of Sarawak, and his *Iban Agriculture*. The first reads like a provisional work, a hint of what would come later as Freeman processed his vast research materials; in the register of his writings it disappeared into oblivion until it was republished as a fuller academic work in 1970. *Iban Agriculture* was much the superior opening statement about his Southeast Asian interests. Reviewers were enthusiastic. Harold Conklin of Columbia University wrote in *American Anthropologist* of "this compact and highly commendable monograph," the "best published description of a Malaysian system of swidden agriculture, and a superior introduction to a long-neglected phase of Bornean ethnography." A young Marshall Sahlins was almost effusive in praise. Freeman's report was "distinguished," "exciting," "of importance far outside the field of Sarawak sociology." Freeman presented a clear picture of agriculture among the Iban, their ecological adjustments, their relentless pressure on rival people, their cognatic group structure. Sahlins had a question about how the Iban were able to organize very large fighting forces if, according to Freeman, there were no large descent groups and no organization above the family at all. And he was bemused by Freeman's outline of the "crusade" the colonial government should adopt to get the Iban to change their wasteful agricultural practices. But this was a "modest miscalculation" in a book that would otherwise "serve a useful purpose in the world of scholarship long after the problems of colonial rule in Borneo have been dissolved."[10] Douglas Oliver, Pacific anthropologist and friend, wrote from Harvard that the book was far ahead of any other description of slash-and-burn culture, and his colleagues were already mining it for their classes.[11]

Other, smaller works followed, including essays on Iban family structure, their system of augury, and their pottery. These pieces culminated in a long essay, "On the Concept of the Kindred," which won Freeman the Curl Bequest Prize of the Royal Anthropological Institute in 1960. In a forensic historical excavation of the word "kindred," Freeman delved back into a dim past of Welsh tribal custom and assorted legal treatises to show what meaning was given to the word in ancient family law. A small part was a defense against Sahlins's skepticism about the organizational capabilities of small Iban family structures (there was no mystery, contended Freeman, given the wide range of kindred networks traversing Iban society). A larger part was Freeman's own crusade, characteristic of his growing scientism, to bring an ever narrowing precision to the definition of anthropology's analytical terms and his demonstration of a severely logical form of argument by winnowing out the various historical and ethnographic uses of the term "kindred."[12]

By now Freeman was in charge of general supervision of Indonesian research in his department, and he returned to Borneo in 1957–58 to round out his Iban studies. He still harbored an intention to return to Samoa and to do a detailed analysis of Samoan society—he made that explicit in his "Kindred" essay, and he had published an essay on the Siovili cult in Samoa in his edited Festschrift for H. D. Skinner in 1959.[13] That dutiful exercise ate into Freeman's time to finish writing up on the Iban, but he was also gripped by a growing intellectual anxiety about the road he was traveling in social anthropology and what he considered its increasingly arid formulas. There is a heavy-footedness in his prose for the "Kindred" essay, as though the concern for accuracy and precision had robbed him of the light and grace that mark his earlier work on the Iban and on Samoa; Jim Davidson noticed it. Freeman sent Edmund Leach a copy of his prize essay with the inscription, "Herewith, this well-dried specimen from my butterfly collecting past."[14] It was an allusion to Leach's description of most ethnography as merely descriptive. A gnawing irresolution meant the great work that Derek was signaling as being on the way—a big book on Iban social structure and Iban religious rituals, already accepted in advance by Cambridge University Press—never appeared; it never even got off the ground.

What made things worse was the sudden death in January 1956, barely a year after Freeman's arrival, of Siegfried Nadel from a heart attack as he was playing chess. Nadel was fifty-three. Stanner reported the "grievous loss" to the ANU Council: "His mind had a large span; his expository gift was remarkable; he was erudite in several disciplines; and he was a cultivated man in the humane fields." The obituaries expressed genuine shock and sadness at the loss of this giant. Nadel was one of Malinowski's "mandarins," a polymath who started life as a concert musician and ethnomusicologist, studied psychology, and combined anthropology, sociology, and psychology in a series of studies on West and North African societies. His real place in anthropology, wrote Raymond Firth, lay in "the comprehensiveness and profundity of his theory." As Derek Freeman would do thirty years into the future, Nadel presented his first general book, *The Foundations of Social Anthropology*, published in 1951, as a preliminary statement of the totalizing synthesis of the social sciences he was planning. He was nothing if not in-tellectually bold and flexible. Firth frowned at the expansive ambition of Nadel's attempts to "push the instrument of anthropological enquiry further into the refractory matter of human behavior," but Firth was no character assassin and only in passing mentioned Nadel's lack of modesty and impatience. It was a typically sideways glance for Firth to end his obituary noting that Nadel played Mephistopheles in a Canberra repertory perform-ance of Goethe's *Faust*.[15]

Behind the scenes at ANU, Nadel's death was less mourned by those who were the victims of his domineering and abrasive manner. But Derek Freeman was not one of them. For him, Nadel's going was the "most griev-ous of happenings and the most deep and bitter of disappointments."[16] He had found in the Austrian a rich, fulfilling echo and was drawn to his rigor-ous logical discipline and forceful personality. Freeman was in thrall to the possibilities Nadel offered for creating a dynamically new anthropology; Nadel's death perhaps did more than anything to disrupt the channeling of Freeman's thinking. Freeman's own obituary for the great man was a paean of praise and heartfelt celebration of Nadel's "remarkable lambency of mind," his incisive analytical intelligence, and his titanic energy (something Freeman's teachers always commented upon about Freeman himself). Derek had known Nadel since 1946 and was one of his first postgraduates; Nadel had got Freeman to Canberra. He considered himself a suppliant son to Nadel and sat with Nadel's wife during the days after his death, consoling her and helping her secure a job that would free her from financial worries. If Freeman modeled himself on anyone outside his own mother, it was probably Nadel, with his "kind of consecration to scientific inquiry" and his "absolute integrity."[17]

Nadel's sudden death also sent the planners at ANU into a state of confusion and exposed as yet unsettled recruitment policies. Who now would lead a fledgling department with such glowing prospects? There proceeded a comedy of egos as first one, then another leading light in international anthropology was marked for luring to Canberra. The person the university wanted was Freeman's old patron, Edmund Leach. Indeed, Freeman was in charge of the department for a short time after Nadel's death and claimed later he had instigated the invitation to Leach to come and look over the university.[18] Leach came, saw, and seemed to conquer; he was offered the chair. But from Ceylon on his way back to England, Leach wrote to decline. To different people he gave different reasons, but to Freeman—possibly because Derek was the one who coaxed him in the first place—he confided that the reason had to do with his wife's reluctance to leave Cambridge and England. When ANU overcame an initial suspicion of Americans as a nonmigratory species and offered the chair to Douglas Oliver at Harvard, he too declined.

Freeman was frustrated at "the long, difficult and profitless interregnum" that followed.[19] He was wrestling with his growing alienation from British social anthropology while becoming himself part of the continuing, messy search for Nadel's successor. In 1957 he tried again to lure one of the giants of the British scene to Australia: Max Gluckman from Manchester University. Gluckman considered coming out, but then one of his students, John Barnes, the disenchanted holder of the anthropology chair at Sydney University, was thrown into the mixture, along with Freeman himself and Stanner within the department. Gluckman would not stand in the way of Barnes.

This occasioned a further round of secret dealings and feelings of betrayal, especially on the part of Stanner, who had disappeared to do research in northern Australia on the understanding that nothing would be done to fill the chair while he was away. Freeman remained on the sidelines, though admitting in later years that his sole motivation in putting his own name forward was to thwart Stanner—a sign of the mutual hostility that was building. The usual eminences in the mother country were asked their opinions. Anthropology's diplomat, Raymond Firth, concluded that neither Barnes, Stanner, nor Freeman was an obvious candidate. Barnes was intelligent, cultured, a good mixer, with competent, elegant work, but Firth still harbored doubts. Stanner was his own worst enemy, forever failing to grasp the big opportunities that came his way. As for Derek Freeman, while acknowledging his drive and theoretical potential, Firth wondered whether his dynamism and self-confidence might undermine the independence of his students. And there was this: "He follows any particular theoretical trail with such abandon that one sometimes wonders whether some perspective has not been lost and the argument pulled out of shape."[20]

Such views had chased Freeman since his London days. "Titanic energy," "passionate enthusiasm," "unusual among his generation"—these phrases were occasionally also uttered in conjunction with "danger." Even Freeman's great promoter, Meyer Fortes, admitted that "men of his temperament, if they are entirely original thinkers and indefatigable workers, can be somewhat intolerant and authoritarian in their general conduct of affairs."[21] But Fortes was more sanguine than Firth that Derek could do the job of professor and was worth the risk. Even Firth accepted that Freeman was probably as good a thinker and organizer as Barnes, "and some would probably rate him as a better anthropologist."[22]

But Barnes got the job. Max Gluckman anticipated that Freeman might feel bitter, and Barnes later wrote that Freeman was disappointed, but that was not the case. Freeman was promoted to a research-only readership after lobbying by Jim Davidson, now dean of the faculty. Barnes was in amiable agreement, although he commented privately to Davidson: "His greatest weakness, I think, is a tendency to oversimplify, to see everything in terms of black and white; but we can't all be perfect."[23]

Looking around among others of my own generation I can discover no one with whom I would rather work than John Barnes, and I shall be most content to have him in charge of our Department." This is Freeman writing to Raymond Firth about the "tangled events" that took up the middle of 1957.[24] Although sincerely meant, Freeman's welcome of Barnes would prove a monumental misstatement, for Barnes was nothing like Nadel, and relations between Freeman and Barnes soured within a few years. The same year, 1957, marks the intensification of Derek Freeman's anxieties and the first of two returns to Sarawak that pitched him into a collision with Tom Harrisson, the museum director in Kuching. Freeman's warmth toward Barnes would disappear in the wake of these encounters.

The return to Sarawak marked a moment when the singularity of Freeman's personality burst into public view for the first time. Rumors of "mental instability," "paranoia," "nervous breakdown," and "straitjackets" attend the stories of the Sarawak incidents, which have been projected back from the Margaret Mead controversy by Freeman's opponents as though the incidents are related and all part of a pattern of Freeman's "madness." These stories circulate when anthropologists talk of Freeman, and they include lurid descriptions of Freeman running wild around a museum lopping penises off carvings, but two published accounts from outside the Freeman camp have captured the high ground.

The first is by Judith Heimann, an American diplomat and writer who deals with the incidents within her vividly written Harrisson biography of 1997; its title, *The Most Offending Soul Alive*, might for many people stand as an apt description of Derek Freeman. Her account is less than four pages in a four-hundred-page work and proceeds outward from her depiction of Tom Harrisson's animosity toward his competitors, especially social anthropologists working among "his" tribes and peoples in the colonial divisions of Sarawak. Harrisson was an Oxford-educated colonial official who was untrained in serious anthropology, but he had become the curator and director of the ethnographic museum in Sarawak. Like Freeman, Harrisson saw himself as an individualist outsider. He had risen to his position and influence through feats of exploration in the interior of Borneo; during the war he was the leader of a successful guerilla team fighting against the Japanese and took on the character of a Bornean head hunter. Tom Harrisson was, in his biographer's words, "a romantic polymath, a drunken bully, an original-thinking iconoclast, a dreadful husband and father, a fearless adventurer, a Richard Burton of his time."[25]

Any anthropologist who entered the country without deferring to Harrisson's "authority" became the target of his animosity. Derek Freeman was always going to be one such target. Heimann characterizes Freeman as "the brilliant but intellectually combative New Zealander . . . tall, rangy, handsome," who "likes to make moral judgments about people and things." Freeman had been in guarded contact with Harrisson since his PhD research days in Borneo. In 1957 Freeman arranged to have an American graduate student installed in an area Harrisson was reserving for himself. The student left Sarawak without completing his research, and in a later meeting with Freeman as he was driving him to Kuching airport, Harrisson viciously attacked Freeman, abusing him in the presence of a young colonial officer.

Then in 1961 Derek sent another student into the jungle, Brian de Martinoir, a Belgian with an aristocratic name, an alleged doctorate from Germany, and fieldwork supposedly done in Mexico. He was to work among the Kajang in northern Sarawak, another of Harrisson's favorite areas. Harrisson, according to Heimann, at first endorsed Freeman's opinion of the Belgian but later turned against the student, accusing him of becoming involved politically and of "various acts of misconduct." Finally, Harrisson went upcountry to oust the now "delusional" Belgian from Sarawak and in a drunken rage publicly humiliated him in the presence of local chiefs.

Enter good Derek Freeman, writes Heimann, galloping to the rescue of his protégé and carrying "a small portrait of St George" as his talisman. With Harrisson temporarily absent, Freeman worked his way around colonial officials to get Martinoir reinstated, pressing them to rid the country of Harrisson at the same time. Walking through the Kuching museum where Harrisson was director, Freeman spied "ithyphallic and copulatory carvings," which a series of deep, interior revelations later that evening convinced him were pornographic fakes and evidence Harrisson was a "madman." He returned to the museum to take photographs, smashing one of the alleged statues in the garden and promptly alerting the authorities to what he had done. Now, he thought, Harrisson would be ejected. When nothing happened, Freeman next went to Harrisson's house, walked in, took more pictures of "pornographic carvings," and pried open a locked drawer, looking for further evidence. When Harrisson's servant called the police, Freeman was able to talk his way out because they were Iban with whom he could converse fluently.

He next rang the authorities to tell them he was leaving for Singapore to resume his study leave and was taken by police escort to the airport. But in Singapore, Freeman changed his plans, resolving instead to fly to England, where he would consult the professor of psychological medicine at Edinburgh University and persuade him to make a submission about Harrisson to the British House of Commons. While he was on the plane, Freeman changed his mind again, deciding this time to return to Australia. He disembarked in Karachi, Pakistan, where he met the Australian high commissioner and was examined by a psychiatrist. While Freeman was telling the psychiatrist that Harrisson's behavior was contributing to a Communist plot in Borneo, the Australian High Commission sent a message to ANU. The person sent to bring Freeman home was John Barnes. According to Heimann, Tom Harrisson later remarked to friends: "It is the only time in my life when I was able to drive someone round the bend without even seeing him."[26]

The Heimanns were friends of Tom Harrisson, and Judith was encouraged by Harrisson's former wife to write her book. In the 1990s, thirty years after the events, Heimann started a friendly correspondence with Freeman to collect her data, and the two met in both Washington and Canberra. Freeman handed her his letters, diary entries, and photographs from the period, and also materials he had sourced from the Australian War Memorial about Harrisson's wartime exploits as a commando officer: it was typical of Freeman's generosity with colleagues working in related areas. But Heimann in the 1990s learned that at this point in Freeman's life, when he was engrossed in the war over Mead, his generosity could come with pressure for fair dealing over interpretations of his earlier life. If she were to use his rich resources, Freeman insisted that Heimann "do me the courtesy" of showing him her draft so that he could check its accuracy.[27] "Fondly," Heimann did so, only to find herself impaled on Freeman's righteous disagreement with her presentation. Her initial draft of the Sarawak affair, almost two chapters long, became three pages, and she agreed to add Freeman's edited version to her notes and sources.

Freeman's editing produced a stripped-down, sterner, and altogether more serious summary in which the emphasis was on the radically different values of the two men, Freeman maintaining the "highest professional standards" and seeing through Harrisson, the "charlatan" and "psychopath." The American student, we are told, was recommended to Freeman by none other than Margaret Mead, while the Belgian was the real fake (Freeman found that the university authorities had taken Martinoir's credentials at face value, while Freeman's own investigations overseas revealed that the student had no doctorate from the university he claimed and had not done any fieldwork with a famous anthropologist in Mexico, and his alleged publications were not to be found). Furthermore, it was Freeman's home university, ANU, that asked Freeman to make a detour to Sarawak on the way to his study leave in Indonesia and investigate what was going on. He found that Harrisson was manufacturing copies for display that had not been collected in the field, a "flagrant departure from professional curatorial practice," and so Freeman broke one of the "inauthentic" carvings on display in a building occupied by the British Council. Freeman in his account does not mention rifling through Harrisson's desk drawer, though he adds that he had experienced in Kuching a "cognitive abreaction: a sudden and deep realization of the inadequacy of the assumptions of contemporary anthropology." Years later he described these traumatic events to Rodney Needham in Oxford as an existential trauma—"my Kierkegaardian earthquake." Freeman agreed almost tongue-in-cheek that Tom Harrisson had driven him round the bend "in the sense that [my] vision of anthropology had been transformed."[28]

The second account from an outsider is by Hiram Caton, professor of politics and history at Griffith University in Australia during the 1980s. Caton, who died in 2010, was something of a polymath—a historian of ideas, an ethicist, a self-proclaimed expert in "political psychology" with publications across extensive fields. Caton collaborated with Freeman in the late 1980s to produce the only comprehensive reader on the Mead controversy. He counted himself a friend who became more of an inquisitor over time. Freeman came gradually to distrust Caton's constant requests for personal information. Freeman's suspicions may have been warranted, for Caton became the first person to make available on the internet a pair of articles "diagnosing" Freeman's deep psychological disturbances, one of which claimed Freeman suffered from a narcissistic personality disorder.[29]

Caton's study of the Sarawak incident is valuable for revealing the archival correspondence between Freeman and his university over the events, along with reports from diplomats, police, and psychiatrists who encountered Freeman during his 1961 mission. Although he loosely follows Heimann, Caton introduces a wealth of extra material to the story: Freeman experiences an "illumination" while pondering events between his student and Harrisson; Harrisson is "in an advanced state of paranoia," according to Freeman; and Freeman has a moral duty to ensure Harrisson's removal from office and from the country. Freeman vouchsafes this revelation to a circle of his contacts in Kuching, one of whom likens him to Don Quixote tilting at windmills. Freeman also consults a psychiatrist, or "alienist," in Kuching and, according to Caton, believes Harrisson's phallic carvings are exercising a degree of mind control that is inspiring a local cult, in cahoots with Soviet Russia, to undermine the Sarawak government.

Freeman's "cognitive abreaction" on the evening before he breaks the false carving flows partly from a feeling of immeasurable compassion for the Iban people, who are living under what he now perceives as a corrupt government. The realization transforms his views "about the nature of man and of human existence." Freeman weeps and resolves to stay in Borneo and live with the Iban. This "abreaction" is a cathartic and liberating emotional experience that leaves him with "an extraordinary clarity and serenity of mind."

According to Caton, these characterizations are from Freeman's own reports, designed to underpin Freeman's insistence that he acted rationally and from his conscience. Caton also introduces a police report from the Sarawak constabulary that documents Freeman's request to see an "alienist," who after a brief examination pronounces Freeman temporarily "mentally unsound."

Caton also describes the Karachi interlude in greater detail, along with Freeman's efforts to safeguard his allegedly damning photographic evidence about Harrisson's carvings. Freeman, still distressed, is examined again by a Karachi psychiatrist who recommends he be escorted home to Australia. The Australian high commissioner to Pakistan (Roden Cutler, later Sir Roden Cutler, governor of the state of New South Wales) is a Victoria Cross recipient who knows about battle stress and shows genuine sympathy for Freeman, listening to his story and ensuring he is taken care of with dignity till John Barnes arrives. Caton emphasizes that Freeman felt a high degree of contentment in Karachi, the result of his "moral action." Barnes endures nine hours of Freeman retailing his story as they fly back to Australia, where Freeman's euphoria begins to dissipate when he realizes his emotional stability is in fact under investigation.

The Caton report is highly suggestive of a deep hole that opened up in Derek Freeman's life and mind, partly through his Sarawak experience in 1961 and partly as a result of other intellectual revelations. Freeman's contradictions and confusions are on display in his reports and protestations. They add weight to the conviction that something happened to him in Sarawak that set him on a different course in his intellectual life. The trouble with Caton's essay is that it contains all the hallmarks he claims to see in Freeman's reports: "a prosecutor's indictment, replete with blaming that leaves no choice but to pronounce the guilty verdict." Everything that came out of the Sarawak experience—Freeman's "manufacture" of "his version" of the events against the reports of others, his new orientation toward anthropology—is judged to be part of a strategy designed to aggrandize Freeman's sense of himself. His dispute with others' interpretations—those of Barnes, Sir John Crawford (the director of his school), and the psychiatrists—is, according to Caton, a malevolent attack (a consistent theme of Freeman's opponents over the Mead controversy; indeed, Caton asserts a connection between Sarawak in 1961 and Freeman's campaign against Mead's research). Caton also rebukes Freeman for not producing scholarly analyses of all these incidents along the psychoanalytic lines that Freeman later devoted himself to, as if this were some betrayal of a sudden new orientation that in reality took years to (incompletely) build.

Although Caton explicitly states that Freeman's Sarawak abnormalities are not the root of what Caton had previously "diagnosed" as a serious personality disorder, his published pieces, with their amateur psychology, effectively raise the specter of a kind of mental illness in Freeman. There are, however, other works in the professional literature that align much more closely with the evidence of the tortuous psychological and physical journey that Freeman was enduring in Borneo in 1961.

As Darian Leader, psychoanalytic practitioner and theorist, explains, the trend in modern psychological medicine has been to rigidly separate mental health from mental ill health, the latter diagnosed from ever more formulaic lists of symptoms outlined in the *Diagnostic and Statistical Manual of Mental Disorders*. These "brain diseases" are often treated almost mechanistically through drug regimes. "Psychosis" is a term applied more frequently to individuals who do not fit within the norms of society, their delusional beliefs about how the world is working, usually against them, regarded as a symptom of insanity.

Yet Leader and many of his colleagues argue that delusions and sanity should not be rigidly separated. True paranoia can manifest itself as delusional thought hand in hand with clarity of intelligence; psychotics can be masters of rational deduction. Following Freud, Leader argues that delusions are secondary symptoms, attempts to repair the hole that has opened up in a life by giving it meaning. They are thus to be seen as positive attempts at healing rather than a pathology in themselves. In paranoia, Leader writes, "a meaning crystallizes: the person knows what is wrong with the world. There is a plot against them, they have a mission to accomplish, a message to disseminate."[30] Characteristic of that revelation, which can come in a sudden moment of insight, is a certainty, an absolute conviction, of some truth in which the subject is central to the meaning and the solution.

Is this not a picture of Derek Freeman abroad in Sarawak and Southeast Asia in 1961? The sudden revelation in Kuching the night before he smashed an "obscene" and faked figure; the plot to subvert Sarawak inspired by the evil genius Tom Harrisson; the absence of doubt; Freeman's own mission to save the Iban; his hastening to the most efficacious source of authority to accomplish his goal—this is Freeman's story, delusional in part but underpinned by a series of real events giving meaning to what had happened to him since his return to Borneo (Southeast Asia *was* gripped by suspicions about Communism; Harrisson's museum *was* no ordinary museum, according to Judith Heimann; Harrisson *did* have many enemies among colonial officials).

Freeman inhabited a strong moral universe—his later opponents would say an extreme universe—inherited from his mother and the conservative Presbyterian background of his New Zealand youth. His notions of integrity and moral virtue were uncompromising. "I am the possessor of certain views about human existence and of a 'humanistic conscience,'" he wrote to Sir John Crawford, "and in the event, after much searching thought, I decided that even though it might involve me in severe personal penalties I had no course as a moral and rational man but to act in a way that would bring the state of affairs which I knew to exist in Sarawak to the attention of those who might do something about it."[31] Freeman seriously believed that he was called to bring order to the world of Sarawak, to be the savior of the Iban against the corrupt regime of which Harrisson was a part. It was an extravagant view, one that allowed later critics to condemn similar moralistic views in his campaign for Samoans against Margaret Mead.

But the slightly ridiculous figure of Freeman riding to the rescue in company with Saint George is a frivolously misleading interpretation initiated by Judith Heimann. It is followed by Hiram Caton, whose Freeman as "moral agent" is diminished in the telling by the underlying tone of incredulity expressed by Caton and his followers. In Caton's eyes, Freeman was exhibiting hubris, but in fact, Freeman's convictions align with the delusional necessity that gripped him after his revelation.

Leader makes the point that such "paranoic delusions" need not be disabling nor generate long-lasting complications in a subject's life. One can develop stabilizing mechanisms that enable normal life pursuits, perhaps with the occasional efflorescence of an episode. That too is Derek Freeman, as we shall see. The key, say Leader and other practitioners, is to listen to the story told by the subject, to respect the interior flow of experience, and to return to the case study of a life lived, all of which modern medicine has increasingly moved away from as a way to understand the psychological complexities of a subject.[32]

Let us therefore look at how Derek Freeman explained the series of events that took him from the bucolic calm of Canberra to the manic happenings in Southeast Asia. It all started, curiously enough, with Samoa, or at least the promise of a return to Samoa once he had satisfied Nadel's insistence that he get his two books on the Iban out of the way. Nadel's death then precipitated a period of malaise in Freeman, and the work on the Skinner book further delayed the big book on Iban social and religious structures. It was in this atmosphere that Freeman received an invitation to give a paper to the Pacific Science Congress in Thailand in November 1957. He grabbed the opportunity: it was a way to get back to Sarawak to recheck his Iban findings. Samoa would have to wait. Around the same time, an American student from Columbia University in New York, Roger Peranio, applied for a scholarship to do doctoral work in Malaysia. Freeman recommended him. Peranio's references were not outstanding, but he had the basic training and was a Quaker, to which Freeman attached "much importance," for it signaled "strong moral character."[33]

Tiptoeing round Tom Harrisson, Freeman got Peranio to work on the Bisaya in the north of Sarawak, a people still living in upriver long-houses. Master and apprentice settled into what was already Freeman's modus operandi: a reading mastery of all the fields the student was covering and intense feedback on field reports reaching Canberra—dense, detailed letters on ideas and practices, with encouraging prompts. Freeman was generous in loaning material for preparation and in answering requests from the field. Peranio was grateful. No teacher of his had ever given his work such attention.[34]

Freeman then made his first trip back to Southeast Asia since his doctorate, to the Science Congress, afterward revisiting his old stomping ground. Sarawak was still recognizably the colony he had left in 1951, but the air of alarm around possible Communist cells had inflamed tension, and native-born Chinese had been deported. Among his Iban, the hill people had suffered inexorable change. "Everywhere," he told Rodney Needham, a fellow anthropologist who worked in Borneo and an old friend from England days, "there are mission educated youngsters who openly jeer at traditional Iban beliefs and values, deriding their elders as ignorant and inadequate fools." The eager cry of progress was on everyone's lips. The days of Iban culture were numbered. "All I can say is that it fills my heart, that had known the Iban as they were, with an ineffable sadness."[35]

Something went wrong when Peranio returned to Canberra in 1959 to write up his research. Within the year he resigned his scholarship for private reasons, claiming also that he had irreconcilable differences with his supervisor and the department. Freeman's opponents might say the Freeman curse was already descending. But the New Yorker, Peranio, seems to have found the Canberra ambience too constricting and conservative. He seemed to bridle at the Australian way of doing things, the lack of cultural activities, and the dress code demanded for dinner at University House; he was sure Freeman and Barnes were prejudiced against Americans.

Peranio may also have come unstuck over the steely intensity of Freeman's demands as supervisor. Freeman went beyond the call of duty to help his students and get the best out of them, but he expected a similar intellectual commitment and high standards. Instead, Peranio had inferred from criticisms Freeman made of the work of Columbia's Marshall Sahlins that he was hostile to all Americans and to Columbia University. In a statement that smacks of the purity of academic rigor he later used in the Mead debates, Freeman dismissed the notion: "Criticism as far as I am concerned, is solely directed at the work being criticized and is entirely without prejudice to its author or place of origin." The fault lay entirely with Peranio. He was, according to Derek, peculiarly touchy, introspective, and brooding. Worse, he was ungrateful in the face of the extra distance Freeman went to offer help and to get him counseling. Peranio packed up and left ANU without a word of thanks to anyone, heading to Europe and then home. ANU later discovered that Peranio was using the material he gathered on scholarship from them to submit a PhD dissertation at Columbia. The ANU authorities were not amused. Derek was outraged: "I shall remember him most for his manners."[36]

Although there appears no obvious connection between this episode and Freeman's 1961 adventure in Sarawak, Freeman himself brackets them together through the menacing figure of Tom Harrisson. It was after Freeman's visit to Peranio in the field, on the drive to Kuching airport in 1958, that Harrisson verbally attacked Freeman and the whole monstrous regiment of anthropologists: "It was the most extreme stuff, 'You fucking cunt of an anthropologist,' and all that sort of thing, and attacking Leach and Firth and Needham and everyone that had been there, and saying, 'You social anthropologists are . . . ,' you know. So when I got to the airport, I very nearly attacked him, and I was shaking afterwards. 'Don't do it. Don't do it.' That's how I felt."[37] Freeman shook all the way home; indeed, the shaking from this incident may never quite have subsided. What happened in 1961, Freeman believed, was a continuation of that earlier trauma. He had gone in 1961 to save another student from *his* trauma with Harrisson. This was the enigmatic Belgian, Brian de Martinoir. Freeman originally set great store in him as an older, experienced student, but Martinoir had become immersed in a menacing environment in which, as several reports, along with Heimann's story, make clear, he became the victim of Harrisson's hostility toward anthropologists. Martinoir's public humiliation in front of his hosts was enough to damage his spirit.

While Heimann and especially Caton give us a detailed and generally accurate account of the sequence of bizarre happenings that followed, they both lack sympathy for the authenticity and life-changing meaning that the experience had for Freeman. Among all the "self-reports" by Freeman about his experiences, which Caton finds merely self-serving, is a document Caton did not view. In Freeman's papers in San Diego lie copies of six pages from Freeman's private diary for 2–22 March 1961, sent to Heimann in 1992 for her research into Harrisson. These are the crucial days of Freeman's (mis)adventure in Borneo and Pakistan. In Freeman's own words, the crowded entries in his crabbed, spidery hand give us a taste of what he was seeing and feeling as the experience was unfolding:

Friday 3 March
In Kuching by morning plane. Met by Smythies and de Martinoir who looks run down and exhausted. . . . Harrisson making charges against Martinoir (they are: incompetence; learning Mandarin; the To'o call; "fondling the breasts of young girls"; breaking through Malay screen; and that cheques had been returned to him). . . . Jakeway [the chief secretary] is correct, formal showing no sympathy . . . slanderous letter by Harrisson against Needham.

Sunday 5 March
Work on drafts until 3 am . . . minute cross-examination of Martinoir lasting until 5.30 am . . . work on letter to Barnes; in afternoon walk in park meet Smythies talk of Iban mythology, visit museum with Smythies with de Martinoir & Smythies see no obscene carvings etc. ie. except traditional ones & *palang*. Continue work on letter; begin to analyze Harrisson's behaviour. At about 1 am after copying words "I have the impression that I am in the presence of a madman in the pathological sense of the term," decide to work on the hypothesis that Harrisson is indeed mad.

[Monday 6 March]
On testing the evidence against this suddenly realize that this is the correct explanation. Go for a walk around deserted streets thinking the position over. At 0900 hrs see Jakeway & report my conclusion that Harrisson is gravely psychotic (ie paranoia). Withdraw request for enquiry and Jakeway

reacts strongly; matter entirely for him etc. . . . go up to inform Bishop that Harrisson is mad; he listens sympathetically but offers to do nothing to help . . . return to long discussion with Brian about state of Kuching society. Make plans to return to Belaga with Brian.

[7–9 March] . . .

Friday 10 March
Read in Sarawak Tribune the letter "Unfair & One-sided: Two young Ibans Look Further": began to weep retire to bedroom and suffer convulsive emotional experience. Brian: "you have found the way." Talked in park with Brian. Develop notion that Jakeway is also involved (? of British Giana) [*sic*]. Decide I must stay; cancel all bookings until June; William S. (a former student at Cambridge) extends my permit until 17.6.61. . . . In afternoon about 1400 hours on way to British Council Library call at main museum see lewd figures; another convulsive experience; smash object by throwing it to floor; there is no sin in you; address attendants; at once call on Bishop; prays says will see God[?]; experience in Cathedral; return R.H.; ring Bishop not religious; Ratcliffe calls are you religious; call on Rozalo and ask for interview with Schmidt [the "alienist"] to be arranged. Article ref de Martinoir appears in Sarawak Tribune + Chinese edition [decide to stay and live with the people].

Monday 13 March
. . . meet Cutler under umbrella at Speedbird House [Karachi]; drive to U.K. High Commission where film is taken from camera and put in sealed envelope; move to Palace Hotel; test for spys [*sic*] by rigging camera; Dr Butterfield calls on my return from walk; he arranges for specialist; I change and tell Cutler I was putting on a performance; 4 pm Dr Habib calls and I accompany him to his clinic where after many delays I tell him the full story until 9 pm. On return to Palace Hotel work on Harrisson document until 12 pm. Sleep for a couple of hours (doors locked) then continue from [?] and test hypothesis of *mass paranoia* or mass delusion; cable to Barnes (watch king cobra; fighting monkeys; cobra and mongoose and have fortune told)—[?] week fulfilling.[38]

A torrent of events and impressions was swirling around Freeman in Kuching and Karachi. He was sick, buffeted by impressions of others (many of whom he felt he could not trust), working till he was overtired, and prone to disorientation. A psychological crisis swelled and overflowed in those early days of March. The diary entries show that 5 and 6 March became fused together in one manic period of introspection, unhappy encounters, and a growing conviction that Kuching was in the grip of some malign force. Derek received a less than sympathetic hearing from Alan Snelus, the deputy chief secretary of the Sarawak government, and from the chief secretary, Sir Derek Jakeway. Both stood upon a stiff-necked colonial authority, and both were cynical of the accusations being made against a senior colonial official (even if they shared Freeman's suspicions of Harrisson's behavior). Snelus accepted without investigation the claim that Martinoir was writing invalid checks, and Jakeway refused to apologize for anything Harrisson might have done, treating Derek and ANU as being in the wrong.[39] These were tense, frustrating moments that added to Freeman's mental strain. His tears for the Iban were real and deeply felt, and they had consequences both immediate and longer lasting in his career. There is a touching innocence and sense of moral rightness behind his decision to stay and fight (though apparently without any awareness of the impact on his family back in Australia). And deep within this delusional experience was a quasi-religious element, with its power of forgiveness drawn from the wellsprings of his childhood.

Although Freeman's mechanistic "testing" of his "evidence" to prove that Harrisson was "mad" is every bit as naïve as Caton's assault on Freeman's own sanity, the genuineness of Freeman's experience is not to be repudiated by later cynicism. If Freeman was undergoing a paranoic delusion, then the identification of Harrisson as being at the center of sinister forces was part of the naming process that allowed Derek to structure his world and bring it back into order. Rather than dismiss such a production as fantastical, says Leader, "the effort to name requires respect and encouragement."[40] A decade after these events, Freeman would be diagnosed as suffering from bipolar disorder (a condition never publicly disclosed), and he was certainly in a phase of manic elation during the time he spent in Karachi. According to his diary, it was not until the plane trip home to Australia that Freeman came down from the mountain of his euphoria and realized that he was being escorted home by John Barnes. Barnes admitted he was tactless in telling Freeman that he did not believe a word of his long story, but Barnes pleaded his own tiredness after thirty-six hours without sleep.[41]

The tug-of-war between Freeman and his university over the Sarawak incidents and whether Freeman was dangerously unstable is amply covered by Hiram Caton. Caton places a hostile construction on Freeman's refusal to be treated as a mentally ill patient and on his disagreements with authorities—Crawford, Barnes, and W. H. Trethowan, the Sydney psychiatrist whom Freeman agreed to meet, though not as a formal patient. But Freeman's diary entries show he saw clearly enough on the plane home the course that events would take once he arrived back in Canberra.[42] Although sick with dysentery, he was determined not to be defined by others' bowdlerized tales about him but to fashion and to insist on a single, true account based on his "scientific" description of the facts. Thus he asserted again and again his rationality against all claims that he "fell apart" in Southeast Asia. Leader suggests this is part of "the litany of self-esteem" and passion for truth by a person suffering a temporary psychosis.[43]

Freeman was still defending himself a year later in correspondence with Stephen Morris, a fellow researcher in Upper Sarawak during the 1950s. All the tropes were there: Harrisson the "near psychotic" had "disrupted a bona fide and scientifically important research project"; Derek was lied to by a regiment of corrupt officials whose blank wall of noncooperation made immediate action all the more urgent; Derek had performed a "highly apposite symbolic act" by damaging the fake carving. Freeman had by now decided that in that act he was speaking the language of engagement against unjust power, an act of "existential involvement."[44]

Freeman had also worked himself into a position of sympathy for Harrisson, "the mongrel, beef-witted madman of Pig Lane, the paranoiac Old Harrovian, ex-cannibal and O.B.E., from the analysis of whose ways I have learnt so much: my *koan* and my Caliban!" In a final irony, unable to foresee his own fate at the hands of others, Freeman proclaimed: "When poor Tom's a-cold, I propose becoming one of his biographers—a life abounding with such clinical interest must not unrecorded go."[45]

5

Remaking Himself

The vanquishing of Tom Harrisson was only half of Derek Freeman's mission. The "cognitive abreaction" he experienced in Kuching on the night of 10 March also inspired a second mission. That was to abandon the structural functionalism of his British anthropological inheritance and to retrain in order to lead anthropology toward a new, unified theory in which psychology and biology played a central role in understanding human social order and culture.

In 1962, nearly a year after his return from Sarawak, Freeman gave a sharp, excited account of this illumination to the director of his school, John Crawford: "Suddenly, quite unexpectedly and with no volition of my own I underwent a spontaneous mental abreaction lasting from about ten to fifteen seconds. As soon as this abreaction ended I experienced an extraordinary clarity and serenity of mind, and I found that my views about human existence had been transformed."[1] Freeman likened this momentous experience to a religious encounter, a metanoia, during which he was made over in mind and spirit to another way of thinking. He acknowledged to Crawford "a quite new understanding of my own self" deep enough to abandon the analytical framework of his thinking for the past twenty years in favor of a new, tortuous reshaping of anthropology's work in the world.

Freeman spent the months after his return to Australia researching the literature around his traumatic experience. William Sargant's *Battle for the Mind* (1959), which included information on battle fatigue, was an inspiration. So too was Gordon Allport's *Becoming* (1955), from which Freeman copied the following quotation, lodging it separately with his papers that went eventually to the University of San Diego: "It sometimes happens that the very center of organization of a personality shifts suddenly and apparently without warning. Some impetus, coming perhaps from a bereavement, an illness, or a religious conversion, even from a teacher or book, may lead to a reorientation. In such cases of traumatic recentering it is undoubtedly true that the person had latent within himself all of the capacities and sentiments that suddenly rise from a subordinate to a superordinate position in his being."[2]

During 1962 and into 1963 Freeman fashioned a grand narrative that explained to his puzzled employer, his colleagues, and the patrons who had nurtured his career the origins and import of this "recentering" of his intellectual being. It is difficult to state succinctly the thrust of that narrative, for its central themes grew progressively with each telling. Freeman's return to psychology was at the heart of it, as he told his old professor Meyer Fortes. He wove a (slightly exaggerated) tale about a sophisticated education in psychology during the 1930s under Ernest Beaglehole, with a basic understanding of psychoanalysis thrown in. Psychology came first, Freeman claimed, and when he turned to anthropology and went to work in Samoa, he retained his interest in psychology; it was Siegfried Nadel's own interest in meshing psychology with anthropology that attracted Freeman to Canberra in 1955.

Then came three key moments of revelation that changed his life. In writing up his Iban research, Freeman had wrestled with the intellectual problem of how to explain the symbolic act when Iban headhunter aspirants acted out the splitting of a trophy head from which spilled the seed of future human heads. He realized he could take the easy way out and simply analyze the social function of Iban headhunting rituals, producing yet another sociological study of religion and another notch in his career belt. But, being Derek Freeman, he fretted at the neat, closed circle of this approach. Again, he was not alone, for anthropologists, especially in America, had begun to shift away from studies of function to studies of meaning in the postwar years. It was on his return to Borneo in 1957 that Freeman came to his first realization: to fully understand Iban religion and ritual he would have to master the psychological ramifications of unconscious symbolism; that realization quickened his desire to find something beyond the arid formulas of social anthropology that explained social phenomena simply in terms of functional cultural structures.[3]

In this partly resolved state of mind, Derek experienced his second awakening. Max Gluckman from Manchester University visited Australia in

1960–61 and read a series of other authors' papers in a symposium examining the artificial boundaries that divided the human sciences. A paper by British cultural anthropologist Victor Turner on interpreting symbols in Ndembu ritual in Africa contained a passage that rocked Freeman. Where psychoanalysts disagree, asked Turner, how can the hapless social anthropologist, without systematic training or experience in psychoanalysis, judge between their interpretations? "This sentence seemed to me like an anthropological *cri de coeur*," Freeman told Fortes.[4] He was persuaded that he would have to do the systematic training in psychoanalysis for which his past education in psychology and his interest in Freud had serendipitously prepared him.

The third and most radical revelation that pointed Freeman to this road was his adventure in Kuching in 1961 and his confrontation with the figure of Tom Harrisson, the so-called psychopath with strong paranoid tendencies. Again Freeman persuaded himself that the key to the whole sorry Sarawak affair lay in the workings of evolution and unconscious psychological processes in human affairs, not the dry, structural explanations of social anthropology. The great irony was (and Freeman recognized this) that "psychopath" Tom was the catalyst. It was Harrisson who helped Freeman make the radical switch in his intellectual approach to human society and to find the right compass by which to chart a new way forward for anthropology.[5]

With gradual additions to his own understanding and subtle variations for different audiences, Freeman's Sarawak revelations became his lifelong apologia for the monumental shift in his intellectual approach to anthropology. He told Ernest Beaglehole that he had learned more in Kuching than from all his years in Samoa and the time he spent among the Iban; he described his experience as "a de-conditioning of my own mind." And Canberra, with its "wonderful climate and an undisturbed country atmosphere," allowed him the freedom to begin the arduous task of reading himself into new fields like phenomenology, ethology, psychoanalysis, and neuroscience.[6] Freeman even gave Beaglehole a little lecture on the literature of phenomenology by Edmund Husserl, Maurice Merleau-Ponty, and Eugène Minkowski. His new anthropology would comprehend the totality of human situations in the field and the experiential data that came out of it—cultural forms, symbolic behavior, psychological drives, and biological instincts. Based on Darwin, exploring all the implications of evolutionary biology, this notion of a unified science of humanity became Freeman's talisman for the rest of his life.

Freeman made his strongest criticisms of contemporary social anthropology in explanatory letters to his old mentors and friends Raymond Firth, Edmund Leach, and Rodney Needham. He had "drunk long and deep at the dusty waterhole of structural anthropology," he wrote to Firth, but he remained "parched."[7] To Needham he confided his dissatisfaction with the "elegant superficialities" and "tautological formulations" of the British approach. It was unscientific, reminding him of a comment attributed to the comedian Shelley Berman: "The reason I smoke so much is that I am such a heavy smoker." The structures anthropologists spun out of custom and rituals were in fact "defensive and symbolic, and a response to quite other forces."[8] These other forces—the elements making up human nature—were what Freeman wanted to understand.

The "baleful" influence of Alfred Radcliffe-Brown's strict structuralism was to blame, he told Edmund Leach in perhaps the most emphatic summary of his discontents. Freeman now found anthropological insights to be "exceedingly shallow." There was no one among the social anthropologists in Australia, certainly not at ANU, which was dominated by functionalist approaches, with whom he could talk much about his ideas. Most of them were

> narrow-minded, defensive and confused. Indeed, when I began expressing the opinion that anthropologists must make some study of psycho-analysis if the nature of ritual behavior is to be understood, this was looked on by some (like Ron Berndt [an Australian anthropologist working on Aboriginal culture]) as a terrible heresy, and a danger to the sacred cause of *social* anthropology—as I suppose it is. Perhaps I will in due course be expelled from the Australian branch of the A.S.A. [Association of Social Anthropologists] that I founded in 1956. It would not perturb me: I now find it much more fruitful to talk to natural scientists, analysts, psychiatrists and historians, than to sociologists.[9]

In the months after his return from Borneo, Freeman's relations with those around him began to sour. Professor John Barnes, a decent man, normally cautious and accommodating in his relations with colleagues, had damaged his and Freeman's relationship by his open skepticism about the Sarawak affair. He believed Derek had been "mentally unbalanced" in Borneo and said so to his face; they had a confrontation over Barnes's refusal to back down from this belief. Bill Stanner also thought Freeman was "not on an even keel" and, as Hiram Caton shows, dismissed Freeman's report on his Sarawak adventure as "grotesque." Freeman also accused the school's director, Crawford, of claiming Freeman was in a mentally disturbed state, though the psychiatrist in Sydney, W. H. Trethowan, had given Derek a clean bill of mental health.[10]

This deteriorating atmosphere carried over into seminar discussions, during which Freeman began raising his new insights about psychological factors and insisted on colleagues and students acknowledging their importance. It was rather too much for some—those who Freeman concluded had become "dependently habituated" to the rules and methods of the social anthropology in which they had been trained and for whom "talk of psychology (any, far less Freudian) is talk to be abjured at all costs, like whisperings of fallibility before the pontiff's chair in Rome."[11] Complaints began to flow to John Crawford's office about Freeman's "belligerency" and his alleged obsession with psychology.

Disentangling the course of events that followed Freeman's return from Borneo equipped with his fresh vision is no mean feat. Personality clashes and the internecine squabbles of a university department were part of the mixture, Freeman only one of the guilty parties. He was certainly beginning to acquire a reputation for being difficult. His response to complaints about him developed a manner that became characteristic of later behavior toward opponents. He would confront his accusers with a series of carefully argued memoranda, stating his credentials and insisting on seeing exact evidence of what he was being accused of. Then he would follow up with a forensic dissection of arguments to show they were wrong, all the while proclaiming the sanctity of "scientific" discussion irrespective of the status or personality of the protagonists. In attempting to defend themselves, his opponents would often find themselves engaged in battles face-to-face or through letters and memoranda without a satisfactory resolution for either side.

Both Barnes and Crawford were bombarded with such Freeman memos, in which he defended his right to raise psychological issues around cultural behavior in seminar discussions. For Crawford, an economist with a distinguished career in the Commonwealth public service before joining ANU, Freeman listed a long line of American anthropologists (Margaret Mead among them) whose approach to the discipline went well beyond a narrow sociological conception. He pointedly reminded Crawford that in Siegfried Nadel's day, the department employed a professional psychologist to instruct students in psychological theory, while Edmund Leach, who had been offered the ANU anthropology chair after Nadel's death, was well known for taking psychology within anthropology seriously.

Crawford warned Freeman against his tendency to twist the meaning of words used in arguments with colleagues to fit his own exquisitely precise interpretation. He also expected Freeman to moderate his seminar behavior. Barnes, too, was not prepared to be bullied by Freeman's serial memoranda denouncing Barnes's lack of training in psychology. He was wearied by Freeman's seeming determination to find a psychological root at the stem of every anthropology problem and was adamant that Freeman's *style* of discourse was the problem in their collegial get-togethers: Derek's vehemence and persistence beyond a decent point of disagreement often outweighed the virtue of what he had to say (a key accusation in the Mead debates two decades later). Barnes stood his ground on these points, though he was disingenuous in declaring that his comments about Freeman being "mentally unbalanced" were nothing to be perturbed about. "Mental illness is not an offence," he proclaimed, a sentiment hardly likely to reassure a protesting Freeman.[12]

Freeman felt he was at a critical juncture in his intellectual life. He had not yet come upon the image of himself as "truth's fool" nor found his way to philosopher Karl Popper's point about truth being the constant elimination of error.[13] But he already considered himself competent at a high level to cross complex disciplinary fields in the pursuit of scientific truth and was not prepared to surrender his right to freedom of thought and expression. Nor, in an institution devoted to advanced thinking, was Freeman prepared to forgo testing conventional disciplinary boundaries by asking questions that might disconcert colleagues. Since Sarawak he had felt liberated from the anthropological paradigm in which superficial formulas sufficed to describe a reality that he saw increasingly as existing beyond such formulations; reality lay beyond theoretical structures. (As we shall see, he was traveling toward his ultimate belief in genetics and biosocial evolution.) Looking back from old age, Freeman thought his ideas had to do with his release from a God-centered Presbyterianism and the deconditioning of his mind that Krishnamurti had encouraged. Ever since, he had been on a pilgrimage "to get through to a point where all substance and illusion would be understood."[14]

In 1962 it is unlikely that Freeman saw the process he was going through exactly in these terms, but since Sarawak he had begun to trace his mind's workings. He was now keeping a diary, in which he plotted each day's thoughts and activities, while gathering in a small notebook quotations from great minds of the past. Cheekily, he sent John Crawford a sample that "might assist you in forming an appreciation of the kind of values by which I live." The sample included lines from John Donne's "Satire III":

> On a huge hill,
> Cragged and steep, Truth stands; and hee that will
> Reach her, about must and about it goe;
> And what the hill's suddenness resists, winne so.

Freeman also included lines from John Milton's *Areopagitica*: "I cannot praise a fugitive and cloistered virtue, unexercised and unbreathed, that never sallies out and sees her adversary, but slinks out of the race, where the immortal garland is to be run for, not without dust and heat." Freeman tried writing a conciliatory letter to Barnes and invited him and his wife to Derek and Monica's Deakin home; he also offered to give up attending seminars until things had cooled down. He wanted Barnes to understand him, pleading that "a man with a conscience greatly different from your own is not necessarily 'mentally unbalanced.'"[15]

This was an age when universities, run according to a collegial rubric with small administrations, worked to avoid if possible bringing the force of legal procedures down on recalcitrant academics, especially those with talent. Both Barnes and Crawford acknowledged that Freeman was a more than competent scholar and should be saved from himself, if he could be. Crawford in particular regarded the Sarawak incidents as an aberration and did not want to proceed with a university enquiry that must embrace those events, for it would do perhaps irreparable damage to a career that held considerable promise. ("Sometimes he treated me like a criminal and other times like a hero," was Freeman's later summation of Crawford.) Barnes too appreciated Freeman's talent, though he admitted forty years later that the thought of having to put up with Freeman for perhaps another decade was the real reason he took up a chair at Cambridge University in 1968.[16]

Freeman spent much of 1961 and 1962 reading through psychoanalytic literature and consulting with psychiatrists in Sydney and Melbourne on theories of mind. In October 1961 he presented a series of papers on Iban rituals to the Melbourne Institute of Psychoanalysis in which he tried to plumb the depths of that symbolic behavior that still eluded him. There is no clear signal how the psychoanalytical fraternity responded, but Freeman wrote to Edmund Leach that the discussions "transcended ordinary anthropological insight," and his paper was accepted for publication.[17] He even embarked on a venture into the Canberra Court of Petty Sessions to observe the preliminary stages and the psychological dimensions of a murder trial. According to Anton Ploeg, a young Dutch anthropologist just back from fieldwork in West New Guinea and an appreciative recipient of one of Freeman's seminar performances, Freeman was in intellectual turmoil; Brian de Martinoir claimed Derek was on pep pills to keep him going.[18]

The denouement of the Martinoir affair added to the disquiet in Freeman's mind. He had returned from Sarawak in 1961 convinced from the days he spent with Martinoir in Kuching that he was in a seriously disturbed psychological state. The university had failed to act on Freeman's recommendation that Martinoir should be brought back to Australia. When he did return in July 1961, he seemed to slip into despondency, failing to respond to any of Freeman's urgings to deliver some written drafts of his work done in the field. The relaxed attitude to the Belgian's dilatory behavior that John Barnes and the university took was indicative of the university's expansive, tolerant atmosphere in the 1960s. They were unwilling to look further into his background, though Martinoir confessed to Freeman that he had been diagnosed with schizophrenia in 1949 and 1955, and he bombarded Derek with pleas to help him in his disturbed state. Freeman did what he could, erring always on the side of too much than too little and in the process persuading Barnes and Crawford that he had too dominant a supervision relationship with his student.

Things came to a head in February 1962. With Crawford giving more and more time to Martinoir to deliver something—anything—that might contribute to his thesis on the Kajang, Freeman became persuaded that they were being deceived. It was his own forensic investigation of institutions, journals, and overseas colleagues that found no evidence of the disciplinary credentials, publications, or fieldwork that Martinoir claimed. Meanwhile, Martinoir was accusing Freeman of breaking his personal confidences and of trying to impose Freeman's personal ethics on him. The university had a consultant psychiatrist talk to Martinoir and declare—after a solitary conversation—that he was not schizophrenic, merely "just an ordinary Frenchman short of a girl."[19] Crawford was ready to let him return to Borneo. Derek was frustrated by the internal politics he deemed the cause of the continuing saga: he had worked Martinoir to the point of agreeing to return to Europe, but ANU kept intervening to haul the student back from the precipice, despite there being no evidence of work done or likely to arrive. Convinced Martinoir was "in the grip of a strong negative transference towards myself," Freeman formally withdrew from his supervision.[20] Better to launch himself wholeheartedly into the enterprise of understanding the psychoanalytic underpinnings of such a state of mind.

John Crawford as director of the Research School of Pacific Studies was generous enough to accept that Freeman might have good reasons for changing his field of specialization and retraining overseas, and he was willing to approve a renewal of Freeman's study leave, lost in the chaotic events of his Borneo visit. Freeman set about asking advice of overseas colleagues like Ernest Beaglehole and his chosen sages of the age—Erich Fromm, Anna Freud, Roger Money-Kyrle—about the opportunities for training in psychoanalysis.

The facade Freeman presented to Anna Freud was of a senior anthropologist knowledgeably trained in psychology, deeply certain of his analysis of the complex events in which he had participated, and who, looking back on his chosen discipline, recognized its bankruptcy of method. Social anthropology had become "a kind of Durkheimian sociology in which the existence of flesh and blood human beings is all but forgotten, and attention is, instead given to statuses and roles, and to abstract principles of social structure." Freeman had succumbed at first, but never completely. Saved by Nadel and by his personal crisis in Sarawak, "I became convinced (not just intellectually—as I had many years before—but deeply and integrally) of the truth of the discoveries of psycho-analysis." Like an eager apprentice he described for Freud the psychoanalytic literature he had recently given himself over to and the entrancement it evoked. He had also attempted a "self-analysis" and had been carefully observing his two daughters and their friends. Where should he go for his study leave so that he could interact with the great minds and undergo a short training analysis—the United States or England? Harvard, Chicago, Pittsburgh, or London?[21]

Within the year he had decided it should be London, for there he could acquaint himself with modern developments in biology through the help of Sir Julian Huxley and learn about the rapidly developing science of ethology from the Dutch ethologist Nikolaas Tinbergen at Oxford. London also had the Tavistock Institute of Human Relations, where Freeman wanted to work with John Bowlby, a psychoanalyst applying ethology to an understanding of human behavior. Freeman was also arranging with the Zoological Society to study primate behavior at the London Zoo and would follow up with paleontology and prehistory at the British Museum of Natural History. In creating this exhaustive and exhausting scenario, Derek seemed to have no sense that he was overreaching himself, though he knew "the establishment" regarded his new mission as an overambitious folly. For good measure, Freeman added a course of advanced training and self-analysis at the London Institute of Psychoanalysis.

Freeman made it clear to the university that while he intended to gain "a full command of the science of psychoanalysis," he had no thought of abandoning anthropology. He was simply acquiring the tools to enable him to join the ranks of senior anthropologists who already recognized the urgency of applying psychoanalysis to the solution of anthropology's problems.[22] His first priority on returning to Australia would be further field research in Samoa to make a study of child development in psychoanalytical terms—a neat, circular route back to his original field of 1940. Significantly, however, Freeman was heading in this direction because, as he told John Bowlby, Margaret Mead's picture of Samoa was "romantic and erroneous," and he wished to lay to rest the illusion that "Custom is King." This, in 1963, is Freeman's first documented statement of the intention his opponents claim was the thread of his entire professional life. It comes later than they have presumed and seems likely to be part of the tide of revelatory impulses that washed to the surface old concerns he held indistinctly before his Borneo conversion. In all the acres of print about Derek Freeman and in interviews with him, only John Barnes seems to have noticed that at this point in his life, Freeman changed his published name from J. D. Freeman to Derek Freeman, dropping his father's name, John, but keeping his surname to reflect his continuing struggle to be "free." "I have been born again," he seems to be saying.[23]

Freeman went to London in 1963 to remake himself so that he could remake anthropology. He was not alone in that mission. Anthropology, particularly twentieth-century British anthropology, was far from a static discipline. The structural functionalism in which Freeman was trained was itself a focus for critical, theoretical argument, part of the "self-awareness and self-accounting" practiced by the discipline and its antecedents since the nineteenth century. But Freeman's urge for a changed discipline was more visceral and more daring, an awakening to a fresh new world not unlike that experienced by the early twentieth-century poet and art critic Edmund Gosse, who famously broke from his naturalist father's narrow religious beliefs to adopt a modern, evolutionary worldview.[24] Freeman was impelled to reinvent himself in the face of colleagues' skepticism and against the advice of mentors that doing so would wreck his comfortable career. In this he was following his father figure, Siegfried Nadel, who had also retrained, going from musicology to psychology to anthropology. The *Problemstellung* was the concept Freeman got from Nadel: following the problem wherever it led, even if it meant going out to get new qualifications.[25] He was coming closer to recognizing himself as "truth's fool."

The formal account he gave to the university of his program in Europe from September 1963 to July 1964 reads like a roll call of famous names and prestigious institutions to persuade his masters that the vast changes he promised in himself were under way.[26] After settling Monica and the girls into a house in north London, Freeman applied to the London Institute of Psychoanalysis and was granted the right to attend courses. He heard lectures ranging from psychoanalytic principles to sexual perversions, depressive states, and manic-depressive psychosis. He also attended Anna Freud's child therapy clinic in Hampstead to listen to her case presentations and a series of seminars on the theory of aggression; he even presented papers at Hampstead on the psychology behind Iban shamanistic rituals.

Hardly drawing breath, Freeman set about pursuing his second objective, to improve his knowledge of ethology. Here he had a stroke of luck, meeting at a symposium Konrad Lorenz, the famed and controversial animal behaviorist. "I have found a new hero," wrote Freeman in his diary at a time when Lorenz's new book on aggression and political activity was, along with a cluster of others, attributing human psychology to an inherited animal nature.[27] Lorenz later invited Freeman to visit him at the Max Planck Institute outside Munich, where Derek gave a paper on aggression and met Irenäus Eibl-Eibesfeldt and other ethologists, who became henceforth his inspiration in developing a new paradigm for anthropology (see chapter 12). Freeman's search for ethologists took him to Amsterdam, Birmingham, and Oxford, where he met and liked Nikolaas Tinbergen. Freeman reported to his ANU masters that he was proposing similar research into human ethology in Samoa when he got back, and Tinbergen was convinced Derek was tackling the field in exactly the right way.

With the help of Desmond Morris and L. Harrison Matthews of the Zoological Society, Freeman also spent some ninety-six hours at London Zoo observing the behavior of primates; he took hundreds of photographs. He also collected photographs from repositories all over Europe for the study of symbolic behavior. Some, along with the numerous images of art in postcard form that Freeman collected with a lifelong fascination, entered his arsenal of materials to be used in coming years in his war correspondence with friend and foe.

In this impressive catalog of unceasing activity and travel, the one area Freeman passes over with virtually no comment is the psychoanalysis he underwent. That may be not only because of its personal nature but also because Freeman was ultimately impatient with the process and unhappy in his relationship with his analyst. The name Harry S. Klein, son of Melanie Klein, the prominent Austrian psychologist, never appears in Freeman's official reports to the university. Yet Freeman spent 138 sessions, from October 1963 to May 1964, with Klein at considerable cost to the family (ANU had refused to fund the sessions) of £552. Kleinian analysis focused on object relations, the emotional bonds people form with instinctual objects, including other people. This put its cocreator, Melanie Klein, at odds with Anna Freud and others of the Freud school, but Freeman had a very high regard for Kleinian psychology when he went into analysis. Melanie Klein made an important provision for inherent childhood aggression in her psychology, and this was a subject that occupied Freeman at this point.[28]

His deepest thoughts about the inward journey he was attempting are not available other than through the summation of entries in his 1963–64 diary made by Don Tuzin. What these make clear is that Freeman was aware of his aggressive tendencies in his relationships with colleagues and family and well before he left Australia for London had begun playing with psychoanalytic themes. Films, parades, criminal trials, his own daughters—all were subject to his voracious reading and newfound gaze. Sessions with Harry Klein made for a slow intensification of his daily life in London.

The sessions started well, Freeman keen to get to the bottom of his Sarawak "cognitive abreaction." But Klein soon began gently nudging Freeman toward examining his relationship with his mother and father. Derek's acknowledgment of his feelings of disgust toward his father jostled with the emotion provoked by the memory of his mother's cloying devotion to himself over against both his father and his sister, Margaret. The attraction to and repulsion from Did created a "feeling of forbidding" and an "infantile fear that Did would disapprove and punish affection for father."[29] There was a certain anguish in his note to himself: "Father not permitted to love me & being so dominated by Did out of frustration & hate opted out and ceased to be a loving father." The realization of "the extent to which I made a bad-object of the old man" was both mortification and catharsis and a clue to the roots of his own aggressiveness toward people.[30]

Contrary to what his opponents believed, Freeman was not blind to this aspect of his character and had been working on it since his confrontations with colleagues in Canberra seminars. Derek's London analysis began to uncover its origins in his "infantile omnipotence and destructiveness," which showed in his merciless teasing of Margaret, in his provoking of Did to the point of nervous frustration, and in his rage when dominated. This latter—the fear of being vanquished—became the key theme in Freeman's battle with himself in the years to come: the ever present struggle to avoid being dominated by conquering others intellectually, and his awareness of the power of this inner drive. Miss Van Stavaren's early punishment of his spelling mistakes leaped into Derek's mind as he struggled to articulate his fear of being found in error or ignorance; any frustration led to an attack on the object. Klein was leading him, albeit not without resistance, to recognizing these alienating tendencies deep within his personality. When Klein told Freeman he was coming five minutes late to their sessions, Freeman registered a "paranoid reaction" followed by a "feeling of depressive guilt." He realized that "I have had primitive notion that something in me that causes annoyance and rage in others; this leads to analysis of my habit of manicuring my nails before I can begin to write = fear that I will not be able to control my aggression in word & thought."[31]

Freeman reexamined his behavior when colleagues and students gave papers in seminars. He explored the aspects of his manner that provoked others and questioned his general touchiness at being threatened—for instance, his readiness to take offense at Barnes and Crawford or at his analyst, Klein, when he lit his pipe in Freeman's presence. An adulation of authority, yet a fear of it at the same time, a sadistic superego that "is very punishing of any lapse"—these were revelations that had Freeman believing self-knowledge could help conquer his fears and his aggression and cultivate decent behavior. His "red-letter day" was 24 November 1963, when he had a breakthrough thought about the significance of dominance striving in human behavior. In fact, Freeman was merging psychoanalytic insights with ideas taken from the extensive literature he was devouring and the personal observations he was making in his ethological research at the London Zoo.

In February 1964 Freeman was writing repeatedly about his "former inability" to admit error and his old anxiety at having to face failure, as though placing unacceptable truths about himself in the past tense was enough to cure him of them.[32] There is no doubting his sincerity in wanting to abandon his dominance striving, and, as we shall see, his struggle was a constant accompaniment to his inner life, but it is also true that thirty years later friends and opponents alike were still chiding him on what they saw as this deeply graven flaw.

By April 1964 Freeman was investing less enthusiasm in the analysis and gradually began to withdraw. He began to see Klein as projecting far too much of himself into their relationship and challenging Derek's belief that he himself could find a rational, scientific solution to the improvement of his personality. Freeman became increasingly resentful of Klein's "dominance." On 8 April he announced his intention to conclude the analysis in early May, prior to his visit to Lorenz in Germany (Freeman did not seem to make any psychological connection between the two). The balance in their relationship began swiftly and subtly to alter. Examining critically his own "unconscious mystic expectation that psycho-analysis will magically bring about a wholly benign state & the accompanying feeling that anything less than this is useless," Freeman told Klein the analysis could no longer do anything for him that he could not do alone (though he felt "somewhat a chump" for leaving).[33] He even felt a distinct lessening of those defensive guilt feelings that had animated earlier sessions and began teasing Klein.

> K talks volubly interrupting me several times reiterating that I am possessed by a wish for perfection; I reply that this is not the case pointing to my action in abandoning the perfect & closed world of social anthropology, facing my enormous ignorance & then actively seeking (at great expense & against marked opposition) understanding of ethology and psycho-analysis, etc; & I compare this to the closed belief systems of many analysts; I also refer to K's past remarks outside the transference (eg ref treatment of children, etc) K states . . . that psychology is not a natural science. I comment "Who is laying down the law now?"[34]

Although their last formal session took place on 8 May, they met again after Freeman's return from Germany, with Klein accusing him of viewing the analysis as "an intellectual game." Freeman did not demur. He walked away believing he had achieved "an admirable resolution of the whole analysis which gives me a sure confidence for the future."[35]

Only Freeman himself could judge the efficacy of this experiment, and then probably only from the vantage point of a life lived in the knowledge of what he had learned about himself. The period of psychoanalysis certainly continued to resonate through the remainder of Freeman's life: according to Monica, he never had a good word for his mother from that day on, and he gained a more tolerant attitude toward his father.[36] But his search for a whole, redeemed self after 1963 at age forty-seven and his struggle to be better than his old self in his relations with others continued for years, though more privately, and was reported in the pages of his diary rather than in a therapeutic relationship.

Freeman's time with Klein did have immediate repercussions because of Anna Freud's antipathy to Melanie Klein and to what Anna considered Klein's distortion of Sigmund Freud's ideas. Though Anna Freud welcomed Freeman to her Hampstead clinic and was pleased with the papers he gave, she dropped him "like a hot potato" when she heard of his consorting with Harry Klein. At home Monica was on the receiving end of Derek's verbal "work-outs" as he tried to understand what was happening in his sessions with Klein.[37]

Although Freeman was in London to build his knowledge of the new behavioral sciences, he was also elaborating his disagreements with old anthropology colleagues in a series of lectures and papers. He remained in sympathy with his mentor Meyer Fortes, whose "increasing interest in phylogeny and psycho-analysis" was gratifying. But Fortes himself was ambivalent about Derek's new approach to anthropology and "could not quite follow the notion of culture as neurotic adaptation."[38]

Others were less gentle in their criticisms. When Freeman reported to the Association of Social Anthropologists' conference that he had good evidence of chimpanzees displaying dominance behavior (this was before Jane Goodall's reports, which changed minds), Leach and Francis Huxley jeered him. Leach took to him again when Freeman gave a paper, "On the Death of an Incubus," in Cambridge, Leach proclaiming that there was no "reality principle" (the mind's ability to assess the reality of the external world), and that states of feeling had no basis in fact. Freeman judged Leach to be guilty of "splitting"—carrying two coexisting attitudes to external reality that functioned side by side without influencing each other. Leach was also guilty of "*passionate* dominance striving" in his explosive out-bursts and repeated attempts to cut Derek down to size.[39]

After giving the same paper at Oxford's Institute of Anthropology, Freeman had to endure the "fiercely anti-psychological prejudices of John Beattie and others expressed in direct attack & with the whimsical flippancy of Ardener & the philosophical defensiveness . . . of Francis Huxley."[40] He forever thought of Oxford anthropology as "that incestuous warren of intellectual bunny rabbits."[41]

These slings and arrows could not dampen the intellectual excitement engendered in Freeman by his Lorenzian turn. He drove on with his reading and research into human aggression, paying particular attention to "the phylogeny of dominance behavior. It's here I believe the answer lies." He was finding a way forward in Robert Ardrey's *African Genesis: A Personal Investigation into the Animal Origins and Nature of Man* (1961), in Lorenz and Tinbergen and Charles Darwin. He was more than pleased when he was invited to give a paper on the origins and nature of human violence in a series on violence run by social anthropologist Ernest Gellner and the psychological historian Norman Cohn at the Institute of Contemporary Arts. Others asked him to lecture on ethology to students at the School of Oriental and African Studies (SOAS). But the summit of his excitement was his visit to Konrad Lorenz at the Max-Planck-Institut für Verhaltens-physiologie (Max Planck Institute for Behavioral Physiology) in Seewiesen near Munich, where he gave a series of talks and joined in discussions with Lorenz, Eibl-Eibesfeldt, and others.

The depressing experience with Oxford anthropologists was counter-balanced by a wonderful discussion with Niko Tinbergen (he was studying Tinbergen's *Social Behavior in Animals*). Right across the road from Tinber-gen's office in Oxford was the Institute of Anthropology. "I thought that was the greatest intellectual abyss in the world," Freeman told Don Tuzin the year before he died. "You see, I was already sold on this by now. It's funny that after that abreaction, it's a deeply intuitive thing. I saw people as different and said, these really are, you know, they're my gibbon. They're not a special creation or anything and we've got to put them back in nature and we've got to understand their behavior as such. That was a deep con-viction that hasn't left me."[42]

Freeman tried to transmit his excitement to John Barnes in Canberra in fulsome letters describing his triumphs and trials. He managed to extract extra funds to subsidize his unplanned but highly productive new activity collecting photographs on "the phenomenology of expressive behavior in the human animal." He had ransacked libraries and art galleries for photo-graphs and cards in the public domain, but his new dedication to a "science" of anthropology led him to the picture vaults of the London newspaper the *Daily Mirror*. With Darwin's classic work *The Expression of the Emotions in Man and Animals* as inspiration ("the best book we have on human ethol-ogy"), Freeman worked out a way to obtain photographic evidence of real behavioral states. He had tried some photography of his own on the way to London, encountering a number of Arabs in passionate argument at the goat market in Aden. But trying to take pictures of the confrontation nearly got him attacked. The files of the *Daily Mirror* delivered up hundreds of thousands of photographs, which Freeman sorted into categories of expressive behavior in infants and children, reactions to accidents, crowd behavior in strikes and riots, behavior under arrest, and even the hysterical reactions of young women to the Beatles. This was material he planned to bring home to Canberra as a repository for a new anthropological assault on ethology and for teaching.

The family left England for Australia on the liner *Fairstar* at the end of July 1964. Derek had gotten through an inordinate amount of work in Europe, as was always the case whether he was at home or abroad; he was never a shirker, and he never took the freedom of academic life as a license to relax. On board he continued his relentless reading program on ethology and behavioral evolution, and in his report to the university, Freeman made clear his intention to proceed to Western Samoa during his next study leave in order to subject Samoan behavior, especially that of chiefs and children, to this newfound ethological approach. There was no mention of Margaret Mead, though he later claimed he reread her classic *Coming of Age in Samoa* on the ship home, annotating it in red ink with a plethora of exclamation marks as he saw through her errors. And when he and the family docked in Sydney on 28 August, waiting for him was a cable that said, "Meeting in Canberra possible in November. Margaret Mead."[43]

6

Face-to-Face with the Incubus

Somewhere in the middle of 1964 the Mead mission crystallized for Freeman. The introduction that he approved for the 1988 Festschrift in his name expressed it thus: "He realized that if he were to return to Samoa it would be incumbent upon him, in the course of his other researches, to re-examine and test the evidence on which Dr. Mead in 1928 based her conclusion that biological variables are of no significance in the etiology of adolescent behavior, evidence of which he was decidedly skeptical as a result of his own Samoan researches."[1] Freeman had returned to Canberra in August 1964 with a sense of dread not of Mead but of the resistance he feared from his anthropology colleagues, who, he knew, remained hostile to his change of direction and the demands he was making on them to follow. His forebodings proved correct and led to new clashes, especially with Bill Stanner, whom Freeman accused of seeking to close off explorations into new territory for social anthropology (see chapter 7).

Freeman spent the rest of 1964 and all of 1965 consolidating his thoughts on how to integrate his new understanding of human behavior with the cultural institutions to which it had given rise. He put his thoughts to the test in a paper to the inaugural congress of the Australian and New Zealand College of Psychiatrists in October 1964. Titled "Psychiatry, Anthropology and the Doctrine of Cultural Relativism," it began as an attack on anthropologists who believed culture was a closed system to be assessed only on its own terms and whose origins outside culture were not to be enquired into.

Freeman was throwing in his lot with the behaviorists. The human—or "man" in the parlance of the time—was an animal evolved from a primate stock who, by use of an invented symbol system and an insatiable curiosity, had embarked on a search for the meaning of existence and the nature of the world. Culture was a "projective system" in which shared fantasies (or myths) and symbolic acting out (or rituals) were "projections of the human animal's impulsive, phylogenetically given nature." Freeman was insistent that man's nature, as a phylogenetic entity, evolved prior to the emergence of culture, a rather crude behavioral scientism that was aimed at this early stage at psychologists and psychiatrists and would have some way to travel in his developing thought. He praised research on the criteria for evaluating behavior (ultimately outlined in the *Diagnostic and Statistical Manual of Mental Disorders*) and supported the definition of mental health as "superior reality perception." Mental health was for Freeman in the 1960s (and ignoring his own past episodes) a zero-sum game in which the neurotic was not only emotionally sick but cognitively wrong.

The 1964 conference paper went over well, with positive discussions and stimulating ideas; the company of psychiatrists was becoming the most congenial for his purposes. Freeman was nothing if not an adventurous intellectual, and he was decidedly more daring than his colleagues. He was prepared even to go beyond the new theoretical ideas he brought back from Europe to consider the possibilities of using lysergic acid diethylamide (LSD) in anthropological research as a way to penetrate the defensive mind systems of subjects in the field. This was a dubious gesture to the narcotic spirit of the 1960s and suggested, rather like Freeman's readiness to deceive the Iban so he could survey their fields, that it was ethnography's duty to break through to objective "truths" about humans in society.[2] He took his developing thoughts to Melbourne in April 1965 to put them before a new audience of psychiatrists.

This provoked a reception radically different from the 1964 conference. Freeman had decided to do a trenchant critique of Freud's 1913 book *Totem and Taboo*, "psychoanalyzing" Freud from various of his papers and providing a psychodynamic interpretation of why Freud insisted, against reason and the advice of his associates, that the "primal parricide," which led to Freud's theory of the Oedipal complex, was a literal historical event. We know little about this occasion, certainly less than the Sarawak incidents, but it seems to have precipitated a second emotional and psychological crisis in Freeman's inner life. A rather wooden statement approved by Freeman for his Festschrift gives a hint of the psychiatrists' reaction: "This paper, when read to a conference of the Australian Society of Psychoanalysts in 1965, provoked a markedly emotional response. Although (as Freeman notes) his paper was based on Popperian principles and had the aim of making psychoanalysis more scientific by the elimination of error, the substantive evidence he had presented was summarily rejected as dangerously heretical and he was pointedly ostracized."[3] Freeman told Frank Heimans three decades later that the psychiatrists were outraged that anyone should do this to Freud and dare to show that he had feet of clay: "They gave me merry hell. It was very severe." So severe that it appears Freeman was hospitalized as a consequence and given electroshock treatments, then put on tranquillizers, which slowed him down considerably. Their effects were only starting to wear off in August, four months later, and according to Monica, Freeman was left with no memory of the period.

The psychiatrists' attack seemingly cut the ground from under Freeman's feet. He had returned from what had been for him a successful period in London. Suddenly, all the investment he had put into "retraining" in psychology and psychoanalysis, all the work he had done on himself, counted as nothing. In Melbourne he was ground down, forced to submit—his greatest fear—in front of serried ranks of experts who believed he had revealed a fundamental misunderstanding of Freudian theory.

There were further attacks from colleagues closer to home, and at the same time Freeman's father back in New Zealand took a "bad turn" and was hospitalized. He ended up in a nursing home, with the family house in Wellington sold for a pittance. Derek's sister, Margaret, blamed him for the sale—unfairly—and they had a hostile falling out in Canberra when Margaret passed through.[4]

And then there was the other Margaret—Margaret Mead. The story of their encounter in the Coombs building where Freeman worked at ANU is one of the set pieces of Freemania that does the scholarly rounds from time to time. David Williamson uses it in his play *Heretic*. Paul Shankman, in his 2009 book, *The Trashing of Margaret Mead*, in which he seeks to rehabilitate Mead, also employs this incident to draw all the venom of the later clash between Freeman's and Mead's supporters back to this moment in 1964. Shankman argues that Mead at this point "had come to occupy a central place in Freeman's psychological universe, representing not only an intellectual challenge but a personal threat to him, to men in general, and to the integrity of Samoan custom."[5]

The reality of the historical moment was much less portentous, though elements of melodrama were certainly present. Freeman told Frank Heimans that Mead came into his office on 10 November 1964, carrying her famous long walking staff, for a discussion of his Samoan work.[6] It was the first time they had met, though they had corresponded in 1961 over the student Peranio. (Shankman claims Mead had known for years that Freeman was critical of her Samoan work, but in what way and to what extent are unclear.) All the accounts agree that Mead swept in, announcing, "You're the one who thinks he knows better than the rest of us, aren't you?" They spoke for two hours and forty minutes, according to Freeman. He had punctiliously set out his Samoa evidence on his desk and then took Mead through it, demonstrating where her account of Samoan adolescence was wrong: "I had got information that really shook her." When Mead asked for a copy of Freeman's 1948 thesis on Sa'anapu, Freeman admits he stuttered as he placed the volumes on his desk for her to take away. "And she said, 'You're trembling like a jelly.' I was a bit scared of her."[7] Freeman then walked Mead back to her quarters.

The next day Mead gave a seminar in the anthropology department that was "just awful," a fanciful flight of ideas full of free association, according to Freeman. At one point she assailed Freeman, asking him why he didn't bring his thesis to her the day before. One later account by a journalist has her having to ask him twice. But Freeman told Heimans that his unconscious suddenly took over, and he sputtered, "'Because I was afraid you might ask me to stay the night.' And that broke the seminar up. That was great."[8]

Shankman and Williamson are surely correct that this was a powerful psychological moment in Freeman's life, full of Freudian slips and shards of symbolic language and gesture. Shankman does his own piece of psychoanalysis on the page: Freeman the dominated, fearing Mead as having a hold over all men; a "castrator," as Freeman put it more than once; and he a victim of the goddess of anthropology, whose spell he had to resist. Interestingly, Shankman does not make any attempt to psychoanalyze Mead's language or her gesture in leaving Freeman's thesis on his desk and her subsequent public challenge of him. Instead, he chooses to emphasize an account of the seminar that has both Mead and Freeman involved in "a very heated public exchange."[9] Shankman's aim is to show Mead as victor in this struggle, refusing to yield to Freeman's aggressive criticisms and adding further fuel to the fire motivating his allegedly long-held and personally vindictive pursuit of her.

But nothing confirms this sense of a sustained mission on Freeman's part. His diary at the time reports that he thought the meeting with Mead in his office went very well. And his accounts of the drama that took place during the seminar, which he gave to interviewers well after the public controversy over his refutation of Mead had broken, do not contradict this. The day after the seminar Derek wrote a letter of apology to Mead that was calm and generous: "I said, 'it's plain to me that our conclusions about the realities of adolescence and sexual behavior in Samoa are fundamentally at variance. For my part, I propose, as in the past, to proceed with my research with as meticulous an objectivity as I can muster. This, I would suppose, is going to lead to the publication of conclusions different from those reached by you, but I would very much hope that however we may disagree, there should be no bad feeling between us. You have my assurance that I shall strive towards this end.'" Mead replied with a little less generosity, brushing off the seminar incident ("you asked for it and you got it") but declaring, "Anyway, what is important is the work."[10] Again, for Paul Shankman this is Mead waving her staff triumphantly over Freeman. And again the evidence is patently lacking, Freeman consistently refusing to read any acidic intent in her reply: "I never quarreled with her except that one occasion." In 1996 he added to a journalist about Mead's reply: "And I thought that was great. It's exemplary."[11]

Looking for winners and losers in this psychological free-for-all does not advance our understanding of Freeman's evolving relationship to Mead and her work. The clearest conclusion we can make from this murky puddle of incidents in 1964 is that, figuratively speaking, here are two cocks strutting aggressively, both striving for dominance in the barnyard of anthropology, the result a kind of wary standoff—for now. Shankman thinks the two of them should have taken the opportunity to talk about psychoanalysis and ethology, but Freeman was already halfway to Samoa in his mind.

He had already begun staking a claim back in the field with a skirmish of articles disagreeing with American anthropologists Marshall Sahlins and Melvin Ember over claims they had made about Samoan descent group structure and political decentralization. Ember was more in Freeman's firing line than Sahlins, with whose views of subtly differing styles of Polynesian hierarchy Freeman was in sympathy. But Ember was guilty of a range of errors about descent group structure and the power and authority of chiefs beyond their villages.[12]

In a classic exercise of refutation, Freeman peeled back Ember's logic, deploying a detailed citation of historical sources from nineteenth-century missionaries and diplomats to show that Ember was wrong. Freeman was able to show that Samoan descent groups had optional rules for establishing succession, though with a major patrilineal emphasis, and that Samoans possessed a kind of ramified descent group system spread across both Western and American Samoa. He carefully explained the traps of language when referring to family and titles and argued that political integration embraced more than one village through well-defined district organizations to which were linked fierce competition for the great titles of the land among the "royal" families. Freeman's argument and subsequent rejoinders to criticisms by Ember were trenchantly logical, founded on a mastery of old Samoan history and expressed in clear prose and firm but not discourteous tones. Mead pronounced his comments "adequate and elegant."[13]

In some respects this series of essays may have been a dry run for the refutation of Mead's *Coming of Age in Samoa* that Freeman undertook twenty years later. Freeman insisted that his treatment of Ember was a refutation and not an alternative reconstruction of ancient Samoan social organization, a testing against the empirical historical evidence of the hypotheses published by Ember (though Freeman does in effect offer a firm view of how social and political integration worked). And just like the refutation Freeman produced in 1983, his measured prose style met with a barrage of hostile, seemingly personal criticisms. Ember asserted that Freeman "does not make friends fast" and claimed his arguments amounted to "pedantic polemic." They were also "authoritarian" and "the antithesis of scientific method," even "churlish" in some instances, according to Ember.[14]

A fair reading of all the essays defies such easy denunciations. Freeman in fact tried before publication to appease anticipated objections to his rather patronizing statement that an "inexperienced ethnographer" with limited exposure to Samoa "might remain wholly ignorant of the closely guarded domain of genealogical knowledge." On Ember's insistence, however, the sentence was published, presumably so that he might have a point of attack.[15] Ember's stated wish to avoid "acrimony" rang hollow in the circumstances, especially as many of his characterizations of Freeman's attitude were presented in a paper to the ranks of the American Anthropological Association (AAA) in Detroit, Michigan, in November 1964. There, he conveniently branded the debate as "acrimonious" and Freeman as a distasteful critic, thus sowing seeds of expectation among American anthropologists whenever Freeman should come into print in the future.[16] In stark contrast to this approach, Freeman had closed his final response to Ember with a gesture of gratitude and without insisting on his point of view, confident instead that Samoa experts would come to their own judgments based on the evidence.

There are still questions to be answered about this controversy, which took place largely in one anthropology journal. Why, for instance, did Freeman list his 1948 thesis on Sa'anapu from the University of London as simply a manuscript? Why did Freeman make a conventional argument about social structure and not attack the entire foundation of social anthropology according to his sudden conversion and retraining? What was his attitude to Margaret Mead six months before their collision in Canberra, her ethnographic study of Manu'a prominently quoted in his essay on Ember and Sahlins but with no mention of her *Coming of Age in Samoa*? The partial answer is that Freeman was still hovering between missions, not yet properly launched on the venture to deal with Mead that his critics would later allege was a personal vendetta stretching back to the 1940s (and which Freeman himself retrospectively traced back to his first visit to Samoa). At this point in 1965, Freeman's views on Mead were still inchoate, and his familiarity with her work was incomplete. He was not yet touting his own work on Samoa as a scientifically accepted study.

Ember's attitude to Freeman was an omen of conflict to come, reinforced by the drama of Mead's visit to Canberra and by stubborn resistance to Freeman's research plans for Samoa on the part of Bill Stanner, now in charge of the department. That resistance was a continuation of the anxiety that Freeman's new approach was causing—at least to Stanner. Freeman had formally advised Stanner on 4 November 1965 that he planned to study five aspects of Samoan culture and history on his research leave in Samoa in 1966. Three of those aspects were a conventional extension of his 1940s work—to study social, political, and economic change in Sa'anapu, along with completing a full-scale examination of Samoan social organization and of chieftainship. The remaining two worried Stanner. Freeman told him there was "substantial evidence to suggest that Dr. Mead's conclusions are, in various ways, at error." His objective was to study socialization among children and adolescents, especially "processes of psychological and social adaptation." Freeman didn't know what the conclusions might be, but they were "likely to be of interest to a wide range of social and behavioral scientists." He also wished to make a proper comparison of social customs between Western and American Samoa, which no one had yet done.

Stanner was opposed to this mix of field ethnography and behavioral analysis: "Here are two radically dissimilar orientations. They mix levels of organization of data. They select different sets of variables. They use different notions of explanation and causality. They lie on different axes of development. They appear to me to lead to different universes of discourse. . . . For my own part I reject any notion that Ethnography + Ethology + Psycho-analysis = Social Anthropology." Stanner informed Crawford that he was reserving the right to withhold further funding if Freeman's plans went too far along these tracks while he was in Samoa.[17]

Freeman utterly rejected this restrictive notion of what anthropology should be, as we have seen. And despite the list of interviews and memoirs that claim his return to Western Samoa was the deliberate reignition point of his mission against Margaret Mead, this correspondence and his diary make plain the crowded program of work he intended, only part of which dealt with a "re-study" of Mead's earliest researches in Samoa, and that with uncertain outcomes. Freeman told another colleague, Jim Davidson, that he was really in Samoa to study "chieftainship in a direct behavioral way and in the general context of dominance theory." He hoped his findings would help support a fundamental understanding of political behavior in general.[18]

He and his family set out for the Samoan islands on 16 December 1965. Like Derek in 1939, they sailed in a "drab tub," the *Oriental Queen*, by way of Auckland and Tonga and arrived in Pago Pago, American Samoa, on 29 December. Here Freeman called on the governor for permission to visit Manu'a during his stay. He also experienced a sudden emotional identification of Monica with Sisi, his long-ago Samoan girlfriend, as they sailed back into Apia, where it all began.[19]

Where, then, to base themselves? Sa'anapu and its rich social life seemed the obvious choice, the ethnographic present that had legitimized his early steps in anthropology. But Freeman had left Australia uncertain whether Sa'anapu would work for him this time, for the village's population had by all accounts become dispersed along the south coast. His own surveys, however, soon revealed that the ancient site of the village still had an adequate and accessible population, and he could reach the remainder of its nine hundred inhabitants by road. Freeman had persuaded ANU to let him bring the family car to Samoa. It meant he had the means to negotiate Upolu's rough, scoured roads and to reach Apia in ninety minutes, a far cry from the four hours or more it took on horseback in 1940.

In 1966 Freeman was far better placed to study Samoan behavior intimately than he had been in the 1940s. He was now professionally trained in social anthropology and was pushing beyond, into the new realm of ethological observation. More than that, he had gained the patronage of Western Samoa's prime minister, Mata'afa Fiamē Faumuina Mulinu'u II, and was given privileged access to government records and the Land and Titles Court so that he might study the result of competition and rivalry among the titled chiefs of the group. Then residents of his old village, Saʻanapu, found him a large *fale* right at its center, overlooking the *malae*, or village green. The *fale* was commodious enough for family living, with a study in one corner and its open sides ideal for observing everyday village life. Trial and error established a tolerable family existence for Monica and the two girls, and they secured a housekeeper, Poto, daughter of Leaʻana Faʻalolo, who had lived in Saʻanapu all her forty-four years and was a valuable informant on the history of the village's families.

Freeman himself was welcomed back as a *matai*, or titled chief, invited to attend all meetings of the Saʻanapu village council. Characteristically, he plunged in without hesitation and by the middle of 1966 had compiled 150 hours sitting cross-legged in village and district *fonos*, or councils (his longest stint was more than eight hours of excruciating discomfort). His proficiency in the Samoan language returned within weeks, and he was able to participate in all the activities of the *fono*, including meeting the customary gift obligations of a chief, a costly addition to his research expenses that he had regularly to justify to ANU.

Never one to sit and muse upon being back in his old field site, by the time Freeman wrote his first report to Canberra in July 1966, he had accumulated notes and analysis at the rate of twenty thousand words a week. Global happenings—America had just made the first soft landing of a craft on the moon, and there were race riots in Chicago—passed them by. The day-to-day problems of the world that Freeman and his family inhabited consumed him. Among the events observed were "the expulsion of a chief (*aliʻi*) from the village; an assault on a chief by a *tauleʻaleʻa* (untitled man); an *ifoga* (ritual submission) by Saʻanapu to a neighboring village; the death of a *Faipule* (parliamentary representative of Safata district), with much consequent political activity at district level; the ceremonial installation of a holder to the high chiefly title of Sanalālā by the neighboring Ala Taua district, and the deaths (and obsequies) of two high ranking *aliʻi* of Saʻanapu."[20]

Freeman was also traveling to Apia to read manuscripts and books in the Nelson Memorial Library and to research the Land and Titles Court records. Add a constant diet of back reading, from Raymond Firth's *Social Change in Tikopia* to Konrad Lorenz's recent book, *Evolution and Modification of Behavior*, plus the challenge of observing and regularly photographing village behavior discreetly, and it is little wonder that by May he and Monica were discussing his "overwrought state."[21]

That overwrought state did not stop Freeman from adding three new research areas to his original plan. First, he wanted to focus on rivalry among *matai* for the highest titles and the way in which they bore on contemporary politics—an extension of his arguments with Melvin Ember, but sparked also by Jim Davidson's recently finished book on the political history of Samoa, which Freeman read in manuscript.[22] Second, in another echo of earlier work, Freeman planned to study religious behavior and changes since the 1940s from his observation point in church each Sunday and through discussions with the wife of the prime minister, Fetaui Mata'afa. Third, he wished to deepen his understanding of the symbolism embedded in Samoan sacred objects, such as chiefly headdresses, fly whisks, and fine mats. This would mean, he told ANU, more historical reading into early missionary writings and the volumes of Augustin Krämer, the German ethnologist—and more time in the field than he had originally budgeted.

The everyday intensity of his field practice and the constantly expanding reach of these interests belie the belief of Freeman's many critics that this Samoa sojourn was all about a consuming mission to show Margaret Mead was wrong. Instead, his frenetic activity points to a manic tendency that drove him to collect, to capture, to analyze, in line with his new behavior-oriented perspective on culture. The Mead mission, though he had been carrying its seeds in his head for some time, came upon him gradually. In July 1966 he was justifying a visit to American Samoa as a way of solving "long-standing ethnographical problems" of the kind he had with Melvin Ember. But he had also met Soloi, the pastor of Fitiuta on the island of Ta'u, where Mead had worked, who promised to help him "in my ethnographical survey of Manu'a." Soloi was originally from Sa'anapu and had written a "critique" of Mead's account of Manu'a's culture.[23]

Mead's name now began to appear regularly in Freeman's diary. The first mention is on 4 October 1966, when Freeman remarked on Mead's "very impressionistic" treatment of Samoan culture. In a letter to Clifford Geertz in December, Freeman wrote of Mead's "projection of her own defenses + a daughterly desire to please 'Daddy Boas.'"[24] The pace quickens from February 1967. Mead's *Coming of Age in Samoa* "takes on more and more the character of an anthropological romance," a "Rousseauian fantasy." Freeman worked excitedly through other Mead writings, taking copious notes. He could finally see an opportunity for reappraising—and rebutting—her thesis, and "I am thinking of giving this task priority on my return to Canberra." By March 1967 he had a tentative title in his head around the unmaking of an anthropological myth.

His reading in other areas and relentless work pace never slackened. To add emotional pressure, his father in New Zealand died on 24 June 1967, making Freeman "unwell and low in spirits." His sister was still fighting with him by letter and would not heed Derek's explanations about the loss of the family home. In August his zeal for anthropological enquiry was at its lowest ebb after the onset of dengue fever. He had to give up serious reading.[25]

This was the environment in which Freeman set out for Ta'u on 1 September. In Ta'u he suffered the third of his "turns" (after Sarawak and Melbourne), that figure in latter-day stories of Freeman's supposed madness. In 2008, seven years after Freeman's death, the anthropologists of the Association for Social Anthropology in Oceania (ASAO) were still trading thirdhand reports that Freeman had gone mad in American Samoa and been taken away by the authorities.[26] Hiram Caton provided more dramatic fare in his 1990 book on the Mead debate, later used by David Williamson in his play *Heretic*. According to Caton in 2008, "Derek lost control and went into a deeply mea culpa state (he covered himself with excrement). This provoked his removal by the US Navy and his confinement for three days."[27] Among these lurid claims, Paul Shankman's book strikes a sober note of caution. He acknowledges that whatever Freeman found in Ta'u upset him greatly and may have precipitated an event akin to his delusions in Sarawak. He *was* found on a beach in a disoriented state. A Coast Guard cutter *was* dispatched to bring him back to Tutuila for observation at the hospital. But he also recovered quickly.[28]

What happened in Ta'u, and what does it say about the emotional and intellectual freight Freeman was carrying in the Samoa of 1967? In the months after the Ta'u episode, Freeman wrote a letter to Lowell Holmes, who had done his doctoral thesis in anthropology on American Samoa and written a book on Ta'u. Holmes was one of the earliest of those whom Freeman saw as Mead acolytes to experience the relentless probing of a Freeman letter. Armed with notes from Mead's work, Freeman questioned chiefs and others on Ta'u about a variety of Mead's claims, including sexual conduct. From two older Samoans he got sworn testimony that Mead had an affair with a Samoan man, code-named Aviata, and that she danced barebreasted with him. These Samoans were shocked, Freeman told Holmes: they saw her behavior as that of a common person; she was "just like a vagrant, like an animal." Freeman expanded to Holmes on the theory that Freeman had been pondering for some time, drawn from his reading in psychoanalytic theory: Mead's account of Samoan sexual behavior in

Coming of Age in Samoa was "a *projection* on to Samoan females of her *own* sexual experiences as a young woman, in the far-away romantic South Seas."[29]

This was an emotional shock to Freeman the puritan anthropologist, whose emotions were already deeply stirred when it came to alleged insults against "his" people and his "family." Freeman acknowledged in his diary that he was overcome by strong feelings and wept at the revelations. The next day (16 September), he spent several hours walking back and forth around Taʻu talking to himself as a way to unload "my own repressed retaliatory aggression." His diary for Sunday, 17 September, has references to God, the admission of error, and the forgiveness of sins.

What added to a heartfelt sense of ownership of the local feelings of humiliation was Freeman's position as holder of the title *lagona-i-taga*, whose ancestral roots lay exactly where he was in Manuʻa. Saʻanapu had been colonized from Manuʻa. Freeman had taken a *tulafale* (talking chief) with him to the island and was received like a long-lost brother, treated with high chiefly deference, feted with special foods, and shown where the ancestor of his title had in ancient times emerged from the ground. He felt deeply and authentically the shame that he now attached to the place and the title because of Mead's alleged actions. More than that, Freeman was at the historical center of the origins of the great title *tui Manuʻa*, one of the oldest Samoan titles with a claim to paramountcy over the entire Samoan group. "All their genealogies go back to there, you see, the true apex of Samoa and Manuʻa. Margaret Mead didn't know that when she went there," he told Don Tuzin thirty years later. "It's the Delos of Polynesia, you know, the sacred island, extraordinary place."[30]

Over the five-day period from 15 to 19 September, Freeman was able to diarize in a remarkably detached manner his psychiatric symptoms: "Abre-actions . . . highly florid behavior. Soloi becomes perturbed, sends signal [19 September] to Moc when I recover after lying on coral at rear of house for 1½ hrs. I ask for signal to be cancelled; I am now quite calm but have notion I am to act as agent for Taʻu; in evening (to my surprise) coast guard cutter arrives nb. onset of physical weakness as soon as I touch ladder; I am given a needle and tken [*sic*] to hospital in Pago Pago."[31] Freeman spent one hazy day, 20 September, under sedation, not three. By 22 September he was back in the office of the governor, asking permission to return to Manuʻa after a rest in Saʻanapu. After talking to Soloi, the governor agreed and Freeman returned to Saʻanapu. There, on 24 September, he heard over the radio that Soloi reported that Freeman had lost his senses, gone mad, and become verbally violent. His permission to revisit Manuʻa was revoked.

Just as in Borneo, Derek Freeman's value expectations were dealt a severe blow in Taʻu. The experience was not the dramatic recentering Borneo was, more a confirmation that he had a moral and scientific task to carry out and a pointer to what he had to do, namely, take up the cudgel against Margaret Mead's portrayal of Samoan culture. But there are striking similarities with the psychological journey Freeman underwent in Borneo: the intense affinity he felt with the Samoan people, taking on their wrongs with a moral force and becoming their agent in a corrupt world (as he had intended to do for the Iban); the sudden mental convulsion that he struggled to cope with; the absence of doubt; and a remarkable figure—Mead, like Harrisson—who was the trigger for the discharge of his emotional energy. Shankman recognizes a pattern adhering to both events.[32]

But as with Sarawak, a diagnosis of "madness," "derangement of mind," or "insanity" is unnecessary. Such conclusions have more to do with the fixed emotions of the long and obsessive campaign around Margaret Mead that followed and the treatment people received at Freeman's hands. We know that Freeman was capable of deep emotional energy and, according to Monica, a totally absorbed manner when he was in the midst of solving a problem. At the end of his life Freeman admitted to Don Tuzin the strength of his emotionalism, dating back, he suggested, to the period of intense living during the 1930s as a student in Wellington writing poetry and dueling with Nazi sympathizers. Sarawak, Melbourne, and Taʻu were all instances of that extreme, "but it's not madness, you know."[33]

At the back end of the long-running Mead campaign it was easy for critics to question the state of Freeman's mind and the reality of what he found or heard on Taʻu. The loss of the "reality principle" is, as one cultural historian reminds us, one of our Western human definitions of madness.[34] Or the mad are those who cannot cope with the daily demands of living and exhibit strange behaviors. Yet other cultures allow such people to inhabit accepted roles and do not dismiss them as crazy. Shankman reports that some Samoans thought Freeman was possessed by spirits, a not unusual phenomenon in Samoa.[35] Darian Leader's reading of the mental states often associated popularly with psychosis or paranoia would suggest that Freeman was concerned with his duty to the Samoan people and with anthropology's place in the intellectual universe.[36] In fighting for the Samoans, he was making an effort to repair that universe, to help bring a new order to anthropology. If that sounds grandiose, then that too is one of the characteristics of the extreme mental and emotional suffering that Freeman experienced in Ta'u. He was truth's fool, compelled to right moral and intellectual wrongs.

That Freeman "stabilized" so quickly after the events, returning to his labors in Sa'anapu and an energetic new correspondence with Lowell Holmes that marks the beginning of the real Mead campaign, suggests two things. First, in American Samoa he was exhausted from overwork and the effects of dengue fever. That partly explains his emotionally distraught condition, as even John Barnes acknowledged.[37] Once Freeman was back in the care of Monica and the girls his outlook on the world recovered. Second, we should be wary of categorizing his mental states as one thing or the other and creating a fable around his identity, as has been the tendency of some protagonists over the years. There is an ambivalence to his subjective being that can be traced through the years, perhaps best summed up in James Clifford's concept, used for another controversial Pacific anthropologist, Maurice Leenhardt, of the *plenitudes* of a life, in which contradictions and ambivalences are held together with seemingly little effort.[38]

The Freeman family left Sa'anapu for Apia and the voyage home in early January 1968. They had been two years in the field, two years that had taken a heavy toll on Derek and Monica (the girls seem to have thrived; Jennifer as a twelve- and thirteen-year-old was given a *taupou*, or village maiden, title and looked after strictly by village elders). Monica nursed Derek through his exhaustion, even drafting his letters sent back to Canberra when he was too weak. As they were leaving for Apia, Freeman wryly noted in his diary a quotation from a nineteenth-century British consul in Samoa, William Churchward: "It is a common saying here that after two years sojourn in Samoa, a man becomes hopelessly mad."[39]

The family spent a month in New Zealand on the way home, touring and visiting the Freeman extended family. It was also an opportunity for Freeman to attend the Australasian science congress, where he listened "with quiet desperation" to a "dull extolling of the Durkheimianism" in a presidential address by a local anthropology professor who, ironically, claimed the discipline was at a crossroads.[40] He himself offered some random reflections on anthropological theory based on his findings in Samoa. The Freemans were back in Australia and Canberra on 15 February 1968 with their collections and over five hundred hours of taped materials from *fono* meetings; it had taken four men to carry the boxes onboard the ship.

Freeman had written to John Barnes from Samoa that he did not quite know what to do with the allegations about Margaret Mead. If they were published, he believed they would cause a scandal. By the time of his return to Canberra, Freeman had decided he needed another bout of retraining, this time on the historical origins of the theories with which Mead went into the field, namely, the culture orientation of her mentor, Franz Boas, and his school.

But it should be remembered that, alongside the steadily building Mead mission, Freeman stuck to his original plan to study the lineaments of dominance behavior among chiefs in Samoa, and he brought home enough material to sustain a new interpretation of customary behavior. This was the other Big Idea that competed with Mead for the rest of his life, as he told Meyer Fortes: to demonstrate, using his extensive data, that "phylogenetically given behavior and emotional states are *integral* (repeat integral) to ongoing customary (or rule-regulated) behavior."[41] Freeman wanted to show that this behavior came prior to the formation of customs and how they were linked together.

The case against Mead's "culture-is-environmentally-determined" claims was a first step toward this wider mission, but it was not the whole mission. When Freeman applied for the chair of anthropology at ANU in 1972, his application did not even mention his plan to refute Mead.[42] By then his reputation was established as the radical anthropologist who wanted to make a new anthropology by denying the old one. A colleague had already likened him to a deathwatch beetle "eating away the cathedral of social anthropology."[43]

7

"The Trouble with Derek Is . . ."

Histories of Freeman's workplace, the Australian National University, tread warily around the subject of Derek Freeman. The official history of the institution, published in 1996, manages to mention him only once, and that merely to quote a line from his obituary for Siegfried Nadel.

The silence was pointed, and Freeman himself noticed. In correspondence with the lead author of *The Making of the Australian National University, 1946–1996*, historian Stephen Foster, Freeman insisted he was not particularly irritated but thought it strange that of the many books by ANU academics mentioned there was not one word on his *Margaret Mead and Samoa*, the book that in 1983 and for years afterward trained a spotlight on the university. Nor was Freeman chosen to be interviewed, though many others had been who had not been at ANU as long or as (in)famously as he had. Was Foster "got at," Freeman wondered? Was Freeman too "unsound" to warrant attention?

Foster's rather limp reply was he did not want to burden the text with names: a roll call of every scholar did not fit the pattern chosen for the history. In fact, Foster told a colleague that after consulting Freeman's ANU staff file (including an intimidating sealed brown envelope), he decided that Freeman's story was too bizarre and complicated to try to unravel.[1]

Freeman fares a little better and a little worse in a memoir about life in the Research School of Pacific Studies (RSPacS), in the Coombs building, where Freeman worked.[2] He is at least named, a succession of academic contemporaries blithely describing him as "neurotic," "brilliantly crazed," "the biggest worm in the paradise." A colleague in anthropology dismissed his "flirtation with biological bases of behavior" and was still unsure whether Derek was joking the day he wore a pair of "dragon fly glasses" to morning tea, solemnly declaring that the black goggles, with half tennis balls pierced with holes in them, were the perfect accompaniment to fieldwork when the subjects did not like to be observed. Freeman's most trenchant critic among former students claimed Freeman's research strategy for his students was to get them to focus on debunking the most prominent researcher in their area and to use a stopwatch during their observations of natural behavior. A few former colleagues and students testified to his kindnesses or to the "sheer intellectual brilliance and adrenalin-producing tension" of a Derek Freeman seminar where the protagonists were equally matched. But the overall message was that here was a driven, eccentric, witheringly dismissive intellect who symbolized the capacious breadth of talent at ANU and the institution's tolerance but who spawned no school of followers.[3]

"The pathogen is nothing; the terrain is everything," urged Louis Pasteur on his deathbed.[4] It is an observation that, lightly adapted, applies to Freeman's work within the university and in the RSPacS. In an institution dedicated to research, not teaching, Freeman's personality and behavior quirks were magnified within the small world of staff and students working intensively together as he applied himself to his mission to build a new anthropology on the carcass of the old while juggling growing responsibilities within the department. "The trouble with Derek is . . ." became a refrain among colleagues and friends over the course of contentious years, intoned whenever stories about Freeman are passed round.

By the time Freeman returned from Western Samoa, Canberra was more truly a city than the bucolic town he had moved to in the 1950s. The population had more than doubled as public servants flooded in from their state outposts in Sydney and Melbourne. New suburbs opened, buildings grew in number and size, the notorious circular road system curved ever outward. The university now stood in its own precinct, with a range of new buildings and student halls built during the 1960s; "the Coombs," a hexagonal, Escher-like building with a complex series of corridors, opened in 1964. Some departments in the research schools were more international than others, but productive work by individuals and teams expanded into the 1970s. In the RSPacS, in anthropology particularly, fieldwork was an expected, if expensive, standard.

Anthropology under Nadel had extended the profession's reach beyond the Aboriginal focus controlled by Peter Elkin at Sydney University. Nadel's energy had helped send anthropologists into Indonesia, Papua New Guinea, and the Pacific islands. But Nadel's death ushered in a decade during which the cohesion he had built up fell away, despite the best efforts of John Barnes. There were those who, like Bill Stanner, had definite, circumscribed views of anthropology's remit; others who were comfortable in a "sprawling profession" developing into broad new fields; and occasionally anthropologists like Derek Freeman who dreamed of a totalizing theory on a grand scale to tie anthropology more securely to the sciences.

Barnes wanted to keep the word "sociology" in the name of the Canberra department and tried to encourage work in Australia's European immigrant society. Linguistics and archaeology were also part of the department in its early days, soaking up funds before they separated into separate entities.[5] Certain figures stood out as mavericks. Derek Freeman was one, a large, vocal, emphatic presence, attracting some of the best minds among students but alienating others, both students and colleagues.

The most privileged years were gone by 1968, and so were the plans Freeman had foreseen for ten years of solid fieldwork in Borneo, the Samoan islands, and Indonesia, with big books consolidating his ethnographic findings. Ever since his time in London, Freeman had felt increasingly isolated within his department. He was starved of seminar time and left out of things happening around him, and his retraining in London and the papers he gave to psychiatrists were omitted from Barnes's annual reports to the university. He found this difficult to live with, even if he was prepared to see it as unconscious behavior by the "sociologically pure at heart."[6]

After Western Samoa his relations with colleagues and some students became worse. "Confrontational, disputatious, and unyielding, prone to deracination, and convinced of having ultimate answers" is how two historians describe Freeman during the Barnes years.[7] This may have dissuaded him from applying for the chair, which Barnes was vacating, but Freeman was also comfortable enough in the intellectual surroundings of ANU to decline an invitation in 1971 to take a professorship in Edinburgh. When the chair position in his department came up again the following year— A. L. Epstein was heading for Sussex—he was still loath to apply. But something changed his mind, even though applications had closed.

Freeman told Meyer Fortes he had gone off to South Australia to study the papers of a missionary to the Aboriginal people. University colleagues and staff at the state museum there persuaded him he had a duty to apply for the chair if anthropological understanding of other cultures had any value at all.[8] Such suasion was most likely connected to Freeman's new interest in Aboriginal affairs, for a progressive new national government was about to take power in Canberra, and perhaps he envisaged having some influence on policy, like the influence Elkin had practiced from Sydney University over decades. But Freeman also realized that as professor he could with more authority promote an anthropology based on a unified science of man.

Throwing his hat into the ring of candidates startled the university authorities, who had calculated against its happening. John Crawford's successor as director of RSPacS, geographer Oscar Spate, respected Freeman's intellectual capacities but worried about his temperament. Spate alerted the incoming director, Anthony Low, who felt that passing over Freeman, even at this late stage, might cause more trouble. If Freeman were to win the appointment, a professorial fellow should be appointed alongside him and the two made to rotate heading the department.[9]

In the end a solution like this occurred. Freeman was appointed, his brace of referees running to fourteen, among them Epstein and Fortes and including Sir Macfarlane Burnet, emeritus professor of medicine; F. J. Fenner, director of ANU's School of Medical Research; professors of medicine or psychiatry or zoology from Harvard and Stanford; and of course Lorenz and Tinbergen. Freeman's application never mentioned Margaret Mead.

Skirmishes broke out around Freeman's candidacy. A group of graduate students pushed his case, highlighting his international reputation, commitment to science, and promotion of student research and welfare. But the selection committee initially advised against his appointment, "in a timid and obscurantist way," Spate told Freeman. Somehow the notion of a co-chairmanship of the department resurfaced, with Freeman expressing willingness to share the office. His old boss John Crawford, now vice chancellor of the university, reconvened the committee, and this time the majority voted for Freeman. Not everyone was enthusiastic, and one colleague, Stanner, asked no questions, would not look Freeman in the eye, and voted against him. Freeman's referees, though, were solidly behind his intellectual power while conceding that he carried a barbed personality. The departing Bill Epstein made no bones about the matter: Freeman was "a notoriously 'difficult' man to whom nothing comes easier than making enemies." Epstein thought it best to appoint Freeman nonetheless in order to preempt any trouble Freeman might cause if someone uncongenial to him got the job. Fortes and the others were kinder.[10] So was Spate, who forecast the dynamic guidance under Freeman that anthropology had lacked for fifteen years.[11]

In October 1972 ANU's *Reporter* published a picture of a smiling Derek Freeman arm in arm with Albert Barunga, an elder of the Worora people in the northwest of Western Australia. It was a signal of the new political and research interest that was beginning to consume Freeman. He had met Barunga at a conference of the Australian Institute of Aboriginal Studies (AIAS) and was at once enthralled by the elder's take on the ecological and human problems besetting Aboriginal communities in white Australia. Barunga was incensed at the arrogance of white men, "because [they've] got a paper from Government," who strode unasked into his country. He pleaded for cooperation around sacred sites and an acknowledgment that Aboriginal people (including Torres Strait Islanders) belonged: "We people, we are Australian people." Freeman wanted to grasp the wisdom he saw in Barunga ("he talks like a stone age St Francis") and to mine the ecological understanding of humans' relations with their surroundings as part of Freeman's own project for a reformed anthropology.[12]

The 1970s were a tense time to enter Aboriginal studies. Anthropology was implicated in years of paternalism toward the Aboriginal population, and the discipline had been laboring under the largely assimilationist strategies of Elkin in Sydney; Stanner at ANU ploughed a lonely furrow. A "resurgence of sorts" began in the 1960s, but the atmosphere in conservative Canberra was at best lukewarm. Aboriginal activists were beginning to flex their muscles inside and outside AIAS. The call for land rights and the establishment of an "Aboriginal Embassy" on the grounds in front of Parliament House raised hackles and the temperature of political debate.[13]

This was meat and drink to Freeman's newfound moral passion. Once he had decided Barunga's cause and that of his people was just, Freeman entered into them fully, seemingly abandoning for the time being his other projects. "I at once resolved to make a detailed study of the Worora," he told Konrad Lorenz. His elevation to the chair—and the headship of anthropology—enabled him to begin his tenure with expansive activities on behalf of Barunga. Freeman helped bring Barunga to ANU in 1973. They worked together classifying rarely seen photographs of ritual and culture. In September Freeman traveled to Barunga's country on the other side of the continent, where Freeman became involved in a study for the Aboriginal Housing Panel and an advocate in the resiting of a settlement.[14]

On returning to Canberra, Freeman had no hesitation in standing with Aboriginal protestors at the tent embassy (it was also a means to connect with his daughter Jennifer, who was active on behalf of the Aboriginal cause). He made statements to AIAS condemning colonial violence and publicly supported an Aboriginal demand that AIAS retreat from its plan for establishing its headquarters in a building belonging to the mining industry. Freeman even flew to Darwin in northern Australia to present a proposal to the Aboriginal Congress for an Aboriginal domain to be sited around Canberrra's Mount Ainslie, where AIAS, art galleries, and even a university might grow.

Freeman's increasingly romantic attachment to the continent led him to purchase an Austrian Haflinger four-wheel-drive vehicle so that he and Monica could head for the mountain and desert wildernesses of the inland: "When one of my Aboriginal friends remarked to me recently . . . 'Bush is best!' I knew exactly how he felt, and at once nodded my silent agreement."[15] The little snub-nosed Haflinger became one of the tokens of Derek's abiding eccentricity among friends and colleagues.

His interventions were, as usual, not appreciated by everyone. Freeman's interference over the location of the AIAS headquarters drew the outspoken anger of its principal. So did his protests at the AIAS conference of 1974, where he was accused of waylaying participants, picketing speakers, and repelling audiences with his domineering challenges. In the most notorious incident, he was accused of "pointing the bone," a form of Aboriginal sorcery, at fellow anthropologist Ronald Berndt, who was outraged at what he took to be a signal that Freeman was trying to damage him. Derek could laugh about it years later with Don Tuzin, claiming all he had done was to show Berndt a beautiful bone from Mornington Island and remark on its psychological power. But the incident followed him down the years, was often embellished in the telling, and was used against him.[16]

Freeman was acting out of a genuine idealism in his intrusions into Aboriginal affairs, albeit with a characteristic touch of righteous moralism. His idealism never ceased, though the interventions did. He and Monica welcomed a long line of Aboriginal activists into their home but the comings and goings of complete strangers who did not share their ascetic lifestyle helped Freeman decide that he should temper his enthusiasm. He was also becoming disillusioned with some Aboriginal leaders, if not with their cause. Several who had been previously warm began to turn on him. He talked it through with Monica: "I am resolved to gradually & discreetly terminate my involvement in Aboriginal politics: it is a jungle too thick with enmity, viciousness and betrayals for the likes of an innocent like me."[17]

Anthropology colleagues had been cynical from the start. Snide cartoons on the departmental notice board poked fun at his relationship with Aborigines. He was accused of defective political judgment, and mutterings about insanity were heard in the corridors. One Canberra anthropologist,

Nicholas Peterson, argues that Freeman wildly overidentified with Aboriginal people and produced nothing substantial to justify his efforts, though Peterson conceded that Freeman was capable of insights. Don Tuzin wondered if this was a phase in Freeman's romantic attachment to the idea of the intellectual indigene: he wanted Aboriginal people to be Paleolithic sages.[18] When they did not measure up to his scale of intellectual values Freeman backed away, a form of snobbery certainly not unique among academics in the circumstances of early 1970s activism.

Freeman's commitment to the principle of righting colonial injustices should not be undervalued. He went out on a public limb for the Aboriginal cause more fearlessly than many of his university colleagues and was willing to confront powerful commercial and government forces. This was honorable and brave in 1974, even if relatively naïve in working with the evolving militancy of Aboriginal politics.

Amid the hubbub, any thoughts of prosecuting the Margaret Mead mission were put on hold. Freeman also had a department to run. John Barnes, before departing for Cambridge, had wrestled with over seventy staff, assistants, and research students straddling anthropology, sociology, linguistics, and archaeology. Social anthropology, with only three staff, was considered among the weakest of the subunits. Freeman as new professor and chair, with only a decade to go to retirement, was charged with renewing anthropology, and he was eager to do so, vowing to Oscar Spate to make him proud of his support. But he was also uneasy about the responsibilities that lay ahead and recognized that "self-mastery" was the key to building his confidence.[19]

The research schools did not have undergraduate students, so Freeman did not have to teach courses. He threw himself instead into the task of evaluating scholarship applications, reclaiming lost graduate students suffering from poor supervision, and putting the administration's backed-up files in order; both he and Spate were appalled at the mess his predecessor had bequeathed them. Within a year, the word "sociology" was removed from the department's title and a second anthropology professor was appointed, the thirty-seven-year-old Roger Keesing, whose father, Felix, was a name to conjure with—alongside Mead and Freeman—as a major scholar of Samoan society.

Freeman put great faith in Keesing to shock the department into new paths. The mandate for the next few years, Keesing told an enquiring colleague, was to do as much free thinking and theorizing as possible in the direction of new paradigms.[20] Other powerful new staff arrived: Michael Young, the future biographer of Malinowski; and James Fox, who, with Freeman's unstinting support, would develop Southeast Asian anthropology. By the 1980s there were twelve permanent staff anthropologists.

Freeman, who in 1973 was elected a fellow of the Academy of the Social Sciences in Australia and chair of the Australian Association for Social Anthropology, did his best to keep pace with the renewed energy in his department. On his initiative, a film unit was set up for studies of human behavior in natural settings—the world's first human ethology laboratory in an anthropology department, he crowed to Edmund Leach.[21] He corresponded with Karl Popper about human nature and culture and seems to have discovered E. O. Wilson ("Sociobiology" was already exercising minds elsewhere as Freeman was ruminating about an anthropology that would respect biology in a nondeterministic way). Although his reading suffered in the midst of intense administrative duties, he managed to experiment during the 1970s with the draft of a book reappraising Mead (see chapter 9); he also had several Iban students and a new project on the "human ecology" of Samoa in the hands of a talented student, Graham Harrison.

Underneath, the uneasiness with which Freeman had approached his chairmanship never left him. He had suffered "anxiety dreams" from the start, even resorting to tablets to help him through sleepless nights. Self-doubt assailed him, though he was careful to mask it in front of students. By the end of 1973 he was feeling numbed and unequal to the task "of being both a super clerk and a super scholar. . . . Feel oppressed by the incessant striving for intellectual superiority which is imposed on me by one's all too clever colleagues: as Professorial Fellow I had a niche in which I felt at home; the diverse and unending responsibilities of a Professor are almost too much for me."[22] Monica was worried about his state of mind.

If anything, 1974 was an even worse year. Nightmares continued. He carried "a heavy heart," so heavy he found it impossible to work in the evenings. His escape in August to join Albert Barunga was one way of dealing with his low mood. The most desperate expression of the malaise that afflicted Freeman through the 1970s came in a letter to a former (hostile) student:

> A senior professor whose moral and intellectual values are most exacting, and said by many to be mentally unbalanced (if not worse) had taken from him by a number of newcomers from the Land of Watergate, and in a room where he spent most of his academic life, a most precious object. It

resembles a soul crystal—it was his confidence in the integrity of his associates. Then a friend saw him searching for it in his garden. . . . He asked where he lost it. "In my room at the university." Then why are you looking here? "Because there happens to be more light here than at my university."[23]

Beneath this rather clumsy parable lay a history of inner torments and outer "betrayals"—Freeman's word for things done to him by colleagues and students while he was in charge and immediately after.

For one thing, there was the seemingly age-old feud with "Brigadier" Bill Stanner. Freeman had no respect for Stanner's conceptualization of the proper limits of social scientific study, while Stanner found Freeman a constant provocation. They sparred over words, concepts, and the deep intellectual roots of each man's anthropology. Freeman's main criticism of Stanner was his argument that Freeman's change of intellectual direction in the 1960s threatened the "coherence" of the department. As Freeman complained to Crawford, Stanner was "laying down procedural rules for the solution of anthropological problems, rules which he considers ought to be made binding on all Departmental members."[24] This was anthropology as a closed system of ideas and for Freeman a great betrayal of fundamental scientific enquiry. His frustration with Stanner never left him ("I was cruel to him in seminars," Freeman confessed), though he did briefly try to make peace when he decided to apply for the chair in 1972.[25]

Then there was John Barnes, who was tarred with the same brush over his less than sympathetic attitude to the Sarawak incident and whose easygoing pragmatism Freeman took for dereliction of intellectual duty. Distress at Barnes's "betrayal" of 1961 troubled Freeman for many years. When Barnes returned as a visitor in 1985, Freeman cornered him to insist on an explanation for his actions twenty years before and remained exasperated at Barnes's refusal to engage with the question.[26]

Roger Keesing's betrayals were the most grievous to Freeman. Keesing, who represented the great hope for Freeman's ideal anthropology department, was a man after his own heart and a partner in pushing anthropology in new directions. In applying for the second chair, Keesing had proclaimed a polymath's interest in neurophysiology and artificial intelligence, systems-theory-oriented ecology, sociolinguistics, grammatical theory, and cognitive facets of social organization; he also wanted to continue working in the Pacific on the emerging political consciousness of island societies in Melanesia.

Keesing arrived with much fanfare in 1974 but was never really on Freeman's side, certainly not in departmental relations. Freeman discovered that Keesing was criticizing him to students behind his back for polarizing behavior and plotting to run a very different ship once he became head of the department. Keesing was a "dissembler," Freeman decided, and at that point in November 1974 he resolved to opt out of future administration and concentrate on his Mead book and the new anthropology. (Freeman wrote to his vice chancellor in April 1975 declining in advance any future invitation to be departmental chair.)

Although Keesing's Pacific work always attracted Freeman's respect, it was unlikely the two anthropologists could ever be compatible partners. They were intellectual rivals, Freeman already the patriarchal elder when Keesing arrived. A faint air of disapproval around Keesing's rather louche lifestyle and complicated personal relations also infected their relationship. Freeman raised a quizzical eyebrow when, in his first meeting with staff, Keesing proposed that seminars be held with a flagon of wine and people sitting on the floor with their shoes off.[27]

Bridges might have been mended had anthropology at ANU been a more coherent body of staff and students. But the discipline was split between the research and teaching faculties, and, as a student and later colleague remarked, there was no single school or authority to regularize knowledge among the theoretical work produced.[28] Certainly, Derek Freeman was not the person to pull the department together. His feelings of isolation from the "interests and conceptual worlds" of his colleagues, which had deepened since the 1960s, only compounded his sense of betrayal.[29]

As well as turning his back on administration, Freeman asked Crawford in 1975 to redesignate him a professor of human science, with a new home in biological sciences. He had lost intellectual confidence in social anthropology, he told Crawford, and was renouncing the field. Unfortunately, the biologists demurred (though a biology colleague offered him refuge in a room nicknamed "Siberia" or "The Professor's Folly"), while his own research school reacted with hostility. Freeman retreated back to his department, Keesing in placatory mood inviting him to stay as a professor without a discipline.[30] These were not just power games on Freeman's part but deeply held convictions over which he agonized in his diary, working his way back from the brink after intense reflection and long talks with Monica.

Power games went on in a fragmented, politically charged atmosphere, with academics competing for advancement and students hungering for time and attention. Freeman contributed to these games, his relationships with colleagues conditional and governed by a complex matrix of personal values involving his concepts of truth, integrity, and expectations of their behavior. The appropriate submissiveness by apprentices and staff, their willingness to listen and learn, made Freeman a cooperative colleague who would sacrifice time and effort to help solve a problem. On the other hand, a too-stubborn adherence to the well-trod paths of an earlier social anthropology or an attempt to contest Freeman's formidable armory of logical thought could result in Freeman's drawing himself up to full height to dominate a conversation, a journal argument, a seminar debate.

Freeman would not hesitate to put his own institution to the sword if he perceived that truth was being sacrificed to a venal purpose. Such was Freeman's reaction when he received an invitation in early September 1979 to the presentation of a replica Aztec calendar stone to ANU by the ambassador for Mexico. What happened next entrenched Freeman's notoriety among colleagues and alerted the wider Canberra community to his idiosyncrasies in a way that haunted him for years to come.

In a state of anxiety over his attempts to focus on the draft of his book about Mead. He was beset by distractions as he wrestled with inner questions about his behavior, and the Aztec stone presented him with another. Perturbed by what he believed was instead a replica of the sacrificial stone on which the Aztecs slaughtered thousands upon thousands of their people to the sun god, Tonatiuh, Freeman began a campaign to prevent its hanging at the university.

In a long and emotion-laden open letter to Anthony Low, vice chancellor of ANU, Freeman castigated the university for its willingness to accept "this monstrous stone." Documenting with his usual detailed referencing of sources the carnage wreaked by Aztec overlords, Freeman effectively accused the ambassador of bribing the university by offering to arrange scientific exchanges with Mexico. Along the way he insulted the local prehistorian who provided the initial briefing to ANU: Freeman was "appalled" that "certain Professors of the Australian National University (acting in woeful ignorance of what it was they were dealing with) should have foisted this barbaric object upon other members of our great University." There was much else besides, Freeman thundering anathemas against Low and warning of internecine warfare between departments if the horrid thing, "which out-Molochs Moloch," were not removed. He also claimed, as "a specialist in the study of human ethology," that the expressive features of the stone had a pernicious physical effect (he had tested the thymus of the vice chancellor's deputy to prove it).[31]

Freeman's insistent, confrontational campaign began a brushfire of outrage across the campus, some for, some against the siting of the stone in the classics building among the treasures of ancient Greece and Rome. The Colosseum, Auschwitz, even the abortion debate were co-opted into the arguments. Freeman remained at the center of the controversy, especially after his letter to Low was leaked to the local newspaper, whose editor poured scorn on Freeman's arguments. Rumors circulated that Freeman was threatening to throw red paint, symbolizing blood, over the object on 21 September, the day of its presentation (the rumors still find an echo today).

Freeman's most egregious act was to seek an appointment at the Mexican embassy, where, he claimed, the ambassador, amid a tirade of furious Spanish, struck Freeman on the arm, shouting at him that he was "an imperialist." Freeman immediately rose and left, but not before he had applied his ethological arts, holding his composure while challenging the ambassador by covering his face to control his desire to laugh. "Tell your Ambassador," he reports himself as saying in a statement to police that documented this theatrical tableau, "that there is not one molecule of my body that is afraid of him."[32]

When the day of the presentation arrived, ANU dignitaries were understandably nervous, especially when Freeman appeared with his dog at the back of the assembly, wearing what the *Canberra Times* claimed was a battle jacket and workman's boots. The official duties were carried out uninterrupted amid pleasantries, Freeman merely drawing Vice Chancellor Low aside to make known his feelings. In accepting the stone, Low adopted a cautious and not altogether unequivocal tone.[33]

The incident of the Aztec stone was testimony to Freeman's dogged persistence that the truth shall prevail. "My *daimon* tells me that to a scholar nothing can be more sacred that [*sic*] the establishment & the safeguarding of the historical truth," he wrote stubbornly to Low well after the dust had settled. His conscience even drove him to resign his Academy of Social Sciences fellowship over its alleged "unscholarly judgment" about the stone (he was reinstated a decade later). As always, his seeming unwillingness to compromise had personal repercussions. Several colleagues and friends, even those in support, were alienated by what they considered his arrogance and self-righteousness in arguing his case.[34] The maligned prehistorian, accused by Freeman of being offered inducements to report favorably on the stone, sued him for defamation. Freeman was forced to withdraw his accusation, apologize publicly, and pay costs.

The incident also fixed in the public mind Freeman's reputation for volatility and extravagance. He might protest to the *Canberra Times* that his so-called battle jacket was in fact a bushman's jacket and his boots mountaineering boots (he had been on Black Mountain behind the university picking wildflowers), that he made no acrimonious comments to the vice chancellor, and that his dog was rather bemused at the human ceremonies, all of which only secured his reputation for eccentricity. The newspaper gleefully reported Freeman's forced apology in February 1981, remarking how the stone still leered over the Greek and Roman displays without any of the deleterious effects Freeman had predicted.

Canberra might have learned about Freeman for the first time through this incident, but inside the university his reputation for overbearing behavior was commonplace. It rested particularly on his performances in seminars, where Freeman continued to intimidate. He was adept at twisting a discussion onto his plane and then, with an apparently unrivaled knowledge of the latest literature, dominating the argument and influencing the dynamic of others' behavior either in his favor or in exasperated irritation against him. His baleful gaze, his occasional reading of the newspaper, or his ostentatious opening of mail as he sat in a direct line with the speaker could be off-putting and distracting. This was Derek Freeman in his continuing battle to overcome anything that threatened his sense of himself as an intellectual.

But relentless logic and forensic dissection of arguments were also features of Freeman's style. Few were able to get the better of him in debate, as the Meadites later discovered. Most successful were those like American anthropologist Paul Shankman, who confronted Freeman's tactics head-on when giving a paper in Canberra, mocking Freeman gently for opening his "important" mail and telling him to pay attention. Explosions against him were reasonably regular in his department, especially during the 1970s, indeed even after his retirement at the end of 1981. Intellectuals who could not in argument put a dent in Freeman's armory of ideas and his veneer of self-assurance had little else but exasperated anger and lasting resentment to deploy against him. Walkouts and "the basilisk glare" of enemies sometimes accompanied his interventions in seminars.[35] In these years an atmosphere of coldness and unfriendliness often accompanied Freeman whenever he was in the corridor; little wonder he carried a heavy heart.

123

Anthropologists Marie Reay and Nic Peterson among his colleagues succeeded Bill Stanner as Freeman's nemeses. Reay, a Melanesianist who also worked with Australian Aboriginal communities, was Freeman's constant foe; the enmity was mutual. Reay confessed to feeling a perennial victim of Freeman's outbursts, cowed by the "sepulchral 'frighten-little-children' tone" he adopted when he was bawling her out.[36] She privately entered the lists against Freeman in the controversy over Mead, writing a review in 1997 even though she admitted understanding nothing about Samoan culture. It remained unpublished because Reay could not bear the inevitable insults she believed Freeman would heap upon her. Even though he was by then long retired, Freeman continued to cast a far-reaching shadow. Nic Peterson adopted a different strategy. He accused Freeman to his face of being a bully, a fraud on anthropology, and mentally unstable to boot. This last taunt, which became a public accusation from several lips in 1974, always deeply upset Freeman, and he strove "to eliminate [Peterson] from [his] consciousness."[37]

Freeman was castigated time and again by colleagues for the vehemence of his counterarguments and the ad hominem barbs his colleagues often spied embedded within those arguments. This was particularly the case if students were involved. Freeman's diary records (and Don Tuzin remembered) British anthropologist Marilyn Strathern shouting "Shame!" at him for one of his caustic put-downs and refusing to allow him to be so threatening. He was openly criticized during an emotional faculty meeting in 1970 for "slamming" students at seminars in his determination to eliminate error. Freeman remained puzzled that colleagues did not agree that all criticism should be welcomed—it was the centerpiece of his conviction about the modus operandi of scientific enquiry.[38]

He had his supporters, even among students. Anton Ploeg refused to take exception to comments Freeman made about his paper on the Western Dani in New Guinea, even though staff members seemed to. During a paper he gave, David Wu found Freeman's suggestions on kinship behavior illuminating despite the atmosphere of hostility to him. Bryant Allen, a human geography student, remembered as tense but brilliant the debate between Freeman and Kenelm Burridge, a contender for the chair awarded to Keesing, with Burridge ignoring Freeman's jibes and calmly answering him point by point.[39] Among staff the Southeast Asianist James Fox, who later rose to be director of the school, became an ally and developed a friendship that lasted the rest of Derek's and Monica's lives.

The supervising of graduate students in and out of the field gave anthropology departments a complex yet more intimate feel than many other disciplines. Anton Ploeg remembers how classes on method run by Barnes and Freeman were central to building confidence that one could achieve a PhD if one carried out a program of close observation.[40] Fieldwork had a science of its own, and the early Freeman took an almost Malinowskian approach to building the scientific results of research. In later years he became less rigid and more expansive, but he continued to work closely with his students, expecting detailed reports from the field and making equally detailed responses. He lent books, corrected drafts, examined students closely, and smoothed the passage to academic appointment where he could. Even his most strident student critic testified that Freeman had a thoughtful, generous side.[41] When necessary he intervened with the university authorities to save students, even flying off to save them from themselves, as with Peranio and Martinoir in Borneo, though the resulting dramas more often attached to him.

On the other hand, Freeman did not suffer the mediocre student gladly—"the ever-present moral problem of choosing between kindness & the truth," he confessed to his diary after some remorseful comments about one who, despite good intentions and affability, possessed, according to Freeman, a "bumbling" mind. In his student supervisions, it was as though he were projecting the father-son relationships that had bedeviled his youth: kind and helpful father, hostile and dismissive son.[42]

Individuals of a certain stamp, however, were drawn to his intellectual power and dark charisma. Don Tuzin was a case in point. He was Freeman's first student in some years when he arrived in 1969. Tuzin swears Freeman bore no animus to Mead as they began work, praising her as a leading intellectual. Freeman walked Tuzin through the Canberra hills, tutoring him in the newly found Popper philosophy and shaping Tuzin's lifelong interest in criticism, the scientific method, and the integration of biological and social anthropology. When Tuzin went to work among the Ilahita Arapesh in Papua New Guinea, they exchanged fulsome reports. Freeman's were detailed, cogent, encouraging, summing up with sharp questions to feed into Tuzin's research. He sent parcels of leisure reading ("outdoor adventures of guys achieving great feats," according to Tuzin's wife, Beverly).[43] Freeman also insisted Tuzin not overdo the hard work: "You must add to your dedication the relaxed gait of the marathon runner who finishes the course still fit for bearing his laurels on a lap of honor. I hope the place is as

125

beautiful to the eye as to the ear: Ilahita sounds like some languorous lotus-land, and very un-Lutheran."[44]

It was an intense, exhausting exercise, Freeman never wasting a thought, extracting as much from the trivial in life as from the serious. Tuzin was exhilarated and uplifted by such engagement, admitting at the same time it was not for everybody. He could handle what others considered Freeman's domineering manner, coming from a family with a military background and conceding nothing in height and posture to the tall, rangy Kiwi. Tuzin knew nothing when he arrived and was prepared to enter into a relationship of trust, even in the face of uncompromising comment on his work; he also had intellectual power to make Freeman relish the challenge—the yang to Freeman's yin.

For others, Freeman's reputation for eating students alive kept them at bay or even drove them away. Weak students were a special liability in anthropology, according to John Barnes: they were either absent in far-flung parts or working in stressful situations where close supervision was impossible, or they fell victim to domination by their supervisor, which is what Barnes surmised happened between Freeman and Martinoir.[45]

Then there were those who, whatever their abilities and talents, matched Freeman's determination not to be dominated and could spark turmoil in Freeman himself. One such was at the head of a student—and staff—revolt when Freeman was in charge of the department. This was a particularly contentious period for students, as two former students reminded reviewers of the anthropology department a decade and a half later.[46] There are cases for the prosecution and the defense in the deteriorating relations that followed in anthropology, and they bear a resemblance to the exchanges that occurred during the Mead debates.

According to Freeman, his withdrawal from supervising this particular graduate student, who, Freeman believed, lacked the vernacular language skills and the dedication to complete his tasks, led to a confrontation during which the student called him a "paranoid schizophrenic," the insult that most grievously offended Freeman. When the school director, soon to be vice chancellor, Anthony Low, hesitated (or prevaricated, according to Freeman) to act on Freeman's request to be psychiatrically examined, the student escaped censure and began a relentless public pursuit of Freeman across a variety of forums that lasted for nearly three decades.[47]

The student tells a very different tale of his ANU years, the fulcrum of which was 1974. His story rests not on his anthropological training (Freeman was wrong about his lack of vernacular fluency) but on Freeman's

126

behavior toward students and staff. The student had presented a petition signed by twelve others, including staff, requesting a meeting to iron out "serious difficulties in the functioning of our group."[48] Freeman, he claimed, reacted bullyingly, demanding to know who and what had led to this and to the satirical pieces appearing on notice boards about his pro-Aboriginal activities. Freeman's goading led to the student's name calling, "the closest term with which I [the student], as a layman, was familiar to describe your behavior as I and others had seen it" (he later confessed that the phrase "paranoid schizophrenic" had come to him from a movie he had watched the evening before). Long hours of meetings between Low, Freeman, and the student resolved nothing, leaving only vague threats that the student's career could be damaged.

This episode is less significant in itself than for the general atmosphere it evokes around Freeman's time in charge of his colleagues and for the signs of the very real personal troubles assailing him. It is from this time that whispers and accusations of "madness," "instability," and "paranoia" resurfaced when talking about Derek Freeman. They intensified during the period of relentless warring correspondence with opponents of his stance on Margaret Mead in the 1980s and followed him into the 1990s.

Derek Freeman retired from his position at the Australian National University at the end of 1981, though not from academic life. He was awarded a visiting fellowship that enabled him to continue enjoying the privileges of his department; it was renewed for twenty years until his death in 2001. The humble joys of retirement—sitting in the back garden reading or listening to music, fiddling with his mass of papers, browsing the shops (a favorite activity)—were at first a release, and the early days were full of excitement and congratulation at his securing the contract with Harvard University Press for his first Mead book (see chapter 9). Yet he was occasionally prostrated by anxiety at the prospect of having to continue contact with those against whom he held "habitual and unconscious resentments," and he became bored with the small talk that accompanied his departure.[49]

Gradually, Freeman was drawn back to attend seminar papers in the department, but his first taste in April 1982 left him "done in" when he became the target of some surreptitious mocking by former colleagues; he resolved to stay away. On the other hand, he was still capable of making wounding assessments of others' performances in his diary, and there was the odd angry exchange with staff in the department or with visitors whom Freeman chose to lecture upon some dereliction of idea or habit; in 1989 one threatened to punch him on the nose for contemptuous comments Freeman made about his beliefs.[50]

Agonies from the old days also occasionally resurfaced, and he gnawed on the events of 1961 or on the actions of Tom Harrisson, Stanner, Barnes, Crawford, and Low. With the publication in 1983 of his first Mead book, a new phalanx of enemies and friends took the place of the old guard. The excitement turned his retirement into a second life and brought forth a second book, though not the big book on the new interactionist anthropology he had been promising the world.

By the 1990s and ten years into retirement, Freeman had gained some measure of acceptance, even cordiality, from most of his former colleagues at ANU. The Festschrift volume in his honor, though criticized for insufficiently probing the great controversies of his life, nonetheless registered the respect and admiration of a range of individuals for whom Freeman had been inspiration, mentor, or goad. There were other, smaller triumphs set among friends and supporters (see chapter 11).

Old colleagues were disappearing. His great mentor Meyer Fortes died in 1983, supportive to the end and before seeing the furor over Derek's first Mead book; Anna Freud had gone the year before. John Crawford, who had ridden the curve of Freeman's life at ANU with support, patience, and frustration, died at age seventy-four in 1984; Freeman never fully reconciled himself with Crawford. His erstwhile competitor in Borneo, Bill Geddes, who went on to hold the chair of anthropology at Sydney University, died in 1989. Edmund Leach, whose intellectual powers and character traits were much like Freeman's own, also died that year. In 1990 John Beattie, Freeman's old functionalist enemy from Oxford, followed, as did Ronald Berndt, object of Freeman's supposed sorcery. "I am now Australia's oldest living anthropologist," he noted in his diary.

In 1973 his historian friend Jim Davidson died of a heart attack while working in Papua New Guinea. Freeman had grown to see Davidson as a rival on Samoan matters and had to fight against his instinctual fears of being dominated by one who had been so close. The first death of a truly close friend was that of Hans Neumann, who had befriended Freeman in Samoa in the 1940s and stayed in touch over the years. Closer to home, Peter Lawrence, anthropology professor at Sydney and a good friend, was gone in 1987. It was Lawrence who had tried to cheer Freeman up in the midst of his fights with Mead opponents, insisting that they were both too old to have any illusions left. "Academic life is supposed to be one of impartiality and untrammeled peace. However, in comparison with us, dog racing is clean," was his sardonic reminder.[51] Family aunts and uncles in

New Zealand passed away in the 1990s, and then his sister, Margaret, living in London. Bizarrely, his own death was prematurely announced in the ANU staff list for 1988. He smiled grimly at that.

His home in Canberra's suburbs remained a haven for family and the occasional close friend. "Things have come to a kind of summation here, now," he said to Don Tuzin in 2000.[52] The daughters were launched on their own careers and had their own families. He and Monica worked through the tribulations they had shared in his bruising intellectual life. Theirs remained a companionable marriage and an intimate partnership in search of a variety of truths, Derek continuing his struggle to see the world through Monica's eyes, not just his own. Monica, who had her sculpting in limestone and metal, took a diploma in art and exhibited successfully. As Derek's life wound down, Monica's wound up. She became a holistic healer, developing their mutual interest in behavioral kinesiology into a home practice of her own; she was also slowly sowing seeds to bring to press her diaries of their life among the Iban in the 1950s.[53]

Monica was also Derek's partner in developing selected Buddhist practices. She had learned about Buddhism from the teachers of her daughter Jennifer, who studied Buddhism in Indonesia. Derek "came in bit by bit," averred Monica. Hostile to institutional religions and the human penchant for gods, Freeman nonetheless appreciated Buddhism for its meditative powers and its aesthetic qualities. His long romance as a young man with Krishnamurti's ideas, reignited in these later years, perhaps signals a predisposition to Buddhism as a spiritual attachment, though it sits oddly against the sternness of his scientific empiricism. But Zen Buddhism to Freeman was a philosophical system that somehow circumvented the relentless overturning of error in the search for truth. It did not require a theism or a dark night of the soul to enter. Instead, Freeman grasped it as a set of disciplines that helped him to a more composed life amid his intellectual and emotional trials, the more so as his health deteriorated into his eighties with diabetes and heart disease.

He learned to meditate—"Zenning" he called it—using the objects he had collected from significant places in his life as prompts. Freeman had learned to do that from the Iban and their perpetual use of charms, he told Tuzin, the miscellany of objects on his study table standing as metaphors for humankind's suspension between nature and culture: "I'm behaving like an Iban when I'm doing that."[54]

Freeman recognized he was in steady decline. He had climbed a mountain in Borneo on his sixtieth birthday and got to the top of Canberra's Mount Ainslie on his eightieth. But his mountain-climbing days were

over. Don Tuzin spent a week with him in June 2000, clearing and arranging Freeman's private papers for transport to the University of California
at San Diego. The completion of the human genome project the same year
seemed to clinch a moment. Freeman regarded it as the final material and
symbolic building block in the mission to know humans biologically so
that a platform could be built for a new theory of culture. He and Tuzin
rehearsed all the great campaigns, fights, and triumphs. Defeats were not
discussed or acknowledged. This was the point where Freeman summed
up his role in life as truth's fool. "I think that scientific truth is sort of like
a god to me or something. It's an external thing," he said to Tuzin, and he
explicitly rejected the notion being spread by some colleagues that he had
wasted his life in pursuing a chimera. And yet, lying on his bed in the
lounge of their home a year later, he said to Monica, "What use is all this
information I have learned?" It was an eerie echo of the question asked by
another anthropologist, Claude Lévi-Strauss, at the end of his book *Tristes
tropiques*: "For what, after all, have I learnt from the masters I have listened
to, the philosophers I have read, the societies I have investigated and the
very Science in which the West takes such pride? Simply a fragmentary
lesson or two which, if laid end to end, would reconstitute the meditations
of the Sage at the foot of his tree." They may both have reached a mountain
peak of self-discovery. Monica thought he might have been ruing some of
the choices he had made in pursuing knowledge for its own sake.[55]

In 2000 the doctors told him he had a 30 percent chance of living for
five more years. Derek thought he might get two or three. In fact, he got
only one, dying on 6 July 2001.

8

On the Edge

For much of his professional life, Derek Freeman was known to colleagues as "the Dragon of Canberra." His vehemence in pursuit of opponents was legendary, his academic life speckled with incendiary encounters and comments, as though his subconscious were always spoiling for a fight. At the height of the controversies around Margaret Mead, his one-time friend and collaborator, Hiram Caton, was unblinking in telling Freeman how others perceived him. "It's impossible to mistake that you send an abundance of dominance signals that no one associates with truth-seeking," he wrote in response to a complaint about how Freeman was being represented in the disputes. "Few can match the aggression that you from time to time project into scholarship and personal relations. The Samoa controversy is, among other things, a monument to your dominance. Derek, EVERYBODY sees that."[1]

Not only did they see it, but some used Freeman's aggressive behavior to assert a pathological condition. Although we are told one cannot defame the dead—biographers have taken refuge in this mantra for years as a defense of their dark art—in Derek Freeman's case there seems to be no statute of limitations. Freeman's chosen title for himself—truth's fool—had in this regard a hidden meaning for others, for the facet of the medieval fool's character that gave him liberty to tell stark truths and poke fun also allowed for a certain madness or mental imbalance that made him a source of amusement and toleration. Accusations were peddled at various times about Freeman's state of mind, not least by Caton in regard to the Sarawak incident. Colleagues at ANU made insinuations, stories and rumors circulated on the conference trail, and judgments were given in print that seemed to give them an air of authenticity and integrity.

There is no doubt that, despite his denials, Freeman did fall apart in Sarawak in 1961. Three reports by professionals (the "alienist" in Kuching; a psychiatrist in Karachi; and the consultant psychiatrist, W. H. Trethowan, from Sydney) speak of Freeman being "mentally unsound," needing to be accompanied home, suffering from "delusion," and being in an "abnormal mental state." The official ANU view ranged from "stress," through "delusional" moments, to a "panic" condition.[2] All agree the trauma was momentary, nonviolent (except for the smashing of a display object, which was a calculated act), and succeeded by a return to productive normalcy. This did not stop people from being convinced Freeman was unstable, which the Samoa incident in 1967 seemed to confirm. That incident had more mundane ingredients, as we have seen, though it must be reiterated that the moral intensity of these experiences was real and transformative, and it set Freeman on radically new paths of ideological development and missionary fervor.

Little, uncanny things continued to count against Freeman's mental health in the eyes of those around him—"pointing the bone" at anthropologist Ron Berndt; the farce of the Aztec stone and the fear of onlookers that he was capable of throwing a bucket of blood over it; the seeming implacability of his argumentative nature. His colleague John Barnes was right that there was an "obsessional component" to Freeman's temperament. Freeman himself admitted it to Frank Heimans in the last year of his life, though he denied he was "neurotically obsessed," just possessed by extreme powers of concentration.[3]

Obsession went hand in hand with a monumentalizing ego and a personalized dominance behavior pattern that Freeman at times exploited in an ethological fashion. That he was able to maintain this was due to his university institution's failing to or being incapable of setting restraints on him. Intellectual bullying was often accepted as part of the cut and thrust of university life, or it was done by letter at a distance that was difficult to bridge. Freeman stopped if he was called out for such behavior in public, if he was laughed at, or if he was discomfited through a legal challenge, such as over the Aztec stone.

The most astringent description of Freeman's personality is not by Caton but by Freeman's main enemy in his university department, Bill Stanner.

There is nevertheless something rather forbidding in his personality. In temperament, he has a large swing: from boorishness to a too obvious suavity. Intellectually, he is extremist and with something like an addiction to system; order, certainty, finality, predictability seem to fascinate him; he seems always to need an unshakable datum. Socially he lacks true civility; he is almost without humor; irony is lost on him. His whole organization . . . is coarse. He has much ambition, and pursues his interest relentlessly. He has aplomb when winning, or when he thinks he is winning. I judge him capable of almost any opportunism. He has a strong punitive streak. He is very quick to sense weakness or confusion or drift, and will then move very quickly. I consider him quite unsubtle, very good at minor tactics of making his way, but not equipped for the large tasks.[4]

This is a graphic and angry thumbnail sketch at one moment in time. Stanner, who was no psychologist, was struggling with his own enmity toward Freeman, who had recently returned from his traumas in Borneo and was challenging Stanner's intellectual status within the department; one senses a Stanner cornered by Freeman's subjugating arts. Again, some elements of Freeman's lasting personality traits leap out at one—an authoritarian intellectualism, the sense of certainty vouchsafed upon him, an elation when in control—but others miss their mark. Freeman had a sense of humor—his papers are riddled with cards and jokes and cartoons that took his fancy, though it is true he lacked self-irony and took himself too seriously most of the time. He carried himself with great dignity and was always civil, almost courtly at times, dangerously so the more he was crossed. His ambitions were not for personal preferment, though his search for "truth" could look like that to bystanders. His "punitive streak" could be followed by a warm and generous hospitality and helpfulness to students and colleagues alike, as we have seen.

One of Freeman's students, we may recall, called him "a paranoid schizophrenic" but admitted it was a throwaway line. No such diagnosis was ever made by any professional. The most extreme interpretation of Freeman's personality in print was probably Caton's claim after Freeman's death that his was a clear case of "narcissistic personality disorder" (see chapter 4). Based on David Williamson's script for his play about Freeman and a parcel of university archive documents whose confidential nature he simply waved away, Caton used a formal, biomedical model taken from the *Diagnostic and Statistical Manual of Mental Disorders* to assert Freeman's pathological condition. Dismissing any ethical consideration of Freeman's family over his "diagnosis," Caton presented Freeman as a person of high self-importance in thrall to his mother's dire religious influence; he lacked empathy with others, was callous to his wife, Monica, and was obsessed with his grandiose mission to unmask Margaret Mead's mistakes. Freeman's "madness" was allegedly apparent in his breakdown in Borneo, with his manic attempt to fly to London and his stuttering recovery in Karachi, then again in his breakdown on Taʻu in American Samoa. Freeman's university, according to Caton, was a place of turmoil, with the institution struggling to contain Freeman's emotional instability, his threats of legal action, and his harassment of colleagues. Derek Freeman, wrote Caton, possessed a hidden self that he never truly sought to find, using his bluster as evidence that he and only he spoke the truth.[5]

Caton's portrait is a stunningly negative, apocalyptic apparition. He ignored the vexed qualities of the documentation on which he based his contentions about the lifelong nature of Freeman's personality. Caton's transliteration of a play's script as an actual factual record of Freeman's life was vastly overdetermined and made no allowances for the creative input of the playwright. The fact that Freeman endorsed the picture of himself presented onstage (see chapter 11) simply meant one of two things: Freeman recognized the freedom to imagine that went with the biographical pact he had made with the playwright, or he only partly understood the play as play, which is entirely in keeping with his empirical spirit.

The flurry of university memos and medical opinions that followed Freeman's return from Sarawak in 1961 ended in a consensus that Freeman did not suffer from an underlying psychiatric disorder. This remained the university's position, as Caton emphasizes. Nonetheless, Caton still claimed that Freeman's behavior was consistent with a diagnosis of narcissistic personality disorder, based on the categorical medical model he used to underpin his analysis. Using the specialized language of clinical psychology, mixing quotations from the play with his own assertions about medical conditions, and riding over the top of any family concerns (who were never consulted in fashioning the analysis), Caton elevated incidents that took place in 1961 to the signature of a lifelong disease. His failure to consider the convoluted history of personal and career development that the present account has laid bare raises questions about Caton's "empathy blindness" and that of those who followed him in accepting his analysis.[6]

Derek Freeman was diagnosed as suffering from bipolar disorder in 1974, the year of the most noise around his running of the department. His diary for that year and the next is full of crabbed, calligraphic script that runs on page after page, gradually easing off to become larger, rounder, calmer, until, a few months later, a fresh burst of energy spills onto the page. Freeman first took medication—lithium carbonate—in that year, but he gradually stopped, because it affected his mental processes. Bipolar disorder was not widely known or discussed at the time, and lithium had only been approved for manic episodes since 1970 in the United States; it was not in widespread use in Australia. Monica Freeman bore the brunt of her husband's manic periods in sleepless, talk-filled nights, but neither spoke about it outside their home. There was enough controversy surrounding Freeman within anthropology as the years went on without adding to speculation and misdiagnosis, though Freeman was not able to escape the ignoble accusations about "paranoid schizophrenia."[7]

As for an explanation of Freeman's mental condition, in addition to in-built chemical causes, one might conjecture about early childhood traumas or the lack of secure parental attachment, based on the constant internal examinations Freeman made of his relationship to his mother, Did, and his father, John. Freeman certainly experienced sufficient life trials and peculiar events to trigger episodes of mania and depression, if he were predisposed to emotional outbreaks. The forms of his disorder, if disorder it was, took perhaps "soft" expression, brief episodes of "hypomania," the likelihood of which even Caton concedes in his otherwise reductionist diagnosis of Freeman's "breakdowns."[8] When so little research into the states of bipolar sufferers has been done it is best to avoid too precise a naming of Freeman's continuing mental conditions. As fellow sufferer and professor of psychiatry Kay Redfield Jamison has said of herself: "Only a sliverish gap exists between being thought intense, or a bit volatile, and being dismissively labeled 'unstable.'"[9]

A form of extreme emotionalism certainly characterized Freeman's comportment toward many issues he considered of utmost scientific or moral importance. He recognized it but when talking to Don Tuzin late in his life could not put a name to it.

> It's my personal characteristic, always is, very strong feelings you know. . . . That has always been the case. This is what happened on these occasions. They mistake it for something that it is not. I'm sure I became very emotional in Sarawak when I broke that thing and so on, but it's not madness, you know. The same thing happened on Manu'a. Now David [Williamson] mentions that briefly in the play. That was a similar event. And the thing

in Melbourne when the analysts attacked me, I became very emotional. This is a kind of—I don't know where that comes from.[10]

Freeman's inability to pathologize his own states masks a certain hypocrisy, because he was ever ready to reduce his opponents to psychiatric formulations. His diaries are full of colorful pseudopsychiatric descriptions of enemies. Although privately made, occasionally, as with Tom Harrisson and certain Mead opponents, those descriptions leaked into his correspondence.

Freeman genuinely acknowledged that he was threatened at times with a loss of control over his emotional states. Not for nothing did he quote in his diary the poet John Dryden: "Great wits are sure to madness near allied, and thin partitions do their bounds divide." And in the depths of disputation with his colleagues in 1974, Freeman recorded his "most fundamental fear: the fear of becoming so maddened that I'll go mad."[11] The affair of the Aztec stone filled him with such anxiety that he considered fleeing Canberra with Monica and settling north of Sydney to be nearer their daughter Hilary. Night sweats and dark dreams accompanied his struggles over what he had done.

Alas, instances of backsliding were as numerous as new resolutions and new forms of action. Entering the 1990s, well into retirement, Freeman was still having trouble resisting his need to win every argument and learning to "let go" the perceived injustices of his opponents in the Mead debates. He admitted to himself that he was intellectually invigorated by opposition, and the temptation remained strong to crow over the routing of an enemy. Tuzin believed Freeman's refusal to accept condemnation from others was fortified by a strong superego.[12] Freeman could recognize that in attributing blame to others' behavior, he was projecting onto others his own blaming of himself, but that did not stop him from continuing to assert his personality forcefully over friend and foe in the face of their anger and frustration.

The family often bore the brunt of this struggle, which included attempts to redirect their actions into a model of his making. "One is painfully encased in the sad geometry of the family," he wrote self-pityingly in his diary as he strove again and again to restore harmony, especially with his beloved Monica, who remained the soul of patience.[13] The worst years were the mid-1970s, when his mood disorder and department troubles converged. "I have no doubt that I am an individual prone to manic-depressive affective reactions & that I have been undergoing one of these reactions since last March," he confessed to himself in August 1975. He remained in a wretched state of self-recrimination until a new specialist took him off the medications in November: "What a deliverance!" was his reaction.[14] But it did not mean the end of his occasional harsh reactions to opponents, though he was always crestfallen and remorseful when they occurred.

There is ample evidence in his diaries that Freeman strove constantly against the more negative effects of his sometimes unsettling behavior. Well before the troublesome years in charge of the department, Freeman was using his diary as "an instrument for self-investigation and self-regulation."[15] The daily diary was designed to keep a watch on himself, and he developed a deep dependency on the interior "conversations" he employed. More than a mere discipline, more than a duty, the diary became his "lodestone," the center and central record of his search for a better self; even Caton acknowledges that Freeman had a relentless dedication to self-understanding. His life was a constant roller coaster of introspection accompanied by the close reading of classical literature on the human mind and spirit, documented every day in the diaries. Speckling their pages is a constant stream of resolutions to be better than the old self, which was forever tripping him up.

16 August 1969: "A very harmonious day: a kind of new beginning: continue with my self-analysis."

15 October 1972: "I realize that all I have to call upon is my courage to be a better man ie. more good or god-like & to this end I can pray for redemption."

28 July 1974: "[His contribution to recent turbulences in the department was] essentially an over-confidence in my own changed state; feel that I have now lived through & overcome this time of adversity and grown in maturity in the process: let me now seek wisdom in my oasis from which I can issue untroubled into 'the wicked world.'"

24 March 1975: "Decide that I must really give up the habitual sequence: anger: anguish: anxiety, by the exercise of inhibition—whatever be the provocation. . . . It is both humbling and enheartening [*sic*] to be moving towards a new maturity in my 59th year."

7 August 1975: "1975 the year of my redemption from the manifold deficiencies of my former character."

9 November 1976: "What a wondrous world to be in and ever more deeply understand—*from the inside out*!; my challenge is to stay on the plateau on the edge of which I now am; this will require vigilant monitoring & active choice; of which I feel I may well be capable with my present insights and understanding."

31 December 1980: "A very full year of inner reckoning, during which I have mobbed [*sic*] nearer than ever before to something approaching a Zen life."

7 May 1984: "Awake feeling in fine fettle at the end of major phase in my response to the obscurantist reaction to my book: I have come through the ordeal with colors bravely flying & in full command both intellectually and emotionally; I must now get to work enthusiastically to cybernetically improve my whole being in the world."

10 October 1985: "How hard it is to get rid of the animal instinct to be first in everything one considers one's world. I fight against envy, jealousy, feel deeply humiliated to have to admit superiority in others."

2 July 1990: "Need to 'let go' of all the injustices of the controversy over my reputation and to persist with my affirmations."

23 September 1990: "I realize that part of my motivation [for domineering behavior] is my apparent defeat at the hands of the ignorant and arrogant."[16]

The sometimes banal quality of these extracts over twenty tension-filled years should not detract from what was the constant struggle for mental equilibrium that Freeman underwent. He was engaged in a relentless project of self-transformation, pursuing himself, challenging himself, and punishing himself, for the diaries make clear how often he was guilty of relapsing and how regularly he needed to renew his vows. Freeman hungered for the ability to transcend his mental and verbal campaigns of triumph over his enemies, whether they were the serried ranks of skeptical anthropologists, the lone thinker daring to voice an unacceptable theory or argument, or even his own family members. His colleagues and opponents saw little or nothing of this interior struggle, but the therapeutic search for who he was and could be, where his negative drives originated, and how he could rid himself of them was real, arduous, and permanent.

Characteristically, his self-scrutiny took inspiration more from external authorities than from a deep, inductive analysis of his inner drives. The diaries were peppered with rallying cries from the Dhammapada, Saint Anselm, and Father Damien ("Be severe towards yourself, indulgent towards others"), from Silvano Arieti ("a man with values closely similar to my own though he does not sufficiently recognize 'the sovereignty of the good'"), even from Simone Weil and Vincent van Gogh. Freeman's readings on human uniqueness and human choice ranged through John Eccles, Aldous Huxley, Sherwood Washburn, Christopher Isherwood, Dietrich

Bonhoeffer, Bertrand Russell, and the film *Dead Poets Society*. Freeman read deeply into classical Greek and Roman literature: his favorite was Marcus Aurelius on character ("one of the most precious & life-enhancing of all the boons bequeathed to me by dear Did"). All experience was grist to Freeman's mill, and he remained alive—tiringly so for those around him—to potential moral or existential lessons wherever he turned, though the mystery of good behavior tending to happiness was for him always grounded in evolutionary adaptation by the human species to the correct choices.[17]

Texts were not his only inspiration. A "red-letter day" occurred in March 1975 when he and Monica discovered the Alexander technique for improving posture, bodily movement, and breathing. Developed by the Tasmanian physiotherapist Frederick Mathias Alexander and taken to Europe, where performing artists and musicians made it popular, the Alexander technique promised a reduction in stress and an increase in confidence. What excited Freeman was the fundamentally important realization that here was a means to transform his behavior by choosing to inhibit himself and his body in ways that neutralized aggressive postures. He was hooked when he discovered that Nikolaas Tinbergen gave his Nobel oration on the Alexander technique. "That's when I really discovered choice," Freeman told Frank Heimans, and he worked on choice intensively from that moment. He and Monica found one of Alexander's pupils in Sydney and traveled there for lessons; they frequently succeeded in "Alexandering" his inner problems, especially those having to do with the family.[18]

In 1979 he discovered the work of medical psychiatrist John Diamond on the thymus. Diamond claimed that the thymus gland was the link between mind and body, as it was the first organ affected by mental stress. It led to Freeman beginning several years of "thymic testing" to "debug" various memories and associations involving persons and places.[19]

Those who knew of this aspect of his home practice, especially his view that the thymus was "a visceral brain," thought it another example of Freeman's "wacky" tendencies, which flew in the face of his renowned skepticism and intellectual strength. So too were his constant attempts at "age regression": "testing" the moments of hurt in his past, naming the villains who generated anger and his repressed aggression in the hope he could lay them to rest. But it is likely that Freeman was as worried about his body as he was about his mind and just as eager to escape his body's biological limits. The Alexander technique, the visceral brain in the thymus, the testing of electric body currents were all weapons in the Promethean struggle to know himself and his past and to control the powers of emotion and intellect that flared in him.[20]

When Don Tuzin was given full access to Freeman's monumental diary collection, Freeman made no bones about the honesty he expected. Tuzin was not to cover up the truth: "In consigning the Diary to me, knowing he was dying, Derek was emphatic that nothing in this record should remain hidden; all of the truth needed to be told. Many of the entries, he knew, were uncomplimentary to Derek himself, and could cause others to judge him harshly in the after-years. This did not seem to bother him, though it was a matter of concern to his surviving family members." Freeman was a man of great moral seriousness—extreme in its reach, according to some observers—and living each day meant a constant attention to the intellectual or humdrum issues he met. Nothing was trivial, and everything had meaning—an expectation that could be wearing on those around him. If there was a narcissistic element operating, "one derived from a doting, ambitious mother and an unsympathetic, anti-intellectual father," nevertheless, Tuzin was convinced, Freeman found in his career a way of sublimating impulses to conquer and overcome, and he worked constantly to be better than his instinctual self.[21] His devotion to anthropology as a science and to the life of the mind was his way of achieving this. His work, his therapy, his routines of reading and writing were both stimulus and release, a way of keeping things in control.

Vague descriptions like "unbalanced" and "unstable" were often used of Freeman. They were—are—laden with implication, at their most extreme implying that Freeman was "mad," if not all the time, then at least some of the time. Madness as a category has been a bone of contention through the centuries. Michel Foucault taught us to "denaturalize" the notion and see it constituted differently at different times and in different places under competing authorities; where we stand relative to those authorities determines our line between sanity and madness. In Western cultural discourse, madness has shifted from being a manifest spiritual sign of sinfulness or of a supernatural visitation by demons through a host of categories of dysfunction to its present-day treatment within medical cultures, responsive to pharmacological and psychiatric interventions. Today mental health lies at the center of Western medical discourse about health in general. Indeed, we are in danger, says psychoanalyst Darian Leader, of being "caught in the ever-expanding field of mental health labels where every surface symptom is transformed into some new diagnostic entity."[22] It reminds one of Caton's diagnosis of Freeman's supposed malady.

The signs of Freeman's personality that Caton presents as symptoms of disease can easily be interpreted in other ways in a full and detailed coverage of the processes of his life, as this book argues. And one does not have to accept Caton's belief that Freeman was perversely blind to his own failings. That he did not hide from himself shows in Freeman's constant struggle, etched in his diaries. Shallow though the process may have been, and obscured by his own self-confidence or fear of what he might find, Freeman in his daily inner investigation nevertheless attempted to plumb the psychic and psychosomatic roots of his character.

This account of Freeman's life and mind refrains from using madness as an attribute of any phase of his life. It has followed an approach to psychological description that remains open-minded and adopts a "reasoned eclecticism."[23] He was certainly a difficult man to many people; accounts of his tension-filled encounters with fellow academics leave one wincing. But the attribution of "madness" stops all further questioning and saves us from having to find an external cause for his moods or behavior. The existential question of what constitutes a normal life is particularly pertinent in regard to Derek Freeman. It is fair to argue that he experienced "mental health issues" in the form of a bipolar condition that was clinically diagnosed, was medically treated, and may have waned. A milder form of mania may have been responsible for some of his responses, though there is no documented clinical evidence. He also experienced several delusional episodes based on a sudden revelation of a world gone sideways, alongside a certainty that he was called to right terrible moral wrongs (against both the Iban and the Samoans). This led to newfound energy to prosecute these missions, whose sometimes egregious events we have examined in detail.

Were these "psychotic" episodes? Here the historian is on shakier ground. If one accepts the definitions of Richard Bentall and Leader that psychosis is a more severe form of mental disturbance in which an individual appears to lose touch with reality, in which the world speaks to that person, even if momentarily, then the answer is a qualified yes.[24] Freeman seemed to have just such an experience in Sarawak in 1961 and again in Samoa in 1967. But psychologists stress that the recovery can be rapid, which it was in Freeman's case, and a perfectly normal life ensue. One of our Western traits is to treat those who undergo such an experience, though they manage to live a fruitful life without needing long-term care, as nevertheless a little mad. And the dramatic, sometimes violent acts associated with such eruptions "prove" madness in the perception of many. Caton used the melodramatic episodes in Sarawak and Samoa in the 1960s to cast such suspicions on Freeman. Yet, as we have seen, these incidents can also be constructed positively, as restorative events, attempts to repair and re-structure one's life. Freeman's "conversion" was real and persistent, the mission to reform anthropology his attempt to reform his world, while his struggle to improve himself in his intellectual relations with others—also real and persistent—was his way of reintegrating himself within that world.

There are no perfect indicators of personality, only ambiguous clues, the possible list of one's personality traits a Tower of Babel, according to some psychologists.[25] Freeman's "turns" were his to experience and make sense from, not Caton's. They were a catalytic force belonging to compart-ments of Freeman's life not definable simply in terms of the remarkable, mentally searing events of the 1960s nor of his war with anthropology of later decades. Critics of Freeman infer his personality from selected exter-nal behaviors rather than from the sum total of his history, his growing up, his changing relations, his intellectual migrations, or his diary intro-spections. These things go together and must be embraced and calibrated one against the other to discover Freeman's biography. "We are more like movies than still photographs," writes Bentall.[26] This is a clue to the impor-tance of tracing Derek Freeman's own evolutionary climb through his life and thought, rather than happily concluding it was from start to finish a finished product and easily understood.

Elsie (Did) and John Freeman with Derek and his sister, Margaret, 1920s. (Freeman Family Papers. Courtesy of Jennifer and Hilary Freeman.)

Mount Evans location where Freeman and two companions fell, January 1938. (New Zealand Free Lance Collection. Alexander Turnbull Library, Wellington, New Zealand.)

It has occurred to me that this lino-cut of mine, which dates from 1938, is a poignant prefiguring of the remarkable reaction of some individuals to the refutation contained in my book Margaret Mead and Samoa (H.U.P., 1983)

TRUTH

Holmes, Rappaport et al who have spilt so much ink in an attempt to blot out the plainly evident truth

the redoubtable Laura Nader who publically condemned Harvard University Press for having published such a disturbing book Derek Freeman 1988

Freeman's long-standing passion for truth. (Freeman Family Papers. Courtesy of Jennifer and Hilary Freeman. Copy in Special Collections & Archives, UC San Diego.)

Young Derek, 1939. (Freeman Family Papers. Courtesy of Jennifer and Hilary Freeman.)

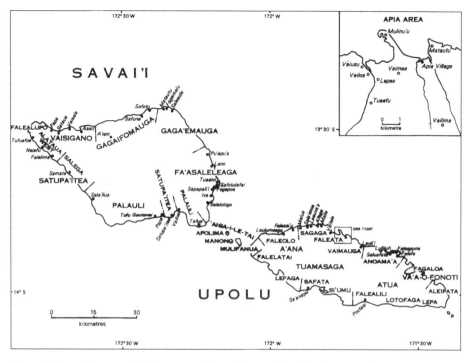

Map of Western Samoa, with Saʻanapu on the south coast of Upolu. (Courtesy of ANU Press.)

Freeman in Western Samoa on the horse he rode to Saʻanapu, 1941. (Freeman Family Papers. Courtesy of Jennifer and Hilary Freeman.)

Lauvī Vainu'u, one of the leading
executive chiefs of Sa'anapu village,
and senior matai of the Lauvī minor
lineage. The staff (to'oto'o) in his
right hand, and the cocoanut fibre
switch (fue) on his shoulder are the
insignia of an executive chief. The
staff is used whenever orations are
made in the open.

Off to war, 1943. (Freeman Family Papers. Courtesy of Jennifer and Hilary Freeman.)

Left: Lauvī Vainuʻu. (Freeman Family Papers. Courtesy of Jennifer and Hilary Freeman.)

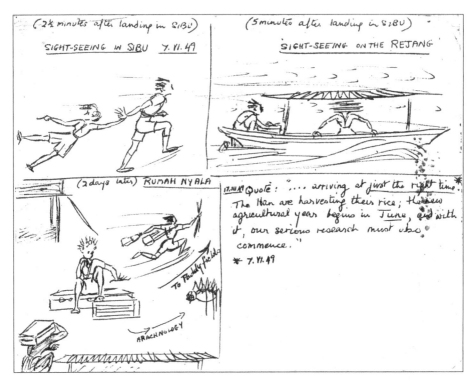

Freeman and Monica waste no time getting to work among the Iban. (Freeman Family Papers. Courtesy of Jennifer and Hilary Freeman.)

Derek and Monica with their Iban family, 1950. (Freeman Family Papers. Courtesy of Jennifer and Hilary Freeman.)

Sa'anapu village center, 1967. (Freeman Family Papers. Courtesy of Jennifer and Hilary Freeman. Copy in Special Collections & Archives, UC San Diego.)

The Freemans with Sa'anapu villagers, 1967. (Freeman Family Papers. Courtesy of Jennifer and Hilary Freeman.)

OTAGO DAILY TIMES

Dunedin, New Zealand

9   February, 1983

Derek Freeman (left) as Dunedin people will remember him in his years at the University of Otago. This photograph is on display in the Otago Museum. Right, Margaret Mead, the eminent American anthropologist whom Freeman attacks in his new book.

Freeman is remembered in Dunedin, 9 February 1983. (Courtesy of *Otago Daily Times* and Allied Press Ltd. Copy in Freeman Papers, Special Collections & Archives, UC San Diego.)

Freeman working at home. (Photo by Frank Heimans. Freeman Family Papers. Courtesy of Jennifer and Hilary Freeman.)

"Me, on an outing with the Saʻanapu *ʻaumaga* manfully resisting the beguiling blandishments of Margaret Mead and Ruth Benedict about Samoa." Freeman caption to *Ulysses and the Sirens*. (John W. Waterhouse. Great Britain, 1849–1917. Oil on canvas. Courtesy of Collection of National Gallery of Victoria, Melbourne.)

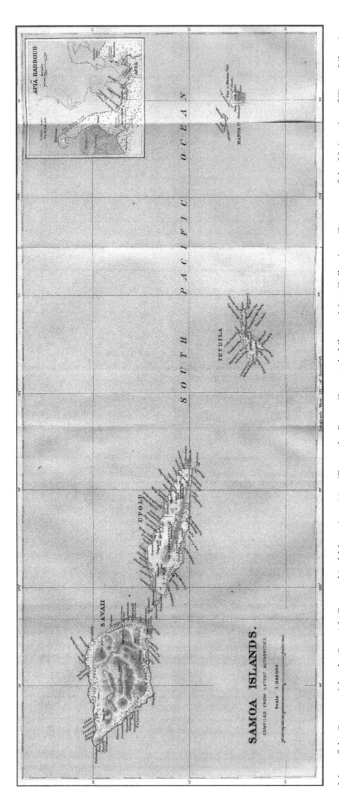

Map of the Samoan islands, *Scottish Geographical Magazine*, 1889. (From the Perry-Castañeda Library Map Collection. Courtesy of the University of Texas Libraries, the University of Texas at Austin.)

Freeman in thoughtful profile. (Photo by Monica Freeman. Freeman Family Papers. Courtesy of Jennifer and Hilary Freeman.)

Freeman at peace in his garden. (Freeman Family Papers. Courtesy of Jennifer and Hilary Freeman.)

sex, lies and

Story by NIKKI BARROWCLOUGH   Photograph by PETER BREW-BEVAN

CENTRE OF
THE STORM:
Derek Freeman
in his garden in
Canberra; opposite,
Margaret Mead in
the early '70s.

Freeman, photographed for an article by Nikki Barrowclough, "Sex, Lies and Anthropology," *Good Weekend: The Sydney Morning Herald Magazine*, 9 March 1996, 30. (Photo by Peter Brew-Bevan. Courtesy of Fairfax Media.)

Part II

The Mead Thing

9

A Not-So-Simple Journey

The compact little book that was the battleground of Freeman's war with anthropology in the 1980s is the most successful work of anthropology ever written, or at least the best selling. Margaret Mead's *Coming of Age in Samoa* was "an account of a part of the world that had long had a place in Western fantasies, at least those of males . . . a picture of relatively carefree sexuality, making that vision of sexual emancipation available not only to young men but to young women."[1] It worked its magic throughout North American society, and though published first in 1928, it was still selling one hundred thousand copies a year in the 1970s. Schools and universities made it a must-read text. Samoan scholars remembered it as compulsory reading in New Zealand university courses in education, psychology, political science, and sociology during the 1950s. *Coming of Age* was also a required text for Pacific Islanders studying at the University of the South Pacific in Fiji in the 1970s. In 1998 Derek Freeman reminded an audience at his alma mater in New Zealand that *Time* magazine in 1969 had called Mead the "Mother of the World," while her biographer asserted she was "indisputably" the most publicly celebrated scientist in America; even an impact crater on Venus was named after her.[2]

What Mead made of Samoa was a simple, unelaborated culture to set against the sophisticated complex culture of America. Her opening vignette, "A Day in Samoa," paints a picture of idyllic village life, the chores and pleasures of men, women, and children matching the rhythms of the unfolding day till sleep descends, and at last "there is only the mellow thunder of the reef and the whisper of lovers, as the village rests until dawn."[3]

Children are educated with simple discipline—"perpetual admonitions" (26)—reinforced with occasional cuffing and ineffectual shouting. Bursts of anger are "nine-tenths gesture" (28). Samoa was an island society "where no one plays for very high stakes, no one pays very heavy prices, no one suffers for his convictions, or fights to the death for special ends" (159). Critically, "adolescence represented no period of crisis or stress, but was instead an orderly developing of a set of slowly maturing interests and activities" (129).

A study of island adolescence was Mead's aim when she set off for the South Pacific in 1925. The question that "sent" her to Samoa was this: "Are the disturbances which vex our adolescents due to the nature of adolescence itself or to the civilization? Under different conditions does adolescence present a different picture?" (17). To answer this she would concentrate on the girls of Samoa in their social setting, describing their life course, the values that guided them, the problems they had to solve, the pains and pleasures of their human lot in this corner of the world. And her answer, the one human gift that this tiny society had developed and fashioned into a unique contribution to the human spirit, was a system for growing up that America must envy and seek to learn from, a system where girls faced no philosophical conundrums, where they were free of perplexing conflicts, and where their ambitions were simple and fixed: "to live as a girl with many lovers as long as possible and then to marry in one's own village, near one's own relatives, and to have many children" (129).

Coming of Age was a psychological study based on a small sample of females in one corner of the Samoan archipelago. It produced an image of Samoans as a set of crudely formed ciphers in the game of life, a shallow, static society that smoothed out all the edges of individual personality in favor of social ends. Precocity was punished, and individual personality was sacrificed to the social, creating a peculiar, passive, unambitious individual. Mead offers vivid portraits of girls growing up in age groups, taking places that were suited to their status and age among titled and untitled women in the village community, learning their work roles before selecting potential partners as they enter the stage of sexual tension and adventure: "But the seventeen year old girl does not wish to marry—not yet. It is better to live as a girl with no responsibility and a rich variety of emotional experience. This is the best period of her life" (37). And girls spend that period, according to Mead, in expending their energy in hidden sexual adventures.

To one side sits the *taupo*, a high-born girl snatched from her age group at fifteen or sixteen and named by the high chief as ceremonial princess to his household. The *taupo* is the village's formal hostess. She is accorded ceremonial titles and presides over visiting delegations, making kava (the slightly narcotic liquid that is drunk during ceremonies) and performing dances for them. She is the treasure of the village and its servant, her marriage a village matter, her virginity a key asset and talisman. The ritual taking of her virginity is performed at her wedding, with repercussions for her and her family if she is found not to be a virgin, though, according to Mead, there were ways around such a transgression: "The attitude towards virginity is a curious one. Christianity has, of course, introduced a moral premium on chastity. The Samoans regard this attitude with reverent but complete skepticism and the concept of celibacy is absolutely meaningless to them" (83).

Mead also described for her readers the "sleep crawling" phenomenon (*moetotolo*), which she differentiated from rape. Mead dealt with *moetotolo* as a kind of game of Russian roulette played out in those silent hours when the village was supposedly resting till dawn, "in which a man stealthily appropriates the favors which are meant for another" (79).

Boys faced greater constraints, wrote Mead, especially those likely to succeed to *matai* titles. Wishing to excel, the boy is ridiculed if he is too slack in his efforts, scolded if he shows himself too prominently ahead of his fellows. Boys develop stronger solidarity than girls in their social communities within the village, but ambition is suppressed in service to the village and its high titled chiefs. The tensions involved in finding a wife and dealing with what Mead painted as the sexual freedom of young females were enough to cause depression and sometimes violence.

Mead's book has been celebrated down the years as a "classic ethnography." But its argument was directed more toward painting a picture of Samoan personality that was a message for American society. Mead went to the Samoan islands influenced by a 1920s intellectual movement seeking to integrate individuals into a distinctive American national culture that would dampen the country's parochial, puritanical materialism. *Coming of Age* had the educational goal (which was equally a political one) to make Americans rethink their cultural assumptions. The Samoa she "found" in Manu'a was a stark and explicit contrast, representing, according to Marianna Torgovnik, what the West most wanted from "the primitive": "a model of alternative social organization in which psychological integrity is a birthright, rooted in one's body and sexuality, and in which a full range of ambivalences and doubts can be confronted and defused through the culture's rituals, customs and play."[4]

Mead identified for American educators a series of lessons in the Samoan scheme of life. Modifying American approaches, particularly around the organization of the family and attitudes to sex, would reduce the stress and anguish of growing through adolescence. Mead ended her book with a little homily on educating children for choice, opening their minds, emptying them of prejudices, and filling them with "the recognition of many possible ways of life, where other civilizations have recognized only one" (197).

In *Coming of Age in Samoa* Mead speaks with sturdy authority, as though she had been in the archipelago for years rather than the eight months and ten days she spent in various parts of American Samoa. During that time she had to settle in, make her observations, and compile her data. Mead's air of specialist expertise is the secret to the lasting value of her book. She was a brilliant stylist (though this is a weapon of uncertain authority in ethnographic interpretations and was a focus for later critics). *Coming of Age* brims with sharp, compelling portraits of individuals and descriptions of landscapes. Mead could sum up a cultural pattern with intuitive flair, her agile syntheses accessible to both the professional and the popular imagination. This gift helped launch her career as a cultural commentator and public intellectual.

But the book is also more complex in its mass of details and methodological appendixes than reviewers and her mentors were wont to see. It was a book written to order—Derek Freeman's great accusation—and followed a line of thinking laid down by Mead's mentor and the "father" of American anthropology, Franz Boas. Mead was writing into a young discipline that was arguing that culture, not biology or race, was the arbiter of human choices. She went to Samoa to test the staunchly held belief that the storm and stress of Western adolescence was a universal, inevitable, biologically based feature of human nature. Boas wanted her to see if cultural conditioning might instead be the key to growing up in an apparently primitive, simple society. A single instance would do. And Mead obliged, said Freeman, with ethnographic "proof" that Samoan adolescence was an idyll of untroubled sexual and temperamental license. Human nature was the rawest of matter till it was shaped by culture. Nurture, not nature, was the key, an idea whose time had come in North America and that was grasped willingly by anthropologists, psychologists, educators, and commentators as Mead's book and her felicitous public advocacy gained traction through the years.

By the time Derek Freeman began his campaign to refute Mead's claims about Samoa, she was not just a famous anthropologist but an icon of

American public culture. Even an anthropologist who disapproved of her scientific status and was a former student of Freeman's could acknowledge her significance as an American figure.

> Mead did embody those critical values that constitute the American ideal. Successful, optimistic, with a fervent belief in the future, she reaffirmed the hope of all Americans that through education everyone could become what he or she wanted to be; and she turned this hope into what people believed was scientific truth through her research. As the result of the proper education, she argued, not only would it be possible for each individual to reach his potential, but it would liberate us all from the past so that all America could believe its utopian vision. This included a society without racism or sexism.[5]

As we have seen, Mead was not Freeman's first priority either during the 1950s or when he went back to Samoa in the 1960s. A self-review by his Department of Anthropology in 1977 does not list anything to do with Mead during those two decades. It makes brief mention of a long-term study of "a Samoan community" stretching over four decades that was due for completion but makes much more of a major new initiative of the 1970s, an ethological laboratory—a Freeman initiative.

The antechamber of the great debate is the period from 1967 to 1980, not the forty years from 1940, which some of his critics allege. Freeman tried to draw Mead into a continuing correspondence not after their 1964 meeting but in 1967 from Sa'anapu, putting detailed queries to her about inconsistencies in *Coming of Age* and her comments on sexuality. But her increasingly exasperated replies pleaded protection of her informants and then stopped. Freeman had remained polite and unflustered in his letters, even courtly in his manner of address, though he was capable of subtle put-downs. However, he took her eventual silence as a "shut out" and decided not to bother her further till he tried again in 1978.[6]

On his return from Western Samoa in 1967 Freeman had plunged into studying the background of Franz Boas and the development of American cultural anthropology. He gave a paper on Margaret Mead's errors a few months after his return, but it was his new social scientific mission that really consumed him, his reading list running more to Hans Eysenck, Erik Erikson, John Eccles, John Bowlby, Géza Roheim, and a hundred other thinkers who stimulated his behavioral and psychological focus.

The first serious salvo of his campaign was fired in May 1968, when he gave a lengthy paper to the Australian Association for Social Anthropology titled "On the Believing of as Many as Six Impossible Things before Break-fast."[7] The light touch of the title, borrowed from *Alice in Wonderland*, belied a serious intent, which was to expose the Boasian assumptions behind Margaret Mead's Samoan enterprise and to counter what he called her "exquisite howlers" about the real nature of Samoan society. His paper contains the road map for what became *Margaret Mead and Samoa* a dozen years later. After sketching a picture of the foundations of American cultural anthropology under Boas and Alfred Kroeber, Freeman moved on to examine the assumptions with which Mead set out for the islands in 1925, the extent to which her findings were keyed into Boas's ideas, and the rapid spread of her conclusions among anthropologists and other professionals in subsequent years.

At this point he zeroed in on Mead's positive depiction of Samoan sexual behavior, which became enshrined in textbooks and public images as "gay pre-marital freedom" in which love between the sexes was "a light and pleasant dance." Freeman in contrast painted a severer picture of rigidly protected virginity, ritualized dominance by high-ranking chiefs, and adolescent practices in which the rate of sexual assault was higher than in Western society. He concluded by returning to the "closed-system anthropology" that had spawned Mead's work and looked forward to the discipline adapting to new discoveries in biological behavior studies.[8]

One of Freeman's most recent critics, Paul Shankman, has placed this paper in a line of descent he claims stretches back many years. Shankman argues that it "linked Mead as a person to her allegedly unreliable professional findings," a peculiar claim, as though her ideas should have developed in some abstract dimension outside herself.[9] Shankman's is part of a cumulative argument that seeks to rehabilitate Mead's findings on Samoa and to destroy Freeman's, suggesting that Freeman carried a highly personal animus against Mead. As we shall see again and again in the following pages, style and the language of implication are at the center of debates by and about Freeman and set a tone of subtle and not-so-subtle denigration of the personalities of the protagonists. Certainly Freeman's language in this early paper flirts with ridicule, its very title suggestive of fairy tales, Freeman describing Mead's prime question about nature or nurture as "ridiculous." While accusing her of making absolute statements, Freeman himself ventures the unqualified judgment that she was "grotesquely in error" and guilty of a "gross and actionable libel" against the Samoan people.[10]

This was an early work-in-progress piece. The language of Freeman's eventual book *Margaret Mead and Samoa* is more restrained, due in part to

162

trenchant criticisms he received when he sent an early draft off to the publishers Holt, Rinehart and Winston in 1971. All three readers who read the manuscript remarked on the tone of his work. The "element of vindictiveness that lurks near the surface" troubled one. Another felt Freeman was guilty of "the most ungentlemanly behavior." The third thought it "a shame to have Freeman's very important message obscured as a personal vendetta."[11] As he reviewed these comments, Freeman was continuing his self-recording and self-examination in his diaries, trying hard to regulate his tendency to win every argument. "Is a mature & true independence of being possible with sufficient nerve, restraints and detachments: yes!" was his encouragement to himself. After reading the Dhammapada—a regular inspiration—in March 1971 he decided "more than ever that my chief interest in life is an 'austere and unconsoled [*sic*] love of the good'—if only I had the strength and purpose to fully realize it." Insecurity enveloped his being every day, for he was never confident he possessed the "right stuff" to do the great thing he was setting out to do. "Have I the capacity to become the Galileo Galilei of anthropology?" he asked in one of his more hubristic moments.[12]

At the same time, Freeman realized that he was intellectually invigorated by opposition—"surely a poor substitute for creativity"—and this showed in the semiregular confrontations that continued during seminars with colleagues and visiting scholars; his old colleague and former boss, Oscar Spate, chided him after one encounter for his "undue vehemence & over-cleverness" after Freeman told the speaker he was "talking through his hat." Others scolded him for having an "overweening manner."[13] About this time, rumors started to spread that Freeman was "dotty" and his anthropology therefore suspect.

If life was becoming burdensome, Freeman did not let it interfere with his formidable reading on the Boas school, on Darwin, and on the history of both biological and anthropological thinking, which was vast and concentrated. He would immerse himself in a cluster of works on a subject he was following for weeks at a time, free to explore every niche. On 27 October 1969 he began drafting the first words of his Mead book. A week later he rejected what he had written in favor of a model of criticism based on Karl Popper's philosophical works. Freeman was struggling to analyze Mead's central argument, but he completed a rough draft of chapter 1 in February 1970. Various distractions and uncertainties about the project meant that it was 1971 before he sent it off to a historian colleague in the Pacific, Ron Crocombe, enjoining him to keep it away from Mead supporters.[14]

The criticisms Freeman received when he also sent the draft to Holt, Rinehart and Winston were a shock. Not only were the readers concerned about the tone of Freeman's language, but, irrespective of their regard for his scholarship (and it was fulsome), all three were concerned he was attacking an idol already dismissed as a popularizer within anthropology and overestimating the degree to which American anthropologists still adhered to cultural determinism. Freeman, they said, was sensibly placed to tackle much larger contexts in the history of anthropology, and his most critical reader argued that Freeman should be tackling the cultural and social anthropology paradigms in Mead's other book, *Social Organization of Manu'a*, as well as classics by Freeman's early British mentors, Raymond Firth, Alfred Radcliffe-Brown, and Bronisław Malinowski. "That is where the paradigms are, not in a popular book which had a vastly different purpose and which—incidentally—achieved it! Or are these too difficult for him; or is he without the necessary parts of the anatomy which define one as masculine." This remark, more acid than anything Freeman ever ventured, incensed him (though he may have mistaken it as referring to his attacking a woman). Even if the remark was designed to intimidate and crush him, Freeman's inner instincts to overcome every opponent only made him stubbornly resistant to such urgings. "They have picked the wrong man, for I will not be daunted," he wrote to a friend. His stubbornness also meant he missed or ignored other substantial advice to focus on empirical cases and argument rather than rely on programmatic statements and appeals to "Truth." At least one of the readers (probably Roger Keesing, soon to be appointed from overseas to a professorship in Freeman's own department) predicted that American social scientists would rally round to defend Mead for personal and emotional reasons.[15]

Mead's *Social Organization of Manu'a* did become a target for Freeman the same year, but only to show the errors Mead had made in her use of Samoan words and symbols, which were reproduced without correction in the edition republished in 1969. Freeman's errata list was an accusation about Mead's carelessness because of Samoans' intense pride in the use of their language and the fact that Mead had various ancient dictionaries at her side in 1925. Strikingly, he said nothing about Mead's introduction and conclusion to the 1969 edition, in which Mead tried to explain the disconnection between her methods in 1925 and various findings about Samoan society since then. Mead explicitly recognized Freeman's work, indeed cautiously approved it while criticizing others (especially Freeman's later bête noire, Lowell Holmes). She was tentatively looking forward to "microcultural" studies like Freeman's "intensive attention" to early childhood experience drawn from his 1960s stay in the islands. Her additions to this 1969 edition have the quality of a thoughtful defensiveness, especially in relation to the social violence among Samoans and changes that may have occurred since her original study. In a plea that strains credulity, Mead suggested that in 1925 "Manuʻa might have represented a special variation on the Samoan pattern, a temporary, felicitous relaxation of the quarrels and rivalries, the sensitivities to slight and insults, and the use of girls as pawns in male rivalries."[16]

Freeman made no mention of these qualifications, which became a focus in the 1980s debate around Mead's Samoan work. Nor did he discuss her account of their meeting in 1964 when he challenged Mead's findings. In her *Manuʻa* book, Mead specifically traced her early intellectual influences back to two New Zealanders who were also deeply influential in Freeman's life: H. D. Skinner and Ernest Beaglehole. Yet ironically, it is as though Freeman did not want to acknowledge this mutual intellectual link. Or perhaps it was not ironic, for, as we have seen, in the early 1970s Derek Freeman was not yet fully armed for an assault on things Meadian. He was working his onerous way through literature and documents and drafting early chapters that were promptly abandoned or subject to vigorous criticism. The "Some Errata" review was mere shadow boxing. His Mead project was a slower-growing monster that consumed the next dozen years.

Freeman's own attitude to Mead fluctuated in these years, between finding fault with her methods and conclusions about Samoa and expressing respect for her prodigious achievements. He advised his student Don Tuzin, now doing fieldwork for his doctorate among Mead's Arapesh in Papua New Guinea, to consult Mead to the full. Derek and Margaret bumped into one another at ANU in November 1971, but she did not acknowledge his nod and smile; instead, she "cuts me dead." In 1973 they met again, and this time Mead said sarcastically, "Hello, Derek, are you recognizing common people these days?" Freeman refused to be vexed, engineering a quite amicable conversation about Samoan behavior. In June 1975 he saw her on current affairs television in Sydney and wrote in his diary how impressive she was at fielding questions.[17]

Some overseas colleagues recognized what he was trying to do in his refutation of *Coming of Age* and agreed with him; others attempted to exonerate Mead. His old mentor and teacher Meyer Fortes lifted Freeman with a praising letter in February 1975, regarding him as "among the two or three most significant individuals in contemporary anthropology," but

Freeman was downcast by Fortes's advice not to proceed with his refutation of Mead, for Fortes still detected hard feelings against her.[18]

The complex play of doubt and deliberation is evident in Freeman's intellectual life through the 1970s. Insecurity and the pursuit of self-knowledge continually wrestled with one another. These were years of anxiety around being appointed professor of the department and its head, of the troubles with staff and students, and of being intermittently cold-shouldered or abused in the corridors. His tribulations caused a series of breaks in Freeman's attention to Mead.

He started the book again, with a new tone and emphasis, in February 1975. It would not be Freeman's first or last attempt to build some momentum. Less than a month later he was writing in his diary: "Decide that the whole enterprise must be rethought with the taking of a much more sympathetic view of Boas, Kroeber, Mead et al." By May he had made up his mind to renounce working on the refutation and to hand all his materials over to doctoral student Penelope Schoeffel, which was a great surprise to her, for Freeman then spent years criticizing her work on Samoan women. But by midyear he had reread *Coming of Age* and decided that Mead, by pursuing the dogma of cultural determinism, "denies to the Samoans the capacity to make choices (except in moral terms) & so, the status of human beings."[19] This moral empathy for the downtrodden—already manifest in the Sarawak episode and in Freeman's Aboriginal crusade during the 1970s—should not be underestimated or cynically discounted in the explanations for Freeman's occasionally egregious behavior. We must also not forget that Freeman returned to the scene of his Asian labors—Sarawak—in the mid-1970s.

Looking back on Freeman's long intellectual life, one might easily conclude that his Iban and Southeast Asian work faded into the background from 1963—the year he strode off to London with an entirely new life plan. But that is not the case. He continued to have a steady trickle of students doing their PhD fieldwork under his supervision—James Masing, George Appell, Michael Heppell among them. In January 1976 Tom Harrisson's death in a road accident in Thailand was a kind of release from Freeman's Sarawak ghosts. Freeman wrote to Heppell about his reawakened enthusiasm for things Iban. His materials on them were "the richest and most scientifically systematic in existence," and he was going to persist with his intention to write a major study of Iban religion.[20] That year Freeman set the Mead project aside and took his study leave in Malaysia, Brunei, Singapore, and Indonesia, giving papers on Iban topics and consulting with colleagues about new projects in Indonesia and Borneo.

Freeman visited his old stomping ground of Kuching in Borneo, where the talk was of "the tyranny of Harrisson." He wrote in his diary that Harrisson's influence still pervaded the museum and the local culture "like some kind of living stain." But Freeman had by the 1970s learned to some degree to control his bitter feeling and was able to find some compassion for "the mongrel, beef-witted madman of Pig Lane." Both men shared a love of mountains. Freeman climbed Mount Kinabalu—conquered it, as had Harrisson—and quoted appreciatively in his diary Harrisson's description of its serried, black, jagged peaks, perhaps apprehending a shared attitude to conquest he was otherwise loath to admit. He even warned an Iban colleague against writing an obituary for Harrisson that told home truths: Freeman had the grace to recognize that just after Harrisson's violent death was not the time to lay into him; ultimately, the truth would come out.[21]

Freeman also engaged in trench warfare against those who would usurp his authority in Iban studies. First there was an upstart book out of Oxford on the Iban and their religion by a young man named Erik Jensen. Freeman reviewed the book sniffily on the grounds that he himself had greater knowledge. Rodney Needham, friend though he was, took exception to Freeman's accusation that Jensen betrayed "an Oxonian approach" when Derek himself had nothing to show for all his years of research into the subject: "Jensen has published a monographic study of certain forms of 'Iban religion': you have not."[22] It was an accusation others would use in future years about Freeman's claim to "own" Samoa. In 1980 he challenged a Canadian scholar named Jerome Rousseau, who argued, contrary to Freeman's original thesis on the unique egalitarian nature of the Iban, that they were a hierarchical, class-based society. Freeman's correspondence and academic rejoinder were trenchant—one colleague said defamatory—but Freeman was concerned to stake a continuing claim to preeminence in Iban studies (he told Edmund Leach in 1980 that he was planning to get back to Iban studies in retirement once he had dealt with the Mead project). Freeman persisted as both patron and critic of Iban scholars like Benedict Sandin, assistant curator at the Sarawak Museum under Harrisson, and drew support and admiration well into his old age from Borneo scholars such as Clifford Sather.[23]

Purging the ghost of Tom Harrisson did not solve the problem of writing when Freeman returned to his book on Mead. Anxiety still gnawed at him, with agonized jottings in his diary questioning his reputation and his self-worth; depressed moods occasionally immobilized him. In October 1976 he formed the idea of writing to Margaret Mead "informing her of my intentions & seeking her comments & possible cooperation."[24] It was a means of getting himself out of his rut. In November he tackled another new direction for the book, but December brought more disquiet over the fact that he was *not* writing.

Freeman vowed to make 1977 the year of the Mead book. In fact, he was juggling work on several fronts, looking after his Asian students, wrestling with the internal politics of the department, and working on a sociobiology paper that became a well-regarded chapter in an Ashley Montagu book.[25] In June he visited Canada and California for a symposium and conversations about his work, as well as for a reunion with Don Tuzin, who was now ensconced at the University of California in San Diego. It was all another distraction, but at least it provided a major lift to Freeman's spirits, for on meeting Jonas Salk in San Diego, Salk invited Freeman to spend some time at the Salk Institute the following year. This was calculated to overcome any of Freeman's self-doubts, and as he flew home across the Pacific he wept a little "at the thought that those who have been calling me mad (since 1960) have been shown to be so very wrong."[26]

Back in Australia, Freeman received another morale boost with an approving letter from Karl Popper, and then he was off again, this time to Europe in October for a symposium with biologists in Bad Homberg, Germany. He gave an ethology paper that was reasonably received. This got his scholarly juices flowing, and a subsequent pilgrimage to Oxford to meet Popper and Nikolaas Tinbergen persuaded Freeman that he should return to his critique of Mead.

In 1978 he wrote again to Margaret Mead—twice—offering to send her an acutely critical essay on her account of Samoa. He had just given it as a seminar paper—"Sweet Analytics, 'Tis Thou Has Ravished Me"—and he was in two minds about sending Mead a copy, "for I have no wish to distress you unnecessarily." He went on:

> It is well possible, it seems to me, that you might be annoyed at the style of my criticism—for I have not hesitated to draw pointed attention to what, after long and careful study of the evidence, I judge to be flagrant inadequacies in your account of Samoan sexual values and behavior.
>
> On the other hand, I recognize that you ought, if you so desire, to be given an opportunity to assess the nature of my criticisms, and to comment on them should you so wish.[27]

Freeman's aim, in the spirit of his strengthened Popperian mood and in the cause of getting closer to a "scientific account," was to get Mead to point out his errors and inaccuracies. It was all too late and may have been futile anyway. Mead was dying and was gone in November 1978.

Her death does not seem to have found any resonance in Freeman's daily diary entries, nor is there any hint that now he had the freedom to proceed with his refutation. Indeed, in February 1979 he was still expressing awe at her prodigious output in various fields across both serious and popular journals. In January 1979 he had given his "Sweet Analytics" paper as president of the anthropology section to the Australian and New Zealand Association for the Advancement of Science (ANZAAS) congress in Auckland. Its rather dismissive conclusion—"Samoa, I trust it will have become evident, is a human domain of great character and complexity, and is no place at all for ethnographers in swaddling clothes"—hid his nervousness at presenting his arguments on Samoan sexual behavior in full public view. Penelope Schoeffel remembers his agitated state and anxiety that he would be attacked.[28]

But 1979 was not yet the year to break the back of the Mead project. Though he withdrew on leave from his department in April for ten months' unbroken work on Mead, it was not until the middle of May that Freeman finished his paper criticizing sociobiology and turned his energies to the writing of the Mead book: "It is quite obvious that if [I] do not achieve this my last years at the A.N.U. & my retirement will be blighted and unhappy."[29] However, periods of listlessness continued to alternate with the interminable distractions that went with Freeman's occasionally manic conviction that he must follow every lead that came at him from any angle: he was reading Nietzsche, Leibniz, Wittgenstein, and Bertrand Russell in June, even waking through the night to talk metaphysics with Monica. He had pulled himself—and his Mead notes—together by July, but the rest of the year was similarly strewn with interior attempts to deal with past controversies, as well as the farce of the Aztec stone at the university.

The year 1980 started the same way, Freeman waking in a sweat on 24 January "with dire forebodings about my capacity to write; come to absolute realization that I must now *really buckle down* & keep at it until the job is done." He resolved to make writing take precedence over everything else, including his bouts of self-analysis and forays into new reading. He was in disarray again in March, with more changes to the plan of the book and with fresh anxieties and avoidances; there were just seven hundred days till his retirement. Finally, in April 1980 he got down to concentrated work and finished a usable draft of the first chapter in eight days. Chapter 2 followed in May, and a newly found serenity allowed him to accelerate. He began waking of a morning brimming with ideas. The Rousseau dispute over the

Iban took him off track for some eleven weeks, but by the end of the year he had reached chapter 7 of his manuscript.

None of this is a picture of a man driven relentlessly by a vendetta against Margaret Mead who sacrificed everything to skewer her work and reputation. Mead shares Freeman's life with several other missions and obligations throughout the 1970s and 1980s, not to mention the constant struggle to understand himself, to identify and free his better nature in relationships with others. Not until the year of his retirement, 1981, did Freeman feel in his bones that he had a book worthy of his scholarly exertions.

He completed chapter 11 in March as the first intimations reached him of the battles to come. Rhoda Métraux, one of Mead's closest, long-lasting friends, wrote him a letter expressing surprise that he was reviewing, "after more than fifty years, the field research of a 24 year old woman who was carrying out her first field task."[30] In June Don Tuzin reported to him the curiosity of observers and the widespread impression that Derek was obsessed with Margaret Mead. No matter, he drove on, buoyed by an expression of interest from Princeton University Press and the offer of a contract from Oxford University Press. July 16 was his red-letter day: Freeman finished typing the manuscript, 20 chapters and 125,000 words, a remarkable achievement considering the number of false starts, anxiety attacks, and distractions.

"Now the matchless deed's achieved, determined, dead [sic] and done."[31] Not quite. Freeman's passion to eliminate errors in the quest for truth had him and Monica setting off for Samoa in September to test the manuscript's contents against the judgment of Samoan scholars. ("I realized that what I was doing was thumbing my nose at the establishment and that they would go for me with sharpened knives," was his claim years later as he looked back at the battles that ensued.[32]) Echoes of his other projects accompanied him: just before they left, James Masing, Freeman's preeminent Iban student, was awarded his doctorate for his work on the great Iban chants. In Western Samoa, Freeman showed the manuscript to the writer Albert Wendt, who praised it, and to colleagues at the new University of Samoa. Freeman's cup of pleasure overflowed when he was appointed as Foundation Professor of Anthropology and consultant on Samoa studies. In American Samoa, Freeman managed to gain access to court records on rape and homicide cases for the first time, and he encountered Napoleone Tuiteleleapaga, who made claims about Mead's sexual behavior with Samoan men. Freeman noted it in his diary as another day of revelation.

From Samoa they headed for the United States for more checking and to finalize a publisher. In Hawai'i, Freeman examined the papers of Māori ethnologist Peter Buck, who was in Samoa in the late 1920s, before he and Monica flew on to meet their daughter Jennifer, now a student in California, and then to New York. The editor at his first choice, Oxford University Press in America, blotted her copybook badly when she returned the manuscript to Freeman, telling him the book would attract no interest whatsoever. Stunned and now at a loss in deepest New York, he and Monica bumped into Jane Howard, a Mead biographer whom Freeman had once helped. She led him to an agent who advised Freeman to put his book before Princeton, Yale, and Harvard University Presses.

From that point on the Freemans' travels through America were a triumphant procession. Derek gave seminars and lectures that were rapturously received at Princeton, Yale, Brandeis, and the College of William and Mary; he felt that he was among friends as they threw profuse blandishments in his direction. He met and connected with biologists John Bonner, John Pfeiffer, and Ernst Mayr. Yale University Press called with a report from one of its readers, saying his book "will become a landmark in the history of American science."[33] Princeton wanted to discuss terms for a special edition. Harvard promised a large print run and a spring 1983 release.

Settling down after all this exhilaration, Freeman finally chose Harvard, a decision he was, on looking back at it at the end of his life, unsure about, accusing the press of cowardice during the backlash to his book.[34] What helped him decide at the time was the motto of Harvard University: *Veritas*, Truth, the virtue Freeman admired above all else and whose meaning was about to be sorely tested in the glare of American publicity. He and Monica returned to Australia elated, there to find an invitation to become a visiting fellow in his old department after his employment with ANU ended on 31 December.

John Pfeiffer, who had enjoyed Freeman's seminar at Princeton, had sent a note to Harvard University Press supporting the publication of the Freeman book: "It is research with passion," he wrote, "involving ambitions and frustrations, bruised and burgeoning egos, in a field noted for vendettas and polemics."[35] This was an echo in advance of the tumult to come. Freeman himself recognized that. On Christmas Eve 1981, at the home of their younger daughter, Hilary, Freeman copied into his diary a quotation from Robert Louis Stevenson, the famed Scottish storyteller who had died in Samoa: "Sooner or later everyone sits down to a banquet of consequences."

10

The Banquet of Consequences

Margaret Mead and Samoa: The Making and Unmaking of an Anthropological Myth is a book with two distinct messages. The core is a refutation of Mead's position on the nature of Samoan society, as well as a critique of the methods she used in researching her portrait of the Samoan people. Freeman's case is built up through a series of building blocks laid out in what for him was a strict progression following the scientific logic of Karl Popper.

First, Freeman dealt with Franz Boas's vision of cultural anthropology, detailing Boas's "mounting confrontation" with eugenicists and others intent on applying notions of heredity to cultural development.[1] In the hands of major figures in the descent line of American anthropology, such as Alfred Kroeber and Robert Lowie, argued Freeman, the paradigm of cultural determinism became an ideology, an ideology into which Margaret Mead and her colleague and companion Ruth Benedict were inducted as students of Boas. In 1925 Mead, doctoral dissertation fresh in her hands, set herself to do field research in the Pacific islands at the instigation of Boas.

Chapters 5 to 7 of Freeman's book examined Mead's research in the Manu'a group of American Samoa in 1925–26 and the way the myth of Samoan sexual freedom was propagated once Mead had reported her "findings." Freeman recounted the chronological sequence of her work, the conditions under which she labored, the people she met, and the places she frequented. He emphasized Mead's own confession that she was excluded from political participation in village life, her inability to witness many social ceremonies, and her reliance on a select list of (mostly young female) informants. The writing of *Coming of Age* that followed was therefore highly constrained and significantly influenced by "Ruth Benedict's vision of culture as 'personality writ large'" (74). Mead's conclusion, said

Freeman, written as an instructive argument for American society, "dismissed biology, or nature, as being of no significance whatsoever in accounting for the presence of storm and stress in American adolescents, and claimed the determinism of culture, or nurture, to be absolute" (78).

In chapter 6 Freeman became more concerned with "the scientific adequacy" (83) of Mead's depiction of Samoan life and turned to her portrait "A Day in Samoa" in *Coming of Age*. Largely by quoting Mead herself, Freeman elaborated on her portrait of an almost perfect society in which adolescents made harmonious adjustments as they passed through life stages. Samoa was a society of "diffuse but warm human relationships" (88), wrote Mead, in which the disciplining of children was not oppressive, competition was virtually nonexistent, and sex, especially in adolescence, was play. This was the "beguiling vignette" (84) that captured the American public's imagination and became the South Seas myth. The romance took flight well into the 1940s and 1950s in centers of higher learning among anthropologists and in the wider public. Mead herself, Freeman made clear, rarely discussed the exceptions she herself had documented and continued to make "extensive claims for the validity of her Samoan researches" (105).

These early chapters were background. The formal refutation began with chapter 8, in which Freeman set out to show that the main conclusions of *Coming of Age* were "the figments of an anthropological myth which is deeply at variance with the facts of Samoan ethnography and history" (109). After reviewing the contradictions between the accounts of explorers, missionaries, and settlers, on the one hand, and Mead, on the other, Freeman set out to show how Samoa constituted one universe from west to east of the archipelago. Mead simply got wrong or she misinterpreted many of Samoa's central institutions and behavioral practices.

Freeman's account ranged over the rank structure among chiefs and people, the competition for titles, the rates of aggressive behavior and affray, and the everyday violence, contained for the most part by the elaborate conventions of the title system. He explored Samoans' devoted religiosity and their strict, moralistic care of girls. "Mead's failure to give due attention to this socio-religious regime (which is accorded great prominence in the accounts of other contemporary observers, such as Judd and Buck)," argued Freeman, "can only be construed as an active—albeit unconscious—denial of the realities of Samoan life" (186).

He did the same for Samoan child-rearing practices, contrasting Mead's assertions of easy, uncomplicated relations with historical accounts of the severe discipline practiced on children and his own researches into attachment behavior during his 1960s fieldwork. Freeman passed on to considering Samoan character, disputing Mead's claims that Samoans possessed no strong passions and discussing various psychological conditions documented by a range of studies. Toward the end of the book, Freeman tackled the question of sexual mores, the most alluring part of Mead's portrayal of Samoa. He described Mead's account of the *taupou* system as "a confused travesty" (228) and emphasized instead Samoans' "cult of virginity" (234). The "fible-fables," or nonsense (252), of Mead's main informant on ceremonial defloration, Phoebe Parkinson, Freeman dismissed out of hand. In chapter 17 Freeman addressed Mead's core conclusions about the easy nature of Samoan adolescence, advancing at some length his own data on rates of delinquency, which matched those in Western countries.

Freeman ended this section of his refutation by examining again the "Samoan ethos" as Mead had depicted it. His own account was based, he claimed, on how Samoans described themselves to him, as well as on his own deep knowledge. He was both admiring and unromantic. Samoans were "a people of exceptional punctilio and grit" (270), a quality particularly in evidence in the 1920s as chiefs and people in both American and Western Samoa fought tenaciously against the demands of colonial authorities. They had "a special genius for restoring order and regaining amity in the face of outrageous fortune" (273).

But obedience and rank were supreme in a system that was anything but casual in atmosphere and tone. A pervasive dependence on the physical punishment of children in particular made Samoans "so disturbingly prone to interpersonal aggression" (275). In refuting Mead's account, Freeman concluded, he was forced to discuss "the darker side of Samoan life" (278), which Mead had ignored to make her ideological point. Samoans shared a dark side with all human societies but remained a "wonderfully hospitable and generous" people whose "devotion to the ethics of Christianity" (278) included a magnanimity of spirit displayed in difficult historical situations.

Not everything in *Margaret Mead and Samoa* was an outright condemnation of Mead's achievements. Indeed, Freeman started with an expression of respect for her (and his diary entries, as we have seen, reinforce his admiration; it was not confected). Moreover, he had no hesitation in dismissing suggestions that Mead lied in her understanding of Samoan culture: "The succession of prefaces to *Coming of Age in Samoa* published by Mead in 1949, 1953, 1961, and 1973 indicate clearly, in my judgment, that she did give genuine credence to the view of Samoan life with which she returned to New York in 1926" (288).

Whether her Samoan informants were telling her lies was another matter, something that at this stage Freeman left open: "We cannot, in the absence of detailed corroborative evidence, be sure about the truth of this Samoan claim that Mead was mischievously duped by her adolescent informants" (291). He would shift ground radically on this question in years to come as he chased down evidence of this very thing happening.

A second message in *Margaret Mead and Samoa* shifted the weight of the argument momentarily away from Mead. Freeman's final section argued the need for anthropology to integrate its studies of culture with the findings of biology and a paradigm that balanced both "genetic and exogenetic" forces to explain human behavior. Here Freeman threw out a challenge for anthropology to concentrate on what biologist colleagues were calling "multiple choice behavior" experiments by primates (299), with cultural adaptations in the human species as the proper field of investigation. Mead made a fleeting return in the last pages, where Freeman bemoaned her "conceptual and methodological" deficiencies (301), but it was to the synthesis of biology and culture that the book was in the end dedicated.

The frontispiece dedication to Karl Popper was in this respect a mishit, for in the final two chapters, Freeman veered away from his scientific refutation approach and onto polemical ground that diverted the reader from his prime objective. As we shall see, it gave his opponents room to attack *Margaret Mead and Samoa* as a case for biological determinism in place of cultural determinism. They attacked it for much else besides.

Despite some later coy reservations, Freeman was convinced his book had the power to change the course of anthropology. He said as much in letters to colleagues. In March 1981 Freeman let his vice chancellor, Anthony Low, know the "big book" was nearing completion and would cause "a major stir" in the human sciences. Elsewhere he referred to its promise as "the greatest denouement in anthropology, so far." Caught up in the euphoria of its completion and acceptance for publication, Freeman even suggested to Harvard University Press that he was exposing "if you like the Piltdown case of the behavioral sciences."[2]

However, no one foresaw the convulsions that followed publication, though one of Harvard's readers (the historian of anthropology George Stocking) had warned that the book would raise hackles and cause controversy. Freeman's enemies, especially Lowell Holmes, later claimed that the publisher had set out to create a sensation in a shoddy campaign to sell books. Freeman himself seemed to accept that he was an innocent bystander in "a planned publication coup."[3] But his early champion turned critic, Hiram Caton, discovered that Harvard was equally surprised and embarrassed by the sudden uproar. The publisher certainly saw its marketing potential: editor Eric Wanner told Freeman it had provoked one of the most spirited discussions he had ever experienced. There had been tussles over the appropriate title (which occasioned a bad dream for Derek in which he and a throat-grabbing interloper struggled for dominance), but prepublication brochures were effusive with praise from Stocking and Irenäus Eibl-Eibesfeldt (this last, from a biologist, was a red flag to many anthropologists).[4]

Detonation day was 31 January 1983. Harvard had already organized its own launch, but Edwin McDowell of the *New York Times*, sensing a story, had received a prepublication copy and persuaded his editor to put his review on the front page. Caton surveyed the carnage that followed: "His story was a masterpiece of investigative reporting which found the professions' dirty linen and displayed it through the words of named sources whose credentials lent the account authority. . . . McDowell's article made all the wire services within hours; columnists were commenting within a day. In forty-eight hours, hundreds of millions throughout the world had been exposed to the story and wanted to hear more." Leaving aside Caton's exaggerations, his summary highlighted the immediate effect on American anthropology: "Thus anthropologists awoke one morning to find their territory ravaged and their citadel under siege by a solitary invader leading the natives into rebellion. They were shocked and perplexed. 'Who is Derek Freeman?' was the first question most would ask; 'why did he do it?' was the second."[5]

The speed of the media blitz in the days before the internet and social media caught anthropologists off guard and led to conspiracy theories that Harvard and Freeman were deliberately laying a trap for the profession. Published copies were not promptly available, but radio and television commentators expected instant reactions. Freeman heard one on the radio in Canberra the day of the Edwin McDowell review: anthropologist Theodore Schwartz in San Diego, who had worked with Mead in Papua New Guinea, attacked Freeman—or at least the extreme statements read to Schwartz over the phone by the *New York Times* reviewer, for Schwartz had not seen the book, only a copy of Derek's "Sweet Analytics" paper. He later apologized to Freeman and, while holding to his opinion of Mead's talent and assiduous research, promised to apologize again in writing if Freeman's book warranted it; Schwartz was as good as his word.[6] Another, David Schneider from Chicago, accused Freeman of bias, again without first having read the book. An interviewer from *Newsweek* phoned Freeman and asked, "Is it true that you have been institutionalized for paranoid schizophrenia (as is claimed by some of your professional colleagues)?" This was the first public snagging of the "madness" trip wire, and it would not be the last. Derek was wary in his initial replies for fear of adding to the "already pronounced irrational opposition to my book."[7]

Friends in the United States reported in March that opposition was massing. A later analyst of the controversy, anthropologist Roy Rappaport, argued that as well as being outraged by what they saw as "the professionally orchestrated hype that apparently animated it," American anthropologists believed Freeman's campaign was designed to discredit American anthropology as a social science that enjoyed public influence. Cultural anthropologists, without reading his book, also feared that it would be used as a weapon by sociobiologists. Richard Basham, an American anthropologist teaching in Australia but observing the furor while in America during 1983, wrote that the knives were out against Freeman before the book's publication; anthropologists who were not Samoan specialists were already deflecting the spotlight from Mead onto Freeman as a person.[8]

Capitalizing on the rush of publicity, Harvard flew Freeman to New York, Chicago, and San Francisco for a series of interviews and breakfast talks on radio and television. Phil Donahue, Studs Terkel, Merv Griffin, and Barbara Walters had him on their shows. Walters's *Good Morning America* pitted him against Mead's daughter, Mary Catherine Bateson. Freeman later claimed he asked to meet Bateson beforehand to assure her he was not personally attacking her mother. He had twice written to Bateson in the months before publication, sending her advance notice and asking her to alert him to errors of fact; he received no replies.[9] Walters too was not interested in reconciliation, forcing Freeman into a "lofty line" on camera that soon got out of hand and forced an early end to the interview. He felt "set up."

He encountered Bateson again on *The Phil Donahue Show*, this time in company with Bradd Shore, a Samoan specialist who had praised Freeman's book lavishly as a reader for Princeton University Press but was already backing away, for reasons we shall explore. Derek felt he earned the sympathy of the large audience when he refused to accept Donahue's challenge that nature was now more important than nurture. Bateson thawed once Freeman asserted that Margaret Mead had a secure place in the history of anthropology because she asked the right questions; Shore wanted nothing to do with Freeman and made a hurried escape.[10]

The book tour was a mixed experience. Freeman believed he received sympathetic hearings and goodwill but with individual occasions outweighed by the hostility radiating from anthropologists. At a talk to the Harvard anthropology department, he heard "sneers and sniggers" at his mention of E. O. Wilson, the biologist with controversial theories about the evolution of the human species. Another colleague from Columbia stormed out in a rage, calling Freeman "highly obnoxious" after a radio appearance.[11] In Chicago, questions about Sarawak and controversies in Canberra cast a shadow.

Once Freeman was home in Australia, the rest of 1983 and 1984 seemed an endless series of onslaughts against him and his book when seen through the entries in his diaries. Harvard University Press sent him a packet of reviews by anthropologists in May 1983. One, by Marvin Harris, he considered "wild"; another was an "enraged outburst." Laura Nader in the *Los Angeles Times* virtually argued for the suppression of his book by questioning Harvard's propriety in publishing it. Anthropologist and psychiatrist Robert Levy in *Science* accused Freeman of having "a dark Hobbesian view of human existence." Mead's first husband, Luther Cressman, attacked "Derek Freeman, the hunter," implying his critique was motivated by an ancient male bias against a strongly ambitious, twenty-three-year-old female student laying the groundwork for her career. A Chicago reviewer accused him of "chicanery" and "deception." The "solid obloquy" of an eighteen-thousand-word draft review by the anthropologist Nancy McDowell made Freeman genuinely angry, but shock was his only response when an article defending Mead by anthropologist Paula Brown Glick implied he was buying the support of Samoans by endowing grants at the National University of Samoa.[12]

While Freeman was attempting to handle the disruptive emotion caused by these writings, worse was being done to his person and integrity back in the United States. Scholars sat in judgment, using the flimsiest of familiarity with Freeman's work or none at all. At the University of California, Berkeley, in April 1983, Richard Basham watched as speakers at a faculty seminar denounced Freeman's book to an audience of students without any attempt to explain the substance of what Freeman was claiming: "*Margaret Mead and Samoa* was presented in brief caricature as the work of a biological reactionary soft on racism." The same month at Barnard College in New York City, speakers insisted there was a personal tone of attack in Freeman's criticisms of Mead, questioned his motivation, and even suggested there was a "sex angle" behind it.[13] A friend sent him the *Denver*

Post with a report of a conference at the University of Colorado at Boulder, during which Bradd Shore described Freeman as "superficial" and Lowell Holmes characterized him as a "self-serving Puritan." Catherine Bateson was reported as saying, "This [Freeman] is not a normal man. This is a man who reacts intensely to topics of sex and violence and who changes the conversation to these topics if he has a chance."[14]

The most inflamed event was the November 1983 meeting of the American Anthropological Association (AAA) in Chicago, where a special session on Freeman's critique was organized; Freeman was not invited—to this or any other of these events. Witnesses attested to the emotion-charged atmosphere and the cult-like denunciations of his work. One noted "what seemed like half the anthropologists in the world" cramming into the room to defend Mead's honor.[15] Don Tuzin wrote to Freeman, describing the occasion as "grotesque . . . [a] feeding frenzy . . . a very slimy business." He remembered:

> A woman from the audience announced, in scandalized tones, that the AAA ought to vote a formal resolution criticizing a book club for having recommended Derek's book for "holiday reading." Most of the audience squirmed at this idea, and the idea was dropped—only to be revived during the business meeting (that day or the next), at which the proposal was passed by a hand vote and subsequently acted upon by the AAA's executive director. This comes close to book burning—if physical copies had been present, I have no doubt that the match would have been lit, and that screaming gyrating scholars would have danced around the flames, like characters out of *Lord of the Flies*.[16]

A visiting student from Canberra reported that the emotions were so extreme as to be "scary."[17] Only one anthropologist seemed prepared to defend Freeman from the floor, Pacific specialist Ann Chowning.

Freeman did receive expressions of support from various sides, both academic and nonacademic. *Time* magazine quoted Pacific anthropologist Douglas Oliver as agreeing that Freeman was "an extraordinarily careful scholar," and "among anthropologists, he's the world's greatest authority on Samoa."[18] Another Pacific colleague, Mervyn Meggitt, believed that Derek's book radically threatened the anthropological establishment. Richard Goodman, who had written a dissenting view of Mead's *Coming of Age* in the 1970s and published it as Freeman's book was coming out, shared with Derek his frustrating correspondence with Mead and encouraged him to relax and enjoy the spectacle of people denying what they knew was true; Goodman believed Freeman's view would prevail.[19]

As "the shockwave of publicity" receded and anthropologists finally had Freeman's book in their hands, specialist journals began to devote space to a detailed analysis of his case against Mead and to the alleged implications for contemporary anthropology. Looking back on the controversy from the 1990s, the doyen among the keepers of the discipline's history, George Stocking, felt that it was one of those episodes in the history of anthropology "when the definition and the boundaries of the discipline are profoundly at issue," proceeding via a war of "citing and counter-citing of quoted passages" in a succession of social science journals and later in full-length books.[20]

The themes at issue were varied, with the pressure applied to Freeman's work at several points, and not equally. Anthropologists in general were insistent that while Mead's work as a cultural commentator and as a spokesperson for anthropology was respected and her impact on American education highly valued, the errors in her pioneering work on Samoa had been known for years before Freeman's book. Some were able to quote critical comments on *Coming of Age* soon after its publication by Lowie, Robert Redfield, and Paul Radin, all prominent in American cultural anthropology of the 1920s and 1930s. Some did an accounting exercise among anthropology textbooks, like Stephen Murray, a sociologist working in mental health. He claimed that only eleven of twenty-seven pre-1983 textbooks incorporated Mead's conclusions about Samoan sexuality (though he offered no indication which books were used by whom, and how, at which institutions).[21]

Derek Freeman could always pull a textbook or journal off the shelf to prove the counterpoint. His argument was, and remained, that Mead's "immature" work and the paradigm of cultural determinism that it helped to secure were continually reproduced as conviction and a stimulus to social policy in American society. Moreover, anthropologists did little to advertise their disagreements with Mead; even Murray had written about the "invisibility of scientific scorn."[22]

Freeman's picture of Samoan sexual behavior, laid beside Mead's, was just as stridently contested, for as anthropologist Annette Weiner pointed out, Mead's picture of Samoan sexuality was at the core of her credibility. Weiner accused Freeman of misrepresenting the significance of traditional Samoan marriage and sexuality. She preferred as an interpretation the views of two other Freeman critics, Bradd Shore and Lowell Holmes, whose own credibility as Samoan ethnographers seemed to be the gold standard for American anthropologists looking on. Weiner refused to see any qualifying comments in *Margaret Mead in Samoa* that might suggest Freeman's views on Samoan sexuality were not as absolute as they were made out to be.[23]

One who was prepared to give ground was Theodore Schwartz in his review of the controversy that delivered Freeman Schwartz's apology of sorts. His field experience—with Margaret Mead on Manus Island in Papua New Guinea, among other places—led him to recognize the possibility of "a public morality and an informal realm of moral definition that governs actual behavior." While Freeman maintained that "at least an ideal of virginity at marriage as a source of prestige and honor to the girl's family applied to everyone in Samoa," he also conceded that few girls actually reached marriage as virgins; Mead, on the other hand, argued Schwartz, privileged information from the sexually active girls of her sample. Schwartz was anxious to reconcile the two views of Samoa: "Aside from our inclination to rally around the memory, work and reputation of Mead, the preeminent leader of our field for decades, we must seek a balance that wastes no insight to be gleaned from Freeman's work."[24]

Separate but similar points of attack revolved around Freeman's use of statistics on Samoan crime to demonstrate how incorrect Mead's claim was that "forceful rape" or sexual assault was "completely foreign to the Samoan mind."[25] Paul Shankman, in later years the most prominent defender of Mead's Samoa work, downplayed the validity of Freeman's statistics, drawn from a range of historical periods and contexts. Lowell Holmes implied that Freeman might have made up his statistics, because other critics of Freeman were unable to find the figures in the archives; Holmes's skepticism was because "Samoans are not very careful record keepers."[26]

Insinuations against Freeman extended beyond the statistical. *Margaret Mead and Samoa* was viewed by some female critics as an underhanded attack on feminism. Freeman's attitude to women is a vexed area of interpretation in the ebb and flow of the exchanges. One reviewer argued that Freeman's claims about male Samoan attitudes to rape were an ethnic slur. Closer to the scene in Samoan villages, Penelope Schoeffel (with her Samoan historian husband, Malama Meleisea) wrote an initial review of Freeman that, while critical of Mead's use of data and misreading of some Samoan practices, took Mead's side that clandestine love affairs were not in the least uncommon. Female virginity was an aristocratic value that Freeman was at pains to emphasize as a public value, but it was not the whole story of sexual custom among Samoans. Freeman, said Schoeffel and Meleisea, was guilty of creating "a new myth about virginity in Samoa." Privately, Schoeffel would later expand on this and claim that Freeman's beliefs about masculine dominance as an outcome of evolutionary development drove his attitude to women, even if he strove to overcome it.[27] Marilyn Strathern summed up her reading of how Freeman saw the world thus: "The 'Samoa' he describes is male-dominated, competitive, rank-conscious. His informants were often high-ranking chiefs or educated persons, very frequently men."[28]

Samoan virginity, Samoan aggression, the harsh rearing of children, the stresses of adolescence, the negative elements of Samoan character—all were themes in *Margaret Mead and Samoa* that Freeman's critics disputed across a range of reviews and journals.[29] Even when the ethnographic data favored Freeman's account, his critics alleged that his counterportrait of Samoa was as dark as Mead's was light. Bradd Shore, it is true, was prepared to accept that Freeman's characterization of a more sober and aggressive human nature in Samoans was not necessarily wrong, but he argued that Freeman's and Mead's pictures of Samoans should be linked together to illuminate "the real complexities and textures of human life." Most critics, however, judged Freeman as presenting "an opposite and equally fatuous stereotype of Samoan life," as one reviewer in the journal *Oceania* put it.[30]

Freeman's methodology was also attacked. Reviewers questioned his use of single cases drawn from the archives of American Samoa to argue a general case about Samoan criminality. They doubted his approach of ranging across historical data from the nineteenth century to the 1960s. Much play was made of his argument that the whole of the Samoan archipelago enjoyed exactly the same cultural lineaments from west to east and that the little piece of Samoa that Margaret Mead studied in 1926 was the same as Western Samoa culture that Freeman knew from the 1940s and the 1960s. They accused Freeman of being highly selective in his use of quotations from the literature, using only those that bolstered his own positions or quoting them out of context (though Marilyn Strathern readily conceded that Margaret Mead was "no keeper of contexts either").[31]

The most widespread pushback by American anthropologists involved Freeman's interpretation of the role Franz Boas played in laying the foundations of an extreme cultural determinism. Freeman argued that the Boas legacy was clear: cultural anthropologists believed that human behavior could only be explained in terms of cultural variables, with biology explicitly excluded. Boas was the real target, not Mead, admitted Freeman at the end of his life: "He's the false prophet. He led the poor children of America into the wilderness, you see, with this false doctrine and he became very powerful. He was the alpha male."[32] As far as American anthropologists were concerned, this was an unacceptably sectarian view of the "father" of American anthropology.

Annette Weiner spoke for many when she accused Freeman of misrepresenting Boas's involvement with biology and distorting the intent of his writings. Boas neither rejected biology out of hand nor excluded it from culture, nor had American anthropology since.[33] Lowell Holmes proclaimed himself "astonished" by Freeman's attacks on Boas, as though Freeman were damning both the earth father of American anthropology and its mother. Theodore Schwartz, prepared as he was to concede much of Freeman's argument about Margaret Mead, saw little value in Freeman's chapters on cultural and biological determinism.[34]

Freeman was wrong about Boas, who had set the foundations for the four fields approach in American anthropology, encompassing physical anthropology, archaeology, and linguistics alongside cultural anthropology. Boas did not view culture fanatically as all-determining but left room for the individual to have an influence on the evolution of cultural forms. In this he was closer to Darwin's complex evolutionary arguments than Freeman realized or was prepared to accept, an irony, given the development of his own thought on evolution and human choice (see chapter 12).[35]

It is doubtful whether concessions by Freeman on this aspect of his argument would have softened the attacks on his ideas. An entire oeuvre of condemnation and censure developed around him. Its language was visceral and much more personal than Freeman's direct descriptions of the ideas he was assailing in Mead and her mentors. *Margaret Mead and Samoa* was "badly written and deeply destructive," according to Annette Weiner; a "bad book," a "dull book," wrote David Schneider. George Marcus declared of "Mr. Freeman's" book, "with its shadowy biological motif," "This is a work of great mischief," as though it disobeyed some commandment of what a book should be. "Turgid, humorless, grudging, uncharitable and sometimes lacking in judgment" was how Adam Kuper, a British historian of anthropology, described it. Marvin Harris resorted to snickering about "a gene for finger-raping" as he dismissed Freeman's arguments about biological inputs to cultural variation. Lowell Holmes laid out a carpet of critical comments by fellow anthropologists—Marcus, Colin Turnbull, Nader, Glick, Harris, and Schneider—in his own dismissal of Freeman and his alleged "lack of professional ethics." Most condescending were

Martin Silverman's ridiculing remarks in *American Anthropologist*, attempting to laugh Freeman out of court with a contemptuous satire on "Daring Derek" and his series of melodramatic plots. Even critics less inclined to carp and seeking some balance, like Bradd Shore, worried about the "dark quality, the intensity and the passion" behind Freeman's book.[36]

False assertions and misrepresentations riddled many of the criticisms made of Freeman: they accused him of engaging in a personal attack on Mead in a vendetta reaching back forty years and of deliberately waiting till she died before firing his bullets. His campaign, abetted by Harvard University Press, was all about self-promotion. He was a closet biological determinist, friend and ally of eugenicists, sociobiologists, and racists. Why had he not written a full alternative ethnography, if he knew so much? Some were ad hominem attacks and pseudoarguments, as one reader of these reviews, a psychiatrist, recognized. "*I* am engaged in critical analysis, *you* are assuming a particular perspective, *he* is ideological" was her caustic summing up of the approach by some of Freeman's opponents.[37] During the most extreme phase of the criticism, Lowell Holmes produced what Hiram Caton, who began collecting the documents of the controversy during the 1980s, called a "visceral statement of what was perceived to be at stake in the cultural politics of the controversy." Holmes told a newspaper reporter that Freeman's book could inspire "dangerous ideas," and the sinister specter of "Nazi racial theories" was invoked; cultural anthropologists like Mead and Holmes were democrats, the implication being that Freeman wasn't. Mead had told Holmes not to worry about Freeman's revelations, because "everyone knows Derek Freeman's crazy."[38]

This language was designed to personally belittle Freeman and to distort what he was saying. It does not fit with a fair-minded assessment of the language of *Margaret Mead and Samoa*. Freeman was direct, sometimes forceful in his criticisms of ideas and motives, but he was not abusive, as some of his critics alleged. Anthropologists at a distance, with a less partisan stake, were able to see a very different work. Margaret Strathern, the British anthropologist and no friend of Freeman's, pronounced it a "cool and polite book" while taking it apart. Two educators from Australia with anthropology backgrounds, while critical of much in the book, believed one of its triumphs was "the way that Freeman's vigorous, clear style has made ethnographic analysis of considerable detail and complexity available to nonspecialists." Another reviewer, the English philosopher Anthony Flew, remarked on its "irenic mildness." Bradd Shore, in evaluating the book for

Princeton University Press, commented that it was "masterfully written" and "stunningly accurate."[39]

For his part, when Freeman had a chance to respond to the "personal obloquy" that accompanied the reviews, a splenetic tone that was confrontational and dismissive, like that of his opponents, overshadowed his replies. This deterioration in his language of address between his book and his later essays provoked more animosity, which only ensured that the tone of exchanges would remain acerbic. In the two lengthiest responses Freeman made to the array of critical reviews, in the journals *Canberra Anthropology* and *Pacific Studies*, Freeman by and large made a meticulous, detailed defense of his arguments. He denied he was attacking Mead personally and pointed to his complimentary judgments; he repudiated the general statements others attributed to him, especially around the sexual behavior of Samoans and his alleged pessimism about Samoan society; and he vigorously defended his statistical surveys and historical research, admitting to some possibility of error but asserting the pertinence of his figures "as an approximate indication of the likely parameters." Most importantly, he defended the final pages on the interaction of biology and culture as the harbinger of things to come for anthropology, though he made no attempt to elaborate on what exactly that interaction meant and how it differed from what his opponents claimed it meant.[40]

In the jousting that went on with embittered opponents, Freeman also let himself slip into his own form of personal obloquy against detractors. Paul Shankman he dismissed for his "pettifogging strictures" about how Freeman should have gone about publishing his findings; Shankman's kind of thinking was "a disgrace to the profession of anthropology." Nancy McDowell, author of a largely contemptuous, personalized, forty-page review, was "unprincipled" and guilty of "unmitigated pedantry" about Freeman's scholarship. Worse, she displayed the "fervor of a fundamentalist" in her shoddy arguments and had the "effrontery" to charge Freeman with going to extremes in his arguments about rape. The young researchers just starting out on their careers, Penelope Schoeffel and the historian Malama Meleisea, were put down mercilessly for their review in *Canberra Anthropology*: "Bizarrely erroneous," "so shoddily inexact as to be ludicrous," and "pretentiously ideological" were some of the expressions Freeman deployed against them. Even Margaret Mead herself, treated respectfully if trenchantly in his book, was now accused of "a flagrantly unscientific maneuver" in dealing with her sample of delinquent girls.[41]

There is no doubting Freeman was unnerved by the force of reaction to *Margaret Mead and Samoa* and upset during much of 1983. One early morning in April he awoke "profusely sweating," convinced it was an unconscious response to the hostile reviews and linked to his fears of inadequacy and rejection. Derek felt that he was the victim of an intellectual mugging campaign, and, using his diary as a diagnostic tool, he worked hard on himself "not to let myself be 'punished'" by these reactions or "to go gently into the dark." His diary bristles with quotes about courage by Thomas Aquinas, Seneca, and Shakespeare and with his resolutions to fight back: "I must, it is clear, continue to offer deliberate and outright defiance to the devotees of cultural determinism who have shown hostility towards my book . . . *while adhering to the highest standards of scholarship and science*, for their intention is to, by their *ad hominem* & other ill-informed strictures, to generate such anxiety in me as to bring about an inner collapse sufficient to silence me and also to create an image of me as a monster."[42] Freeman was practicing the same determination he displayed after the Sarawak incident of 1961: he refused to let others define him by their criticisms; instead, he would assert his own identity and mission among anthropologists. In his heightened sense of persecution, Freeman saw himself as a Galileo or a Johannes Kepler, fighting to bring the sanity of a rational science to his obscurantist enemies. This suggests his continued need to affirm his ego and his unwillingness to accept criticism, both of which had plagued him for much of his career. At the same time, the language of some of his opponents and the continuing bombardment of negative reviews help explain his reaching for weapons to protect his mental defenses; he was in an exhausted state by the end of 1983, with numbness down his right side. He noted in his diary the remark of his Australian colleague working in America, Mervyn Meggitt, that Derek was regarded as the antipodean Antichrist who had killed the American earth goddess. In addition, he had to endure hostile reviews from anthropologists in Australia in those first couple of years. At a packed seminar at Sydney University in May 1984, he squirmed when the chairman, as introduction, read out in full the AAA resolution of November 1983 criticizing the book club for having selected Freeman's book. He was then attacked relentlessly by one of his former students.[43]

Uncompromising attack thus became Freeman's method of defense. His modus operandi was similar to that fashioned in disputes with colleagues during the 1960s. He would bombard his circle of opponents with letters demanding explanation or retraction and with questions regarding their specific knowledge of Samoa or its language, each time repeating a mantra: Mead reached her "preposterous conclusion" that biological variables played no part in the processes of adolescence. (He was using "preposterous," he noted punctiliously, in the dictionary sense of "contrary to nature, reason or common sense.")[44] Her conclusions were "extreme," an example of "absolute cultural determinism." He would retail again the story of Boas's complicity. Rarely did he go beyond the points he had made in *Margaret Mead and Samoa*; much of his response was devoted to exposing the seemingly willful misrepresentation of his views and issuing blunt challenges. All this would be conveyed in Freeman's characteristic calligraphic handwriting, yet with a fastidious attention to the formalities of address; supportive colleagues received copies.

In 1986 the anthropologist Roy Rappaport wrote a long essay in the journal *American Scholar* on Freeman's refutation of Mead. Much of it meandered through Rappaport's own scholarly work, showing Mead's mythic status within American culture. But it was also what one lay reader called a "lengthy grinding of Derek Freeman into the anthropological turf." Although recognizing that the appearance of Freeman's book was "a cultural event of genuine importance," Rappaport by subtle degrees managed to associate Freeman with the illiberal agenda of eugenicists and racists while expecting him—a frequent demand by critics—to have written a proper ethnographic study of Samoa to counter Mead.[45] In reply Freeman accused Rappaport of "intellectual deviousness" and "anthropological mystification," forcing a partial apology from him. Rappaport eventually threw his hands in the air at the "tiresome controversy over contexts."[46] The exchanges epitomized the talking-past-one-another that often took place as each purported to expose the self-delusion of the other.

Another exchange occurred with the fierce critic Stephen Murray, who carried on a correspondence with Freeman into the 1990s over Freeman's seemingly endless refusals to concede to criticisms of *Margaret Mead and Samoa*. At first Derek replied with patient and detailed arguments, thanking Murray for his engagement. But the back-and-forth tired Freeman, which was unusual and a sign of creeping old age. A series of muscle-bound exchanges characterized their correspondence. Murray wrote in frustration about Freeman's unwillingness to accept correction: "If cognitive dissonance existed, you should be in pain." At one point in 1991 Freeman referred to Murray's "bumbling, purblind scholarship." Even when Murray admitted he was more and more drawn to Freeman's critique of Mead's methods, Derek's reply conveyed a "told-you-so" tone.[47]

Freeman was also not beyond stray threats of legal action or suggestions that a career might be damaged if he chose to take matters further. When New York anthropologist Eleanor Leacock gave a public lecture in Fiji in 1985 that was highly critical of Freeman's book, Freeman's response, refuting her claims, pointedly mentioned sending copies of his letter to the vice chancellor of the University of the South Pacific in Fiji.[48] Such threats did not always work. Jeanette Mageo, a student of the cultural studies critic James Clifford, had taught in American Samoa and was married to a Samoan, and she wrote an article exploring the issue of Samoan aggression as treated by Mead and Freeman. She claimed that Freeman confused cultural and ethological arguments about aggression and, citing Nancy McDowell's critique, that his manner of writing had given "ample excuse" to anthropologists to see him as the "bad guy." Incensed at yet another willful misreading of him, Freeman accused Mageo of "polemical and political aims," of "intellectual defamation," of being "misinformed," "puerile," and "unscholarly in the extreme." He sent a copy of his letter to her departmental chair at the University of Hawai'i and threatened to refer her to the ethics committee of AAA. Mageo refused to be bullied and signaled she would herself send their correspondence to the committee. In a lengthy, Freemanesque reply to all his points (though ignoring the aspersions she had cast on him through McDowell's work), Mageo showed sympathy for his plight and for some of his views, but she challenged Freeman to move beyond rebuttal.[49]

His two most frequently targeted critics were Lowell Holmes and Bradd Shore. Holmes bore the brunt of Freeman's ire because he was the only anthropologist who had done a restudy of Samoa in the very place where Mead had resided and who had made Samoa his life's work, so his endorsement of Mead's overall reliability helped make *Coming of Age* a classic entrenched in anthropology. In *Margaret Mead and Samoa* Freeman criticized Holmes for missing a golden opportunity to retest Mead's conclusions. Holmes had picked out contradictions between *Coming of Age* and his own findings, yet he went on to claim a very high reliability for Mead's results. He was thus in Freeman's eyes no innocent bystander.

Holmes became Freeman's most tenacious critic in the war of words of the 1980s. His reviews of *Margaret Mead and Samoa* savaged Freeman's motives, his methods, his scholarship, and his integrity. He wrote his own book-length counterattack in 1987, *Quest for the Real Samoa*, which was a sustained argument against Freeman's depiction of Franz Boas and a staunch though not unqualified defense of Mead's findings. A mixed bag of a book,

Quest was part ethnography, part literature review, part denunciation of Freeman by both Holmes and Eleanor Leacock; a quarter of it came from Holmes's 1954 study. Holmes scored some points against Freeman over the latter's use of historical data to convey the impression of one stable period in Samoa, and Holmes pointed out the arguable basis of some of Freeman's statistics. Holmes also agreed with others that Freeman weakened his refutation by including his interactionist coda.[50] But Holmes's personal animosity leaked into his language and led him to assertions about Freeman's motives and methods that were not substantiated and carried an air of prejudice. At one point, Holmes insinuated that Freeman's New Zealandness, with an implied edge to it of puritanism, colonial rigidity, even racism, helped explain his interpretation of Samoans against those of more easygoing American scholars.[51] Littering the pages were the usual red herrings about a vendetta against Mead and Freeman's waiting to act until after she was dead.

Freeman and Holmes had corresponded since the 1960s. Although Holmes claimed Freeman was the initiator, Holmes had first contacted Freeman in 1960 to gain some advice from an experienced fieldworker. Freeman then began a serious bout of writing to Holmes from Samoa during his 1966–67 study leave. He shared his thinking on his own observations of chiefly behavior compared to those in Holmes's reports and tried valiantly to draw the American into a professional engagement, even sending him information about evidence of Mead's sexual affairs while in Samoa. When Holmes finally replied to Freeman's insistent letters, Holmes claimed he differed with Mead mainly on matters of interpretation, not "fact," but he admitted that Mead "finds pretty much what she wants to find" and that he was "forced by my faculty advisor to soften my criticism." This was a red rag to a fool for truth, and their correspondence took an increasingly negative turn. Holmes had already decided in 1967 that Freeman was out to discredit him, Mead, Boas, and all of American anthropology. Holmes wrote Mead that Freeman seemed more interested in gossip than ethnography, though the letter Freeman wrote Holmes about Mead's affairs reads like the gifting of confidential information to a fellow professional and was deliberately not used in *Margaret Mead and Samoa*.[52] Freeman laid bare their correspondence in his *Pacific Studies* response to critical reviews, exposing the hollowness of Holmes's argument that his mass of data contradicting Mead did not require him to find her unreliable; Schwartz had also commented on this in 1983. Holmes's attacks on Freeman looked more like a defense of Holmes's own contradictoriness; other commentators thought the same.[53]

Lowell Holmes became a fresh whipping boy through the 1980s, Freeman taunting him with an increasing air of triumphalism. When Freeman visited Kansas in 1987 with a film crew to interview Holmes, Freeman let his domineering side take over, staring Holmes down, giving him "the Manjusi treatment; reducing him to quivering hulk, then embracing him." Freeman spoke to Holmes's university class the next day, trumpeting it as "a complete triumph in ethological terms. . . . Holmes has become submissive to me, sitting abjectly in [a] corner while I take over his class & shrinking from facing me & looking me in the eye."[54] Two years later, Freeman sent Holmes a selection of comments on his performance in the film, remarking, "Have my sympathy. Samoan controversy not gone well with you."[55] Freeman would still send Holmes a card for his sixty-third birthday a few months later, wishing him the best, though Freeman's own animus toward the anthropologist had not cooled.

Bradd Shore did not display the kind of unyielding certainty that Holmes and Freeman's other critics brought to the controversy or that Freeman himself displayed. Shore could see there were two sides to every position. For Freeman — "truth's fool" — this was Shore's besetting sin, and Freeman accused Shore of a disabling dualism in his review of *Margaret Mead and Samoa*. Shore had praised the book to Princeton University Press, yet as soon as it was published he began stepping away from his earlier position. He could agree that Mead presented an oversimplified picture of Samoan society yet argue that her version was also insightful. Freeman's work, on the other hand, had "the makings of a fine book," but his motives were suspect. Freeman's characterizations of Samoan personality were basically correct, but he gave Mead too little credit for her portrayal. With regard to sexual behavior, Shore agreed that *moetotolo* was a form of rape, but he was prepared to paraphrase what Mead meant in gentler terms than he accorded Freeman's message. Shore also complained about Freeman's "radical de-contextualization of Samoan behavior" but at the same time ignored Mead's. In all these elements of the Samoa question, Shore was making a plea for a more complex cultural image than either Mead or Freeman had presented to the world. "Contradiction is the stuff of life," he wrote, and his portrait of Samoan life stressed structural dualities and layered realities that both culture and biology produced in Samoa.[56]

Freeman would have none of this, accusing Shore of being an "arch inductivist" who went to Samoa with a ready-made theory about culture as a symbolic system and found what he set out to find.[57] Freeman was referring to Shore's 1982 book, *Sala'ilua: A Samoan Mystery*, his major ethnography, in which he applied a symbolic analysis to the account of the murder of a high-ranking talking chief in Salaʻilua village on Savaiʻi. Shore argued for a multifaceted sense of the Samoan self, depending on the context of relationships. In his retort from Canberra, Freeman criticized Shore for his basic ethnographic failure to contact and interview his main subject— the killer of the chief. With his empiricist spirit in a world he saw as presenting basic moral choices, Freeman regarded symbolic analysis as the refuge of a soft anthropology that betrayed the discipline's aspirations. He himself had sought out the murderer on parole and discovered a more prosaic ethnographic explanation: the Samoan "would, in all likelihood, have been so inebriated [at the time of the murder] as to have lost cortical control of his actions."[58]

Freeman had no time for Shore's playing with "a fundamental cultural template for ordering contexts." He argued that Shore got completely back to front the Samoan concepts of *aga* (nature) and *amio* (culture), extravagantly denouncing it as the greatest ethnographic blunder in the entire literature on Samoa.[59] He also pilloried Shore for being an "intellectual chameleon," an "anthropological Vicar of Bray" who altered his opinions to stay in with the crowd and was guilty of "breathtaking illogicality" in his judgments of Freeman's book.[60]

Shore tried hard to find the middle ground in his criticisms, though they invariably ended up more critical of Freeman than not: "Freeman knows as much about Samoa as any non-Samoan in the world and he has had a 40 year vendetta against Margaret Mead. He is a brilliant man, but one wonders about the dark quality, the intensity and the passion behind the book."[61] Shore's attempts at compromise did not stop Freeman from resorting to disdainful language and the tarnishing of Shore's work in letters to Freeman's Samoan colleagues. Their relationship retained a bitter edge through the 1990s.

In 1988 Shore wrote a letter that poignantly expressed the anger and sadness that underlay much of American anthropology's relationship with Freeman. Shore was exhausted by Freeman's continual demands for answers to his letters probing Shore's arguments. He was convinced in the end that Freeman operated "on intellectual principles and motivations quite alien to me." Critical of what he called Freeman's "rigid, doctrinaire, unsubtle and intellectually flaccid" approach to Mead and Samoa, Shore accused him of arguing by elision, decontextualizing others' statements, ignoring uncongenial evidence, and repeating the same hackneyed phrases again and again. "While claiming the high ground of science, you have never, so far as I know, betrayed any scientific humility or self-doubt about any of your pronouncements, even in the face of some very cogent criticism."[62]

Shore was not above snide asides that Freeman's campaign was all about self-promotion and media grandstanding. His anger showed when he criticized Freeman's attempts to keep the "ludicrous debate" over Samoan chastity alive and when Freeman sent Shore news snippets of empirical data to reinforce the complex theoretical arguments that were in play. Such "trash" was naïve at best and made Shore chuckle, though Derek, with a "not so" scribble on the letter, could see that Shore's anger was still there.[63]

But Shore was more sad that Freeman persisted in seeing Shore's position as "fuzzy or weak and unmanly," as though only Freeman's strongly masculinist interpretations told the truth about Samoa. Shore believed that "my basic commitment is to a view of human nature that stresses contradiction at the heart of human experience." His interest was in the dialectical, encompassing contradictions to find the subtle whole. Why Freeman should continue to caricature Shore's arguments and mischaracterize him puzzled Shore. "I really do wish you well," he ended. "In some way, I have always quite liked you and have always felt sad that a friendship and profitable intellectual bond appeared so far from possible."[64]

Freeman's answer to this letter exemplifies all that made the ranks of his enemies gnash their teeth. Completely disregarding what Shore was saying about the overall effect of Freeman's handling of criticism, Freeman simply requested Shore to be more specific about the arguments Freeman was supposed to be ignoring and referred him to the recent Festschrift that had come out in his honor.[65] It was an insistence on the wild purity of his scientific method.

Robert Levy has argued that the anthropology profession was upset with Freeman for "miscellaneous reasons," but their counterattacks were due mainly "because he hit us squarely on our passionately held and blinding paradigm—'culture' as the exhaustive explanation of human behavior, denying a deeper and truer and incorrigible biological human nature."[66] Margaret Mead was at the heart of that paradigm. She was a totemic figure in American twentieth-century social history, and she held a mirror to American society, furnishing from her own studies and commentary "a repertoire of human possibilities" with which Americans might modify and improve their own culture. As one of Freeman's American supporters wrote, "Clad in a red cape and carrying a forked stick, she became the interpreter, healer and prophet that she had once been for South Seas native cultures. She spoke to us about us as she had spoken to us about them."[67]

Derek Freeman was guilty of desecrating this mythic figure, claimed Roy Rappaport. Others saw him attacking the integrity of cultural anthropology and, by extension, that of American anthropology in general.

According to another of Freeman's supporters, anthropologist Tim O'Meara, his opponents came from all corners of the American anthropology scene: "feminists defending Mead at all costs, xenophobiacs defending America, mediocre anthropologists . . . banding together to defend themselves against rising standards of fieldwork and analysis, misguided anthropologists defending anthropology's public image, antiscientists and obscurantists who don't want to be awakened from their dreams, antisociobiologists and anti-racists who are (understandably) nervous about reopening the door to biology, and apologists of all kinds who don't want to admit that they or their mentors were so obviously wrong for so long."[68] All of this suggests that 1983 was a moment of interior disciplinary significance for many American anthropologists. Freeman's refutation of Mead came after a decade of crisis for anthropology over its identity and methods, and it paralleled a resurgence of biological determinism in the sciences. Since the 1960s the humanistic disciplines had struggled in conflicts over their identity and methodologies. The seemingly permanent values of modern civilization were, among intellectuals, melting into thin air in the tumult of self-referential, politicized critiques of reality by philosophers, linguists, and social scientists; anthropology as a discipline was particularly susceptible to, and ripe for, reappraisal of the solidity of its ethnographic findings.

Like all intellectual and emotional communities, anthropology organized its discourse through leaders and institutions, enabling what could be said and patrolling what should not. Loyalties ran deep.[69] Although Mead was already on the periphery of the discipline's scholarship, with many anthropologists averring that they had disagreed with her findings for decades, her reputation had still to be defended as the most visible sign of American anthropology. Freeman was probing the reliability of the ethnographer's magic and seemed to be wantonly undermining the place of cultural "maximalism" as an essential feature of the social sciences. He was therefore a disruptive and disreputable force. Samoa, once an emblem of the brave new world of cultural contentment and sexual liberation, had become, in the words of Hiram Caton looking back on the Mead–Freeman disputes, "the hair shirt of disillusion."[70]

The fragility of liberal cultural politics in the Reagan years of the 1980s and a whiff of American exceptionalism heightened the outrage against Freeman. He was, after all, a product of British social anthropology, heir to the culture and practice of Malinowski, Radcliffe-Brown, Firth, and Fortes and their emphasis on social organization rather than culture. Levy made an offhanded comment about Freeman's "study of our culture, viewed from Canberra and the Antipodes," which was perhaps not as barbed as Lowell Holmes's crude suggestion of a particular New Zealand worldview that drove Freeman. But even George Stocking ventured to suggest that Freeman was motivated by jealousy of Mead's reputation over Samoa, reinforced by identifying with another New Zealander critical of Mead, her second husband, Reo Fortune.[71]

Many antipodean anthropologists in fact shared American feelings about Freeman, though he had his defenders. The Europeans were more generally bemused, recognizing a peculiar Atlantic righteousness in the attachment to Mead and the way Freeman was treated. Edmund Leach in Cambridge, friendly to Freeman but no friend of his ideas, proclaimed that Mead's social science was "faintly ridiculous" among European intelligentsia, while Freeman's book, though narrow and polemical, was a genuine contribution to the history of twentieth-century anthropology. Thomas Bargatzky of Germany marveled at the political conformity of some anthropologists who argued that Freeman's book should never have been published, as though criticizing Mead was un-American.[72]

What of the Samoans themselves, around whose culture and emotional behaviors this controversy swirled? The smorgasbord of judgments by Samoan commentators left the debate poised in terms not dissimilar to those reached by the books, articles, and reviews that appeared in the mid-1980s. Younger Samoans were distressed by Mead's disfigurement of their culture, reported Hiram Caton. Derek Freeman had turned them into "a race of sex starved rapists," according to Lelei Lelaulu, a correspondent to *Pacific Islands Monthly*. Lowell Holmes's *Quest for the Real Samoa* provides a fair rendition of the opposing choruses: Napoleone A. Tuiteleapaga, an associate of Mead, said she was "100% right"; Le Tagaloa Leota Pita Ala'ilima, member of Parliament and friend of Freeman, stated, "Freeman makes us human, Margaret Mead makes us unreal"; Fetaui Mata'afa, wife of Western Samoa's prime minister, believed neither was right.[73] In New Zealand, journalist Michael Field felt that Freeman's book was being used by local tabloid newspapers to demonize the sizeable Samoan population in Auckland. Field, author of a respected study of the Mau movement in Western Samoa and married to a Samoan, had his own reservations about both Mead's and Freeman's portraits.[74] The Samoans he knew personally could not be summed up in one book—or in two.

Samoans were saved from one myth only to be subjugated by another, Robert Levy claimed. There were always those who said Derek Freeman wasted the moment in which he could have written a proper counterethnography that would give rounded flesh to a portrait of the Samoan people. Freeman's answer was that if he had set out to write a general study on Samoa, Mead's errors would have gone untreated, and "the ideational fabric of cultural anthropology" would have persisted for another generation.[75] He had to start with his refutation, and he chose his battleground carefully, though not as early as he claimed. In the preface to *Margaret Mead and Samoa*, he told the world that he knew he would have to refute Mead as early as 1943, his magisterial Iban work just a diversion. This statement may have led to the belief that he was fulfilling a "vendetta" against Mead. Yet in his long answer to critics in *Canberra Anthropology*, Freeman retreated from that claim, presenting a tale in which the veil was lifted gradually from his eyes. The history of his life and work to that point shows this is a truer version.

Margaret Mead and Samoa works as a refutation that also contains elements of an ethnographic account. It was not the world-shattering manifesto Freeman was wont to claim it was, but it balanced out Mead's more idyllic picture of the South Seas. Viewed as an exercise in scholarly argument free of the noise from the battles of emotion and vilification, the book's contents were neither dangerously heretical nor demeaning to Margaret Mead. They were merely subversive of what even anthropologists agreed had become a mythoideological text in American social science since the 1930s.

On the other hand, the "interactionist" end to the book was a distraction whose relevance was lost in misguided accusations that Freeman was trying to remodel the social sciences into the biological sciences. The book's concluding chapter was no help to Freeman's refutation of Mead. At the end of his life, Freeman was still convinced he had done the right thing in bringing the book forward, but he agreed with Don Tuzin that the clumsily titled last chapter, "Toward a More Scientific Anthropological Paradigm," should have been called "Beyond Determinism." Despite these and other individual points on which he may be criticized, the cumulative effect of Freeman's refutation-portrait was, as Theodore Schwartz concluded, "ineradicable," and Samoa would never be the same again for social science or in public understanding.[76]

The aftermath might have been engineered differently. Freeman expected that critical attention would lead to progress toward the new interactionist paradigm, a generation of bridge building, perhaps, ending in a new heaven and a new earth. He was dismayed and upset by the initial reactions, which cannot be laid at his door. Should he have refused to come to the United States in 1983 to promote his book or meekly and passively tried to dodge the bullets being fired at him by serried ranks of anthropologists? It was not in his temperamental nature to avoid conflict, nor would it have been characteristic of him to make desperate attempts to avoid subjugation. He could have been more generous, both to Mead and to his critics. After all, the first evaluations of his manuscript ten years before had warned him that the North American establishment would react badly. But his opponents too could have found more generosity and self-insight. Their many-sided attacks on multiple flanks were an extraordinary dissipation of professional energy.

What Freeman hated most was the impugning of his integrity as a scientist devoted to rooting out error in the search for "truth." He saw himself as a "truthmonger." Every assault on his truth-seeking mission had to be turned back, every position defended, the enemy routed altogether from the field. As his closest but hard-eyed supporter Don Tuzin summed up, "For Derek, this was the way to resolve the issue, to ferret out ill-informed or corrupt opinions, to get at the truth, and to do justice to an issue that he was convinced had historic proportions. . . . [His opponents] lacked the High Sense of Purpose that drove Derek, and therefore it was easy for them to dismiss Derek as being either messianic or crazy."[77]

At various points during the 1980s Freeman thought the Great Debate was over, his opponents vanquished, and he could move on. With various rejoinders to critics coming out in *American Anthropologist* in 1985 and 1986, Freeman told his closest supporters in Samoa, "I would regard the whole controversy as having been decisively settled in my favor."[78] These were benign years in his personal life. His eldest daughter, Jennifer, finished her master's degree in psychology in the United States and brought her future husband home to meet the family. Derek felt contentment with his and Monica's peaceful house and bird-filled garden. His diary is punctuated with comments on art, gardening, excursions to the coast south of Canberra, and his wide reading, along with his new interest in Buddhism.[79]

In 1984 he received a "marvelous" letter from Hiram Caton, a professor of politics and history at Griffith University in Queensland who wrote an article defending Freeman in the conservative Australian magazine *Quadrant*. Caton was an American, a graduate of Chicago and Yale in Arabic civilizations and philosophy, and he had a keen interest in Freeman's project to unite the social and biological sciences; he had also written on cultural politics and political psychology. The Samoa debate, with its questions about how to evaluate knowledge and its emotional rhetoric, intrigued him. He and Freeman met and began a correspondence. By June 1985 Caton had become one of Freeman's champions on the sidelines, preparing draft articles and crossing swords with critics. It led to his collecting as much of the written substance of the debate as he could, even traveling to the United States to meet and interview some of the protagonists. His proposed book, *The Samoa Reader*, seemed like another sign to Freeman that the debate was closing down. Monica certainly wanted him to get off the Mead thing and onto the big book on the new anthropology, even though Derek, now in his seventies, was well into retirement.

But the Buddhist statue prominently displayed in their quiet house kept proclaiming to Freeman the purity of truth. His critics kept up the barrage of articles attacking this or that aspect of his refutation, and he found it difficult to ignore them. He learned that Lowell Holmes was bringing out his own book to challenge him. This set the juices flowing again: he would write a book about the whole "irrational reaction" of American anthropology and this time compose a more positive picture of Samoan society.[80]

As if to validate his decision, Australian filmmaker Frank Heimans approached Freeman in the middle of 1986 with a proposition to make a film about the Mead controversy. They journeyed to the Samoan islands in November 1987 to interview witnesses. There, in Fituita on American Samoa, the eighty-six-year-old Fa'apua'a Fa'amu Tagia testified that she and other girls who had been constant companions of Margaret Mead in the 1920s jokingly told her exaggerated stories about free love under the palms, never supposing she would write them down or believe them. It was another epiphany in Freeman's life, a moment that, in the past, would have acted as a moment of liberation and change. But instead of enjoying peace in his time and sitting down to model the new anthropology, Freeman resumed his war footing and set out on another decade of fevered hunting and writing.

11

Hunting Heretics

Frank Heimans's film *Margaret Mead and Samoa* premiered on Australia's public television channel in September 1988. Although its title was the same as Freeman's book, the film was not a simple visual replay of his arguments but showed the views of both supporters and opponents in "the greatest controversy in the history of anthropology." The film presented Freeman as a sober, articulate, well-spoken authority, confident without being overly confident. He sat in his Canberra garden, leaning on a table that held one of Monica's small sculptures of reclining figures—they might have been Samoan girls. Margaret Mead was depicted as a plain, bright student needing to belong to her "family" of Franz Boas and Ruth Benedict, her picture of idealized sex in a lax, primitive Samoan culture clearly elaborated for viewers alongside her image as the most publicly celebrated scientist in America.

Among commentators, Mead's daughter, Mary Catherine Bateson, took the lead, setting a picture of an unpredictable Freeman who her mother worried would damage anthropology and the people of Samoa. According to another early critic, Laura Nader, Freeman wanted to ruin Mead's reputation and fundamentally attack anthropology. Lowell Holmes struggled to answer a question about the contradictions in his arguments and ended up agreeing that Mead possessed a romantic view of the islands, distorting the facts and using an artist's license in writing for a popular audience. Those who spoke positively about Freeman, like Robin Fox, made it clear that American anthropologists were discomfited by this antipodean who they believed would curl up and crawl away in the face of dismissive reviews of his book. But "Derek doesn't just go away."

The interview with Faʻamu (Faʻapuaʻa was her nickname after she became a *taupou*) occupied mere seconds, but she would occupy much of Freeman's attention and energy for the last decade of his life. He had not known she was still alive when he and Heimans arrived in Samoa. Faʻamu, born in 1901, had been living in Hawaiʻi since the 1960s but in the 1920s had lived in Siʻufaga in American Samoa, not far from Margaret Mead. She had become a close friend and confidante to Mead—her closest, Faʻamu claimed. With another friend, Fofoa, Faʻamu accompanied Mead on a *malaga* (a ceremonial visit to a neighboring village, district, or island) to the small islands of Ofu and Olosega in March 1926, where the two women acted as Mead's "talking chiefs" in exchanges with local Samoans. It was on this trip, Faʻamu claimed, that they answered Mead's importunate questions about a topic Samoans never discussed openly—sexual behavior—with a series of joking references to nightly trysts with boys. Only on her return from Hawaiʻi after twenty years did Faʻamu realize the import of what they had done, as Samoans were disputing Mead's claims in the wake of Freeman's book.

None of this is evident in the Heimans film. It ends suggesting Freeman was the victor in his quest, though the film pointedly depicts him as an eccentric presence as he climbs into his odd-looking little truck, funny hat on his head, and trundles off to walk in the mountain bush. Freeman had great expectations for the film even before it was released—"epoch making" and better than his book, he advised Samoan friends.[1] Faʻamu's revelation satisfied him that the Mead controversy was at an end. Her story became the touchstone of every piece on Samoa he wrote from that moment to his death more than a decade later.

As the film garnered awards and showed across Europe and the United States, Freeman began the task of setting out this new revelation in authoritative articles, first in *American Anthropologist* in 1989. In a "brief communication," he reported this "crucially *new* evidence on Margaret Mead's Samoan researches of 1926." Resting his thesis on the use by Samoans of a form of "recreational lying," Freeman now advanced beyond his noncommittal comments in his 1983 book about Mead's duping by Samoans to give full credence to Faʻamu's story.[2] Faʻamu had been interviewed in 1987 by the secretary of Samoan affairs (later lieutenant governor), Galeaʻi Poumele, with Freeman as bystander. Freeman now arranged for a Samoan student writing his PhD under Freeman's guidance, Leulu Felise Vaʻa, to interview Faʻamu again, using a long list of directed questions and getting Faʻamu to swear on a Bible that everything she said was true.

"Never before can a prank have had such far-reaching consequences in Academe," Freeman gleefully reported a colleague saying. Thus were Samoans' "farfetched" stories translated into the literature of anthropology, at the same time explaining how Mead's account of Samoans' sexual mores was radically at odds with accounts by other ethnographers. Though Freeman took Fa'amu's oath on the Bible as the strongest of affirmations, he emphasized that his argument confirming Mead's error did not depend on Fa'amu's story, only explained it (while validating his own). He even excused Mead to some extent, for she could not be blamed for a prank.[3]

Friends and defenders lauded the film and the new disclosures. Hiram Caton, with light ambiguity, likened Freeman to a "Wise Elder to whom Cosmic Messages have been vouchsafed—very much like Mead herself." Robin Fox thought Freeman came over "as a prince of sweet reasonableness." Freeman's university colleagues were generally positive. James Fox believed the film would be good for the discipline, though another colleague with whom Derek had dueled for years told him to his face that he had "achieved nothing in anthropology."[4]

Freeman was soon left in no doubt that his overseas opponents thought much the same and that his hopes that "the Mead thing" would now disappear were sorely misplaced. British anthropologist Adam Kuper struck back in the prominent science journal *Nature*. Kuper could not see what all the fuss was about. Recycling hoary tales of a campaign beginning in the 1940s and not surfacing till after Mead's death, Kuper presented an altogether zanier Derek Freeman, "padding through the woods in gloves, driving what seems to be an armored personnel carrier through quiet suburban streets, wearing funny woollen hats, dressed as a Samoan and as a naval officer—all the while pressing his charges against Mead and her defenders." Kuper was openly incredulous that his colleagues would believe "the testimony of [Fa'amu,] a confessed liar." Kuper's primary purpose was to defend his profession to outsiders because he was worried that recent "reflexive" tendencies of a postmodern kind were eroding the authority of decent ethnography. Freeman's "crusading style" was a "disservice" to a troubled discipline even if his "dogged polemics" at least made outsiders recognize the issues at stake in contemporary anthropology.[5]

This was the style and temper of much of the discussion that continued to swirl around Freeman despite his repeated attempts to proclaim the Mead debate over and resolved. The Fa'amu moment became an obsessional theme, repeated over and over in a variety of exchanges with old and some new challengers. Hiram Caton's *Samoa Reader*, appearing in 1990, did little to quell the skepticism of critics. Ivan Brady, who as book review editor of *American Anthropologist* in 1983 had organized the American critique of *Margaret Mead and Samoa*, thought the collection too convoluted and clumsily organized. But he pounced on Caton's descriptions of Freeman's vehemence and used them to make an attack on Freeman's "relish of the fight" and "sense of retribution far beyond the ordinary."[6] The *Reader*, he believed (correctly), would simply confirm the suspicions of the various combatants. Bradd Shore had refused permission for Caton to quote abridgments of his writings because he saw the project as biased toward Freeman. Shore dismissed the Fa'amu interview as a public relations ploy.[7]

Ironically, Freeman and Caton fell out over the style and tone of parts of *The Samoa Reader*, not least Caton's own depictions of Freeman. Caton wrote of Freeman's "towering confidence and his relish for taking on all comers," his "aggressive attacks" and "impulse to dominate opponents," his "fits of rage" at editors who thwarted his demand for space and time to answer his critics. Freeman, "wrapping himself in the flag of Science," accused hostile anthropologists of negligence, even misconduct, suggested Caton.[8] In reply, Freeman rejected Caton's "melodramatic" presentation of Freeman's personality and his resurrection as a kind of Saint George figure who had come to slay the dragon on behalf of the Samoan people. His scientific persona, he told Caton, did not speak in a Samoan accent; he was not "an attention-seeking maverick but rather one of truth's fools." Caton had seriously misconstrued Freeman's positions, especially on sociobiology. Freeman wanted *The Samoa Reader* to acknowledge that he fully recognized "the scientifically demonstrated mechanisms of both nature and nurture."[9]

Their relationship faltered during the ensuing decade as Caton tried to get Freeman to face the fact that others perceived him as ferocious in pursuit of his enemies, no matter how moderate the provocation. Caton found it hard to fathom why Freeman was still concerned what others thought: "You have won the battle, you have no career interests to protect, you have been invited to the Salk Institute, you have an important book or two to write. The devil take reputation."[10]

It was good advice, but instead of building his statements about his "interactionist anthropology" into case studies or choosing to relax into a second decade of retirement, Freeman embarked on a new aspect of the old mission during the 1990s: to show exactly *how* and *why* Margaret Mead went wrong in Samoa, always leaning on the "probative" significance of Fa'amu's revelations. This was a much more historically focused mission, arising out of Mead's own research materials and letters archived in America. And Freeman was more openly critical of Mead's methodological failings, the way she cut corners to achieve her personal desires and her personal failing in accepting multiple *taupou* titles despite being married.

Freeman laid out this new approach in 1991 in an essay titled "'There's Tricks i' th' World,'" designed partly as an answer to Kuper's skeptical attitude to the Heimans film. Praising the "historic importance" of Heimans's work in Samoa, Freeman told in dramatic detail the story of the sudden appearance of Fa'amu with her admission she and Fofoa "'just fibbed and fibbed'" to Mead.[11] Drawing on a range of new biographies and from correspondence between Boas and Mead that had come into Freeman's possession, Freeman proceeded to expand the argument from his 1983 book. He had already shown that Mead set out on a mission for "'Papa Franz'" to make a "'study of heredity and environment'" around adolescent behavior in a "'primitive'" culture (106). Mead wanted her own eastern Polynesian island to study, but in a compromise with Boas, who worried about her safety, she went instead to American Samoa in western Polynesia.

What was new in Freeman's argument was the mixed context of instructions, advice, private agreements, and preconceptions with which Mead arrived in Samoa. Crucial to Mead's later conclusions—and to Freeman's argument—was her stopover in Hawai'i and time spent at the Bishop Museum with its director, Herbert Gregory, and with Edward Craighill Handy, an ethnologist who had studied the Marquesas Islands in eastern Polynesia. Handy's work on what he called "'the youthful libertines'" of the Marquesas, with their rampant sexual freedom during adolescence, coalesced with Mead's own romantic notions about lax Polynesian cultures (109). In addition, Mead entered into an agreement to produce an ethnology of Manu'a in order to help complete the museum's study of Polynesian cultures. It was this promise, along with a series of fateful decisions once in Samoa, said Freeman, that distorted the momentum of Mead's mission for Boas and led her off the track.

Freeman also wrote disapprovingly of Mead's acceptance of three *taupou* titles, though she was married and not a virgin: gratifying events, he said, that helped lead her into the hands of the two Samoan girls who "hoaxed" her. Making no progress on a systematic study of adolescent girls' sexuality and "lured by thoughts of ethnological gain," Mead went on a visit to outlying small islands with Fa'amu and Fofoa, where she fell victim to their "recreational lying" (113–14). Mead then hastened to depart Samoa for a sojourn in the south of France.

Freeman was more judgmental of Mead in this article than in *Margaret Mead and Samoa*. Mead's researches on the problem laid down by Boas were, "through neglect, in a state of disarray" (115). She was "reckless" in giving priority to her ethnological gathering and taking the word of Faʻamu and Fofoa, then cutting short her stay to sail for Europe (117). He also aired for the first time a report of an affair Mead is supposed to have had with the son of a high chief. This was the rumor Freeman reported to Lowell Holmes during Freeman's 1967 stay in Western Samoa but decided against divulging as part of his refutation. Caton's *Samoa Reader*, however, had published a copy of Freeman's letter to Holmes, so he felt justified in using it now to reinforce his judgment of Mead's sins.[12] He went on to show the "romantic bilge" of the depiction of Samoan sexual desire on the cover of the 1928 edition of *Coming of Age*, "exquisitely true to the preposterous fantasies by which she had been hoaxed" (118).

"'There's Tricks'" is not an unqualified demolition of Mead. In a fascinating excursus that was an unconscious explanation of his own experience in Sarawak had he but seen it, Freeman wrote of Mead returning to New York "in a state of cognitive delusion," a condition in which someone comes earnestly to believe in a mistaken idea "and for which . . . the 'sole authority' is an uncritical certainty that belief in this mistaken idea is fully warranted" (117). Cognitive delusion became a favorite stick with which Freeman beat several opponents during the 1990s, but in Mead's case it was a way of absolving her from any intent to deceive, a belief to which he held for the rest of his life. Besides, her little book was a tribute to the "infinite facility" of Mead's brain and to her "extraordinary literary skills" in synthesizing such a tangle of conflicting evidence into a "spell-binding" work for "humanly laudable ideological ends" (117, 118).

No such concessions applied to Adam Kuper in his dismissal of the Heimans film. Kuper had got it wrong attacking Freeman in 1983, wrote Freeman, in failing to recognize what Mead's mission to Samoa was really about. Now, as editor of the influential journal *Current Anthropology*, Kuper had the temerity to attack this new evidence without even mentioning the filmmaker, Frank Heimans, which only showed his entrenched admiration for all things Mead. Freeman wanted Kuper to deal with the Faʻamu evidence and Freeman's own call for a new science-based anthropology, not dwell on threats from so-called postmodernist anthropology, "the most anti-scientific 'school' in the entire history of anthropological thought" (121). This was Derek Freeman's traditional mode of argument, as we have seen, trying to draw opponents into an argument of *his* making rather than theirs. In an irony he did not seem to recognize, he also deplored Kuper's categorizing of individuals into types, the very thing he had just done in adding Kuper to the ranks of the "cognitively deluded" (120).

"There's Tricks" encapsulates all of Freeman's lasting arguments about Mead's work in Samoa. It anticipates what would become his final book on the subject, *The Fateful Hoaxing of Margaret Mead*, published nearly a decade later. The same year as the article, 1991, Freeman gave a public lecture at ANU, published later as a pamphlet by his research school and adapted as an article for the American journal *Academic Questions*. The article, titled "Paradigms in Collision," represents a synthesis of the state of knowledge around "the Mead thing" and was designed as a pivot to the last phase of Freeman's intellectual life as he developed his new "anthropology of choice."

"Paradigms" trumpets the significance of the Fa'amu revelation, "one of the most spectacular events in the intellectual history of the twentieth century," its scientific credibility attested by her sworn deposition lodged with AAA in Washington, D.C., and Freeman's two detailed accounts in leading American journals.[13] The significance of Fa'amu's revelation lay in the fact that the whole world fed off Margaret Mead's belief in the cultural plasticity of human nature argued in *Coming of Age*, and that belief was subsequently propounded for decades by deluded professors. In coy modesty, Freeman presented himself as taking away the cornerstone of that cultural determinist model with his 1983 book. Freeman also told the story of his victimization by an anthropological establishment that accused him of being "crazy" and "fueled by accumulated venom" (27). He endured, however, their "futile attempt to conjure me and my perturbing refutation right out of tribal consciousness," and now the controversy was "in effect" over, with moves afoot even to rescind the AAA motion of 1983 condemning his book (28). Mead and her ilk were consigned to "the trash cans of human error" (31) as the fully interactionist paradigm gained pace. Molecular geneticists were studying humans' primate background, and fresh research was connecting environmental variables to the evolutionary history of the human species and its capacity for making choices.

"Paradigms in Collision" remains a hinge between that which had ruled Freeman's intellectual life for some decades and what might have been conquered in the final decade of his life but never was. He was seventy-five, had cleaned out his university office, and was less and less connected to that theater of his life. His and Monica's retirement prospects were hit hard by the 1987 stock market crash. That added to the sapping of his already failing physical energy: Derek was on medication for diabetes, followed a strict dietary regime, and was suffering the beginnings of heart trouble. He still had intellectual energy aplenty to make things happen, but as the 1990s proceeded, events unfolded that changed the calculus of the decisions he made about where to concentrate that energy. A key event was an invitation to visit Canada in March 1990 to give a series of lectures at Simon Fraser University in British Columbia.[14]

This trip became an energizing eight-week tour down and up the West Coast of North America. At Simon Fraser Freeman met Douglas Cole, a historian completing a biography of Franz Boas who delivered into Freeman's hands copies of Boas's correspondence with Mead. Traveling south, Freeman gave well-regarded talks on various campuses, meeting supporters and some of the "cognitively deluded" and ending in San Diego. He spoke again to packed seminar rooms and met Francis Crick and Jonas Salk. Salk seduced Freeman with a hint that the Salk Institute might support a project searching for "a unified understanding of human behavior." When Freeman left, the two men embraced: "We both have tears in our eyes & are walking on air." Freeman decided there and then that he and Monica would move to the United States.

By the end of April they were back in Canberra, where the fantasy about moving to America promptly dissolved. But the "priceless boon" of the Cole materials made Freeman envisage a wholly new-old future that lay in front of him.[15] "That really was the beginning of *The Fateful Hoaxing*," he told Don Tuzin in 2000. "You have to proceed with this book," he told himself, although he was telling everyone else the Mead debate was over, and he remained convinced that further opposition to his arguments about Mead's failings in Samoa was mere sophistry.[16]

Girding his loins—again—Freeman traveled to Washington, DC, in 1992, returning with two thousand copies of key documents from Margaret Mead's papers in the Library of Congress. The trip enhanced his admiration for her: "She emerges as an immensely ambitious young woman of genius," he wrote to one of his supporters. "What happened to her in Samoa is quite remarkable and I should, if I put my mind to it, be able to write one of the books of the century. Oh for the pen of a Tolstoy!" It also emerged that "by March 1926 she had a very good command of the Samoan language. Indeed I would suppose that she talked to Fa'apua'a and Fofoa in Samoan."[17] The new book initially sported a bland academic title, but

Don Tuzin persuaded Freeman that "Fateful Hoaxing" conveyed a double message: fate led Mead to find what she wanted in Samoa with results that were fateful for twentieth-century anthropology.[18]

A roller coaster of small triumphs and signs of recognition kept Freeman at his desk to finish a manuscript. He had already appeared on a card in the game of Trivial Pursuit in a question about Margaret Mead. Now correspondents were reporting that his work was being taken up in classrooms, sometimes in approval, sometimes as the target for criticism; at least he was being discussed. In March 1996 he was invited to address the National Press Club in Canberra. His speech was titled "A New Evolutionary Enlightenment," and the event was televised across the nation. He also gave talks to the Sydney Institute and the Australian Skeptics, who voted him their inaugural Skeptic of the Year. Richard Dawkins listened to that talk and praised him as "one of the great scientific heroes of our age." The same year his 1983 book was reissued in paperback as *Margaret Mead and the Heretic* and promptly went to the top of the best-seller list in the journal *New Scientist*. A review in the *Canberra Times*, which had previously pilloried him, considered the book a "courteous rebuttal of a classic test," according to Freeman. On 1 August Freeman had a private meeting with Chicago anthropologist Marshall Sahlins, who, according to Freeman, recognized that Boasian culturalism had had its day and was doomed. Off to one side, a triumph by one of his Iban students, James Masing, had Freeman's name prominently connected to it in the publication of an ancient Iban chant that he had helped translate.[19]

In 1996 a larger triumph set Freeman's name literally in lights. The previous year Freeman's interest had been piqued by a controversy involving the playwright David Williamson. Williamson was regarded both in Australia and abroad as a serious comic dramatist with a rapier-edged feel for dialogue and a wicked eye for the ambiguities of class aspirations and faddish ideologies in contemporary Australia. He had studied psychology at university, which toughened his native belief that "human nature" was a universal condition in which greed, ambition, self-deception, and male aggression wove a solid core.[20] In 1995 his play *Dead White Males* persuaded some commentators that Williamson had fallen victim to the temptations of prosperity and stardom and was now intent on lampooning the politically correct values of his intellectual contemporaries.

Dead White Males had its germ in Williamson's own encounter with a turgid paper on literary deconstruction by a young academic at a writer's conference.[21] No one could understand what the paper was about, said

Williamson, who, while accepting that postmodernist approaches offered some insights, firmly rejected the argument that "truth" was just a series of textual effects, always driven by a conservative, gender-loaded political ideology. His play has as villain the literature professor Dr. Grant Swain, for whom culture is everything, biology nothing. The resonances with Freeman's picture of Margaret Mead were powerful. Swain rages at the notion that there is any biological difference between the impulses of men and women: "Nothing is biological, nothing! . . . There are no demons in the brain. Everything can be changed and will be changed! There are no demons! None!"[22]

When the play was first performed, controversy erupted in the letter pages of national newspapers over Williamson's treatment of feminist issues. Enter stage left Derek Freeman, who read about the playwright's argument with a prominent feminist in a weekend newspaper and wrote to him. Freeman sent Williamson a copy of "Paradigms in Collision" and a brief history of his life and of the bruising encounters he had endured over Mead. They had things in common, especially an interest in evolutionary thinking. "The next thing I knew," Freeman said later, ". . . three excited faxes arrived, right on top of one another, saying this would make a marvelous play and 'would you possibly be agreeable to it?'"[23]

He certainly would. A play would be vindication well beyond the academy, the kind of recognition his colleagues had always denied him. Freeman immediately said yes. Driven by his fervor for truth, though perhaps not giving sufficient thought to the kind of truth a dramatist might find, he turned his personal papers and correspondence over to Williamson. The two did not meet until the script was completed. Williamson traveled to the Freeman home in Canberra, along with director Wayne Harrison of the Sydney Theatre Company, where the play's premiere would be staged. The meeting was accompanied by its own moments of melodrama, choreographed by Derek. Freeman, "a vision in beige," according to Harrison, eased tensions by staging a Pacific islands–inspired welcoming ceremony. Freeman gave Williamson a statuette of Maat, the Egyptian goddess of truth. He promptly dropped it, breaking it in two. "In the stunned silence that followed," said Harrison, "I think we all decided not to see this as an omen. In retrospect it was." For whom was not entirely clear, though there was enough in the finished play to give all sides pause. Derek had marked the play's script with over ninety notes but nonetheless accepted Williamson's depiction of him as a flawed character different from (and less flattering than) his own conception of himself.[24]

The play carried the portentous title *Heretic*. Derek willed the cast on in its preparations. In February 1996 he and Monica visited the Sydney Theatre Company to meet them and watch the dramaturgical adjustments as the play came together. Freeman gave fully of himself in these encounters. He wrote letters to the actors, went to the previews, discussed changes, and loved it all. At the final preview he sat with pen poised over a large, clean notebook but failed to write a word, so entranced was he by this flesh-and-blood incarnation of his heretical life.

The Derek Freeman who emerged from *Heretic* was "a pedant and a moralist and a chip-on-his-shoulder Australian" spoiling for a fight, particularly with Margaret Mead. Onstage, Freeman's argument over her work became a personal conflict with Mead herself. Although traced by his psychoanalyst in the play to Derek's relationship with a domineering mother and a consequent ambivalence toward all women, Freeman's pursuit of Mead was portrayed as rooted in righteous, scientific indignation at an international reputation built on deeply flawed work. But a litany of more selfish reasons also occupied the background: his moral puritanism toward a young woman liberating herself in the 1920s, the alleged humiliation he suffered at Mead's hands at their 1964 meeting, a little sexual jealousy, and some professional envy. A narrator had Freeman "consumed with seeking your own personal glory and crushing your competitors." Mead herself was portrayed as the naïve believer in a human utopia where "we've got infinite choice. We can shape society any way we choose." Ironically, the play had her driven by her own sexual expression and by a desire for power and status that was instinctually, biologically driven.[25]

The play also dared to raise the question of Freeman's mental state, making the accusation that he experienced moments when he was mentally unbalanced, especially on the occasion of his Sarawak misadventure thirty years before.

Audiences loved what was a surrealist, dream-based set of episodes stretching over the life of a young and an old Derek. But critical reviews followed thick and fast, disdainful of the cartoonish, cabaret-style production that Wayne Harrison concocted and lapping up the tensions that had emerged between Harrison and Williamson over its staging.[26] However, the play was true to Williamson's conception of and appreciation for Derek Freeman's personality: a "passion to control and dominate, nurtured by his mother's ambitions and his own genetic drive," together with a certain tendency to paranoia. Despite these singularities the dramatist celebrated Freeman's cognitive strengths and dedication to unpopular findings in the face of hostility. Williamson regarded Freeman in 1996, and continued to regard him, as "one of the bravest intellectuals of the twentieth century, and one of the most important."[27] David Williamson's fool was still truth's fool.

Freeman was much taken with the title of "heretic." "In science, if you're a heretic, it's a terribly dangerous thing because you're making a leap in the dark, and if you come a cropper you're finished," he told a journalist in 1996 in a magazine article that described him as "an impassioned, idiosyncratic, uncompromising man, who stalks hallowed doctrines like the grim reaper."[28] In the accompanying picture, in which he sports long, gray hair, he stares pensively at the reader from a dark cave in his garden among a smothering embrace of ivy. It is the face of a mystic or a medieval alchemist.

His assertion that he had "got it right" only inflamed the rage of "true believers," according to Freeman.[29] As the 1990s wore on the disputes drew in new players, each of whom Freeman felt compelled to drive off. James Côte, a Canadian sociologist, produced in 1994 the most aggressive attack on Freeman for some time. His small book examining the controversy attributed ulterior motives to Freeman, one of which was "trying to prove that traits such as human aggressiveness are universal human 'biological imperatives' that cannot be mitigated by culture."[30] Côte framed his arguments through a legal metaphor, involving "charges" laid by Freeman against Mead's "crime," the readers invited to be judge and jury to decide the "culpability" of the parties. It was a format wherein Freeman could never expect justice, let alone mercy. Côte "cross-examined" "expert witnesses" like Lowell Holmes, generally conceding all their points against Freeman and ending by finding Mead's arguments "persuasive." Witnesses for Freeman's "defense," like Caton and his *Samoan Reader*, were simply dismissed as proxies for Freeman's hostility to Mead and American social science.

Freeman's Fa'amu argument was treated with equal dispatch: Fa'amu was the victim of pressure to "confess" before her high-titled Samoan interviewer, while Freeman was guilty of contaminating the way the information was collected. Côte's argument was all in terms of "maybes" and "possibilities" and strained the credulity of any fair-minded reader. In one of his characteristic open letters, Freeman in reply demolished Côte's "jury" artifice and the "plethora of misinformation" Côte had assembled—the length of time Freeman had spent in the islands, the false accusation that he had not considered social change, the confected charge that Freeman was trying to prove a universal human aggression and that he was "determined to disgrace Mead." He repudiated yet again the claim that his Samoan title was only symbolic and vigorously defended Faʻamu, her Christian seriousness, and the various investigations of her claims.

Freeman's strictures against Côte were delivered with an incautious rhetoric that had now become the currency of exchange among contenders. Côte was guilty of "baseless aspersions," "utterly shoddy scholarship," "crass inanity." He was "an unprincipled polemicist" who had "flagrantly monkeyed" with the evidence for his ideological ends. Although Freeman ended on an upbeat note, with his usual good wishes to his assailant, he was guilty of departing from the cool, calculated discourse of his previous arguments about the defects in Mead's scholarship.[31] Côte too was guilty of provocation: Freeman's attempt to provide historical grounds for his conclusions was "soap opera science"; he was intransigent, smug, out to settle scores. Côte condemned Freeman's followers for the same approach.[32]

One of the authorities Freeman drew to his defense against Côte was the American anthropologist Martin Orans, whom Freeman counted among his little band of backers who found Mead's work less than scientific. Their relationship, like many others, started well, with a respectful request from Orans in 1988 for information on Freeman's research. Orans had worked in Salamumu, the village next door to Saʻanapu, and he knew the respect in which Derek was held among Samoans. "Call me Derek" was Freeman's friendly reply. Their relationship developed amicably, both exchanging materials and insights, Derek even staying with Orans and his family during his 1990 trip to the West Coast.

Things began to sour after Orans sent Freeman drafts of his forthcoming book, drawn from a detailed study of Mead's Samoa field notes. Orans was traveling beyond the argument, agreed to by Freeman, that contradictions abounded between Mead's field data and her conclusions. Now Orans claimed Mead was deliberately misleading her supervisor and readers when she presented her findings. Freeman could not accept that. "I do not for an instant suppose that Margaret Mead was capable of such highly unethical behavior," he wrote in some agitation to Orans.[33] He asked Orans repeatedly if his "heavy words" were his real belief. Scholarship and morality went hand in hand in Freeman's intellectual universe, that universe of choices that human evolutionary history had delivered. Historian Geoffrey Elton and philosopher Iris Murdoch were Freeman's oracles in this. He even sent Orans an excerpt from Murdoch's novel about fundamental moral choices, *The Good Apprentice*, in which a character expressed the basis of Freeman's own scholarly morals: "Being objective is being truthful, making right judgments is a moral activity, all thinking is a function of morality, it's done by humans, it's touched by values right into its center, empirical science is no exception."[34] These were sentiments Freeman's critics may have found hard to identify in his exchanges with them, but they were at the core of his way of looking at the world. They meant that friends could become enemies if they did not share his obdurate certainty.

Orans found that out when Freeman sent him twenty-five pages of close-grained comment on the prepublication draft of his book, *Not Even Wrong*. Mead, wrote Orans, knew perfectly well that adolescent females in Samoa faced more restrictions in their sexual behavior than her generalizations implied. Her generalizations in fact proceeded from hunches that fitted what she wanted to find. Hence her conclusions were "not even wrong," just entirely inconsistent with what she knew from her defective researches.

This was a serious enough departure from the script Freeman allowed. But Orans also claimed that Fa'amu was never the main informant for Mead, nor could Mead ever have believed her and Fofoa's fibbing; Fa'amu, after all, was a *taupou*, her sexual activities severely guarded. Orans also disagreed with Freeman's explanation for Mead's hasty departure from Samoa.

Orans's book may have been seen to give some comfort to Freeman's side of the argument, but Freeman himself was having none of it. The American now found himself condemned in the strongest terms for a "polemical and casuistic" assault on Fa'amu, since he had dismissed evidence that Freeman conveyed to him privately. In an irony Freeman recognized, he was now in the position of defending Mead against Orans. Far from ignoring who Mead was as a person—Orans's approach—Freeman insisted on studying her character, values, and actions. She may have been a "fervent ideologue, brilliantly clever and highly ambitious, who went to Samoa with an unquestioning belief in Boasian culturalism," but "a deliberate cheat she *most certainly was not*." With the kind of dismissive sarcasm both sides now employed, Freeman denounced Orans "as one of the illustrious Humpty Dumptys of American cultural anthropology," joining the likes of Lowell Holmes on "the Wall of Bewilderment."[35]

Côte and Orans became part of a group whose sniping rejoinders to Freeman followed him all the way to his death in 2001. Freeman had nicknames for this group—"the Four Horsemen of the Apocalypse" and "the Pensacola Crackpots" after a conference they attended in Florida. Including at different stages Lowell Holmes, Paul Shankman, and French anthropologist Serge Tcherkézoff, as well as Côte and Orans, they constituted the Grand Inquisition against Derek Freeman's brave Heretic, who, despite his assurances that the great debate was over, continued to fight on many fronts against those who impugned his motives, misread his arguments, or refused to accept his clinching revelations.

Adam Kuper was another who remained in Freeman's sights well after Kuper had dismissed the significance of the Heimans film. In 1992, when Kuper, as editor of *Current Anthropology*, refused to publish the latest Freeman revelations about Mead and Fa'amu, Freeman tried to bully him into submission: "I was doing field research in Samoa before you were born. And, I am now Australia's senior living professional anthropologist." Colleagues around the world were invited to join the campaign. Kuper was guilty of "unhistorical fictions," his refusal to publish "a clear instance of the political construction of anthropological knowledge, and is thus, in scholarly terms, corrupt." Freeman even approached his old teacher Raymond Firth, who, with his Old World courtesy, would have none of it.[36]

Ivan Brady, who, like Kuper, rejected the hoaxing argument, was likewise the recipient of an "open letter" in Freeman's continual, wearying effort to correct his enemies' basic facts. Brady's review of *The Samoa Reader* contained a catalog of factual mistakes but also, to Freeman, betrayed Brady's "snide proclivities" toward a willing misinterpretation of Freeman's actions: "You are so obviously intent on scoring cheap points and showing off to your like-minded readers: bully for Brady."[37]

This obsessional carping—from both sides—continued throughout the decade. Some whom Freeman tried to engage deflected his barbs with good humor or witty ripostes, like James Clifford, the cultural theorist. Others, like Clifford Geertz, simply stayed silent. Behind the fluctuating levels of invective lay anguish on Freeman's part. His opponents' brains, he told Don Tuzin, seemed hard-wired against his continually mounting evidence. At one point in the debates, Freeman identified with the stricken Black Knight in the Monty Python movie *The Holy Grail* who, despite having his limbs comically cut off, keeps on prodding his enemies to fight. Freeman felt like a victim of personal attacks while pursuing fair and robust criticism of ideas; he believed, shortly before his death in 2001, that "their casuistry and their sleazy opprobrium" were getting worse.[38] One stands out in Freeman's declining years, the student-become-anthropologist who had stood up to him in the 1970s. He practiced Freeman's rhetorical tactics in a continual goading through letters and publications that did not let up until shortly before Freeman's death. Freeman might complain of "spiked animus" and "ideologically inspired malevolence," but he was being treated as others felt he had treated them in the battles over Mead.[39] It is a curious blind spot in Freeman that in his struggle to transform himself he never seemed to recognize this dark symmetry of revenge. One can see in the mutual, sad hostility the negative energy that continued to plague Freeman's reputation long after his death.

Freeman's absolutist principle of replying to every written criticism was not a recipe for normal life and relationships, even within a scholarly community. It would be a biographical cliché to write this off as a "tragic flaw," but it does raise the issue of the state of his psyche at various points during this extended war of words. Unfortunately, Freeman's diaries for the last ten years of his life are not presently available, so it is difficult to assess whether the struggle to be better than himself that so occupied him before 1990 still mattered in the heat of these late battles. Only small glimpses appear either in correspondence, such as with his old friend Douglas Oliver, with whose admonitions against extravagant responses Freeman agreed, or in the extended interview with Tuzin, a year before Freeman's death.

As we have seen, Freeman was on medication for manic behavior during the 1970s, before the bipolar condition was widely known or accepted. Freeman admitted to his former vice chancellor, Anthony Low, in 1995 that he still suffered from feelings of injustice that he believed Low was responsible for twenty years earlier.[40] "The Mead thing" was the other great trial of Freeman's life, during which he struggled to retain a civilized discourse with those who attacked his every argument. Don Tuzin, who knew him better than anyone outside his immediate family, thought Freeman "did behave occasionally in a manner I would call manic. His behavior was truly eccentric, but I never thought it crossed over into pathology." However, Tuzin conceded that others felt Freeman was "crazy," and Tuzin could see why they would think that.[41] Their suspicion was that Freeman's priority was to defend his sense of himself as "truthmonger" and wounded heretic, rather than broaden his sympathies and try to understand his adversaries.

In 1999 *The Fateful Hoaxing of Margaret Mead* finally appeared. Freeman had tried to get either Harvard, Yale, or Norton to publish the book, but they all declined. It adhered too closely to the arguments of 1983, said the letter from Norton, and "hence would not be regarded in the trade world as news."[42] But with the help of Tuzin and Freeman's agent, Philippa

Sandall, Westview Press, based in Colorado and in Oxford, picked it up and published both hardback and paperback editions.

Fateful Hoaxing fleshes out the arguments of "There's Tricks" into a gripping, sometimes rollicking tale that is part detective story, part scholarly argument. Freeman begins with the dramatic moment when Frank Heimans found Fa'apua'a Fa'amu and the account she gave of her and Fofoa's time spent with Mead. He then launches into a historical analysis of Mead's preparations for and experience of fieldwork in Samoa, the sequence of events, their causes and effects, and the varied contexts surrounding the decisions she made and the revelations that emerged. It was, he argued, an "intensely human" tale, important for both Samoa and for anthropology in general.[43]

Mead's hoaxing was "fated" by a set of interlocking factors: her fervent belief in Boas and Benedict and their theories; her commitment to ethnological collection rather than the systematic study of adolescent behavior Boas wanted; the preconception, absorbed from Edward Smith Craighill Handy, that premarital promiscuity was the cultural pattern throughout Polynesia; her need to satisfy Boas; and finally the resort to joking behavior by Fa'amu and Fofoa (14–15). Freeman marches Mead and the reader through her Samoan adventure and her mistakes, the tone of his language returning to the studied, neutral style of his earlier *Margaret Mead and Samoa*, though marred this time by a constant, finger-wagging repetition of his main points.

But *Fateful Hoaxing* is not the demolition of Mead his 1983 book set out to be. Throughout, Freeman stresses Mead's "exceptional abilities" (99), the difficult circumstances of her environment, and the catastrophes of weather and illness that beset her. What emerges is a portrait of the practical difficulties of a young woman pioneering her way into a workable fieldwork practice, testing, abandoning, and retrying a variety of methods to extract information, learn the language, survive the climate, and produce something that would satisfy her ambitions and solve the tasks set by her supervisor. Freeman continues firmly to absolve Mead from the charge made by Orans of deliberately misleading her readers. She may have been guilty of denial and rationalization, but she was no falsifier (212).

Mead does not escape some censure. Her information on adolescent girls was "highly unsystematic and anecdotal," the information in her notebooks "arbitrary and equivocal." She was also waylaid by her "major and illicit involvement with the Bishop Museum" (154–55). Finally, "Margaret Mead's Samoan research will go down in the history of the behavioral sciences as an example of the way in which a highly intelligent investigator can be blinded to empirical reality by an uncritical commitment to a scientifically unsound assumption" (212).

The book goes well beyond the hoaxing episode and what led to it. The focus, as one reviewer pointed out, was also on "how the Boasian mindset and other features of Mead's biography set her up to be hoaxed."[44] The final chapters explore the phenomenon of *Coming of Age*; the campaign that its publisher, Morrow, put into preparing the ground (a "stunt" that prefigured the accusations made against Harvard University Press in 1983, though Freeman did not seem to notice the similarity); and how the book became standard reading in the behavioral and human sciences, with Mead herself the mythic figure Rappaport had recognized in reviewing Freeman's earlier book.

If Freeman thought he had said the final word and his detractors would now fall into line, he was, again, sorely disappointed. Ten years after pronouncing "the Mead thing" over, nearly two decades after his original book, he found himself in new skirmishes with friend and foe. Reviews of *Fateful Hoaxing* divided roughly on ideological lines. Outsiders accepted it as a good book with a humane edge to its appraisal of Mead, but insiders like Martin Orans and James Côte refused to accept it as any kind of step forward. Both men disdained as speculative and implausible Freeman's painstaking story of the "hoaxing." Orans wanted to know why Freeman hadn't provided a full list of all the questions and answers of the interview his student had carried out with Fa'amu (a recurring point of attack in future years). Côte, in the kind of personal slap for which Freeman was often criticized, wrote that the rich journey that Freeman had provided through Mead's myth and his own life was "like being shown through the henhouse by the fox." Freeman's positions were becoming more and more "outlandish and illogical."[45] In shades of 1983, Côte tried to damn the book by resurrecting suspicions of a publishing conspiracy to make money and enhance Freeman's fame. Even sympathetic reviewers like the anthropologist Donald Brown in California agreed that the evidence for the hoaxing was circumstantial at best. So too the Janus-faced Hiram Caton, who, while accusing Orans of "vintage anthropological twaddle" in his playing with words, nonetheless took Orans's side on the unlikelihood of the hoaxing and the "travesty" of Mead's findings.[46]

Freeman could not hold back his pen, though now in his eighty-fourth year. His method was to keep hammering his essential hoaxing argument in a variety of ways in different places, adding new twists that surely must persuade naysayers. The startling new evidence that for Freeman clinched his theory was his rediscovery of an article by Mead from 1931 that he had first read in 1968 but discarded. "Life as a Samoan Girl" speaks of "reverend scientists" who sent Mead to study adolescent girls with no clear idea how to do it. She journeys to Ofu and Olusega with two girls, who serve as her helpers and from whom she receives "whispered confidences" that answer the scientists' questions. Triumphantly, Freeman laid out this "definitive evidence" alongside the preconceptions Mead had imported via Handy about Polynesian sexuality.[47]

Neither Côte nor Orans would have any of it. There was no hoax, no Meadian epiphany. Mead had sufficient evidence from earlier notes and enough time to put it all together in *Coming of Age*. Freeman's claim that her ethnological work was illicit was plain wrong, his re-creation of Mead's state of mind mere speculation, his approach polemical, and his methods too rigidly empirical. From these accusations they would not budge, despite Freeman accusing Côte of behaving like a bigot. Côte continued deriding "the pat ideas he [Freeman] has flogged for the past decade" and his "hood-winking" tactic of moving on to a new discovery when all else failed to convince.[48] Language was warfare now, and both sides practiced open aggression.

In the first year of the new century and the last year of his life, Derek wanted it all just to stop. Although the constant battles had kept him alive, he didn't want to go on looking up any more new material for ammunition. The Samoa controversy was over, as far as he was concerned—"finis coronat opus" (the end crowns the work) was the phrase he chose—and from the middle of 2000 he began packing up his vast archive of notes, correspondence, and papers to send off to Don Tuzin for deposit in the University of California, San Diego, library. "I have reached a kind of contentment," he told Frank Heimans in February 2001. "I don't read books much anymore. I used to read books avidly, but I'm quite content just being in the world, sitting in the garden looking at the world." He had signed off to his closest supporters in Samoa with the same sentiments.[49]

In 1998 a public lecture in the city of his birth, Wellington, laid down the version of his master story that he was most comfortable with: the heretic who had punctured the complacent errors of anthropology's "sacred woman" with a momentous discovery of innocent lies by two young women and who could laugh at his enemies. Now, advances in genetics and molecular biology and in primatology, ethology, and the neurosciences were ushering in "the new evolutionary enlightenment." Had he been killed in that climbing accident in January 1938, he ventured, "it is unlikely in the extreme that the Mead myth about Samoa would ever have been exposed."[50] The Zeitgeist was flowing in his direction: the queen was dead; long live the new anthropology.

Except that off to the side his adversaries were continuing their campaign to bring him down. Hiram Caton was now trying to manufacture a different life story for Derek, finding a pattern in Freeman's personality: the intensely serious truth-seeker who invests the trivial event of the hoax with high dignity in a chain of events wherein Freeman discovers Mead's mistakes and Boas's error. "The grandiosity of this narrative is the stuff of legend," wrote Caton, "because the narrator emerges as the protagonist in this century's most important quest for truth." Caton claimed to diagnose in this narrative "some symptoms of a personality disorder."[51] With mock sincerity he would not name it, though he was confident enough to proclaim its existence, despite having no clinical training. This became Caton's favorite construction after Freeman's death, and it was taken up by others seeking to enforce Freeman's destruction.

Serge Tcherkézoff, French anthropologist, was different and took a middle path through the labyrinth of "the Mead thing." As founder of Samoan studies in France and director of a center for research on Oceania, Tcherkézoff knew the islands well and had a Samoan family. He had met Freeman in 1983 and corresponded with him during the 1990s, agreeing about Mead's mistakes but defending cultural anthropology's mission to explain the human world. Friendly and cooperative at first, their relationship began predictably to cool as Tcherkézoff disagreed with Freeman's reconstruction of why Mead was wrong. Freeman erred in seeking a silver bullet in *Fateful Hoaxing*, said Tcherkézoff. He gave too much individual agency to Fa'amu over the cultural reasons why she might make her claims. He was also wrong to look for Samoan perpetrators of a hoax and wrong to try to turn cultural explanations into sociobiological ones.

On the other hand, Tcherkézoff agreed that Mead was wrong about much of Samoa because she went there with three centuries of European preconceptions about Polynesian sexuality in her head, as well as pressure from Boas and Benedict to find one dominant cultural attitude to adolescence. Mead's field notes demonstrated that in fact she found plenty of other attitudes toward sexual freedom than her book displayed. Orans was also wrong. In fact, everybody was guilty of playing "Popperian logical games."[52]

Tcherkézoff outlined these arguments formally in 2001 in an essay titled "Is Anthropology about Individual Agency or Culture? Or Why 'Old

Derek' Is Doubly Wrong" in the *Journal of the Polynesian Society* after a bout of acrimonious correspondence between Australia and France had forced some changes in Tcherkézoff's thinking. Despite his assurances that he was finished with the whole mess, Freeman continued to be driven by his compulsion on "scientific" grounds to correct every error. He had to get Monica's physical help now to write letters, and he took Tcherkézoff seriously enough to keep up an angry exchange.

Tcherkézoff had accused Freeman of unethical behavior in making Faʻamu the center point of his hoaxing argument, and he suggested that Freeman should be drummed out of the community of scholars. Freeman's first reaction was outrage at this "entirely false and defamatory accusation." He had already threatened legal action against the *Journal* if it proceeded to publish Tcherkézoff's article, and he genuinely wondered what "ideological frenzy" was driving the Frenchman with the "Durkheimian world view." Tcherkézoff made his apologies and agreed to make small changes, but he would not retreat from his accusations that Faʻamu was under great stress during her interview and that Freeman should have done everything to prevent her from becoming the scapegoat for all the wrongs suffered by Samoans since the publication of *Coming of Age*. Nor would Tcherkézoff accept the hoaxing argument.[53]

Derek Freeman did not want another exhausting altercation or a public spat about the guilt or otherwise of Samoans; that would only upset their mutual Samoan friends. But he could not accept the interpretation of Faʻamu's state of emotions and mind that Tcherkézoff was confidently embracing, the kind of speculation Freeman himself was being accused of in relation to Mead's frame of mind. Their stiff-backed letters to one another continued until shortly before Freeman's death on 6 July 2001.

Tcherkézoff tried to distinguish his agreement with and admiration for Freeman's original 1983 refutation of Mead from the debacle that he considered the "second debate" (Freeman's "ridiculous detective-style inquiry") had become. He could not understand why Freeman had spent ten years on the hoaxing theory, reducing the ground of Mead's errors to the joking lies of two girls on one day in March 1926. It diminished the power of Freeman's original refutation, narrowing "the grand debate to a poor lonesome 'smoking gun.'" Mead, he said, would have written exactly the same book even if she had never met Faʻamu.[54]

Tcherkézoff continued to send encouraging, friendly notes, not in appeasement but to reconcile with another and more senior Samoa expert whom he knew to be fatally ill. It was too late and of little use in clarifying a debate whose ground had been plowed over so many times that the original argument was difficult to remember. Tcherkézoff's essay was duly published to the accompaniment of one last, forceful counterattack by Freeman in the following issue. Its substance repeated Freeman's historical analysis of Mead's sojourn in Samoa and the circumstances that led to her conclusions, but its language was directed against Tcherkézoff as "a plethoric ideologue with a Durkheimian bee in his bonnet" and "a Durkheimian spin-doctor who fabricates his own version of history" who was himself guilty of unethical behavior and "beyond the pale of honest and trustworthy scholars."[55]

Even then Freeman did not get the last word. In a letter to the *Journal* after Freeman's death, Tcherkézoff felt compelled to explain Freeman's "verbal violence" in terms of his long and deep emotional devotion to the Samoa people. Tcherkézoff now revealed all the "facts" and interpretations he had agreed not to put in his article as a way of explaining the "Freemanian passion" with which Freeman had responded to Tcherkézoff's accusations. Had Freeman been alive he would surely have questioned the ethics of such a response, since Tcherkézoff bared Fa'amu's supposed cultural embarrassment for all to see. It was an odd way to protect Samoan feelings.[56]

In bidding Freeman farewell, Tcherkézoff could still pay him a well-meaning, if left-handed, compliment. Freeman's loss of "self-control" revealed how important these matters were to the scholar. He "more strongly resented an accusation of mistreating a Samoan than one of making historical errors about Mead's notes."[57] It was the sincerest compliment any of Freeman's opponents paid him.

Coda

In 2003 an anthropologist argued in the pages of *American Anthropologist* that the "Sturm und Drang" of the Freeman–Mead controversy was past, making it safe to begin appraising some other differences between Mead and her colleagues over her New Guinea ethnographies.[58] It was wish rather than fact. Admittedly, anthropology was being rocked by other, more deadly controversies, including the campaign against Napoleon Chagnon, accused of inoculating Yanomamö indigenes in the Amazon with a measles vaccine in a kind of genocidal quest. His argument that "men who killed the most also had the most offspring" was far more shocking than arguments about Samoan sexual behavior or Margaret

219

Mead's supposed naïveté, though Freeman's name was brought into the same orbit when accusations flew about him giving comfort to sociobiologists. There were also cleavages within American anthropology between the growing prominence of evolution-influenced scientific approaches and reflexive, text-based studies, leading to what one observer termed "fractal divisions"—structural polarizations with their own inherent "rhetoric of contention."[59]

But the contentiousness of the Freeman–Mead controversy was still a live issue, if frozen into textbooks for students to choose who was right and who was wrong. This was also evident in events in 2001 to celebrate the centenary of Margaret Mead's birth, with sessions devoted to her at a conference in Miami, Florida, and at the AAA meeting in Washington, DC. The Library of Congress mounted an exhibition of treasures from the Mead archive. At the Florida conference on Mead's Pacific ethnography, some of Mead's greatest supporters and Freeman's most forthright critics were free to pronounce upon both without fear of reproach from either side. Their papers were later gathered into a special issue of the American journal *Pacific Studies*.[60]

Understandably, opinion centered on Mead and her manifold contributions to the field. Attitudes to Freeman remained locked into a familiar pattern of hostility. Catherine Bateson was there to defend her mother by dismissing Freeman's refutation as a distraction that obscured Mead's lifelong work, the clear target, in Bateson's eyes, of Freeman's "opportunistic" attack (165). Nancy McDowell had hardly moved beyond 1984: she recognized the "tit-for-tat" nature of the arguments but scolded Mead's detractors for "essentializing" her work while simultaneously essentializing Freeman for his "deception, which surely must be conscious and in some ways intentional" (10). McDowell argued that a just evaluation of Mead meant seeing her as a historical figure growing intellectually within the twentieth-century discipline. However, McDowell made no such demand on behalf of Freeman, impugning his motives and writing off his supporters as "conservatives, simplistic sociobiologists, and his students" (14).

James Côte displayed the most patent antagonism to Freeman, claiming to see "an escalation of harassment" of Mead by Freeman during the 1960s. Côte's technique was to take two sets of letters, one from the early 1960s, the other from late in the decade, and then "speculate" that the "chain of events" he found between these two periods—Freeman's supposed resentment of Mead for failing to help him into an American psychiatric training program—explained Freeman's turning against her (65–68). Côte also joined the band of untrained amateur psychologists in mixing a dose of David Williamson's play with a dash of text from Nikki Barrowclough's magazine article of 1996 to produce a confused and repressed Freeman who had to punish the wanton Mead and yet forgive her as a mother figure (69–70). The "craziness" and "menace" of Derek Freeman were being made the real event.

The most authoritative Samoa figure at the conference was Paul Shankman, one of "the Pensacola Crackpots," though Freeman's also naming him as a member of "the Four Horsemen of the Apocalypse" more truly described his influence. Shankman was Freeman's most sober-minded critic, patient and well versed in Samoa's cultural history sources. Shankman, a cultural anthropologist who had worked in Samoa since the 1960s, was unafraid to stand toe to toe with Freeman either in his presence in Canberra or in a series of essays on key areas of Freeman's argument about Mead. He breached Freeman's defenses in tracing the decline of the *taupou* class among Samoans, in pointing to changes to sexual behavior patterns among some Samoans during World War II, and in asking why Freeman had so undervalued Mead's other Samoa book, *Social Organization in Manu'a*. Shankman was the only anthropologist to explore Freeman's professional backstory to some degree and attempt to make connections between Freeman's motivations and the lineage of his writings.[61]

But the sobriety of Shankman's dissections of Freeman's ideas seemed to take a new, more personal turn in 1998 with an article in the scientistic journal *Skeptical Inquirer*, in which Freeman himself had featured. This was a direct attack, making Freeman and his scholarship the center of a new narrative—Freeman the misguided and unscholarly enemy of Margaret Mead, with whom he had more in common than he wished to acknowledge on the question of evolution. Shankman suggested that Freeman's attacks were driven by a devious ambition to make himself the centerpiece of the controversy, and in a new tone of contempt, Shankman dismissed Freeman as "an intellectual speedbump in the way of our understanding Samoa, the work of Margaret Mead, and the state of anthropology today."[62]

In 2009 Shankman probed more deeply into the chronology underlying Freeman's critique of Mead. He was able to expose the inconsistent narrative Freeman himself had constructed in 1983 of a mission to unseat Mead that stretched without deviation back to the 1940s. Shankman recognized that Freeman's path was "less direct and more haphazard."[63] But Shankman proceeded to ignore the complexity of memory and the variable contexts of Freeman's life that this implied, instead painting a picture of a Freeman who allegedly disliked Mead personally from the 1940s, despite not having met her yet, and was from the 1960s engaged in a conspiracy to bring her down behind her back. Freeman's sins of omission and his attempt to cover a colorful, multifaceted life with a personal story to justify his mission were made crimes with which to charge him. Shankman—like other Freeman critics—seemed to believe he could identify and condemn the motives of a twenty-something-year-old Freeman by quoting him at the age of seventy-six.

While he was alive Freeman had made several, largely ineffectual attempts to bully Shankman into submission. He never properly addressed Shankman's criticisms, talking past the latter's arguments and focusing on those aspects he could control. Their arguments about historical sources on Samoa had about them a scholastic tone in which Samoans themselves, participants and scholars alike, seemed to play little role. Freeman possessed typically unflattering views of Shankman. He was "a dyed-in-the-wool Meadophile," "unprincipled," civil on the surface, but underneath engaged in "academic skullduggery" against Freeman's views.[64]

After Freeman's death, Shankman came gradually to assume the mantle of Mead's central defender and Freeman's definitive scourge. His climactic statement came in a book eight years after Freeman's death, *The Trashing of Margaret Mead*. Modestly termed by Shankman himself as a piece of "housekeeping," not an academic endeavor, *Trashing* was in fact a thoroughgoing academic examination of the controversy and an effectual "trashing" of Derek Freeman, who became the central event around which the book revolved, though his name appeared nowhere in the book's title.[65]

The stage was set with an anti-Freeman foreword by the editor of the series, Studies in American Thought and Culture, which in itself signaled a certain nationalistic concern. Shankman proceeded to build on the "onslaught" of criticism against Mead after her death, a relentless campaign allegedly engineered by Derek Freeman and in which he was the main player.[66] Freeman, according to Shankman, had the effrontery to criticize Mead even though Freeman had written so little about Samoa himself. His campaign was the "culmination of decades of research and single-minded effort" (8), capped with a note to himself about a matchless deed, dared and done. Shankman dissected Freeman in a forensic exercise that left Mead virtually untouched; Mead was not on trial, for she was dead. But then, so was Freeman. *Trashing*, shorn of its academic apparatus, had many of the hallmarks of a show trial with Shankman as prosecutor.[67]

Thus, the media frenzy around *Margaret Mead and Samoa* became Freeman's fault, a marketing conspiracy prosecuted in a detailed plot. The reactions of American anthropologists, on the other hand, were a virtuous, puzzled stutter of righteousness to be taken at face value, with no partisanship, no agendas inherent in their attitudes to Freeman. Yet all of Freeman's deficiencies—and there were many in both argument and attitude—were apparently sleights of hand and acts of deception.

Shankman treated the contents and tone of Freeman's two books about Mead as though they were exactly the same in content and tone as the rough-and-tumble of the controversial arguments that occurred after their publication. This allowed Shankman to characterize everything about Freeman as "confrontational," "adversarial," and "an intellectual sledgehammer" (66), with Freeman displaying a highly personal dislike for Margaret Mead. Freeman's personality was made to look a finished product from the beginning, rather than a historically developing process that required probing Freeman's personal life, his interior struggles, the varied contexts for the sources from which Shankman derived his judgments. *Trashing* did not allow for contradictions and inconsistencies in a personality that had not only extreme features but also a consistent moral compass. Freeman was as much "essentialized" as Mead ever was.

Shankman, however, demolished the hoaxing argument with precise and measured skill. It was always a highly weighted gamble by Freeman to base his argument on a single evening's conversation by Mead with two Samoan women. The Heimans film and subsequent interviews with Fa'amu raised the suspicion that Freeman's own sense of absoluteness prevented him from factoring in issues of aging memories, cultural proprieties, and the "probative" significance of an oath taken at the end of the proceedings, even by a Samoan Christian. Shankman showed that many of Freeman's conclusions were in fact conjectures, interpretations rather than fact.

But Shankman and other anthropologists showed no respect for *Fateful Hoaxing* as a competent deconstruction of the varied contexts in which Mead did her work on Samoa. It is the ultimate paradox of the book that Freeman did not need to belabor the hoaxing argument. His most persuasive point was that, even with Margaret Mead's extraordinary powers of synthesis and expression, there was not enough time, nor occasions, nor statistical data underlying her fieldwork to make her definitive conclusions about growing up as an adolescent in Samoa. *Fateful Hoaxing* worked best as a historical study and a limited essay in biography, not as an anthropological breakthrough, and in it a fair-minded reader will not find the caricature of Mead that Shankman claimed.

Both *Fateful Hoaxing* and *Margaret Mead and Samoa* were on the whole well-mannered and even-tempered books. They were separate life forms from the divisive rancor that surrounded them in the pages of anthropology journals and in correspondence between Freeman and his enemies. Shankman is right about Freeman's obsessiveness over "the Mead thing," which delivered him into an intellectual cul-de-sac for the last ten years of his life. Freeman's invective against stubborn critics was real, at least in exchanges separate from his books, and it was worse at the end of his life than earlier in the controversy. But alongside the picture of the "virtuoso of the personal epithet who was energized by controversy" (56) must be balanced the insults Freeman suffered in exchanges with adversaries, some of whom implied, if they did not say so to his face, that he was "mad," "crazy," "unstable." Shankman himself was ready to reveal that these judgments had been made (counting it a courtesy to Freeman that they had not been previously published!) and to follow Hiram Caton's musings about Freeman's state of mind as evidence against him (53–55).

An air of disbelief in Freeman's sincerity pervaded *Trashing*.[68] There was no allowance for Freeman's lifetime of extreme but real moral passions; his dedication to the Samoan people; his mission for anthropology; or his skewed sense of honor, which was tied intimately to the search for "truth," idiosyncratic and self-absorbed though it was. Shankman was open and honest about the personal nature of *his* mission and brave in revealing his own experiences at the hands of Freeman. But *Trashing* is of only marginal utility in a historical understanding of Derek Freeman, of the range of his professional and workplace activities, and of his inner struggles.

While Margaret Mead was undergoing rehabilitation, Freeman in the years after his death was being progressively banished, and not only by Shankman, from the emotional community of (American) anthropologists. *The Trashing of Margaret Mead* was part of that process, not unlike the "mythic process" by which *Coming of Age in Samoa* entered into the cultural consciousness of modern America. Reviews of the book and educational media coverage supported Shankman's modest representation of his work, adopting into the bargain Hiram Caton's "diagnosis" of a narcissistic personality disorder afflicting Freeman, aided and abetted by musings spread by anthropologists on the internet.[69] Freeman had his supporters, though many anthropologists saw them as dupes of a contrived publicity campaign sustained by Freeman himself. Even Shankman indirectly credited "the Mead thing" with increasing interest in the lessons anthropology had to teach.

The debate has an assured place in the history of ideas in the twentieth century and in the history of anthropology's internecine wars. Historians of the people of the Pacific islands and of Samoa in particular can find within it object lessons about disciplinary warfare, biographical complexity, and the intellectual and emotional nature of engagement by Western scholars with what Mead's generation saw as "the primitive Other." Let Robert Louis Stevenson, who lived and died among Samoans, the patient victims of a decades-long exercise not yet ended, have the last word. Freeman quoted Stevenson in his final sortie against critics: "It is hard to reach the truth in these islands."[70]

12

"We Are Kin to All That Lives"

The final chapter of Paul Shankman's book *Trashing* seeks to belittle Derek Freeman's vision of an "interactionist anthropology." Freeman wanted anthropologists to combine aspects of the biological sciences, especially the influence of human genes, with the interpretation of cultural evolution to explain human behavior. Only then could anthropology truly lay claim to being a human science. Shankman claims that the interplay between nature and nurture had been one of the "cornerstones of American anthropology since its inception," and Freeman had misread—deliberately and systematically—both Boas's and Mead's acknowledgment that biology was a key factor in cultural behavior patterns. Freeman's two books on Mead, argues Shankman, made her into a pawn in the nature/nurture debate, with "intelligent people" interested in biology, genetics, sociobiology, and evolutionary psychology misled into believing Freeman's arguments.[1]

The anger against Freeman, as against Napoleon Chagnon, helped expose those "fractal divisions" within anthropology around the specter of racism and the notion that human nature might not be perfectible through cultural evolution. Earlier critics of his 1983 book, as we have seen, accused Freeman of being a crude sociobiologist who was soft on racism. In its entry on Margaret Mead, the *Macmillan Dictionary of Anthropology*, published in the mid-1980s, dealt with Freeman's criticisms by claiming he "attempted to exploit the weaknesses of Mead's ethnographic data in order to argue a case for the biological determination of behavior and social institutions."[2] David Williamson's play in 1996 presented Freeman's critique of Mead as explicitly the combat of biological science against the obscurantism of cultural interpretations of society. In the year of Freeman's death, Serge

Tcherkézoff was still arguing that Freeman was in danger of seeing culture as dominated by the neuropeptides of the brain.[3] Even those who did not stray so far took the line that Freeman was talking obsolete nonsense, because anthropology was already well aware of biology and active in studying its effects on culture. More than one critic used the "four fields" argument, that ever since the 1930s the discipline had been divided into four productive fields that were "interactive": ethnology or cultural anthropology, linguistics, archaeology, and physical anthropology, the latter dealing consistently with biological aspects.

In vain Freeman asserted that he abhorred racism and was no sociobiologist. And what critics claimed was "interactionism" was not what he meant. So what *did* Freeman mean, and how and where did he come to this conception of anthropology that others claimed was the core of his mission in unseating Mead?

Freeman ended both *Margaret Mead and Samoa* and *The Fateful Hoaxing of Margaret Mead*, as Shankman points out, with little lectures about the significance of biology in human behavior and the need for a new scientific prototype for anthropology. The theory of evolution by natural selection had reemerged as the "unifying paradigm" for the biological sciences, from biochemistry to ethology. *Homo sapiens*, as a primate, was, like all living things, a product of that evolution, and the coded information stored in human genes was crucial for understanding human behavior. A new pattern was emerging, driven by evolutionary biologists, geneticists, neuroscientists, and evolutionary psychologists, "in which it becomes possible to view culture in an evolutionary setting and to take account of both the genetic and the exogenetic in a way that gives due regard to the crucial importance of each."[4] It was time for anthropology to abandon the model embodied in Boas's cultural determinism and relativism and give full cognizance to biology and culture together. Freeman went on to ponder the possibilities of studying "multiple choice behavior," which, as we shall see, he tried to develop into a distinctive "anthropology of choice." This was the discipline's task for the twenty-first century.

The story line of how Freeman found this conviction and its formulation is as long and as tortuous as his journey through "the Mead thing." But, like the "official" line that he laid down in his first book on Mead, Freeman himself presents a much simpler, straightforward tale around his rejection of British structural functionalism and his conversion to an ethology-based, biocultural anthropology. This charter story is set out most coherently in the introduction to the Festschrift his students dedicated to him in 1988.

There, the "recognition of choice" was a "kind of slow fuse" that finally assumed significance for Freeman during the 1970s.[5] Freeman was very precise that the major watershed in developing his thinking was the period from July 1960 to March 1961. To that point he had worked within the framework of Boasian cultural explanations.

But Freeman was discontented on several fronts, first, because of his unhappiness at being unable to decipher the symbolic act at the center of Iban head-hunting in other than conventional Durkheimian terms. He recounted the revelation vouchsafed by Max Gluckman and Victor Turner, which, combined with the "cognitive abreaction" Freeman experienced in Sarawak, set him firmly on the track of the self-analysis that would make him a better anthropologist. At the same time he began a systematic reading into the fields of ethology, evolutionary biology, primatology, the neurosciences, psychology, and genetics. He had discovered that his approach to the science of man was that of the "natural historian" (23) and that evolution and biology were the basis for understanding humans: "We must begin with the human animal, and never let him slip from our sight when studying social systems" (24).

This new position meant Freeman abandoning cultural relativism and the Durkheimian notion dominant in British anthropology that culture explained itself in cultural terms only. Drawing a veil over his flirtation with psychoanalysis in London, Freeman's official tale highlights his growing in ethological knowledge; the crucial encounters with Konrad Lorenz, Irenäus Eibl-Eibesfeldt, and Nikolaas Tinbergen; and the behavioral research on primates he began tentatively at the London Zoo.

As we have seen, after his return to Australia in 1964 Freeman took this naturalistic approach to psychiatrists' conferences to test his ideas, the 1965 experience in Melbourne, where he was attacked for his paper on Freud, leaving him unnerved and emotionally bruised. He was convinced thereafter that psychoanalysis was "very much a belief system in which doctrine was accepted merely on authority" (31) and consequently inimical to scientific understanding. From this time on, Freeman became enthralled with the ideas of Karl Popper and their relevance to the scientific method.

Freeman's conviction of the importance of ethological approaches met stiff resistance among anthropologist colleagues in Canberra, but that resistance did not derail him. In Western Samoa in 1966–67, he studied attachment behavior among children and discovered the serious deficiencies of Margaret Mead's account of Samoan society (Freeman does not mention the trauma he experienced on Ta'u in this official story line). On his return to Australia, Freeman was increasingly critical of social and cultural anthropology in general. He began arguing for a new "interactionist paradigm . . . that gives recognition to genetical and environmental feedback and interaction both in the ontogeny of individual organisms and in the phylogeny of breeding populations" (35). By the 1970s these calls had become more frequent, and Freeman was beginning to emphasize the human capacity to make choices as the focus for future studies. He laid out his thinking on choice behavior to the Australian and New Zealand Association for the Advancement of Science (ANZAAS) conference of 1979, but from that point on Freeman became caught up in the controversy over his first Mead book.

This "official" story ends in 1988, with Freeman hoping his work on Mead will become "a landmark portending a significant, paradigmatic shift in the theoretical perspective of anthropological inquiry" (48). Once "the Mead thing" was resolved he wanted to get back to the study of his seminal proposition: "In that a wise and free choice is a creative act determined at the moment it is exercised, it will be necessary to develop a scientific paradigm able to accommodate choice as an independent variable" (49). We know he never did. Nor did he reach this point without many twists and turns in his thinking amid struggles to persuade fellow anthropologists—and a range of scientists in other fields, including psychiatry—that he was on to something different from the classic "four fields" approach.

It is important to reiterate that Freeman took an authentic, giant leap of faith into an alternative way of thinking from his position in a comfortable, well-respected career. His intellectual anxiety over the deficiencies of the anthropology in which he had been trained, his struggles to explain the meaning of Iban head-hunting rituals in other than symbolic terms, the "Kierkegaardian earthquake" he experienced in Borneo—all these events contributed to the recentering of his mind and set him on this new path. "I think I walked out of the cave in 1961," he told Don Tuzin in 2000. "I had this blinding kind of thing when I looked at people at the airport and saw that everything . . . , I was seeing it in different behavioral terms."[6] And he remained remarkably consistent in sketching out the sequence and consequences of his great epiphany, whether in the "authorized" version laid down in Appell and Madan or in correspondence with colleagues such as Ernest Beaglehole, Raymond Firth, Edmund Leach, Rodney Needham, and the writer Judith Heimann.

Freeman maintained his stance despite opposition from various quarters. Besides unsympathetic colleagues in Canberra, he was acquiring American critics, especially David Schneider at the University of Chicago, who would later join the throng attacking Freeman's 1983 book. In 1963 Schneider and Freeman were tussling over the latter's turn away from the structuralist study of kinship, which had helped cement his international reputation. Schneider was unimpressed with Freeman's biological turn and scornful of his plans to do ethological studies in Samoa. Equally significant for helping explain the reception Freeman received in 1983 was the beginnings of a ridiculing tone in Freeman's correspondence, which only provoked Schneider.[7]

Meyer Fortes was another who never accepted his star pupil's turning his back on social anthropology. Fortes remained sympathetic to Freeman's intellectual strivings but expressed a fundamental disquiet about ethologically based studies of human behavior. Humans had rules that Fortes could not see existed among primates of the forest: "I am still nervous of jumping straight from the wordless, physiologically based discontinuous 'dominance' of the ape or baboon family head so-called to Hitler." Fortes also thought Freeman's heroes—Lorenz, Tinbergen, and Julian Huxley—were naïve about human affairs.[8]

"Human Nature and Culture" was the beginning of a series of papers to proclaim his new vision that Freeman gave in seminars or published in journals during the 1960s and 1970s. He would not be moved by Fortes's gentle observation that Freeman's argument was "empty of the kind of significance I find in, let us say, the discoveries of Mendel a hundred years ago or the experimental work of the Harlows. Forgive me if I say that it seems to me your paper is full of such generalizations of width and little specificity."[9] Freeman was unapologetic in return: generalizations were his intention. They were no broader than—indeed, they were a world removed from—those of Boas and Alfred Kroeber and were based on a mass of experimental evidence from the biological and evolutionary sciences, which anthropologists were yet to take seriously. Freeman had specific data from his Samoa researches, which he would eventually publish. At least he was talking to biologists as an anthropologist in a common scientific language: "It might be argued that anthropology is in no need of a new paradigm, and there are many, as I well know, who are well content with the cosy comfort of a closed system. For my part I have quite a different vision of the kind of science that anthropology might be, and, in my judgment, we have no choice but to come to terms with the momentous advances in the biological sciences of recent years."[10]

In America the Cold War and the hunt for un-American activities had already begun to implicate liberal intellectuals and social scientists, drawing in the anthropologists. There were precedents for the AAA's outburst against Freeman in 1983, in divisive debates and votes during AAA meetings from the 1950s, over the organization's failure to support anthropologists caught up in McCarthyite accusations of Communist influence. The Vietnam War in the 1960s saw similar divisiveness, involving, ironically, criticisms of Margaret Mead for her support of counterinsurgency work in Southeast Asia.[11] Hand in hand with this dissension went what Eric Wolf called "universalizing and scientizing tendencies" in the social sciences, which led by one path to the return of sociobiology as a flash point among anthropologists.[12]

Historian of anthropology George Stocking says the 1960s saw in America the onset of "the 'crisis of anthropology': an interrelated series of observational, methodological, epistemological, theoretical, ethical, and demographic problems."[13] In 1961 Margaret Mead had identified five areas where anthropologists had failed to grasp hands with other disciplines. They included cybernetic model building around the central nervous system, ethology, genetics, and evolution. Physical anthropology—the field closest to the biological—was one of the areas that, according to zoologist and physical anthropologist Sherwood Washburn, was a matter merely of measurement and description, with no experimental method and little interest in probing primate behavior.[14]

But evolution was in the air. Crick and Watson had discovered the double helix structure of the DNA molecule. *American Anthropologist* had begun publishing articles on human genetics—Theodosius Dobzhansky, the evolutionary biologist, published there on the operations of natural selection on human beings. Nobel Prize biologist Peter Medawar's 1959 book, *The Future of Man*, with its positive vision of population genetics and general biology, was favorably reviewed.[15]

Down in Canberra, Australia, Freeman was beginning exactly the cross-disciplinary explorations that Margaret Mead had called for in 1961. His poetry writing, indulged since the 1930s, became a sacrifice to his new scientific mission and mind-set: "I realized that it really didn't have to do with the truth, that the truth lay somewhere else." This was the period in which he began to acquire a reputation for relentless questioning in seminars and a deep seriousness that would not let others off the hook. In 1959 his paper "Social Anthropology as a Form of Nomothetic Enquiry" had been full of Alfred Radcliffe-Brown's structuralism and "high-flown social anthropology of that period." By 1962 and his return from Borneo, Freeman was repudiating that paper as "entirely mistaken and wrong-headed."[16]

He began writing reviews of works on human evolution and produced a paper, "Human Aggression in Anthropological Perspective," which he gave to the Institute of Biology in London during 1963. In 1964, the year of his brush with Margaret Mead in Canberra, he presented a paper to the Australian and New Zealand College of Psychiatrists on psychiatry, anthropology, and cultural relativism;[17] the next year he had his more serious confrontation in Melbourne. He was also taping the cries of apes and playing them in Canberra's city center to test people's reactions: observing the human animal was part of the tool kit he was developing. Contrary to the view of later critics who see him only through the lens of the war over Mead, Freeman was interested in much more than Mead and working on several fronts.

The statement in which Freeman nailed his new colors to the mast after his "awakening" was the 1966 paper "Social Anthropology and the Scientific Study of Human Behavior," drafted in Samoa. He published it in *Man*, the journal of the Royal Anthropological Society of Great Britain, at the heart of the British tradition of social anthropology, in which he had been trained. Derek began by dismissing Max Gluckman's "closed system" approach to the study of human beings. His new heroes were Huxley, Tinbergen, Harry Harlow, and the behavioral scientists, among whom he counted himself—indeed all anthropologists. Although in later years he dismissed Émile Durkheim outright for his view that there were "social facts" separate from psychological and biological facts, here Freeman took the softer view that there were not only social facts but "phylogenetically based forms of social response which decisively determine . . . the course of social behavior." It was a cardinal error to oppose the two types of behavior as though they were entirely distinct. Durkheim's "procedural rule" that social facts can only be explained by other social facts must be abandoned in favor of ethological observations of human behavior and the use of evolution theory. Behavior came before culture: "Socially inherited customs (in Durkheim's sense) must have gradually evolved from the phylogenetically given behavioral repertoire of the hominids."[18]

This was the paper that prompted Freeman's colleague Bill Stanner to oppose Freeman's new direction and try to limit funding for his research in Samoa. Freeman claimed that Stanner was ready for him when he gave the paper in the department in 1965: "When I'd finished talking he put his hand in his waistcoat and drew out a critique of it, which he had obviously prepared before he'd heard it. I said to him, 'You didn't even listen to what I said.' The bottom fell out of that seminar."[19] There is a characteristic lack of self-insight in Freeman's triumphalism over this incident: he had made the point in his paper that social rules were best studied "in the breach," when the behavioral proclivity against which the rule was a defense showed itself most explicitly. Stanner's behavior may have been exposed, but Freeman did not seem to notice his own behavior and his determination to dominate his colleague; his diary notes pass over the incident with a resigned shrug.

Derek went to Samoa at the end of 1965 to test theories on human behavior. That was his prime goal, rather than Margaret Mead. He spent hundreds of hours observing the ritual rivalries and dominance behavior of the Samoan *matai*, the lineage title-holders, and the attachment behavior of children in Saʻanapu "within a frame of reference derived from ethology, social anthropology, psychoanalysis and various cognate disciplines," as he told Meyer Fortes.[20] We know that his findings about Margaret Mead and the traumas that this set in train led him to concentrate on his refutation when he arrived back in Australia. But we also know that he returned more convinced than ever that social customs and the symbolisms embedded in cultures were intimately connected to biologically derived behaviors.

Freeman was also continuing to process his Iban materials and to follow his psychoanalytical interests while preparing the ground for his Mead campaign. A trilogy of essays appeared in the late 1960s in which Freeman seems to be working out his early ideas on the road to his "anthropology of choice." The first, the conference paper that caused such outrage among the psychiatrists in 1965, asserted that several of Freud's assumptions about early humans' living arrangements and the real, historical basis of the Oedipal neurosis were mistaken.[21] A series of phylogenetically given impulses— the sexual drive, dominance, aggression, and fear—could be traced back to our remote primate ancestors, and these impulses, together with the symbolizing brain as it evolved, led to social practices, dreams, and fantasies passed down through the ages. Rivalry, contention, and struggles for dominance, especially between sons and fathers, were intrinsic to human nature. Freeman may as well have been thinking about his own nature and his relations with his parents. The paper reads like an intellectual substitute for the therapy Freeman had undergone—and broken off—in London. It records his recognition of the "naturalness" of dominance behavior, which he was at the very same time attempting to inhibit in his own relationships.

The second paper, "Shaman and Incubus," reveals a driving narrative style that distinguishes Freeman at his ethnographic storytelling best. It is an eye-witness account of an Iban shaman, Manang Bungai, attempting to slay an incubus molesting an Iban woman through her dreams. Freeman explains its evolutionary relevance: "I hope to reach a sympathetic under-standing of the mystical notions of the Iban and of the social role of the shaman, as well as a naturalistic explanation of a cultural adaptation which in evolutionary terms is of an archaic kind." Freeman goes on to apply a psychoanalytic approach to the incubus as "a cultural precipitate of this kind of dream"—behavior before culture again—and to document the "dominance strivings" of the Iban. In an essay where Freeman demonstrates a new level of learned, specialized vocabulary, his characters nonetheless have a lively, rounded quality in their cultural form.[22]

The final essay in the series carried the dramatic title "Thunder, Blood and the Nicknaming of God's Creatures." This was a play on both the title of an influential essay by Rodney Needham on the Penan of Borneo and a line from Shakespeare's *Hamlet*. Freeman pondered the phenomenon of the Semang people of Malaya stabbing at their legs to draw blood during tropical thunderstorms, then scattering the blood mixed with water to the sky gods to stop the storm. In a wide-ranging, eloquent essay replete with comparative examples and references to Melanie Klein, Dante, Shakespeare, Aristophanes, and the poet Dylan Thomas, Freeman argued that "human projective beliefs about thunderstorms have been evolved from a similar kind of emotional response in the proto-hominids."[23]

This essay was Freeman's most developed exploration of the link between culture and primordial impulses in the brain and emotions. Al-though it ends without any general resolution, it was the closest Freeman came to the kind of interactionist study he spent the next two decades wishing upon anthropology. He was ahead of most anthropologists in the 1960s in trying to bring together biological and cultural themes in a con-temporary case study. Indicative of the times, though, Freeman had again to place the article with a psychoanalysis journal, for *Current Anthropology* would not publish it, claiming the "comparative method" was no longer acceptable.[24]

Freeman was writing at full speed during these years, enough to fill "10 PhDs," he claimed in his diary, and switching direction with seeming ease: from his critiques of orthodox social anthropology to tilts at Mead and Boas, an essay in defense of Charles Darwin, a study of dominance behavior among Samoan *matai*, even a tentative start to an article on Oedipus in Samoa. He was taking initiatives to drive forward his vision for the new anthropology. In 1969 ANU created a series of open lectures titled Man and the New Biology, which, under Freeman's influence, would explore the implications of recent advances in the biological sciences. "We'll get a planck [*sic*] across Kroeber's 'eternal chasm' yet!" he crowed to a friend.[25]

Freeman was invited to give the last lecture, which became the essay Fortes frowned upon: "Human Nature and Culture," published in 1970. In it Freeman declared evolution as the unifying paradigm of all the biological sciences. He showed how Franz Boas had departed from Darwin in the 1920s and why Darwin must rise again, flanked by the new generation of scientific heroes like Dobzhansky and Washburn. Human beings were not tabulae rasae at birth but intrinsically variable, courtesy of their genes, before culture began its differentiating work. Of all the primates, *Homo sapiens* was an "embodied paradox" of primitive brain stem and advanced neurological processes, which enabled humans to "exercise preferences," that is, to make choices. Where choice was concerned, values were also inescapable, and a science of human values based on human adaptive choices was a rich prospect for anthropologists, according to Freeman.[26]

Fortes may have made his disapproval apparent, but some colleagues at ANU congratulated Freeman for the combination of anthropology, history, science, and philosophy he was able to mix so eruditely. Tinbergen wrote him that plenty of people in Oxford were "vividly interested" in his work. Hiram Caton later identified this essay as "the anchor" of a half-dozen essays over the next decade dealing with anthropology's mission to integrate natural evolution and culture into a unified science. They were conveyed in a "voice of reckoning" that would distinguish Freeman in the coming controversies.[27]

The 1970s contained reckonings of another kind. His dark years of administrative upsets, alleged betrayals by close colleagues, and accusations that he was "mad," not just eccentric, led Freeman twice to try to have his professorship redesignated away from anthropology and into biology; both attempts were unsuccessful (see chapter 7). Freeman plowed on, continuing to immerse himself in the scholarship of population and behavioral genetics and to study the history of his discipline's alleged turn away from the integrative science he now championed. He joined the Human Biology Group, made up of natural scientists. After he became head of his department he founded an ethology laboratory, though encountering resistance from within and without. He was also building up ideas for his Mead refutation, which he had flagged in his 1968 paper "On the Believing of as Many as Six Impossible Things before Breakfast." Margaret Mead visited Canberra again in 1971, though this time Freeman did not meet with her. He was instead critical of her declaring that anthropologists' informants were sacred, and if they did not want to answer questions, then the anthropologist was finished. "That's an extraordinary admission," Freeman told Tuzin, "because if you're an ethologist, you don't begin with the informants, you begin with the behavior."[28]

The ANZAAS symposium of 1972 on ethology and human behavior firmed up his conviction that the key to a successful anthropology on the new platform was to focus on human choice behavior as a biological phenomenon. He had heard the Nobel Prize virologist Frank Macfarlane Burnet say as much at the meeting; Burnet was impressed with Freeman's ideas. The next year a Nobel Prize for Konrad Lorenz and Tinbergen legitimized the new field of ethology and convinced Freeman he was part of the coming wave. He published papers on aggression as instinct and on anthropology as both scientific and humanistic, and in 1978 he gave a seminar in Sydney, "A Precursory View of the Anthropology of Choice." In it he explored the origins of the human capacity to make choices and declared anthropology to be both a moral and a natural science. "Choice" as the secret to humans' evolutionary history was still far from an acceptable idea, especially among scientists: the year before, Freeman had been refused permission to speak on choice at an ethology conference in West Germany.[29]

Freeman gradually became disillusioned with Konrad Lorenz's more deterministic view of the effects of biology on behavior. It caused him an uneasy ambivalence, for they had had "a kind of friendship" since 1963. But not even friendship could trump Freeman's zeal for truth.[30] He was also actively involved in the intense controversy that exploded with the publication of E. O. Wilson's *Sociobiology* in 1976.

Freeman's contribution to the debate was a chapter in Ashley Montagu's 1980 book, *Sociobiology Examined*, in which he argued against the closed behavioral programs of the sociobiologists while holding to a scientific materialist approach in favor of evolution. He rejected Wilson's genetic determinism and argued that humans had a highly developed capacity to make choices. That was "one of the defining characteristics of the human ethogram." Most importantly, the human capacity to learn came through the "exogenetic process" of cultural choices that led to cultural adaptations, which, in turn, led to evolutionary changes in the human brain. Sociobiologists failed in not taking account of cultural variables and in trying to reduce everything to genetic information. "Was there ever such pseudoscientific flummery?" Freeman exclaimed of some of their grosser claims. He was specifically critical of Wilson's contention that "the genes hold culture on a leash."[31]

Freeman was aware of the irony in the journey he had made to this point. In the 1960s he found himself trying to show "cultural determinists and structuralists" that they could not leave out the biological. Now, in the late 1970s and 1980s his task seemed to be to try to convince sociobiologists that they could not comprehend human action while ignoring the "exogenetic."[32] That did not save him from being accused of being a fellow traveler because of *Margaret Mead and Samoa* in the 1980s and in particular of being an ally of E. O. Wilson.

Wilson's 1976 book brought out the kind of militant response from anthropologists that Freeman himself would suffer nearly a decade later and under the same imprint of Harvard University Press. A survey of anthropologists across the four fields in 1989 found that fewer than half of cultural anthropologists accepted core sociobiological concepts, though most accepted some interaction between genes and environment. Wilson wanted to push evolutionary biology into the mainstream of the human sciences, including anthropology. Instead he found himself attacked by what he called a Marxist-influenced antiscience movement at his own university, Harvard, with water thrown over him at the annual conference of the American Association for the Advancement of Science and students invading his classes to demand his dismissal. Even his colleagues on the Harvard faculty, some of whom privately sympathized with what he was saying, showed him little or no open support.[33]

Freeman's own relationship with the American "father of sociobiology" remained an up-and-down affair that often provoked both men's enemies. He seems to have made his first encounter with Wilson's work through Douglas Oliver, who gave Freeman a paper in 1974 on human evolution. Initially, he was excited by the biological arguments but became as disillusioned as most anthropologists by Wilson's *Sociobiology* and his *On Human Nature* for their biological reductionism.[34] He wrote to Wilson, and they began a correspondence that lasted throughout the next two decades, increasing in warmth. Wilson finally agreed with Freeman that choice by humans was a critical factor he had not allowed for. Derek was flattered by Wilson's likening them to the hedgehog and the fox—Wilson the hedgehog who knew one big thing, Freeman the fox who knew many things.

When Freeman visited the United States on his book tour in 1983, the one Harvard celebrity he asked to see was Wilson, and they talked long and hard, although without finding total agreement. But Freeman berated those anthropologists who dared snigger at the mention of Wilson's name, because Wilson was at least ready to change his mind. They remained friends, and Wilson became one of Freeman's staunchest supporters in the resistance to his Mead book, exchanging letters sometimes two or three times a week.[35]

Considering Freeman's decades-long background of work and thought on a new anthropology, his *Margaret Mead and Samoa* of 1983 can be judged a missed opportunity, though his critics did not see it that way. Amid his explanation of what his refutation was intended to do, Freeman's additional goal of arguing that a new, more scientific paradigm must replace the "antiquated doctrine" of cultural determinism occupied only two lines in his opening. His actual argument was his last chapter, a mere nine pages in a large book, containing his now-standard refrains about evolution as the unifying paradigm, the importance of genetic codes alongside culture, how anthropologists must change, and why multiple choice behavior was the area with the best prospects for human scientists to explore. The effect of placing this addendum at the back of the book, as Gil Herdt, anthropologist and shrewd judge of what Freeman was trying to do, understood, was to bury a key part of his critique: the need to look critically at what constitutes anthropological knowledge.[36]

Although, as we have seen, most of the hostile catcalls against Freeman and his book were related to his criticisms of Mead, few missed targeting for extra condemnation what was essentially a coda. They ranged from the most arguable, frequent objection, which was that Freeman had misread Boas's downplaying of the biological and that the four-fields approach constituted a long and honorable record of "interactive" anthropology, to Mary Catherine Bateson's bizarre suggestion that Freeman was drawn to sex and violence, the message seemingly being that this was his behavioral obsession.[37]

Ivan Brady, in introducing the special forum on Freeman's book in *American Anthropologist*, recognized that to dwell on the issue of biological determinism was inappropriate. However, this did not stop Martin Silverman in the same issue from cynically claiming that the book's "popular subtext" was that common sense dictated that biology had a role in Samoan adolescent behavior. Silverman expected Freeman to provide this evidence. So did Lowell Holmes, both in his reviews and in his later book on the controversy. Nancy McDowell condescendingly claimed that a Cambridge, UK, scholar (meaning Freeman) would not necessarily know that the new paradigm was already in action among physical and biological anthropologists in America. Several American anthropologists, like Nancy Scheper-Hughes and Eleanor Leacock, feared that the specter of social Darwinism or, worse, racism lurking in the biological arguments would rise from the miasma if not exorcised at once.[38]

Anthropologists had been "startled" by how the public reacted to Richard Dawkins's "selfish gene" message and to E. O. Wilson's ambitious arguments. Hiram Caton was not the first to point out that the dust jacket of *Margaret Mead and Samoa* carried endorsements by a range of biologists and ethologists—Tinbergen, Ernst Mayr, John Pfeiffer—or that the *New York Times* article that started it all highlighted the nature/nurture arguments that might arise from Freeman's work. Caton was right that biological explanations for human behavior had become more visible by the 1980s. The opening to biology had been happening in the social sciences since the 1950s, especially in sociology. By the 1980s, most research was being done outside sociology, among ethologists and primatologists; even political scientists were turning to the view that evolutionary theory based on biology might offer new insights. Historian Carl Degler notes that genetics research, freed from its dubious association with eugenics, was making giant advances into the mystery of heredity.[39]

Therefore, had he made more of his interactive argument in the body of *Margaret Mead and Samoa*, Freeman would have had oracles on whom to draw and a body of literature at hand. But he did not. That final chapter acted for Freeman's many critics as a no-longer-original afterthought, a distraction from the main message of the refutation, and an added gallows on which to hang him. Don Tuzin was right that the book needed a different title.

The Fateful Hoaxing of Margaret Mead fifteen years later failed to correct Freeman's mistake, simply repeating, with slight variation, the urging on anthropology to follow the new route to an integrated human science. In the interval, Freeman's "anthropology of choice" remained a sketch for a program, a vision, rather than a concrete, testable possibility, at least in his hands.

The vision had already been brought half to life in 1979, in that nervous presidential address to the ANZAAS conference in Auckland.[40] It fastened on the question: What was humanity's ultimate nature? The study of human beings remained riven over the answer, said Freeman, neither Mead nor Wilson providing the ultimate clue. That answer lay in linking biology and culture through human choice behavior, "both intrinsic to our biology and basic to the very formation of cultures." Freeman pointed out that Richard Dawkins himself agreed with him that the human capacity to make choices was the fundamental starting point. Choice was a biological phenomenon, "phylogenetically given," since human choice behavior was different from the instrumental choices primates made. It emerged from the decisions early hunting and gathering humans had to make to survive. Those choices in time created strong selective pressures for the evolution, through genetic flows, of the biological capacities required to develop technological and cultural innovations. The key was language, with its own biological basis. Humans transformed into "a *zoon phonanta* or language animal." From that point on, roughly forty thousand years BCE, human evolutionary history became mainly cultural. The key for a "scientifically informed and humane anthropology" in the present day was to apply a critical approach to cultural practices and values. Some choices in some cultures had negative and destructive effects—this was Freeman's answer to the cultural relativists among anthropologists who argued that cultures were not open to critical evaluation or to one universal set of value judgments. Wrong, said Freeman: a human being was "a self-defining animal" worthy of a scientific, moral anthropology that viewed cultures as "experiments in living" so that "we might gradually learn to select our values with greater wisdom."

This was as much a philosophical as a social scientific argument. A curious disjunction exists between Freeman's sense of the ideal anthropology as a moral undertaking judging between humane cultural values and his view, stridently proclaimed over decades, of anthropology as a science rooted in causal laws and possible universals. Freeman normally clung to a rather legalistic, narrow view of the truths a scientific anthropology presented in the testing of propositions—witness his faith in the statements of Faʻamu Faʻapuaʻa under oath. He was confident that ethnological science was not a belief system but a process grounded "in the art of unclouded observation." In defending his Mead work to George Stocking, Freeman claimed that his own psychoanalytical experience had protected him from observer bias. That was why he could not understand the failure of his enemies to accept his ever-mounting evidence against the methods and findings of Mead; he attributed it to fixations in their brains.[41]

When Stocking accused him of possessing a "strident scientism," Freeman protested, challenging Stocking to quote examples back to him; the Popperian master logician would not tolerate inexactitude in descriptions of his style of argument. Yet in his adoration of Popper, Freeman missed Popper's subtleties about historical events, which Popper argued were not governed by laws or testable propositions; even natural science, said Popper, was explained more by "trend-like regularities" than laws.[42] Freeman, for his part, seemed incapable of accepting people's inconsistencies or recognizing that scholarly life was littered with contradictions. When Stocking ruefully warned him that the world was full of paradoxes vis-à-vis truth and facts, Freeman responded: "The world may well, as you say, be 'full of paradoxes.' The work of scholars, surely, should never be."[43]

Predictably, therefore, Freeman was no friend of the trend to reflexive, interpretive anthropology associated with the postmodern condition that gripped all the social sciences and the humanities from the 1970s onward. The idea of culture, especially in America, had been for more than a century "the single most powerful cohesive force in anthropological enquiry."[44] Culture had developed a particularly idealist conception as a set of patterns, ideas, and values expressed in symbols that was peculiarly open to subversion by the linguistic turn flowing out of Europe. The dissolving of old certainties about reality manifest in philosophical and linguistic discourse, the highlighting of authorial strategies, the fictive qualities of textual production itself—all plunged the social sciences, anthropology especially, into a period of instability that straddled the generations. How best to reconstruct fieldwork in the text when exotic otherness was now an insult on the page and due attention must be paid to the subjectivity of the observer and the intersubjectivity of the observation process?[45]

Much of this was not central to Freeman's earlier scientistic form of ethnographic representation and analysis; indeed, the postmodern approach was anathema to it. Although some of his oldest colleagues, like Raymond Firth, could recognize the intellectual justification for such changes, others saw in the new developments a form of questionable alchemy, producing a babel of voices and a loss of ethnographic will; Eric Wolf thought the developments signaled a Zen Buddhist–like withdrawal from a fraught world. For his part, Freeman deplored the slide of ethnography into multiple texts and multiple selves. He thoroughly rejected the statement by James Clifford and George Marcus in their seminal text for the new age, *Writing Culture*, that his picture of Samoa was another Western myth, as authentic an allegory concerning human nature as was Margaret Mead's. One irony in the host of ironies surrounding Freeman's sustained war with anthropologists was that he had more in common with an avowed critic like Adam Kuper over the true nature of anthropological thought and practice than he (or Kuper) would ever admit.[46]

Freeman only joined the debates on the fringes. When AAA asked him to write something for its newsletter on the subject, he pleaded that he was too busy trying to finish the *Hoaxing* book, adding that Clifford Geertz and Roy Rappaport were scared of "science in anthropology" and "thick" on "thick description." Geertz, whom Freeman could never truly draw into debating with him, he saw as central to the "demonstrably false assumptions" of the American school of cultural anthropology; he was a "word monger," Freeman told an American PhD student studying in Canberra. He never forgave Geertz his claim that the human nervous system was as cultural a product as ideas and values.[47] After hearing a talk by George Marcus in Canberra in 1989, Freeman wrote it off in his diary as "the most ghastly rhetorical and barmecidal bilge, ie. he suffers from superfetation of the left hemisphere evinced as logorrhea & post-modernist gibberish; I tell him that he is the great mischief & and will in time became a mere curiosity."[48]

Freeman the "truthmonger" felt less under siege than most. He might agree with Andrew Strathern that postmodernism had created a crisis within anthropology that went beyond Boasian cultural relativism, but again he felt protected by the analysis he had done on himself. Freeman remained unrealistically confident that none of his evidence in his arguments over Mead could possibly be affected by any projection of his personality.[49]

Although Freeman later decided "holistic" was a better epithet than "interactionist" for the kind of anthropology he was advocating, and he published a much elaborated version in Caton's *Samoa Reader*,[50] his "mission statement" remained essentially the same into the last years of his life. He kept noting in his diary the prospect of a "New Anthropological Ark" and wanted ten more years to complete this project. There was his momentary excitement in 1990 when Jonas Salk seemed to be offering him a base at the Salk Institute in San Diego to develop the new field of "Humanology." He was prepared to move there to make that happen, but, as we have seen, nothing came of it. Twelve months later his "Paradigms in Collision" proclaimed another moment ripe for revolution with the collapse of the Soviet Union. He saw in it vindication that the Boas-Meadian belief that human nature was entirely malleable in favor of some grand social design was deeply flawed. The time was "conspicuously at hand" for the new paradigm to triumph. Hiram Caton was urging Freeman to join him in a "new revolutions project" to trace what Caton called "the ethology of the crowd."[51]

All to no avail. *The Fateful Hoaxing* absorbed the months and years Freeman would have had to devote to another retraining in order to produce an ethnographic example of his holistic approach. He was also following new and distracting trails in pondering how humans chose to do "right," or what made biological sense. This led him to the thymus, whose significance he had picked up from the writings of John Diamond and Frank Macfarlane Burnet. The same route led him to behavioral kinesiology and the testing of muscles against a range of stimuli to produce physical and emotional effects. He began testing himself and Monica against a range of foods, chemicals, plants, even people, much to the bemusement of colleagues.[52] This was Freeman's way of searching for mechanisms that might mediate the interaction between genetic and "exogenetic" information.

It was a serious endeavor on Freeman's part to follow the problem where it led in the sense he had learned from Siegfried Nadel while he was simultaneously wrestling with the second phase of his Mead campaign. His interest in the physical workings of body and mind also helped address the problem of a system of ethics to complement his evolutionary worldview. Freeman had worked his way to a materialist view of the cosmos from his early Presbyterianism at about the age of fifteen. He rejected a personal God, even the kind of deism that E. O. Wilson was content to consider. Krishnamurti had taught him to spring-clean his mind of the world's fantasies—he was still doing that regularly in his seventies—and gradually, through an early influence on his evolutionary thinking, the agnostic Thomas Henry Huxley, he was drawn to Zen Buddhism.

Huxley, whom Freeman saw as the true founder of interactionist anthropology, recognized that evolution could not provide a foundation for morals. Humans must construct their ethical systems for themselves. In his Romanes Lecture of 1893, "Evolution and Ethics," Huxley chose Buddhism as an example of a value system that could combat the cosmic processes of natural selection. Buddhism encouraged the mental habits that helped conquer the appetites and passions of the body. Buddhism cultivated an active skepticism that was the essence of the scientific spirit. Through Buddhist practice one strove to acquire the freedom to choose as one ought to choose.[53]

Thus, in the final decade of Freeman's life, Buddhism became the mix of ideas and practice that best suited his personal attempt to marry nature and nurture. It also armed him in his struggle to rid himself of the continuing impulse to dominate others. The will to overcome the dominating self was very much an old mantra. Ever since the 1970s and the diagnosis of a bipolar condition, Freeman had fought to maintain himself on a plateau with the help of inhibitory behavior and active choices. He continued to exist on the edge of that plateau, relentlessly workshopping his mind, taking one step forward in self-knowledge and two back. At times he practiced "age regression" in discussions with Monica, identifying "blockages" in individuals and experiences that haunted his past. Whether valid or not, these exercises helped to reveal so-called preconscious memories stretching back to childhood that kept eating away at Freeman.[54]

Many of his early strategies were mechanical. They found expression in listening to music, in meditative moments within the calming sanctuary of his home, and in the carrying of small objects, his "mood prompts." These objects included a Samoan adze blade he excavated in Samoa on his first visit in 1940, a pebble from the Thinking Path at Charles Darwin's home, a *vajra*, or Hindu brass wand, used to hurl thunderbolts against Shiva's enemies. He didn't "worship" objects, wrote Tuzin, but he found these pieces "useful as mnemonics and attention focusers."[55] Again, brain function and cultural adaptation blended together to create efficacious symbols. Buddhist practices gave him a way of trying out new ways to be the whole human being he valiantly struggled to be. Already at the beginning of the 1980s he was writing in his diary: "I want as far as I can to become ever more resigned and indifferent to, and, at the same time, accepting of, the 'murmurous world.' . . . I must have then wit and wisdom to direct my energies to the realization of a more cohesive self, that is very much *in* the world (in a Zen sense) but not of that world which is not of my making."[56]

A decade later, in 1989, on the fiftieth anniversary of his first meeting with Krishnamurti, Freeman was still articulating that mission to himself and seeking understanding from a visiting Buddhist monk. But within a year he was crowing in his diary at a perceived triumph over Adam Kuper in one of their testy exchanges: "He is mine! and obviously seared."[57] His gloating was instantly succeeded by new resolutions to reject such behavior in the future.

The year 1990 is the last for which we have summaries of Freeman's diaries, but there is no reason to believe his diaries for the last ten years of his life do not continue to document this battle with himself, evident since the 1960s. When, after *The Samoa Reader* came out, Hiram Caton raised a toast—"here's to dominance, may it ever increase"—Freeman refused to drink. "See, that's the Huxley point," he told Don Tuzin. "Dominance is something we have to control, not . . . 'may it ever increase.'" For all his appreciation of Buddhism and attempts to harness its ways of being in the world, Freeman remained the scientific materialist. That was his real "theology," he told Tuzin at the end of his life: "All you can do is recover core consciousness and be in the world, and that's it. . . . All I know is that evolution occurred and it's not God that made the Genome. It's G-O-D, generation-of-diversity, which is natural selection and it just happens to be how the world is."[58]

The completion of a rough draft of the human genome in June 2000, a year before his death, was a red-letter day for Freeman. In it he saw the triumph of Darwinian method and philosophy, a scientific breakthrough that won the case for an unassailable biological appreciation of the underpinnings of culture. Freeman believed it signified the bankruptcy of Boasian culturalism, and he would brook no protest by Don Tuzin that antievolutionists and creationists in the United States would fight bitterly to resist its implications for understanding human nature. Anthropology had to change. This was its chance to become that moral science, exploring the biocultural mechanisms of choice and their consequences for humankind. He called it "the anthropology of wisdom . . . an analysis and an examination of the consequences of certain choices," which sounded a lot like old-fashioned moral philosophy and the place he was moving to in the end.[59]

Freeman could rightly regard himself as a precursor to all that, an early anthropologist pioneer of such integrated thinking, even if it involved struggling against the worst aspects of himself in the process. In his eighty-fourth year he was still of a mind to "have a crack" at moving evolutionary biologists beyond their determinisms and bringing the accelerating discoveries of the neurosciences into anthropological data. He did not live to see the criticism of his failure to bring any of this to fruition or the dismissal of his ideas as already out of date. As Freeman was wrestling with the Meadites over his refutation of Mead in 1984, Paul Shankman was writing in another context: "As theory watchers in anthropology know, anticipation and the contemplation of possibility are only the first tentative steps in the stalking of the elusive paradigm shift."[60] Shankman was speaking about Clifford Geertz's effect on the theoretical ground upon which cultural anthropology worked. But, paradoxically, he might well have applied it at the other end of the spectrum, to the paradigm-shifting aspirations of Derek Freeman, whose work Shankman would diminish after Freeman's death.

Conclusion
Truth's Fool?

"Truth's fool" was Derek Freeman's self-chosen appellation. He was in-ordinately proud of and very stubborn about his reputation as the one who would brook no fooling with the "truth," and he was continually assuring his university colleagues that he spoke "the complete truth and only the truth."[1] He was the jester at the court of cultural anthropology, teasing and taunting the royalty of the discipline with realities they did not want to hear.

Some anthropologists accepted that Freeman was speaking truth to the power of cultural anthropology in carrying out his assessments of its ideological roots in Boasian culturalism and in his refutation of Margaret Mead's Samoa work. There is little evidence, however, that any shared his view of himself as inhabiting the historical, ritualized character of the medie-val jester or fool, except in a pejorative sense. Some, indeed, made a point of conceding nothing to his influence. The student who led the rebellion against his chairmanship in 1974 and who remained a lifelong critic summed up his view of Freeman's contribution to anthropology thus:

1) Detailed fieldwork (the *Iban Agriculture* book of limited circulation);
2) The kindred [Freeman's 1961 prize-winning essay] (that nobody ever took up);
3) Getting anthropology on the cover of *Time* magazine (on the Mae West principle) [any publicity is better than no publicity].

The rest, as far as he was concerned, were just footnotes.[2]

The truth about "truth's fool" lies somewhere in between. That Free-man was a great ethnographer whose best students produced outstanding work is an appreciation widely held. Colleagues at his university agree on this when they agree on little else about him. The promise that his British mentors—Meyer Fortes, Edmund Leach, Raymond Firth—saw in him they always affirmed, regretting only his later intellectual turning. Freeman's work on the Iban is his crowning glory, and his failure to complete it with a study of religion counted as a tragic shortfall for twentieth-century ethnography. What he might have achieved had he set his mind to writing the great ethnography on Samoa has exercised several commentators. Penelope Schoeffel believes he was far ahead of Pacific historians in plumbing the cultural richness of the archipelago's history and could have—should have— produced the kind of monumental study that his friend and anthropology colleague Douglas Oliver did for ancient Tahitian society.[3]

Freeman made his name as an anthropologist through his ethnographic work on the Iban of Borneo. This was the area of his greatest promise, marked by award-winning essays and precise ethnographic analysis, work that Meyer Fortes believed was circulating almost unconsciously among admiring colleagues from the moment Freeman was awarded his doctorate.[4] Freeman was set for stardom in the contemporary atmosphere of British social anthropology, especially in the structuralist area of kinship studies, but among American anthropologists he was also highly regarded. His genuine creativity shows through in the absorbing *Report on the Iban* and in his ingenious symbolic interpretations in "Shaman and Incubus," itself a superbly told human drama.

But in the story line of his life Freeman did not brandish his reputation in Iban studies as dramatically as his work on Mead, though during the 1970s he showed that he was prepared to guard his territory against all comers, even when he was working full time on his Mead refutation. Freeman never wrote up the major work on Iban religion that others wanted and that he had planned; the research data still lie in great abundance among his papers in San Diego. He confined himself to helping others—Iban students like James Masing, and colleagues in the field, Michael Heppell, Benson Saler, and Cliff Sather. Part of the reason, his wife, Monica, suggested, was that Derek was never integrated as intimately into Iban longhouse society as he had been in title-wielding Samoa.[5] But mainly the Iban detracted from the main message of Freeman's professional and life self-narrative: he was the seeker of truth over against the army of anthropologists who believed in cultural determinism.

The Iban, however, remained important for Freeman's life story. It was his intellectual anxiety over interpreting the symbolism surrounding head-hunting, as well as the traumatic set of events in Sarawak in 1961, that led him away from British structuralist approaches, with their reifications, abstract systems, boundary definitions, and what Freeman regarded as intellectual insularity. We have followed him as he plunged into a program of retraining in psychology and an incomplete, ultimately unsatisfying experience of self-analysis with a professional. This conversion was real, agonizing, and courageously undertaken, though the question remains open whether the psychoanalysis he underwent bit deeply into his interior life afterward. Nonetheless, Freeman's newly found cognitive armaments opened up a fresh battle front alongside that which was developing as Margaret Mead and her alleged deficits became the focus.

Freeman's work on Mead attracts the most vexed appraisals, as this book demonstrates. They range from the total acceptance by his hero, Karl Popper, of the demolition work Freeman did on the underpinnings of Mead's work; through those who appreciated that Freeman opened up the sacred, myth-ridden status of Margaret Mead for reevaluation by Americans; to those who argued that it didn't matter whether Freeman was right or wrong, for he had highlighted, perhaps unwittingly, the question of what anthropology was really about and how it should go about its business in the postmodern world.[6]

His war with North American anthropologists over Mead claimed most of his attention, excessively so as the years went on. He believed that his highly structured refutation of Margaret Mead's iconic Samoa study had sunk "the good ship Boasian culturalism" with a "torpedo at the waterline," as he told Frank Heimans.[7] Freeman had the highest regard for his first Mead book and continued to defend it against all criticisms, whether by anthropologists who were Samoa experts or by those who were not. His work contained empirical flaws, as we have acknowledged, and created a picture of Samoan custom that was as dark as Mead's was light, but it was "99% right," according to Schoeffel, the anthropologist who had lived in and studied Samoa herself (and who lives there now) and who bore the brunt of Freeman's dismissals.[8]

Although who was "right" and who was "wrong" captured much of the public attention, among anthropologists themselves "the Mead thing" was more revealing of disciplinary conventions and their limits, of the ways of dealing with dissenters, and of the edges of personality that showed when egos and intellects clashed. Motive and language are the areas in which Freeman has been most faulted during this longest-running and often vituperative controversy in anthropology. Yet the same charges can be laid against many of his opponents, and these charges strengthen the argument that American critics in particular were reacting as much to the assault on the "sacred woman" that Margaret Mead was to the profession (undervalued though she might have been in private) as to the details of the arguments. As a shrewd outside observer commented, Freeman's dispute with American anthropologists was "entangled with profound intellectual disagreements, turf wars between schools of thought, ideologically and politically motivated maneuverings, all obscured by personal animus."[9]

Freeman's refutation was not a full-scale attempt at a revisionist ethnography of Samoan society, though his critics claimed it should have been. There was no necessity for that in what he set out to do, even if Freeman was the anthropologist best able to give us an overarching portrait utilizing his extensive knowledge of the archipelago's history. The other accusations against him, that he pursued a malicious vendetta against Mead and that he waited till after her death to launch his campaign, are not borne out by the evidence. Wrong too is the conspiracy theory about Harvard University Press deliberately engineering the most damaging launch of *Margaret Mead and Samoa* it could; the press was simply caught up in its own marketing campaign.

Conspiracy theories extend to alleged subtexts lurking in Freeman's work. More than once critics expressed in print the belief that he was a closet sociobiologist peddling a discredited and dangerous theory about the behavioral drivers of culture. Yet the final chapter of each Mead book was no more than a summary position on the need to integrate both cultural and behavioral approaches, a position he had reached over decades of reading and thinking. As a platform for the future, the chapters were unexceptional statements. Their major value lies in being a tantalizing glimpse of one project among several that Freeman never completed.

This at least can be held against him. A curious paradox plagued Freeman's intellectual career: in several fields of anthropological endeavor, he became obsessed with the One Big Idea and insisted on preparing himself to pursue it with relentless scientific study. Yet he failed to bring any of these ideas to a resolution that satisfied him — or others — and that allowed him to go on to other Big Ideas.

Words were Freeman's most powerful weapon and his undoing. He loved words and knew their power. The poetry of Gerard Manley Hopkins, with its visions of nature's grandeur and its stippling rhythms, was a favorite. Deep in his arguments with James Côte in the 1990s, Freeman sent Steven

Pinker a letter thanking him for sending a copy of *The Language Instinct* and enclosing a poem by Siegfried Sassoon:

> Words are fools,
> Who blindly follow once they get a lead
> But thoughts are kingfishers that haunt the pools of quiet.[10]

Freeman possessed the darting, flashing thoughts, but he also let his words run wild on occasion. Language and style—on both sides—provide some of the reasons for the supercharged atmosphere that surrounded the Mead–Freeman debate. Although the language of both Freeman books on Mead is much more precise and less aggressive than his enemies give him credit for, the style of writing on both sides in the subsequent review controversies certainly raised the temperature. Freeman was continually provocative in his defiant refusal to be cowed, to stay silent, and to be humble in the face of attacks on him. This was as much personal need to secure his sense of himself as determination to win the argument. Much of what came from anthropologists in America was warlike and in some cases blind to what Freeman was saying. It was fed by biases with roots in hearsay about how "difficult" Freeman was and by the academic rumor mill, which retailed "Derek" stories of confrontations in seminars or in writing. But the anthropologists' belligerence was also a defiance of Freeman's mode of debating.

In the campaigns in which Freeman locked horns with anthropologists, several formats operated. His verbal brawls with colleagues in seminars or in public forums in the United States were ethological in character. Freeman set out to dominate, to win, sometimes to cow opposition. Even when that was not his intention it could be an effect. His language in writing was more precise, exact, and exacting: he was scrupulous in choosing the correct word, wanting words to say what they meant, and demanding the same of correspondents.

We can discern three types of Freeman writing in the war of words over Margaret Mead. First was the language of his books, which was forthright and direct in explication and argument and more measured and less vitriolic than his critics contended. Second was the language in his journal and magazine responses to those critics: this was uncompromising and astringent, uttering challenges and demanding retraction or recantation. Third was his correspondence with opponents and journal editors and newspapers: this could be provocative, even accusatory, sometimes derisive or contemptuous, as when he dismissed George Stocking's ruffled feathers with the quip that at Stocking's age Freeman was just starting research for his *Fateful Hoaxing* book.

There was no dressing up his responses to academic criticism in respectful or jocular fashion. Freeman made blunt, earnest challenges, often quoting back to a correspondent his or her exact words and interpreting them on Freeman's ground. His encounter over Samoan social structure with Melvin Ember in the 1960s was a good example and a dress rehearsal for much of the Mead debate. As Ember became more terse and self-righteous with every exchange, Freeman became more dogged, continuing to probe Ember for answers, insisting on reply after reply. This was Freeman's modus operandi, chasing correspondents for replies until they succumbed or walked away. Judith Heimann experienced it over her version of Sarawak events, Freeman insisting that she adhere strictly to versions of his role that he approved and jollying her along with gifts of postcards and invitations to book launches. He would not countenance departures from his version of events, could not stomach contradictions or compromises that required him to admit a defeat, however small.

His impassioned reactions, occasional bombast, and unwillingness to concede ground were also mirrored by a selection of North American anthropologists. Allegations were bandied about that did not speak to the facts being argued but conjured up an atmosphere of doubt and distrust of everything that Freeman stood for. Lowell Holmes claimed that he knew from the "tone" of Freeman's correspondence with him in the 1960s that Freeman was engaged in something more devious than a scholarly endeavor. Holmes could quote single instance after single instance of criticisms against Freeman that created the impression of an avalanche: George Marcus claiming Freeman had nothing new to say about the relation of biology to culture; Colin Turnbull declaring that the nature/nurture issue had nothing to do with what Mead set out to investigate; Laura Nader complaining that Freeman's book was not a systematic restudy of the Samoan islands; Paula Glick too wondering why he had not written the book she thinks he should have; David Schneider panning it as "a commercial enterprise not a contribution to knowledge" and seeing it as part of the dreaded "materialist, biologistic thinking" of the time.[11] As we have seen, much of the coverage of *Margaret Mead and Samoa*, as of Freeman's *Fateful Hoaxing* book, struck the same tone.

On both sides the language of the debates was the language of rolling warfare. E. L. Doctorow's novel *The March* has an image of the American Civil War that puts one in mind of the battle between Freeman and

American anthropology: "And so the war had come down to words. It was fought now in terminology across a table. It was contested in sentences. Entrenchments and assaults, drum taps and bugle calls, marches, ambushes, burnings, and pitched battles were transmogrified into nouns and verbs. . . . No cannonball or canister but has become the language here spoken, the words written down, Sherman thought. Language is war by other means."[12] Freeman's claims that the great controversy was over, even before he wrote a word of *The Fateful Hoaxing of Margaret Mead*, just provoked more conflict.[13] However reasoned and telling the second book was as an account of Mead's own mode of operating and of the preconceptions with which she entered the field, Freeman's enemies portrayed it as an exercise in stale scholasticism, overkill, evidence that Freeman had spent his life in rebuttal. He had become a prisoner of the Great Debate. He may have won the initial battles over his refutation, but, not knowing how to sue for an honorable peace by compromise with his enemies, Freeman made the war continue, till after his death he lost control of it altogether, the rhetoric of condemnation continuing unabated. The nature/nurture argument rolled on, Mead's rehabilitation was begun with the momentum generated by the centenary of her birth, and rumors continued to be circulated about Freeman's eccentricities, or worse.

Some of his friends, like anthropologist Douglas Oliver, and his sparring partners who were not sworn enemies, like the Oxford anthropologist Rodney Needham, chided Freeman for the forceful techniques he employed—the use of italics, boldface, emphatic adverbs, and exclamation points. They might be signs of Freeman's "irrepressible energy and wonderful determination," but his arguments were better served without them, urged Needham.[14] But many other commentators, especially in North America, reacted in hostile form, which contributed to the acerbic nature of the Mead debate and provoked Freeman to continue his assaults. We have seen how Ember's responses paved the way for a hostile reception of anything Freeman said on Samoa (chapter 6). Judith Heimann conceded ground in her biography of Tom Harrisson but had the last laugh in keeping anecdotes that cast Freeman in the guise of a deluded fanatic (chapter 4). Others gave up in frustration and contented themselves with retailing anecdotes against Freeman privately or, like James Clifford, the cultural studies critic, met Freeman's dour, forensic analysis by letting Freeman have his way but in a joking, friendly manner that ultimately dismissed him.

Perhaps Hiram Caton got under Freeman's skin most acutely. As a political psychologist and at first a friend and collaborator, Caton was close enough to challenge Freeman's perceptions of the language he employed with a bluntness not even Freeman used. "No one could possibly mistake your intention to execute not only the errors, but the reputations of the erring," Caton observed of Freeman's style of address.[15] He deplored Freeman's use of defamation threats against Adam Kuper in 1992, pointing out that this put an instant stop to scholarly communication. Kuper stood accused by Freeman of "subverting and flouting fundamental principles of science, of bizarre, aberrant, absurd and biased judgments, of lying, of malice toward yourself, of slandering your character: what an indictment! The letter hardly promotes dispassionate scholarly discussion, which is what you purport to espouse against Kuper's silence and evasion."[16]

Such honesty, too seldom articulated by friends or colleagues, cooled their relationship, though Caton refused to be cast into outer darkness and continued to proclaim his "precious friendship," even affection, for Freeman. Caton unsettled Freeman, who expected either transparent support or opposition. He was unsure whether Caton was friend or enemy and was alarmed at the end of his life that Caton might be maneuvering to become his biographer. Although thwarted in that, Caton's two articles after Freeman's death do look like biographical attempts to solve the puzzle of Freeman's personality.

It is true Freeman could have handled the exchange of ideas better. He sanctified "criticism" and "the elimination of error," but his responses and occasional threats were designed to channel criticisms into areas that he controlled so that he could dispose of them. This eventually stifled discussion altogether and hardened animosity. Whether a more sparing, conciliatory engagement with his antagonists would have eliminated some of the visceral hostility toward him remains an open question, for a reputation had preceded him, and he was dealing with a discipline already jittery from a decade of crisis around sociobiology.

Freeman's interventions were a momentary disruption to American cultural anthropology. Freeman may have been naïve in thinking that one book or even two, however well argued, could kill the myths that surrounded Mead's role in American society, particularly as he did not directly address Mead's wider role in American society as the prophet of a freer social, sexual, and educational environment. But it is an irony that he moved (some) anthropologists to begin the process themselves through their trashing of his own contribution and the building of a new mythology, which was based on half truths and outright falsehoods, of Freeman the wrecker, the cheat, the monster. Freeman liked to see himself as anthropology's heretic or as "the deathwatch beetle of cultural anthropology" who brought down the spire of the discipline and along with it an array of false prophets—Durkheim, Boas, and Mead most prominent among them. Anthropology, or at least many critical cultural anthropologists, regarded him instead as a disconcerting alien presence, a villain, and a perpetrator, not just for what he did to Mead's early work but for the threat he represented to liberal campaigns in the United States against a resurgence of sociobiology and the ugly racial implications conservative forces drew from it.

Derek Freeman will always be linked to Margaret Mead in anthropology's history, "spinning through space with Margaret Mead forever," as Freeman himself told Frank Heimans.[17] But his obsession with "the Mead thing" obscures the relevance of Freeman's all-round arguments and the value of his other work. His Samoa work in particular runs the risk of being underestimated. The 1948 study of village Saʻanapu is a lively analysis in the classical British tradition of structural functionalism that is based on observations Freeman made as an independent amateur ethnographer. It is underpinned by a unique set of data collected in the early 1940s. But the Saʻanapu study contains no hint of where Freeman was heading in his own mind, and it languished unread and underused for decades, a relic of a bygone age of ideas, perhaps, but the foundation for a canonical text on village Samoa, something that Freeman had ample time and resources to create. This was his greatest failing, according to Penelope Schoeffel. Because he never exploited his return to Samoa in the 1960s to compare changes since his first visit and write the definitive book on social and cultural change, Freeman ended up being "the great ethnographer manqué of Samoa."[18]

Even his relations with Samoans were made part of the criticism of his work in the 1980s and 1990s. He was accused of settling scores for the Samoan people by his attack on Margaret Mead but also of dishonoring them by "studied distortions of Samoan realities."[19] He was blamed for further damaging their image by making Faʻapuaʻa Faʻamu the moral scapegoat for Margaret Mead's failings. He was unfairly attacked for having a clear conflict of interest in his campaign against Mead because he was a great supporter of Samoa's fledgling attempts to build a university and a generous donor. These were grievous blows, and they hurt Freeman deeply. This work shows several instances where he felt Samoans' indignities personally and viscerally, and he paid for those feelings with another "abreaction" in 1967. Freeman deplored the patronizing comments made by

James Côte, that not even Samoans could understand their own culture, and made no apology for defending the new university and its senior staff, working tirelessly behind the scenes writing references and promoting prizes.[20] Freeman's moral empathy with the Samoan people was real, and it was deeper than he felt for the Iban or for Australia's Aboriginal people. He felt at home in these islands, they owned him, and he had planned to have his ashes sprinkled in Samoa after his death.

Nonetheless, a higher purpose drove Freeman even beyond his Samoan sympathies. When he told Hiram Caton that the Freeman persona did not speak in a Samoan accent, Freeman was alluding to his utter dedication to the truth. The wider scientific issues were always more important to him than setting the record straight on Samoa. "General ethnographies in my view have virtually nothing to do with the solution of scientific problems," he wrote to the anthropologist Tim O'Meara, which may partly explain Freeman's failure to write the Great Book on Samoan society.[21] Anthropology was an empirical science; science was the one true reliable knowledge that proceeded from the testing of hypotheses till error was whittled away. Thus was truth attained.[22] "I do not think of myself as clever, though I hope I do have a modicum of what T. H. Huxley calls 'the divine afflatus of the truth-seeker,'" he wrote to another colleague. "All that I will admit to then, is to being one of truth's fools, with perhaps a glimmering of *sunyata*, who has learnt not to bite!"[23] This last comment would have amused his critics, for it was his persistent chasing of those who disagreed with him (and foolishly kept corresponding) that resulted in Freeman being accused of harassment.

In fields remote from "the Mead thing," Freeman did brilliant work of clarification and synthesis, said one of his critics, Nicolas Peterson, who nevertheless believed Freeman was, if supremely well read, essentially uncreative. This is a highly colored judgment dependent on a limited definition of creativity. Freeman's Iban studies—and indeed his books on Mead—cannot be dismissed as uncreative. James Fox, a closer colleague and friend, thought him a "big picture man" who set the agenda for a newly bicultural anthropology in a very general sense during the 1960s and 1970s but was too thin in his knowledge of biology and psychoanalysis to fit the components together with anthropology.[24]

In any case, Freeman's form of scientific theory was regarded by many anthropologists as old-fashioned and positivistic (though he abjured positivism and thought himself immune from, because well aware of, observer bias). Freeman was part of an older scientific tradition in the discipline, even if he was abandoning its social-structural theorizations as part of his conversion to a more behavioral stance. To revisit the ironies surrounding his relationship with his noted adversary Adam Kuper, Freeman was an unconscious ally in Kuper's continual assertions that social anthropology was a social science, not a project in the humanities. Indeed, in Freeman's prosecution of Popper-like scientism, whether over Mead or in promoting his "interactionism," he was a contemporary manifestation of the phase of neopositivism that Kuper was predicting for anthropology in the early 1990s and the perfect Enlightenment Puritan to sit beside Kuper's hero, Ernest Gellner.[25]

Freeman's call for a new style of "interactionist" anthropology was certainly not old-fashioned. Although he was dealing with perhaps the oldest question in anthropology, the nature of being human in society, he was during the 1960s and 1970s ahead of the curve in the discipline (though not "centuries ahead of my time," as he bragged just before his death).[26] Social and cultural anthropologists were slow to grapple with the questions linking their studies with the more subtle aspects of human biology. By the end of the 1970s, the decade that saw the furor over E. O. Wilson's sociobiology, few anthropologists were even considering the integration of genetics, neuroendocrinology, and neurophysiology into their discipline, according to the applied anthropologist Eliot Chapple, himself a keen collaborator with biologists. A decade after that again, says Leonard Lieberman, cultural anthropology was still divided within itself over sociobiology; while there were cultural anthropologists who dealt with evolution, most had gone the cultural materialism or ecology route. Even in the twenty-first century, a decade after Freeman's death, biological anthropologists and those devoted to cultural frameworks and political economy were still talking past one another, operating within lively niches of their own and admitting cross-flows of theoretical thinking but without the benefit of ethnographic studies to harden their perspectives.[27]

So Freeman before his death could still with respectability dream his dream—he called it "Dilthey's Dream" after Wilhelm Dilthey, the nineteenth-century hermeneutical philosopher—of fusing the humanist and natural science aspects of anthropology together to study human beings, not as fallen angels but as risen apes, kin to all that lives.[28] He himself remained an armchair revolutionary in that he never developed a realistic case-study method or series of facts within a conceptual framework, as Charles Darwin did, that might allow him to pose testable hypotheses. Given the time scales involved in biocultural evolution, that may well have been an insurmountable obstacle, but his obsession with Margaret Mead and her Samoa researches certainly held him back, the messianic promise in his programmatic statements never realized.

"Reformers intent on changing humanity's habits have made the same mistake again and again, forgetting that new habits of mind cannot be put on like a clean shirt," says the historian of emotions Theodore Zeldin.[29] It is an apposite warning of the mammoth size of the task that faced Derek Freeman, which even for him would have entailed career-long dedication. Since his death the task has only ballooned. Freeman was mistaken that the mapping of the human genome would of itself revolutionize the human sciences. Attention has shifted to the processes of gene expression, to the developing field of epigenetics, to questions of distributive systems or modularity in the brain, while biological anthropologists continue to develop models for coevolution of the human organism with the environment.[30] Don Tuzin recognized both Freeman's eagerness for anthropology to climb aboard the accelerating train and his own limitations.

> DF was always insistent that the Nature/Nurture debate is jejeune; that reality emerges from the interaction of these domains. What he didn't fully realize—actually, nobody did—was how thoroughgoing that interaction is. The Cartesian dualism he rightly decried is so embedded in our language that it's almost impossible to think about the depth of that interaction. . . . DF, like everyone else, was partly a captive of the very dualism that he rejected. One thing I can say for sure, however: if he were here, he would be enjoying these developments in genetic science and would have no trouble assimilating them to his long-standing convictions.[31]

Critics of Freeman, especially in Australia, point out that Freeman founded no school of anthropological training in the new paradigm, no pool of students to pursue it. It is questionable whether any other anthropologist did either; anthropologist champions in Australia were at the time thin on the ground. Freeman did, however, strive to develop a form of biological anthropology in Australia, taking the initiative to at least establish resources at his home university as a way of moving the field along. One should remember also that Margaret Mead did not found a readily identifiable school.

Contrary to Caton's belief, Freeman did inspire some of his students: Don Tuzin is an exemplar of the new approaches, which he learned from Freeman. Tuzin's "Miraculous Voices" essay of 1984, which suggests a link between humans' auditory apparatus and supernatural apprehensions, using as an example the Ilahita Arapesh of Papua New Guinea and their fear of thunder, drew its inspiration explicitly from Freeman's paper "Thunder, Blood and the Nicknaming of God's Creatures." Tuzin argued, without apology and drawing on studies into the effects of sound on human cognition, that feelings, memories, and brain states are experiences that possibly precede meaning and cultural conditioning. His paper attracted the sort of criticism Freeman's arguments did—a refusal to concede that sensations might come before culture and warnings about dogmatism (though there is not a hint of inflexibility anywhere in the essay). Tuzin had insisted that "the paradigm of an anthropology *integrated* around cultural, biological, and environmental variable has not yet been delineated, and in the nature of the case it may never be."[32] It did not stop the warriors of cultural anthropology forming up a phalanx against him, twenty years before Freeman died and with Tuzin having to make the same kind of vigorous defenses as Freeman had against claims that seemed deliberately to miss the point.

Freeman too may never have been able to bring his new paradigm to birth or have brought his many Big Ideas to the sort of closure that his initial ambition foresaw, but he was a solvent force in anthropological history nonetheless. He helped U.S. anthropologists see themselves, at least that part of themselves reflected in the image of Margaret Mead, as social scientists socialized into a particular ideology about culture's dominance in human development. On the other side of the Atlantic, while claiming that Freeman's crusading style was a disservice to anthropology, Adam Kuper was still able to admit that Freeman's "dogged politics" pushed the discipline to reflect on the sacred character that anthropologists bestowed on the ethnographic enterprise. The Freeman–Mead controversy even fed into the growing "reflexive" tendencies in anthropology that challenged the objectivity of traditional ethnography. Ten years after Freeman's death, Kuper was still invoking Freeman's name—and notoriety—as he bemoaned anthropology's descent into silence concerning the great matters of the day: "Anthropologists hardly bother any longer to take issue with even the most outlandish generalizations about human nature. Not their business."[33]

In that respect, Freeman was unusual for the vision of anthropology as a moral science that he held out for at the end of his life. He would not subscribe to the politicomoral teachings of postcolonial anthropologists-cum–cultural critics who regarded ethnography as an oppressive science. Rather, he took the side of American philosopher Daniel Dennett, who, out of a hardline materialism, wrestled with the questions surrounding free will and moral responsibility that Darwin's evolutionism threw up. He was of one mind with Roy D'Andrade, who celebrated the coming of the evolutionary paradigm in the social sciences and believed the field of cultural anthropology would become more peripheral, ceding ground to sociology and especially social psychology.[34] Freeman's oeuvre will continue to live comfortably among such critiques.

Don Tuzin found Freeman the confirmed materialist musing at the end of a long life about whether there was some ultimate external agency; he even expressed himself open to it, surrounded by his Buddhist symbols and reminders. Being kind mattered enormously to him now, refusing to drink to "dominance," and recognizing that the struggle to control dominance behavior was his struggle for survival. Freeman's embrace reached out to Margaret Mead, whose wisdom in her later years he acknowledged and whose integrity he was prepared to defend: "I would as soon believe in unicorns than that she was a cheat. I'd seen no evidence of that at all."[35]

Derek Freeman was glad he had not become Mr. Southeast Asia or an ordinary social anthropologist. He saw himself as "a bit of a buccaneer," roving around the discipline, and he was happy where he had ended up. Most of all, he wanted to be remembered as a good scholar and an incorruptible scientist with, at the end of his life, a touch of Buddhist tranquility about him.[36] One is reminded of Edmund Halley of comet fame, an iconoclastic earth scientist and astronomer who did not believe in God:

So imperceptible the line of chance—
"Is this the best of worlds?" Perhaps. I've been
At best a brave appendix to events,
But feel that chance and choice affect our view.
The Earth revolves more understandably,
Descanting an old music. Hear it hum:
Ideas, ideas, indelible ideas—
Continuous, pervasive, circumscribing
Discovery shall measure all. It can.[37]

Notes

Abbreviations

ANUA	Archives of the Australian National University
ANZAAS	Australia and New Zealand Association for the Advancement of Science
ASAO	Association for Social Anthropology in Oceania
F/UCSD	Derek Freeman Papers, Special Collections & Archives, University of California, San Diego (cited by box number / folder number, e.g., 1/1)
IT	Island Territories
NA/NZ	National Archives New Zealand, Wellington
NLA	National Library of Australia
TS	Tuzin summaries and notes on Freeman diaries, 1963–90

Introduction

1. Caton, "The Mead/Freeman Controversy," 587; Shankman, "The Samoan Conundrum," 38.

2. Tuzin, interview by the author, 29 June 2004.

3. Byatt, *The Game*, 230.

4. "Margaret Mead," *New World Encyclopedia*.

5. Waterford, "Capital Times."

6. Caton, "Exalted Self."

7. The result was Mein Smith et al., *Remaking the Tasman World*.

8. These details are from the introduction to the Festschrift for Tuzin: Lipset and Roscoe, *Echoes of the Tambaran*, 1–12.

9. Tuzin, "Margaret Mead and the Heretic."

10. Don Tuzin moved back to the United States in 1973, to the University of California at San Diego, where he fashioned a reputation as "an anthropologist's anthropologist." He

was known as a sophisticated practitioner and thoughtful philosopher of culture, the "dean" of Melanesian experts on the Sepik, and a writer of authoritative and dramatic texts. See Lipset and Roscoe, *Echoes of the Tambaran*, 1. Tuzin's major works include *The Voice of the Tambaran* and *The Cassowary's Revenge*.

11. Lepore, "Historians Who Love too Much," 134; see also Malcolm, *The Silent Woman*.

12. Freeman to Margaret Brock (sister), 26 June 1994, 153/5, F/UCSD.

13. Tuzin to the author, 7 August 2006.

Chapter 1. The Man-Most-Likely-To

1. Appell and Madan, "Derek Freeman"; Freeman, "In Praise of Heresy"; Freeman, interview by Tuzin; Heimans, "Recorded Interview."

2. Heimans, "Recorded Interview," 2–3.

3. Freeman, interview by Tuzin, transcript 5, p. 69. Monica Freeman told me that one of Did's English ancestors had been "the hanging judge of Bath" (interview by the author, 9 October 2002).

4. Freeman to Tuzin, 21 August 2000, 160/1, F/UCSD. The social atmosphere of this period in Wellington is evoked in the short stories of the acclaimed novelist Katherine Mansfield.

5. Freeman, interview by Tuzin, transcript 5, p. 69.

6. Margaret Brock to Freeman, 8 August 1992, 153/5, F/UCSD. Margaret left New Zealand in 1947 for America, though she finally settled in the UK, where she died in 1995.

7. This educational journey is outlined in "Derek Freeman: Notes Toward an Intellectual Biography," which became the opening chapter in Appell and Madan, *Choice and Morality*. Throughout the present book, I have used Freeman's annotated copy of this manuscript (loaned by the family) rather than the Appell and Madan chapter, since the manuscript represents his "authorized" version.

8. The material on Freeman's early life, when not separately documented, comes from the following: interviews with Monica Freeman; Freeman's interview with Doug Munro; Tuzin's obituary for Freeman, which appeared in *American Anthropologist* ("Derek Freeman [1916–2001]"); and my own discussions with Tuzin.

9. Barrowman, *Victoria University*, 51.

10. Ibid., 57. Ernest Beaglehole wrote works on the Cook Islands, Hawai'i, and Tonga, as well as on New Zealand. On J. C. Beaglehole, see Beaglehole, *A Life*.

11. Munro, *J. C. Beaglehole*, 17–30.

12. Barrowman, *Victoria University*, 53.

13. Heimans, "Recorded Interview," 8.

14. Freeman, "Nursery Rhyme."

15. "Free Discussions Club," Freeman Family Papers; see also Beaglehole, *A Life*, 230.

16. "Our Plunket Babes," 1.

17. Tuzin, interview by the author, 8 August 2006; see Belich, *Paradise Reforged*, 121–25.

18. Freeman, "(love)ution," 45.

19. "Judgments, 1937."

20. The full story is in Heimans, "Recorded Interview," 5–7; see also Freeman, interview by Munro. See Freeman's "Poem for a Friend Killed on Mt. Evans."

21. Freeman to David Mackay, 21 November 1997, Freeman Family Papers; Tuzin, "Derek Freeman (1916–2001)," 5.

22. See Mehta, *Nameless Experience*, 1–62.

23. Freeman, interview by Munro; see also Openshaw and Ball, "New Zealand Teacher Education."

24. Heather Packer (née Morrison) to Freeman, n.d. [1998], 157/32, F/UCSD.

25. For these facts and their suggestiveness, I am indebted to Caroline Thomas, personal communication to author, 4 January 2013; see her *The Sorcerers' Apprentice*. Freeman identifies Calverton's book, published in 1931 for social scientists who knew no anthropology, in his diary for 1990: TS, 18 December 1990.

26. Heimans, "Recorded Interview," 10.

27. Freeman to Meyer Fortes, 20 September 1962, 8/9, F/UCSD. On Hunter's approach, see Ernest Beaglehole's 1964 Hudson Lecture to the Royal Society in Wellington, "The Third Culture in New Zealand: Human Nature and Conduct," copy in 118/27, F/UCSD; see also Freeman to Money, 13 August 1986, 15/2, F/UCSD; and Ross Papers, Alexander Turnbull Library. Ross, a playwright, was at Victoria with Freeman.

28. Freeman, interview by Tuzin, transcript 4, pp. 22–23.

29. Freeman to Rosenberg, 7 January 2001, copy in author's possession. The quotation is from Rosenberg, interview by the author.

30. These details are taken from a report titled "Education in Samoa," written after the war. It was based on a visit to Western Samoa by the director of education in New Zealand, C. E. Beeby, in June 1945 to report on the state of affairs that prevailed during the war. See Beeby to Secretary of External Affairs, 18 July 1947, IT1, EX13/1, NA/NZ; Beeby, *Biography of an Idea*, 212–18.

31. Memo for Secretary of External Affairs from Permanent Head, Education Department, n.d., IT1, EX89/3, NA/NZ.

32. Sinclair, *Halfway*, 62.

Chapter 2. Preparing for a Heretical Life

1. See Hempenstall and Rutherford, *Protest and Dissent*, 18–43; Field, *Mau*; Campbell, "Resistance and Colonial Government."

2. Stanner, *South Seas in Transition*, 324.

3. Freeman, "In Praise of Heresy," 81; see also Heimans, "Recorded Interview," 15–21.

4. "I loved" is in Freeman, interview by Tuzin, transcript 4, p. 26; Te'o Fairbairn, personal communication to author, January 2016. Fairbairn's sister, Mabel Barry, was taught by Freeman in Samoa.

5. "Interview with Mr McKenzie, Supt. of Schools Samoa, 20 May 1947," copy in Davidson Papers, NLA. I am indebted to Doug Munro for ferreting out this document.

6. "The Falemaunga Caves"; "O le Fele o le Fe'e"; "The Vailele Earthmounds."

7. Freeman, interview by Tuzin, transcript 4, p. 24; Heimans, "Recorded Interview," 14. Freeman was partly projecting back in the shadow of David Williamson's play about him and Margaret Mead, *Heretic: Based on the Life of Derek Freeman.*

8. "The Seuao Cave."

9. Freeman, *Mead and Samoa*, xiii–xiv.

10. Information from Serge Tcherkézoff, January 2006. Tcherkézoff, a French anthropologist, was in correspondence with Freeman about Samoa shortly before Freeman's death in 2001. The account of Freeman's activities in Sa'anapu is based on Heimans, "Recorded Interview," 14–18; Freeman, interview by Tuzin, transcript 4, pp. 24–28; and Freeman's own ethnographic notes, box 50, F/UCSD.

11. Details are in Freeman's December 1946 seminar paper at the LSE, "On Samoan Social Organization."

12. Freeman to Sylvia Neumann, 11 July 1987, 16/7, F/UCSD.

13. Heimans, "Recorded Interview," 18; see also Tcherkézoff to the author, January 2006.

14. Turnbull to Secretary of External Affairs, 2 October 1941, IT1, EX89/3, pt. 4, NA/NZ.

15. Freeman to Field, 22 November 1984, 8/1, F/UCSD. Jim Davidson, the constitutional advisor and professor of Pacific history, encountered the same problems with expatriates in Samoa in the late 1940s and early 1950s: see Munro, "J. W. Davidson," 107–8.

16. Mulgan, *Man Alone*, 9.

17. For a detailed examination of this aspect of New Zealand history, see Wood, *New Zealand People at War*, 25–27, 111; see also Cookson, "Appeal Boards," 181; and Scott, *Harry's Absence.*

18. Wood, *New Zealand People at War*, 67–89, 215.

19. Stanner, *South Seas*, 324–25; see also McKay, *Samoana*, chaps. 15–17.

20. Stanner, *South Seas*, 327. Stanner was a later colleague of Freeman's in Canberra and fell out with him over their approaches to anthropology.

21. McCulloch to Secretary of External Affairs, 31 August 1942, IT1, EX89/3, pt. 4, NA/NZ.

22. Dennerley, "The Royal New Zealand Navy," 110–11. Some eleven hundred Scheme B personnel were sent overseas.

23. Heimans, "Recorded Interview," 19. Freeman's other mentor, H. D. Skinner, ethnologist and director of the Otago Museum, also dismissed his misgivings.

24. The account of Freeman's time overseas follows Sinclair's robust autobiography, *Halfway*; for "fanatic," see p. 85.

25. Freeman to Sinclair, 15 October 1993, 21/9, F/UCSD. Freeman also agreed that his work might have him accurately described as an intellectual extremist.

26. Denoon to the author, 23 June 2006.

27. Heimans, "Recorded Interview," 99.

28. Freeman, interview by Tuzin, transcript 5, p. 28.

29. Sinclair, *Halfway*, 100.

30. Freeman to Firth, 13 January 1983, 8/4, F/UCSD.

31. This set of circumstances can be traced in Firth's correspondence in Freeman's papers: Firth to Freeman, 22 February 1945, 28 May 1945, 1 July 1946, and Dean of Postgraduate Studies to Firth, 11 April 1945, all in 8/4, F/UCSD. The confusion seems to have been Firth's fault.

32. Sinclair, *Halfway*, 86.

33. See Freeman to Sinclair, 15 October 1993, 21/9, F/UCSD; see also Dennerley, "The Royal New Zealand Navy," 118–20.

34. Freeman, interview by Tuzin, transcript 2, p. 63.

35. Freeman to Firth, 1 February 1945, Firth Papers. I am indebted to Geoff Gray for extracts from these papers.

36. Heimans, "Recorded Interview," 24. Freeman's ship carried troops back to Australia probably via Singapore, which figures in another typically picaresque tale from thirdhand sources by anthropologists after his death. In a series of postings on the internet site of the Association for Social Anthropology in Oceania (ASAO) in 2008, one member claimed that an unnamed informant had been told by Freeman that he had witnessed with shock an Australian naval officer telling his men that they might rape and loot but not disturb any official records they might find (5 March 2008). This is nowhere corroborated in writing or interviews, though Freeman told Tuzin in 2000 that he had witnessed his crew grabbing contraband from captured Japanese troops in Indonesia, while the administrative records of the Japanese unit were simply thrown overboard; see Freeman, interview by Tuzin, transcript 2, p. 63.

37. Freeman to Firth, 22 March 1946, Firth Papers.

38. See Gibbings, *Over the Reefs*.

39. Freeman to Firth, 2 June 1946. Freeman was able to collect for New Zealand's national Turnbull Library a valuable collection of glass plate negatives of photographs of European settlement on Samoa.

40. Heimans, "Recorded Interview," 24. The last stages of Freeman's wartime experiences and the immediate years thereafter are covered by Heimans on pp. 24–28.

41. The quotes and material in this section come from Freeman correspondence in the Firth Papers.

42. The story and other details are in Heimans, "Recorded Interview," 25–26; see also correspondence with the Bishop Museum, 3/14, F/UCSD. Freeman organized and edited a memorial volume for Skinner titled *Anthropology in the South Seas*, and wrote an appreciation of him.

43. The New Zealand Rehabilitation Board had expected Freeman to complete the diploma in a year. He had to persuade the board that two years of comprehensive study had practical value for New Zealand's knowledge of its small colonial empire. Firth went to bat for Freeman again, pronouncing him a man of "very great capacity." Firth to Director of Rehabilitation, New Zealand, 26 May 1947, with Freeman enclosures, Firth Papers.

44. The quote is from Mills, *Difficult Folk?*, 6. The account of the tensions between the LSE and Oxford is summarized from Mills; see also A. Kuper, *Among the Anthropologists*, 117–18, 141.

45. Freeman found his copy again in 1987 and recorded it in his diary: see TS, 16 February 1987.

46. See Appell and Madan, "Derek Freeman," 3–10; Heimans, "Recorded Interview," 26; Freeman, interview by Tuzin, transcript 2, pp. 14–15. The paper was titled "On Samoan Social Organization." A copy was accessed in Freeman Family Papers, now with F/UCSD.

47. Shankman, *Trashing*, 50–51.

48. Freeman to Fortes, 28 February 1948, 8/9, F/UCSD.

49. A. Kuper, *Anthropology and Anthropologists*, 69–70.

50. Beaglehole to Freeman, 25 February and 23 June 1948, 181/37, F/UCSD.

51. Freeman, interview by Tuzin, transcript 2, p. 13; Heimans, "Recorded Interview," 27–29.

52. Heimans, "Recorded Interview," 25–29.

53. Freeman to Freud, 28 June 1962, 154/34, F/UCSD.

54. Malinowski described his senior students as "mandarins": Mills, *Difficult Folk?*, 35.

55. McCall, interview by the author, 1 November 2016. McCall was a longtime critic of Freeman.

56. Freeman, *Social Structure*.

57. This was *Fateful Hoaxing*: see chap. 11.

Chapter 3. Mr. Southeast Asia or Mr. Pacific?

1. Freeman, "Notes towards an Intellectual Biography," 14.

2. Freeman, interview by Tuzin, transcript 1, p. 41.

3. Mills, *Difficult Folk?*, 69–91.

4. Seymour-Smith, *Macmillan Dictionary of Anthropology*, 165; Gray and Munro, "'Leach Would Be First Rate,'" 2–3; Tambiah, *Edmund Leach*.

5. Heimans, "Recorded Interview," 29–30; see also Leach's foreword to Freeman's *Iban Agriculture*; and Mills, *Difficult Folk?*, chap. 5.

6. The details of Monica's background are from her daughter, Jenny's, eulogy at Monica's memorial service after her death in 2012; see also Monica's introduction to Appell-Warren, *The Iban Diaries*. On Davidson, see Munro, "The Prehistory of J. W. Davidson."

7. The government of Sarawak published this later, longer report without consulting Freeman. Raymond Firth and Anthony Forge persuaded him to republish it in 1970, because copies of the original edition, though sought after, had become rare; Freeman's own copy had disappeared from his shelves.

8. Appell-Warren, *The Iban Diaries*, 155.

9. Ibid., 105.

10. Ibid., xxxvii, 129.

11. Freeman, *Iban Agriculture*, 30–31.

12. Appell-Warren, *The Iban Diaries*, 63.

13. Incidents taken from a range of Monica's observations; see ibid., 4–5, 8–9, 15, 108, 179, 184, 219, 227.

14. Monica continued to record her notes as the illness ran its course; see ibid., 511–27. The Iban women believed her illness was brought on by failing to feed the crocodile spirit of the weaving she was making at the time.

15. Ibid., 73.

16. Ibid., 323.

17. Monica to her mother, 24 November 1950, in ibid., 482.

18. Monica to her mother, July 1950, ibid., 358.

19. Monica to her mother, 11 August 1950, ibid., 392.

20. Quotations are taken from Monica's letter of 21 April 1951 in ibid., 571–79. The southern trip is covered from page 453 onward. W. R. "Bill" Geddes (1916–89) was a fellow New Zealander and almost exact contemporary of Freeman's, with a similar trajectory through the LSE but with his PhD already in hand in 1948. He became a professor of social anthropology at the University of Sydney in 1959 in a career that paralleled Freeman's in both interests and controversies. See "Geddes, William Robert (Bill) (1916–1989)."

21. Appell-Warren, *The Iban Diaries*, 551.

22. Mills, *Difficult Folk?*, 89; this section is based on Mills, chapters 5 and 6. See also Eriksen and Nielsen, *A History of Anthropology*, chap. 4; A. Kuper, *Anthropology and Anthropologists*; Stocking, *After Tylor*.

23. Leach, quoted in Appell-Warren, *The Iban Diaries*, 392.

24. Freeman to Firth, 16 February 1949, Firth Papers.

25. See Appell-Warren, *The Iban Diaries*, 206, 270.

26. For "I was looked on," see Heimans, "Recorded Interview," 44; Firth examiner's report, 8 October 1953, Firth Papers.

27. Freeman's grief is recorded in TS, 14 March 1964; offer of lectureship is in Freeman to Firth, 2 July 1950, Firth Papers; see also Heimans, "Recorded Interview," 45.

28. Freeman to Davidson, 5 April 1954, Davidson Papers, 57-58, ANUA.

29. All quotations are from his letter of 25 February 1954. The draft in Freeman's papers in 8/4, F/UCSD, is subtly different from the version that reached Firth, whose letter of 9 February 1954 and Freeman's reply are in the Firth Papers.

30. Munro, "J. W. Davidson," 98–116.

31. Davidson to Freeman, 8 February 1950, Davidson–Freeman correspondence, Freeman Family Papers. I am indebted to the family for copies of this correspondence and to Doug Munro for alerting me to it.

32. Freeman to Davidson, 5 April 1954. Davidson–Freeman correspondence, Freeman Family Papers (italicized words underlined in original).

33. Nadel to Freeman, 12 April 1954, Davidson Papers, 57-58, ANUA.

34. Leach to Registrar, 22 June 1954, and Fortes to Hohnen, 25 June 1954, Davidson Papers, 57-58; see also 57-30, ANUA. Fortes highlighted Freeman's "meticulous respect for scientific accuracy."

35. Freeman to Davidson, 21 June 1954, Davidson Papers, 57-58, ANUA.

Chapter 4. "My Kierkegaardian Earthquake"

1. "That dreary place" is from Passmore, "Interview."

2. For a short summary of these 1950s growing pains, see Gray and Munro, "'Leach Would Be First Rate.'" Raymond Firth was invited to join, along with Howard Florey of penicillin fame; both declined.

3. Gray, *A Cautious Silence*, 1–29; see also Wise, *The Self-Made Anthropologist*.

4. Foster and Varghese, *Making of the Australian National University*, 4–41.

5. For Worsley's impressions, see Gray and Munro, "'Leach Would Be First Rate,'" 4; Davidson to Freeman, 17 August 1953, Davidson–Freeman correspondence, Freeman Family Papers.

6. Gray, "W. E. H. Stanner." Stanner's 1968 Boyer Lectures on Australian radio, *After the Dreaming*, brought him to public attention as a thoughtful, sensitive interpreter of Aboriginal life to the wider community.

7. For "rabble," see Gray and Munro, "'Leach Would Be First Rate,'" 6; Davidson's quotes from his letter to Freeman, 17 August 1953; Hempenstall, *Meddlesome Priest*, 287, 290.

8. Firth to Registrar ANU, 6 July 1954, Firth Papers.

9. A. N. Wilson's phrase for the sacred hearth of another twentieth-century provocateur, Hilaire Belloc (*Hilaire Belloc*, 203).

10. Conklin review in *American Anthropologist* 59, no. 1 (1957): 179–80; Sahlins's review in the *Journal of the Polynesian Society* 67, no. 3 (1958): 311–13.

11. Oliver to Freeman, 18 January 1957, 157/29, F/UCSD.

12. Freeman, "On the Concept of the Kindred," 192–220. The "approved" introduction to Appell and Madan, "Notes towards an Intellectual Biography," argues that this article dispelled once and for all "much of the conceptual confusion over the nature of cognatic societies" (13). In 2013 Sahlins published a long essay on kinship (*What Kinship Is—And Is Not*), which, though never mentioning Freeman or his essay, reverberates with concepts that are alive in Freeman's "Kindred" essay.

13. Freeman, "The Joe Gimlet or Siovili Cult."

14. Davidson judgment in promotion reference for Freeman, Davidson Papers, 57-30, ANUA; for "Herewith," see Freeman, interview by Tuzin, transcript 3, pp. 12–13.

15. Stanner's comments are from "Report of the Council of ANU, 1956," 39, ANUA; Firth's are from "Siegfried Frederick Nadel."

16. Freeman to Vice Chancellor, 9 May 1956, Freeman, Staff Files, 19-6.2.2.6, pt. 1, ANUA.

17. Freeman's obituary for Nadel is in *Oceania* 27, no. 1 (1956): 1–11. Freeman's help to Mrs. Nadel is in Freeman to Fortes, 25 January 1956, 8/9, F/UCSD. For a very different view of Nadel, see Reay, "An Innocent."

18. Heimans, "Recorded Interview," 48–49. The Leach affair is covered in Gray and Munro, "'Leach Would Be First Rate.'"

19. Quoted in "'Leach Would Be First Rate,'" 802–11.

20. Firth to Registrar, 25 July 1957, Davidson Papers, 57-30, ANUA. Details about the search are in Gray and Munro, "'The Department.'"

21. Fortes to Hohnen, 9 July 1957, Davidson Papers, 57-30, ANUA.

22. Firth to Registrar, 25 July 1957, Davidson Papers, 57-30, ANUA.

23. Gluckman to Freeman, 8 July 1957, Davidson Papers, 57-30, ANUA; Barnes on Freeman's disappointment is in Barnes, *Humping My Drum*, 345; Barnes's comment is in letter to Davidson, 5 August 1957, Davidson Papers, 57-30, ANUA.

24. Freeman to Firth, 28 August 1957, Firth Papers.

25. Heimann, *The Most Offending*, 4.

26. All quotations from ibid., 332–35.

27. The Heimann–Freeman correspondence between 1992 and 2000 is in 10/6 and 155/17, F/UCSD.

28. The Freeman account is in Heimann, *The Most Offending*, 443–45. His investigations of Martinoir are laid down in correspondence in 6/22, F/UCSD; see especially a detailed memo to ANU, 24 April 1962. "Kierkegaardian earthquake" is in Freeman to Needham, 13 September 1971, 157/22, F/UCSD.

29. See Caton, "The Exalted Self"; "Conversion in Sarawak" was posted on 19 January 2006; see also *The Samoa Reader*, edited by Caton. Caton was also a serious advocate (along with Freeman) of biological perspectives in the analysis of culture.

30. Leader, *What Is Madness?*, 77. See similar arguments in Bentall, *Madness Explained*. The discussion on madness and paranoia follows broadly themes fleshed out by these theorists.

31. Freeman, "Mr Tom Harrisson." I am grateful to Dr. George Appell for a copy of this report.

32. Leader, *What Is Madness?*, 4–7.

33. Freeman to Morton Fried, 4 September 1957, 17/13, F/UCSD.

34. Peranio to Freeman, 14 October 1958, 17/13, F/UCSD.

35. Freeman to Needham, 24 April 1958, 157/22, F/UCSD.

36. The quotations and detail are from a confidential report on Peranio to the university, n.d., 18/1, F/UCSD.

37. Freeman, interview by Tuzin, transcript 1, p. 20.

38. Select excerpts only. The entire set of diary entries for 2–22 March 1961 is in Freeman to Heimann, 24 June 1992, 10/6, F/UCSD.

39. Freeman, "Mr Tom Harrisson."

40. Leader, *What Is Madness?*, 87.

41. Barnes, *Humping My Drum*, 351.

42. Caton, "Conversion in Sarawak," 8–10; Freeman diary, 17 March 1961, 10/6, F/UCSD.

43. "Fell apart" are Cutler's words in the Australian High Commission's cable to Crawford, 16 March 1961, 19-6.2.2.C, pt. 1, ANUA; Leader, *What Is Madness?*, 82.

44. Freeman to Morris, 9 August 1962, 157/16, F/UCSD. It took a decade, until 1971, for Freeman to concede in a letter to Rodney Needham that he had gone too far in his

actions in Sarawak (157/22, F/UCSD). He admitted the same to Don Tuzin forty years later, in 2000 (Freeman, interview by Tuzin, transcript 1, p. 21).

45. Both quotes are from Freeman to Morris, 9 August 1962, 157/16, F/UCSD. In a tragic twist, Harrisson was killed in a road accident in Thailand in 1976 after being banned from reentry to Sarawak through the efforts of a female archaeologist. A "farrago of half-truths and undocumented rumors" accompanied his banishment, of the kind Freeman accused Harrisson of spreading about him and his students; see Heimann, *The Most Offending*, 356, 362. *Koan* is the term for a paradoxical statement or question used for meditation in Zen Buddhism.

Chapter 5. Remaking Himself

1. Freeman to Crawford, 15 February 1962, quoted in Caton, "Conversion in Sarawak," 5. Caton refused to accept the sincerity of this "conversion experience," interpreting it as a self-deceiving set of rationalizations to counter the embarrassment of Freeman's losing Borneo as a research field (Freeman was banned from reentering Sarawak, though that did not last).

2. Allport, *Becoming*, 87. The quotation is on a separate card in a folder titled "Abreaction" in 26/1, F/UCSD; see also Sargant, *Battle for the Mind*.

3. George Stocking explores the breakout from structural functionalism and makes the point that Freeman was not alone in his return to psychology as part of the foundation for anthropology: see *Functionalism Historicized*, 131–91. Lindstrom also points to several well-known anthropologists who were rejecting British anthropology's aversion to history and psychology: Peter Worsley, Kenelm Burridge, Ian Jarvie, and Peter Lawrence. Lindstrom, "*Trumpet* and *Road*," 184, 188; see also Eriksen, *Small Places*, 19–20.

4. Freeman to Fortes, 20 September 1962, 8/9, F/UCSD. The Turner passage is in Turner, "Symbols in Ndembu Ritual."

5. Freeman to Fortes, 20 September 1962, 8/9, F/UCSD.

6. Freeman to Beaglehole, 23 January 1962, 152/25, F/UCSD.

7. Freeman to Firth, 16 January 1963, 8/4, F/UCSD.

8. Freeman to Needham, 22 May 1963, 157/22, F/UCSD.

9. Freeman to Leach, 5 March 1963, 156/21, F/UCSD. In a mocking draft letter of 1 July 1963 he never sent to Leach, Freeman commented of Leach's and Lévi-Strauss's approach to symbolism: "So many fabled fish slip unnoticed through the gaping mesh of your Durkheimian net." Ron Berndt had a severe falling out with Freeman a decade later (see chapter 7).

10. Correspondence between Barnes, Freeman, and Crawford is in Freeman, Staff Files, 19-6.2.2.C, pt. 1, ANUA: Barnes, 26 May, 13 and 27 June 1961; Crawford, 26 May and 21 June 1961; see also Caton, "Conversion in Sarawak," 12.

11. Freeman to Fortes, 10 January 1963, 8/9, F/UCSD.

12. Freeman to Crawford, 8 June 1961, and Barnes to Freeman, 27 June 1961, Freeman, Staff Files, 19-6.2.2.C, pt. 1, ANUA.

13. See Popper, *Conjectures and Refutations*.

14. Freeman, interview by Tuzin, transcript 2, p. 70, transcript 3, pp. 26–32.

15. Lines of verse are in Freeman to Crawford, 8 June 1961; see also Freeman to Barnes, 27 June 1961, Freeman, Staff Files, 19-6.2.2.C, pt. 1, ANUA.

16. Crawford draft memo to Vice Chancellor, 26 June 1961, Freeman, Staff Files, 19-6.2.2.C, pt. 1, ANUA. In a letter that reveals the administration's view of academic quirkery, the ANU registrar also enquired of Oxford University whether it had procedures in place to deal with "these indeterminate mental cases, which, after all, cannot be very unusual." Hohnen to Sandford, Oxford, 27 June 1961, Freeman, Staff Files, 19-6.2.2.C, pt. 1, ANUA; Freeman's summation of Crawford is in Freeman, interview by Tuzin, transcript 1, p. 27; Barnes, *Humping My Drum*, 356, 368.

17. Freeman to Leach, 5 March 1963, 156/21, F/UCSD.

18. Ploeg to the author, 15 August 2013.

19. Barnes, *Humping My Drum*, 356. If accurate, this seems a flippant, throwaway line, but it may exemplify the attitude of universities at the time toward mental health issues.

20. Freeman's comment is at the end of a long chronological summary of the events surrounding Brian de Martinoir dated 1959–62. The above outline is taken from this report and correspondence with Crawford in 154/2, F/UCSD, and from Barnes's memoir. Brian de Martinoir died in Troyes, France, in 1990.

21. Freeman to Freud, 28 June 1962, 154/34, F/UCSD.

22. Freeman to Crawford, 20 May 1963, Freeman, Staff Files, 19-6.2.2.C, pt. 1, ANUA. Freeman argued that he was not alone among anthropologists in accepting the relevance of psychoanalysis and implied that Firth, Fortes, and Gluckman were right behind him in his venture. Ploeg also remembers that the urge to find a "new" anthropology was common at the time. See Ploeg to the author, 15 August 2013.

23. Freeman's letter to Bowlby, 22 January 1963, 3/20, F/UCSD. I am indebted to Lamont Lindstrom for this reading of Derek's name change as a "free man"; see also Barnes, *Humping My Drum*, 352.

24. The "self-awareness" quote is from Mills, *Difficult Folk?*, 178; Gosse's *Father and Son* is considered one of the most influential, early psychological autobiographies in the English language.

25. Freeman, interview by Tuzin, transcript 1, p. 15.

26. Freeman's study leave report, 17 September 1964, Freeman, Staff Files, 19-6.2.2.C, pt. 1, ANUA.

27. Freeman's diary entry, TS, 21 October 1963; Lorenz, *On Aggression*; see also Smith, *Between Mind and Nature*, 250.

28. I am indebted to Tuzin's notes in TS for Freeman's views on this subject. See Colman, *Oxford Dictionary of Psychology*, s.v. "Kleinian," 405–6; and "object-relations theory," 519; see also Stephen, "Klein in Bali."

29. TS, 15 January 1964.

30. TS, 4 and 5 March 1964.

31. TS, 14 November 1963.

32. This is Tuzin's insight from reading the diaries and observing the life: TS, 13 April 1964.

33. TS, 16 April 1964.

34. TS, 30 April 1964.

35. TS, 18–19 June 1964. Klein's comment is noted on 5 June. From the historian's viewpoint it is fiendishly difficult to determine whether this personal analysis was a successful exercise. Partly an experiment to prepare himself for his journey into the human sciences, analysis presented Freeman with a set of interpretative possibilities about himself on which to ponder and take action. At first glance he seemingly failed to do so, for his treatment of Klein suggests a return to the very dominance behavior he had identified and resolved to jettison. On the other hand, Derek's notes on the sessions suggest that Klein was occasionally too absorbed in the effects of the process on himself and blind to the countertransference onto Freeman that was taking place.

36. Monica Freeman, interview by the author, 28 November 2002.

37. For "hot potato," see TS, 27 February 1964; "work-outs" is from Tuzin to the author, 4 September 2006.

38. "Phylogeny" is in Freeman to Barnes, 6 February 1964, 2/20, F/UCSD; Fortes's doubt is in TS, 1 February 1964.

39. Leach and Huxley jeers is in Freeman, interview by Tuzin, transcript 3, pp. 37, 42; Leach in Cambridge and "*passionate*," TS, 19 February 1964 ("passionate" is underlined in original); see Colman, *Oxford Dictionary of Psychology*, s.v. "splitting," 723. Freeman was wont to practice his newfound vocabulary of psychoanalysis in snap judgments about his associates: at dinner with the Astors he met Arthur Koestler, "who is revealed as a deeply schizoid personality with pervasive depressive formations and repressed sadism" (TS, 15 January 1964).

40. TS, 28 April 1964.

41. Freeman to Les Hiatt, 18 March 1971, 155/22, F/UCSD.

42. Freeman, interview by Tuzin, transcript 3, p. 41. It is uncertain, but Freeman's gibbon may have been a reference to their family pet in Borneo, which Derek had trained in certain behaviors.

43. Heimans, "Recorded Interview," 54.

Chapter 6. Face-to-Face with the Incubus

1. Freeman, "Notes towards an Intellectual Biography," 30.

2. Freeman to Fortes, 27 November 1964, 7 February 1965, 8/9, F/UCSD.

3. Freeman, "Notes towards an Intellectual Biography," 31. Freeman was referring to Popper's scientific method for testing hypotheses.

4. "Merry hell" from Heimans, "Recorded Interview," 57; the details of Freeman's conflict over his father and the section on his reception by psychiatrists are from TS, 1 March–25 December 1965, and from Tuzin's correspondence with Monica Freeman, "Questions for Monica," 25 Sept 2006, in author's possession.

5. Shankman, *Trashing*, 61–62.

6. Heimans, "Recorded Interview," 54–57.

7. Barrowclough, "Sex, Lies and Anthropology," 37.

8. Ibid.; Heimans, "Recorded Interview," 55.

9. Shankman, *Trashing*, 61.

10. Freeman quoting from a copy of his own letter in Freeman, interview by Tuzin, transcript 5, p. 59; Freeman's diary entry on his talk with Mead in TS, 10 November 1964.

11. Barrowclough, "Sex, Lies and Anthropology," 37.

12. See Freeman, "Some Observations on Kinship"; Ember, "Reply to Freeman"; Freeman, "Samoa: A Matter of Emphasis"; Ember, "Samoan Kinship and Political Structure"; Freeman, "Anthropological Theorizing." A perusal of the issues of *American Anthropologist* in which these articles appeared reveals an assortment of language by other anthropologists in mutual disputation that is far more feisty and personal than in this debate.

13. Mead, *Social Organization of Manu'a*, 1969 ed., 219.

14. Ember, "Reply to Freeman," 620–21; Ember, "Samoan Kinship and Political Structure," 164, 167.

15. Freeman, "Samoa: A Matter of Emphasis," 1536.

16. Ember, "Samoan Kinship and Political Structure," 167.

17. Stanner to Crawford, 12 November 1965, 181/25, F/UCSD. Freeman's memo to Stanner of 4 November 1965 is also here along with other correspondence.

18. Freeman to Davidson, 28 February 1966, 57-114, ANUA.

19. Details and quote from TS, 19–30 December 1965.

20. Details and quotation from Freeman's "Report on Researches in Samoa," 14 July 1966, copy in Freeman to Davidson, 15 July 1966, 57-114, ANUA. In 1978 Freeman published an essay detailing the assault on a chief by an untitled man; the essay clearly reflected how the order of dominance in a Samoan village dealt with this incident. Freeman, "'A Happening Frightening.'"

21. TS, 7 May 1966.

22. Davidson, *Samoa mo Samoa*.

23. Freeman, "Report on Researches," 11.

24. TS, 4 October 1966. The letter to Geertz and quotation are from an entry on 21 December 1966, reported by Tuzin.

25. This section is based on entries in TS, 1967: quotations are from 17, 18, 19 February 1967; "unwell" on 24 June 1967.

26. Emails, March 2008, ASAO Intrnet forum Thread (asaonet@listserv.uic.edu).

27. Email, Caton to Tcherkézoff, 28 February 2008, ASAO Intrnet forum Thread.

28. Shankman, *Trashing*, 63–64.

29. Freeman to Holmes, 10 October 1967, in Caton, *Samoa Reader*, 318. In the same letter and in a separate report to John Barnes, Freeman claimed the Samoans told him Mead would be tied up and thrown to the sharks if she returned. Freeman to Barnes, 27 September

1967, 2/20, F/UCSD; see also Shankman, *Trashing*, 63, where the tone is slightly more hostile to Freeman's report.

30. Freeman, interview by Tuzin, transcript 3, p. 19.

31. TS, 15–19 September 1967.

32. Shankman, *Trashing*, 63.

33. Freeman, interview by Tuzin, transcript 3, p. 17. Monica and "absorption" from interview with the author, 9 October 2002.

34. Partner, "Historicity," 32.

35. Bentall, *Madness Explained*, 136, makes the point about other cultures' acceptance; Shankman, *Trashing*, 63.

36. Leader, *What Is Madness?*, 68; see also Bentall, *Madness Explained*, 300.

37. Barnes, *Humping My Drum*, 357.

38. Clifford, *Person and Myth*, 216, 7.

39. TS, 28 December 1967.

40. TS, 25 January 1968.

41. Freeman to Fortes, 19 June 1968, 8/9, F/UCSD.

42. A copy of his application is in Freeman, Staff Files, 19-6.2.2.6, pt. 3, ANUA.

43. Freeman remark in TS, 13 December 1968. The colleague was Michael Walter; see also Freeman, interview by Tuzin, transcript 1, p. 48.

Chapter 7. "The Trouble with Derek Is . . ."

1. Munro to the author, March 2013, corroboration by Foster to author, 23 November 2016. The correspondence with Foster in September and October 1996 is in 154/29, F/UCSD. The official history is Foster and Varghese, *Making of the Australian National University*.

2. Lal and Leys, *The Coombs*. The building is named after H. C. "Nugget" Coombs, former governor of the Reserve Bank of Australia who was one of ANU's founding fathers and later became its chancellor. RSPacS later became the Research School of Pacific and Asian Studies and was then combined with other disciplines into a college as various restructurings took place.

3. References to Freeman in ibid., 75–76, 85, 121, 266, 276–77.

4. Quoted in Sachs, *Awakenings*, 228.

5. "Sprawling profession" in Eriksen and Nielsen, *A History of Anthropology*, 112; Barnes, *Humping My Drum*, 325–26. But at least funding was adequate at ANU in the 1960s, as Barnes found out after moving to the comparative poverty of Cambridge. One contemporary view of anthropology's evolution is Lawrence, "Ethnographic Revolution."

6. Freeman to Fortes, 7 February 1965, 8/9, F/UCSD.

7. Gray and Munro, "'The Department,'" 160.

8. Freeman to Fortes, 31 July 1972, 8/9, F/UCSD. It was typical of Freeman to be moved by a direct appeal to his ethical responsibilities, even if colleagues in Canberra believed that was exactly what was missing in his relations with them.

9. Spate to Low, 2 August, and Low to Spate, 14 August 1972, Low Private Papers. The Spate–Low correspondence has details of the selection committee's deliberations.

10. "In a timid," Freeman note in TS, 1 September 1972; referees' reports in Freeman, Staff Files, 19-6.2.2.6, pt. 3, ANUA; "Memo to OHK Spate by students," 27 July 1972, copy in 159/12, F/UCSD; other accounts from Freeman's remarks, TS, July–September 1972.

11. Spate to Low, 13 October 1972, Low Private Papers.

12. "We people" in Barunga, "Sacred Sites," copy in 152/24, F/UCSD; Freeman to Fortes, 31 July 1972, 8/9, F/UCSD.

13. Gray and Munro, "Australian Aboriginal Anthropology," 365–66.

14. Freeman wrote an article for the *ANU Reporter* on Barunga's Canberra stay, copy in 152/24, F/UCSD; Freeman to Lorenz, 27 July 1972, 13/11, F/UCSD; Freeman, interview by Tuzin, transcript 1, p. 2.

15. For correspondence with Aboriginal authorities, see 152/19, 154/23, and 158/2, F/UCSD; Freeman to Leach, 21 July 1975, 156/21, F/UCSD.

16. Freeman, interview by Tuzin, transcript 1, p. 5.

17. TS, 30 September 1974.

18. Departmental atmosphere evident from TS, 1973–74; Peterson, interview by the author, 10 July 2003; Tuzin, interview by the author, 29 August 2006.

19. Events in the department and Freeman's state of mind contained in TS, 1972–75; "self-mastery," TS, 3 October 1972.

20. Keesing to Rappaport, 10 October 1973, 18/21, F/UCSD.

21. Freeman to Leach, 3 May 1978, 156/21, F/UCSD.

22. TS, 17 November 1973.

23. Freeman to John [Haviland], 28 April 1975, 161/9, F/UCSD.

24. Freeman to Crawford, 18 November 1965, 159/15, F/UCSD; see also Freeman, "Notes towards an Intellectual Biography," 33; Gray, "W. E. H. Stanner."

25. Freeman, interview by Tuzin, transcript 1, p. 43.

26. Barnes, *Humping My Drum*, 432.

27. TS, 13 August 1974; Keesing's background interests are in Keesing to Freeman, 14 December 1972, 156/11, F/UCSD; see also Heimans, "Recorded Interview," 66, and Freeman, interview by Tuzin, transcript 1, pp. 7–9, and transcript 3, p. 59; "dissembler" is in TS, 7 November 1974; see also TS, 24–28 April 1975. One suspects Freeman was also disappointed that Keesing never got round to reading the draft of the Mead book Freeman offered him.

28. Robinson, "We, the Ethnographers," 121.

29. Freeman to Leach, 21 July 1975, 156/21, F/UCSD.

30. Correspondence is in Freeman, Staff Files, 19-6.2.2.6, pt. 3, ANUA; see also TS, 5 May–29 July 1975. Freeman rescinded both his request and his withdrawal from administration in July 1975. He tried again in 1979 to be redesignated, this time as professor of human ethology, with a similar result.

31. Quotations from Freeman to Low, 6 September 1979, 150/13, F/UCSD; see also Freeman's "A Brief Note on the So-Called 'Aztec Calendar Stone,'" 23 October 1979, copy

in 112/20, F/UCSD. Moloch was an ancient god of the Canaanites, associated with child sacrifice. It is not clear *how* Freeman went about testing a thymus, though he was later involved in kinetic muscle testing.

32. "Police statement by J. D. Freeman," Canberra, 17 September 1979, copy in 150/13, F/UCSD. This folder also contains thick files of letters documenting support for and opposition to the stone, as well as correspondence and newspaper reports upon which this reconstruction is based. TS, 1979–1981, is also instructive.

33. *ANU Reporter*, 28 September 1979.

34. "*Daimon*" is in Freeman to Low, 28 February 1981, 150/13, F/UCSD (*Daimon* underlined in original); Charles Price to Freeman, 15 September 1979, 150/13, F/UCSD.

35. Shankman riposte is in TS, 29 May 1984; "basilisk" is in TS, 24 September 1980.

36. Reay memo [to Low?], 10 April 1974, 440-892, Reay Papers, ANUA. I am indebted to Doug Munro for making copies of these materials.

37. TS, 31 March 1976.

38. Freeman's diary is peppered with wounding assessments of scholars' ideas and papers. Even Don Tuzin expressed his surprise at Freeman's "dyspepsia" when it came to criticizing colleagues' work.

39. TS, 17 December 1970; Ploeg to the author, 15 August 2013; Allen, "Seriously but Not Solemnly," 85.

40. Ploeg, "The Culture of Fieldwork." One of Freeman's American students, George Appell, after settling into his career at home, wrote that the British tradition of training maintained closer and more concerned contact with students in the field than the American, where students were left to themselves. *Anthropological Newsletter*, September 1989, 48–49, copy in 118/7, F/UCSD.

41. McCall to the author, 13 October 2016.

42. "Bumbling mind" is in TS, 16–31 October and 7 November 1980; father-son insight by anthropologist Lamont Lindstrom.

43. Details on Tuzin are in the introduction to Lipset and Roscoe, *Echoes of the Tambaran*; see also Tuzin, interview with Hempenstall, 29 and 30 June 2004; "outdoor" is in Lipset and Roscoe, *Echoes of the Tambaran*, 3.

44. Freeman to Tuzin, 15 October 1969, 161/15, F/UCSD.

45. Barnes, *Humping My Drum*, 281, 295, 354–55. On the other hand, Barnes admitted late in life that he took far too casual an attitude to the supervision process and was constantly engaged in rescue missions as a consequence. Another anthropologist, Penelope Schoeffel, who knew Freeman well from the war around Mead, believed his sense of masculinity was absolute and made him hostile to female students. Schoeffel, interview by the author, 8 December 2012.

46. Macintyre and Jolly response to review, 1989, copy in 154/30, F/UCSD; for changes in social sciences in the 1970s, see Eriksen and Nielsen, *History of Anthropology*, 111–12.

47. Freeman's version is in several places, most concisely in Heimans, "Recorded Interview," 66–68.

48. The student's version and quotations come from his memo to Freeman, 18 July 1974, Freeman, Staff Files, 19-6.2.2.6, pt. 3, ANUA. Notes by Anthony Low are in the same file.

49. TS, 18 March 1982; "habitual" is in TS, 4 January 1982.

50. "Done in" is in TS, 21 and 22 April 1982; confrontation is in TS, 8 August 1989.

51. "Oldest living" is in TS, 9 July 1990; "Academic life" is a note by Freeman in TS, 31 July 1986.

52. Freeman, interview by Tuzin, transcript 5, p. 81.

53. Details on Monica are in a eulogy by Jennifer Freeman, 14 April 2012; see Appell-Warren, *Iban Diaries of Monica Freeman.*

54. Freeman and Buddhism are in Monica Freeman, interview by the author, 9 October 2002; and in Tuzin, interview by the author, 29 June 2004, 30 June 2004; "I'm behaving" is in Freeman, interview by Tuzin, transcript 2, pp. 45–46.

55. "I think" is in Freeman, interview by Tuzin, transcript 4, p. 71; Lévi-Strauss (1964) quoted in Williams, "Professing Culture," 290; Monica Freeman, interview by the author, 8 December 2005.

Chapter 8. On the Edge

1. "Dragon" is in Caton to Freeman, 27 June 1990, 5/13, F/UCSD; Caton to Freeman, 17 February 1989, 184/1, F/UCSD, capitals in original.

2. Ross Hohnen (Registrar) to Oxford University, 27 June 1961, Freeman, Staff Files, 19-6.2.2.6, pt. 1, ANUA; see Caton, "Conversion in Sarawak," 3–8.

3. "Obsessional" is in Barnes, *Humping My Drum,* 354. Freeman stressed he wanted to be rid of his obsessiveness; see Heimans, "Recorded Interview," 89.

4. Stanner memo is quoted in Caton, "Exalted Self," 378.

5. Ibid., 359–84.

6. "Empathy blindness" is the term Caton used as part of his characterization of Freeman; see "Exalted Self," 382; see also Shankman, *Trashing.*

7. I am grateful to Monica Freeman for showing me the writing in the 1974–75 diaries. She believed Derek's condition softened into the 1980s and 1990s and did not need medication: Monica Freeman, interview by the author, 8 December 2005. Details on lithium are in Jamison, *Unquiet Mind,* 81. See also de Moore and Westmore, *Finding Sanity.*

8. Caton, "The Exalted Self," 374. Bentall, *Madness Explained,* 273, contains a definition of hypomania taken from Jamison's textbook on manic depressive illness. He also discusses environmental causes. Ironically, a psychiatric examination, such as Freeman called for, may not have picked up such episodic soft expressions.

9. Jamison, *Unquiet Mind,* 202. Jamison also gave up taking lithium because of the deadening effect it had on her mind.

10. Freeman, interview by Tuzin, transcript 3, p. 17.

11. Dryden quote is in TS, 8 November 1970; "fundamental fear" is in TS, 2 April 1974.

12. For Freeman's struggles, see TS, 6 February, 20 March, 14 June, 23 September 1990; Tuzin belief is in TS, 3 June comment.

13. TS, 23 March 1975; see also 11 September 1976.

14. TS, 20 August and 18 November 1975.

15. TS, 11 April 1979; the diaries begin in earnest in 1961–62.

16. Extracts from TS, 1969–90; Tuzin's summaries end with 1990 (italicized words underlined in original).

17. "All experience" is Tuzin's point; diary rallying cries: 13 March 1971, 20 December 1973, 16 March and 12 May 1974, 4 April 1975, June–July 1979, 8 June and 16 July 1980, 12 November 1989.

18. "Red letter day" is in TS, 7 March 1975; Heimans, "Recorded Interview," 68; TS, 11 September 1976. For the Alexander technique, see Barker, *Alexander Technique*; see also Colman, *Oxford Dictionary of Psychology*, s.v. "Alexander technique," 22.

19. The following analysis is based on entries in TS, 1979–85. Diamond's book that inspired Freeman was *Your Body Doesn't Lie*.

20. I am indebted to Lamont Lindstrom for the insights about Freeman's bodily concerns.

21. General comments on Freeman's diary are in Tuzin to the author, 7 August 2006.

22. Leader, *What Is Madness?*, 136; see also Eghigian, *From Madness to Mental Health*. Foucault called the issues around madness "metaphysical": Clark, *History, Theory, Text*, 117.

23. This is the approach of Gordon W. Allport, who was one of the founders of personality psychology and an influence on generations of psychologists: Allport, *Becoming*, vii; Allport was one of Freeman's "authorities."

24. Bentall, *Madness Explained*, 12; Leader, *What Is Madness?*, 43; see also De Masi, *Vulnerability to Psychosis*.

25. Funder, *The Personality Puzzle*, 143.

26. Bentall, *Madness Explained*, 415.

Chapter 9. A Not-So-Simple Journey

1. Rappaport, quoted in Caton, *The Samoa Reader*, 252.

2. Faanafi Aiono le Tagaloa to Freeman, 10 April 1991, 7/22, F/UCSD; see also Crocombe to Freeman, 3 March 1971, 6/7, F/UCSD.

3. Mead, *Coming of Age*, 23. Hereafter cited parenthetically in the text.

4. Torgovnik, *Gone Primitive*, 240. On 1920s American culture, see Molloy, *On Creating a Usable Culture*.

5. Appell, "Freeman's Refutation," revised version, 13. I am indebted to George Appell for making this available.

6. A copy of the 1977 review of the department is in 181/28, F/UCSD; "shut out" is in Freeman to Pfeiffer, 27 January 1983, 18/4, F/UCSD. This letter lays out the chronology of his contacts with Mead. Copies of the actual correspondence from 1964 to 1978 are in 141/7, F/UCSD.

7. The full title is "On the Believing of as Many as Six Impossible Things before Breakfast: An Analysis of the Consequences of Cathecting Assumptions in Cultural and Social Anthropology." A copy is in 112/7, F/UCSD; "exquisite howlers" is on p. 40.

8. Ibid., 25, 35, 48.

9. Shankman, *Trashing*, 65.

10. Freeman, "On the Believing," 15, 37, 33.

11. The readers' comments were sent to Freeman, and copies are in 112/13, F/UCSD. All three readers were North American anthropologists.

12. Quotations are in TS, 18 July 1970, 13 March 1971, and 26 August 1971, respectively.

13. "Creativity" is in TS, 14 October 1972; "talking through hat" is in TS, 7 August 1969; "overweening" is in TS, 19 May 1972.

14. Chronology of Freeman's writing attempts are in TS, 1970–71; Freeman to Crocombe, 14 March 1971, 6/7, F/UCSD.

15. The "anatomy" remark is in the report dated 8 June 1971, 112/13, F/UCSD; see also the report dated 13 April 1971. Freeman's friend was Eliot Chapple, who wrote a book on culture and biology in 1970: Freeman to Chapple, 25 May 1971, 153/19, F/UCSD.

16. Freeman's "Some Errata" was rejected by *American Anthropologist* as "most inadvisable" in an article section; for Mead on Manu'a's conditions, see Mead, *Social Organization*, 227–28.

17. Observations and quotes are in TS, 5 May 1971, 10 November 1971, 24 May 1973, and 30 June 1975, respectively.

18. TS, 27 February 1975. Raymond Firth also tried to dissuade Freeman from his course.

19. "Whole enterprise" is in TS, 20 March 1975; for the offer to Schoeffel, see 3 May (Schoeffel confirmed the offer in an interview by the author, 8 December 2012).

20. Freeman to Heppell, 29 January 1976, 155/20, F/UCSD.

21. "Stain" is in TS, 31 May 1976; Harrisson on Kinabalu is in TS, 26 June 1976; Freeman to Mulok Kedit, 24 February 1976, 156/20, F/UCSD.

22. Needham about Jensen is in 157/22, F/UCSD; see especially Needham to Freeman, 19 July 1976.

23. Rousseau, "Iban Inequality." Freeman's reaction can be followed in his correspondence with Stephanie Morgan, on whom Rousseau drew, 1 and 2 August 1980, and with Richard Salisbury in Rousseau's Canadian department, 11 August 1980, 19/12, F/UCSD; Freeman to Leach, 23 September 1980, 12/19, F/UCSD.

24. TS, 9 October 1976.

25. Freeman, "Sociobiology."

26. TS, 26 June 1977.

27. Freeman to Mead, 23 August 1978, 141/7, F/UCSD. He told John Pfeiffer that he had written to her in April 1978, without reply: 18/4, F/UCSD.

28. "Sweet Analytics" 112/19, F/UCSD; Schoeffel, interview by the author, 8 December 2012. Schoeffel had her own worries that Freeman would attack her when she gave her first ever conference paper at the same time. He did not.

29. Unless otherwise noted, the sequence of events and all quotations in this section, including some of Tuzin's comments, are in TS, 1979–81 (italicized words underlined in original).

30. Métraux to Freeman, 5 March 1981, 150/18, F/UCSD.

31. In a Freudian-like slip, Freeman wrote "dead" when he meant "dared": Freeman, interview by Tuzin, transcript 1, pp. 32–33. The quote is from the eighteenth-century poet Christopher Smart. The original reads: "And now the matchless deed's achieved, / Determined, dared, and done" ("A Song to David," verse 86, 215).

32. Heimans, "Recorded Interview," 72.

33. TS, 23 November 1981. Unless otherwise stated, all descriptions and quotations are in TS, 1981.

34. Heimans, "Recorded Interview," 73; Freeman, interview by Tuzin, transcript 4, p. 56.

35. Quoted in Freeman to Pfeiffer, 27 January 1983, 18/4, F/UCSD.

Chapter 10. The Banquet of Consequences

1. Freeman, *Margaret Mead and Samoa*, 31. Hereafter cited parenthetically in the text.

2. Freeman to Low, Freeman, Staff Files, 19-6.2.2.6, pt. 4, ANUA; "denouement" is in Freeman to Stephen Morris, 19 January 1981, Freeman Family Papers; see also Freeman to Bishop Museum, Hawai'i, 14 August 1981, 3/14, F/UCSD; Freeman to Gayle Treadwell, Harvard University Press, 28 April 1982, 10/1, F/UCSD. *Life* magazine, May 1983, quoted Freeman making the same claim; see the copy in 150/10, F/UCSD.

3. Stocking warning in Caton, *Samoa Reader*, 324–26; Freeman, "Notes toward an Intellectual Biography," 47.

4. Harvard's surprise is in Caton, *Samoa Reader*, 208; Wanner is in Freeman remark in TS, 26 March 1982; Freeman dream is in TS, 30 December 1982.

5. Caton, *Samoa Reader*, 207.

6. Schwartz, "Anthropology"; Schwartz to Freeman, 14 February 1983, 20/9, F/UCSD.

7. Freeman's notes are in TS, 1–14 February 1983.

8. Rappaport quoted in Caton, *Samoa Reader*, 223; see also TS, 24 May 1983; Basham comments are in Caton, *Samoa Reader*, 218–21.

9. Freeman to Bateson, 13 January 1983, 3/4, F/UCSD.

10. "Set up" is in Heimans, "Recorded Interview," 79; TS, 14 March 1983.

11. TS, 7 and 11 March 1983.

12. Freeman on reviews: TS, 26 May, 20 April, and 23 May 1983; Cressman in *New York Times*, 3 May 1983, and Freeman remark in TS, 31 May 1983; McDowell, "Derek Freeman"; Glick, TS, 30 September 1983.

13. Basham, "Anthropology's Adolescent Dilemma," quoted in Caton, *Samoa Reader*, 219. In TS, 2 May 1983, Freeman notes that newspapers reported that his book was described at Barnard as "a shoddy piece of work." For "sex angle," see Caton, *Samoa Reader*, 230–32.

14. Quoted in *Denver Post*, 18 October 1983; also mentioned in TS, 9 November 1983.

15. Robert A. Paul in Caton, *Samoa Reader*, 230.

16. "Feeding frenzy" is in TS, 18 January 1984; Tuzin memory in note to author, inserted in TS, 18 November 1983 (italicized words underlined in original).

17. TS, 3 January 1984.

18. Quoted in Leo, "Bursting," 51; see also Herdt correspondence, 1983, 10/10, F/UCSD. Gilbert Herdt, an American anthropologist at San Francisco State University, had received his PhD from ANU and worked with Freeman in Canberra. He consistently supported Freeman's work.

19. Meggitt, TS, 24 June 1983; Goodman quoted in Freeman entry, TS, 8 June 1983; see also Caton, *Samoa Reader*, 135–42.

20. "Shockwave," in Schwartz, "Anthropology," 919; Stocking in *Ethnographer's Magic*, 278. Three special issues were devoted to arguments, mainly against Freeman: *American Anthropologist* 85, no. 4 (1983); *Canberra Anthropology* (now *Asia Pacific Journal of Anthropology*) 6, no. 1 (1983); and *Pacific Studies* 7, no. 2 (1984). Freeman contributed substantial rejoinders to the latter two.

21. Murray, "On Boasians," 450; see also his "Problematic Aspects," 405.

22. See Freeman to Caton, 13 August 1991, 5/13, F/UCSD; and Freeman to Wanner, 29 April 1982, 10/1, F/UCSD. Freeman's papers hold two crammed folders of quotations in books and articles from 1928 to 1983 that repeat Mead's Samoa claims: 107/2 and 3, F/UCSD; "invisibility" is in Murray, "Problematic Aspects," 407.

23. Weiner, "Ethnographic Determinism," 915.

24. Schwartz, "Anthropology," 920, also 923, 925.

25. Quoted in Freeman, *Margaret Mead and Samoa*, 244.

26. Shankman's critique is in "Samoan Conundrum," 48–49; Holmes, *Quest*, 153.

27. Ethnic slur is in Nardi, "The Height"; "new myth" is in Schoeffel and Meleisea, "Margaret Mead," 68; Schoeffel, interview by the author, 8 December 2012.

28. Strathern, "The Punishment," 77.

29. The *Canberra Anthropology* special issue included a "select bibliography" of 237 items on the controversy in the first eighteen months.

30. Shore, "Paradox Regained," 25; Hooper, "Book Review."

31. On selective quoting, see McDowell, "Derek Freeman," 112–16; Holmes, *Quest*, 154–55; "no keeper" is in Strathern, "The Punishment," 73.

32. Heimans, "Recorded Interview," 77.

33. Weiner, "Ethnographic Determinism," 910–11; see also Harris in *Sciences*, July–August 1983, quoted in Caton, *Samoa Reader*, 236; Murray, "Problematic Aspects," 401–3.

34. Holmes, *Quest*, 1, 139, 174, 177; Schwartz, "Anthropology," 920–23. An extension of these Boasian defenses was the rejection of Freeman's argument that American anthropologists had adopted from Boas a doctrine of "absolute cultural determinism." R. E. Young and S. Juan argue instead that "cultural maximalism" best represents the dominant view ("Freeman's Margaret Mead Myth").

35. On Boas's influence, see Degler, *In Search of Human Nature*; and Lewis, "Boas, Darwin."

36. Weiner, "Ethnographic Determinism," 918; Schneider quoted in Caton, *Samoa Reader*, 223; Marcus, "One Man's Mead," 3; Kuper in *Times Literary Supplement*, quoted in Freeman to Kuper, 20 May 1983, 12/9, F/UCSD; Harris quoted in Caton, *Samoa Reader*, 237–38; Holmes, "Margaret Mead's Samoa," 541–44; Silverman, "Our Great Deception"; Shore in *London Observer*, 6 February 1983, quoted in Caton, *Samoa Reader*, 283.

37. Colleen Clements to Letters Editor, *Science*, 18 May 1983, 13/8, F/UCSD (emphasis added).

38. Quoted in *Wichita Eagle-Beacon*, 20 February 1983; see Caton, *Samoa Reader*, 226–27.

39. Strathern, "The Punishment of Margaret Mead," 79; Young and Juan, "Margaret Mead Myth," 64; "irenic" quoted in Freeman, interview by Tuzin, transcript 4, p. 71; Shore quoted in Freeman to Treadwell, Harvard University Press, 28 April 1982, 10/2, F/UCSD.

40. "Personal obloquy" is in Freeman to Levy, 23 May 1983, 13/8, F/UCSD; Freeman's responses: Freeman, "Inductivism" and "Response: Derek Freeman"; "approximate indication" is in Freeman, "Inductivism," 124.

41. Comments on Shankman: Freeman, "Inductivism," 112, 157; on McDowell: Freeman, "Response: Derek Freeman," 160, 158, 145, 175; on Schoeffel and Meleisea: Freeman, "Inductivism," 160, 162; on Mead: Freeman, "Inductivism," 118.

42. TS, 27 April 1983, also 14–22 April and 6 January 1984 (italicized words underlined in original).

43. On Freeman's numbness, see TS, 22 December 1983; Antichrist, see Freeman summary in TS, 5 August 1983; Sydney seminar, TS, 3 May 1984.

44. Freeman in Caton, *Samoa Reader*, 192.

45. "Lengthy grinding" is in Cornell, "Reader Replies"; Rappaport, "Desecrating," 319.

46. The Freeman–Rappaport exchange is in "Reader Replies," *American Scholar* 56, no. 1 (1987): 157–60; and "Reader Replies," *American Scholar* 56, no. 2 (1987): 303–4.

47. Murray letter, 12 December 1990; Freeman letter, 16 November 1991; their correspondence is in 15/15, F/UCSD.

48. See Freeman and Leacock correspondence, 12/20, F/UCSD, esp. Freeman letter, 12 June 1985.

49. The Freeman and Mageo correspondence is in 14/1, F/UCSD, and in Caton, *Samoa Reader*, 295–300. Mageo's article is abridged in Caton, *Samoa Reader*, 84–98; another appeared in *Oceania* 59, no. 3 (1989). Freeman had tried to persuade the editor to have it checked by Samoans.

50. Holmes, *Quest*, 151–53, 170–74.

51. Ibid., 129.

52. Holmes correspondence with Freeman quoted in Caton, *Samoa Reader*, 281: original letters from 1967 to the 1990s are in 10/17, F/UCSD; Freeman, "Inductivism," 130–48, includes his treatment of Holmes; see also Caton, *Samoa Reader*, 280–81, 315, 320–21; Holmes to Mead, 23 October 1967, 10/17, F/UCSD. Holmes told Mead he thought Freeman was a very sick man.

53. Thomas Bargatzky's review of *Quest* in Caton, *Samoa Reader*, 255–63; Stocking, *Ethnographer's Magic*, 325, argues that Holmes's posture was "roughly that of the general anthropological community for the next several decades"; in a letter to Freeman dated 19 September 1978, Holmes admitted he did not want to draw the anger of Mead by being involved in controversy: 10/17, F/UCSD.

54. TS, 1–2 November 1987. Manjusi (or Manjusri) refers to the pose of the Buddha of Wisdom in Asian art.

55. Freeman to Holmes, 4 February 1989, 10/18, F/UCSD.

56. These judgments are taken from the amplified version of Shore, "Paradox Regained," in *Canberra Anthropology*, 17, 21, 25, 29, 32–33.

57. Freeman's comment is in his "Inductivism," 148.

58. Freeman, "Inductivism," 150.

59. Shore made two detailed responses to Freeman, in both of which he argued that Freeman had distorted Shore's use of the term "nature." "Reply to Freeman," *Oceania* 54, no. 3 (1984): 254–60; and 55, no. 3 (1985): 218–23.

60. Freeman, "Inductivism," 148–55, esp. 151, 152. In a review of *Sala'ilua* in 1984, Freeman explained his case against Shore in detail, praising Shore's account as "by far the best outline of the social structure of a village community in the published literature on Samoa" but disputing Shore's complex cultural explanation in favor of Freeman's own, simpler account of intoxicated anger. Shore made an effective reply, though shying away from the fact that he had not interviewed the murderer, and, like many of Freeman's critics, Shore questioned Derek's motives. Exchanges went on for the usual lengthy period till editors were sick of the issue. Freeman, "The Burthen," plus Shore's replies in the following issues of *Oceania*. See also Freeman to Le Tagaloa Leota Pita Ala 'ilima, 1 May 1985, 13/1, F/UCSD. The Vicar of Bray was the satirical description of a clerical figure, dating to the sixteenth century, who cut his ecclesiastical cloth according to whichever regime was in power.

61. Shore in *London Observer*, 6 February 1983, quoted in Caton, *Samoa Reader*, 283.

62. Shore to Freeman, 14 June 1988, F/UCSD, 21/2.

63. Ibid.

64. Ibid.

65. Freeman to Shore, 1 July 1988, F/UCSD, 21/2.

66. Levy, "Mead, Freeman and Samoa," 85. Stocking, *Ethnographer's Magic*, 338, concurs that cultural determinism was central to the (American) discipline's self-definition during the twentieth century.

67. "Repertoire" is in Tuzin, "Margaret Mead and the Heretic"; "clad" is in Lefkowitz, *New Republic*, 1984, quoted in Caton, *Samoa Reader*, 241.

68. O'Meara to Freeman, 28 April 1988, 16/14, F/UCSD.

69. See Clark, *History, Theory, Text*, 122, for Michel de Certeau on controlling disciplines; see also Mills, *Difficult Folk?*, 178.

70. Caton, *Samoa Reader*, 4.

71. Levy comment is in "Mead, Freeman and Samoa," 85; Stocking, *Ethnographer's Magic*, 333.

72. Leach quoted in Caton, *Samoa Reader*, 245, 217; Bargatzky comments are in ibid., 261.

73. Caton, *Samoa Reader*, 11, for young Samoans; for other Samoans, see ibid., 6, 7, 13; Levy, "Mead, Freeman and Samoa," 87, for Lelei Lelaulu.

74. Field to Freeman, 14 December 1985, 8/1, F/UCSD.

75. Levy, "Mead, Freeman and Samoa," 87; Freeman, "Inductivism," 109.

76. Schwartz, "Anthropology," 925.

77. Addendum to the author, TS, 27 September 1983. Freeman saw all anthropologists ideally as "truthmongers"; see TS, 21 October 1983.

78. Freeman to Le Tagaloa Leota Pita Alaʻilima, 16 December 1985, Freeman Family Papers.

79. TS, 1985, passim.

80. Freeman to Le Tagaloa Leota Pita Alaʻilima, 6 August 1986, Freeman Family Papers.

Chapter 11. Hunting Heretics

1. Freeman to Aiono Dr. Fanaafi Le Tagaloa, 27 March 1988, Freeman Family Papers.

2. "Faʻapuaʻa Faʻamu and Margaret Mead," 1017; see also Freeman, "On Franz Boas." "Recreational lying" was adopted from anthropologist Tim O'Meara.

3. Ibid., 1020–21.

4. Comments recorded in TS, 24 February, 16 April, 20 July, 23 September, and 4 November 1988.

5. A. Kuper, "Coming of Age," 454–55.

6. Brady, "*The Samoa Reader*," 499.

7. Shore to Caton, 14 April 1989, 21/3, F/UCSD.

8. Caton, *Samoa Reader*, 207–8, 268.

9. "Attention-seeking maverick" is in TS, 30 November 1989; Freeman to Caton, 11 January and 7 February 1989, 184/1, F/UCSD.

10. Caton to Freeman, 27 June 1990, 5/13, F/UCSD. For Caton on Freeman's personality, see Caton letters, 27 April 1992, 5/14, 17 February and 21 April 1989, 184/1, 27 June 1990, 5/13, and 13 March, 8 April, 15 April 1992, 5/14, all in F/UCSD. Ironically, Caton faced questions about his own personality and unorthodox opinions within his university community during the 1980s: personal communication, Lyndall Ryan, September 2014; see also TS, 23 October 1985.

11. "'There's Tricks,'" 104. Hereafter cited parenthetically in the text. Quotes enclosed in both single and double quotation marks are quotes Freeman used from others.

12. Schoeffel believes Freeman was only too happy to see this rumor published. Shankman spent energy and ink arguing the affairs never happened.

13. "Paradigms," 25. Hereafter cited parenthetically in the text; page numbers are from the article in *Academic Questions*.

14. The previous material and the following paragraphs, including quotes, are drawn from TS, 1990, the last year available for scrutiny from Tuzin's summaries of Freeman's

diaries; see also Freeman correspondence with Appell, 1990, 152/11, F/UCSD; Freeman to Herdt, 2 July 1990, 10/10, F/UCSD. Freeman was Woodsworth Visiting Scholar at Simon Fraser, and his series was titled After Margaret Mead: An Antipodean Rethinking of Anthropology, 181/23, F/UCSD.

15. TS, 16 March 1990.

16. Freeman to Salk, 3 June 1990, 19/24, F/UCSD; quotes to Tuzin in Freeman, interview by Tuzin, transcript 3, pp. 14–15.

17. Tolstoy quote from letter to Mary Lefkowitz, 7 September 1992, 12/12, F/UCSD; "by March" is in Freeman to Sather, 30 September 1992, 20/6, F/UCSD.

18. Tuzin to Freeman, 19 October 1994, 23/1, F/UCSD.

19. Details are from Freeman, interview by Tuzin, transcript 5, pp. 9–45.

20. For Williamson's career, see Zuber-Skerritt, *David Williamson*; and Kiernan, *David Williamson*.

21. Williamson tells the story of the play's genesis in the preface to the 1995 Currency Press edition of the script.

22. Quotations from the Currency Press edition, 94–95.

23. Heimans, "Recorded Interview," 92.

24. Account of meeting and quotations are in Harrison manuscript, "Derek and Monica."

25. Quotations from the Penguin edition of *Heretic*, respectively, 18, 89, 63.

26. Examples: McGillick, "Heresy"; John McCallum in *Australian*, 1 April 1996. See also Freeman, "Heretic Draws on 50 Years of Research."

27. Williamson to the author, 21 February 2012; "a passion" is in the introduction to the Penguin edition of *Heretic*, 10; "one of the bravest" is in Williamson to Freeman, 16 July 1997, 24/20, F/UCSD.

28. Barrowclough, "Sex, Lies," 31; see Freeman, "The Science of Heresy." At times, Freeman implied that his fate mirrored that of Galileo, Michael Servetus, or Giordano Bruno, heretics of former centuries. He had also in mind Dr. Peter Cameron, a Presbyterian cleric in Sydney tried as a heretic by his church in the 1980s.

29. Freeman to Robin Williams, 6 October 1997, 24/18, F/UCSD.

30. Côte, *Adolescent Storm*, 20–21. The essential arguments are contained in the first sixty-four pages; the rest is devoted to an assessment of the needs of contemporary young Samoans. See also Côte, "Was Mead Wrong."

31. Freeman to Côte, 10 September 1994, Freeman Family Papers. Freeman sent Côte a postcard of an Australian peregrine falcon in flight, telling Côte he should think of himself as the "pigeon."

32. "Soap opera science" is in Côte, *Adolescent Storm*, 8; examples of Côte's provocations: 4, 8, 12, 15, 21–24.

33. Freeman to Orans, 3 April 1993, 16/17, F/UCSD; Orans's 1988 correspondence is in 184/5.

34. Freeman to Orans, 11 November 1992, 16/17, F/UCSD; Stuart Cuno quoted in Murdoch, *The Good Apprentice*, 29.

35. Quotes are from Freeman to Orans, 5 August 1995, 17/2, F/UCSD (italicized words underlined in original). See also Freeman, "Margaret Mead, Martin Orans."

36. Quotes and descriptions are from Freeman to colleague, 20 December 1991; Freeman to Silverman, 3 February 1992; Freeman to Kuper, 20 February 1992, all in Firth Papers. I am indebted to Geoff Gray for copies of this correspondence.

37. Freeman to Brady, 16 December 1991, 4/1, F/UCSD. Brady's review is titled "*The Samoa Reader*: Last Word or Lost Horizon?"

38. Freeman on enemies' brains is in Freeman, interview by Tuzin, transcript 2, p. 22; see TS, 24 May 90; "casuistry" is in Freeman to Tuzin, 21 February 2001, 160/1, F/UCSD.

39. Freeman forced an apology in 1996 after threatening legal action, but the barbs continued. Freeman's papers contain much evidence: 14/13, 155/22, and 157/6, F/UCSD; "spiked animus" is in Freeman to *Journal of Polynesian Society*, draft in 155/2, F/UCSD; "malevolence" is in Freeman to Low, 3 January 2000, 13/1, F/UCSD.

40. Freeman to Oliver, 4 March 2000, 141/31, F/UCSD; see also Bentall, *Madness Explained*, 428–38; Zeldin, *Intimate History*, 380; Freeman to Low, 12 May 1995, 156/31, F/UCSD.

41. Tuzin to the author, 10 July 2006.

42. Norton publishers to Freeman, 3 October 1997, 158/25, F/UCSD.

43. Freeman, *Fateful Hoaxing*, 14. Hereafter cited parenthetically in the text.

44. Brown, review of *Fateful Hoaxing*.

45. Orans, review of *Fateful Hoaxing*; Côte, review of *Fateful Hoaxing*.

46. Caton, review of *Fateful Hoaxing*; for other reviews, see Ings; Gerrand; and Walter.

47. Freeman, "Was Margaret Mead Misled"; another Freeman essay asserting his final position is "Margaret Mead's Coming of Age," published in three different journals. Mead's "Life as a Samoan Girl" is in the edited collection *All True!* See also Handy, *The Native Culture*.

48. Côte, "Correspondence Concerning"; "bigot" is in Freeman to Côte, 28 February 2000, Freeman family archives. I am indebted to Doug Munro for obtaining a copy of this letter.

49. Freeman, interview by Tuzin, transcript 5, pp. 67–94; Heimans, "Recorded Interview," 97; Freeman to Aiono Dr. Fanaafi Le Tagaloa, 11 September 2000, Freeman Family Papers.

50. Freeman, "In Praise of Heresy," 90, 92.

51. Caton, "The Mead/Freeman Controversy," 599–600.

52. Tcherkézoff to Freeman, 17 December 2000, 159/24, F/UCSD. A full folder of their correspondence is available.

53. Freeman quotes in letters of 3 and 4 January 2001, 159/24, F/UCSD; see also Freeman letters, 22 February and 23 March 2001, and Tcherkézoff to Freeman, 7 February 2001.

54. "Ridiculous" is in letter to Freeman, 28 February 2001; "the grand debate" is in Tcherkézoff to Freeman, 26 March 2001, 159/24, F/UCSD.

55. Freeman, "'Words Have No Words,'" 301, 310, 302.

56. Tcherkézoff, "Correspondence: Samoa Again," 431–36.

57. Tcherkézoff, "Correspondence: Samoa Again," 435.

58. "Sturm und Drang" from Roscoe, "Margaret Mead," 581.

59. On Chagnon, see Horgan, "Hearts of Darkness"; and Wallace, "The Left Hand of Darkness"; "fractal" is in Tarrow, "Polarization."

60. Tiffany, "Reflections on Pacific Ethnography." Hereafter cited parenthetically in the text. For a typical college-level presentation of the Mead–Freeman debate, see Endicott and Welsch, *Taking Sides.* I am grateful to Robert Welsch for a copy of this text.

61. Shankman cannot point to any evidence that Freeman knew what was happening to loosen Samoan society during World War II and relies on a book by W. H. Stanner, who was there on a rushed visit during a nine-month tour of three British Pacific dependencies and for his judgments relied on government officers and official publications. Shankman also quotes Mary Boyd, a political scientist making general academic points from New Zealand. He ignores the eye-witness memoir about Samoa during the war by the New Zealand official C. G. A. Mackay (*Samoana*), who says there was no "loose behavior" in public during the war. With Freeman spending as much time as he could on the south coast away from Apia, it is perfectly possible he did not observe significant changes of behavior. In any case, there is no diary or correspondence to shine a light on the situation.

62. Shankman, "Margaret Mead, Derek Freeman," 39. Shankman and Côte were now arguing against the puzzling public acceptance of Freeman's critique; see also Shankman's "Margaret Mead's Other Samoa."

63. Shankman, "Derek Freeman," 204.

64. Freeman to Lefkowitz, 31 January 1999, 12/22, F/UCSD; see also Freeman, "'All Made of Fantasy,'" which includes Shankman's reply, 977; see also Freeman, "Controversy: Derek Freeman Replies."

65. "Housekeeping" from Monaghan, "The Battle of Samoa Revisited." Monaghan also sided with Shankman in "Boffins Behaving Badly" and with Caton's speculations in "An Australian Historian."

66. Shankman, *Trashing,* 5. Hereafter cited parenthetically in the text.

67. The argument about Mead being dead and being put on trial by Freeman is in ibid., 17. I have turned his image on its head. The "matchless deed": Freeman, as was his habit with any task completed, was quoting from a literary source, this time the eighteenth-century poet Christopher Smart. Shankman used it, as did Caton, without attribution to suggest an overweening arrogance in Freeman.

68. For example, Freeman's entire "interactionist anthropology" was seen in this light (ibid., 223). Shankman also could not see any sincerity in Freeman's excusing Mead for being hoaxed.

69. See Shankman, "The 'Fateful Hoaxing.'" Shankman adds the accusation that Freeman deliberately misused the Fa'amu interview data to mislead; see also LeVine, "Cutting a Controversy." In February 2008 and again in early 2017 a series of postings on the ASAO list server spread a new generation of "Derek" stories.

70. Freeman, "Was Margaret Mead Misled?," 609. Freeman was quoting from a letter Stevenson wrote: see Colvin, *The Letters,* 14.

Chapter 12. "We Are Kin to All That Lives"

1. "Cornerstones" is in Shankman, *Trashing*, 211; "intelligent people" is in ibid., 206.

2. Seymour-Smith, *Macmillan Dictionary of Anthropology*, 186.

3. Tcherkézoff, *Le mythe occidentale*, 209–10.

4. Freeman, *Mead and Samoa*, 298, see also chap. 20.

5. Freeman, "Notes towards an Intellectual Biography," 16. Hereafter cited parenthetically in the text. The annotated draft listed in the bibliography is Freeman's authorized version; page numbers in the text are from this version.

6. Freeman, interview by Tuzin, transcript 3, p. 73.

7. Schneider correspondence is in 20/8, F/UCSD.

8. "I am still nervous" is in Fortes to Freeman, 27 December 1967, and Fortes to Freeman, 11 September 1969, 8/9, F/UCSD. Earlier than many, Fortes identified a feature of Freeman's writings that others observed later: Derek's were "programmatic statements" rather than applications of theory to a specific body of cultural and social data.

9. Fortes to Freeman, 11 September 1969, 8/9, F/UCSD.

10. Freeman to Fortes, 7 February 1970, 8/9, F/UCSD.

11. Patterson, *Social History of Anthropology*, 106, 125–27.

12. Eric Wolf quoted in Stocking, *Ethnographer's Magic*, 337.

13. Ibid., 7.

14. Mead, "Anthropology among the Sciences," 479–82; Devore, "An Interview with Sherwood Washburn."

15. Dobzhansky, "Does Natural Selection?"; Thieme, review of Medawar.

16. "I realized" is in Freeman, interview by Tuzin, transcript 3, p. 31; "high-flown" is in transcript 3, p. 9; "mistaken" is in transcript 3, p. 13. The whereabouts of the 1959 paper is unknown.

17. This 1964 paper became the article "Anthropology, Psychiatry" published in 1965. The whereabouts of his 1963 paper is unknown.

18. Freeman, "Social Anthropology," 331, 333, 338, 339.

19. Heimans, "Recorded Interview," 59.

20. Freeman to Fortes, 19 June 1968, 8/9, F/UCSD.

21. See Freeman, "Totem and Taboo"; Freeman, interview by Tuzin, transcript 3, p. 13.

22. Freeman, "Shaman and Incubus," 334, 335.

23. Freeman, "Thunder," 356.

24. Rejection noted in diary: TS, 30 December 1966. In 1984 Freeman's example inspired his student, Don Tuzin, to test Freeman's ideas about thunder and noise and human responses among the Arapesh of New Guinea, which by then *Current Anthropology* was prepared to publish: "Miraculous Voices."

25. "10 PhDs" is in TS, 31 December 1966; "planck" is in Freeman to Lawrence, 21 November 1968, 156/20, F/UCSD.

26. "Human Nature and Culture," quotations from reprint in Freeman, *Dilthey's Dream*, 16.

27. Colleagues included John Crawford and the historian Keith Hancock; Tinbergen is noted in TS, 29 August 1969; "anchor" is in Caton, *Samoa Reader*, 102; "reckoning" is in ibid., 106.

28. Freeman, interview by Tuzin, transcript 3, p. 53.

29. Correspondence with Frank Macfarlane Burnet is in 5/1, F/UCSD; a copy of "Precursory View" is in 112/18, F/UCSD. The other papers were "Aggression: Instinct or Symptom?" and "Towards an Anthropology Both Scientific and Humanistic." See also Freeman, interview by Tuzin, transcript 4, p. 16.

30. Freeman to Reynolds, 27 April 1977, 19/3, F/UCSD.

31. "Sociobiology: 'The Antidiscipline,'" 198–219, quotations (including about Wilson) from 200–201, 213, 214.

32. Freeman to Fortes, 2 April 1980, 8/9, F/UCSD.

33. The survey is reported in Lieberman, "A Discipline Divided"; see Wilson, "Science and Ideology."

34. See Wilson, *Sociobiology* and *On Human Nature*.

35. The Freeman–Wilson correspondence is in 160/18, F/UCSD; see also Freeman, interview by Tuzin, transcript 1, p. 33, 3, pp. 60, 71, and transcript 4, p. 76; and Tuzin to the author, 13 March 2007.

36. Herdt to Freeman, 8 August 1985, 10/10, F/UCSD.

37. Tuzin thought Bateson might have a point, but the point was that Freeman knew that sexuality and violence are two of the most significant parts of the human behavioral repertoire and therefore ripe for study (Tuzin to the author, 4 February 2007).

38. See "Special Section: Speaking in the Name of the Real"; see also Scheper-Hughes, "Margaret Mead Controversy"; Leacock, "Anthropologists in Search."

39. "Startled" is in Caton, "The Mead/Freeman Controversy," 593; Dawkins, *The Selfish Gene*; Degler, *In Search of Human Nature*, 226–41.

40. This was brought fully to life by Tuzin in "Miraculous Voices." Freeman's "The Anthropology of Choice" was published in *Canberra Anthropology* 4, no. 1 (1981): 82–100. The following quotations are from the version republished in *Dilthey's Dream*, 23, 25, 32, 37, 39, 38.

41. "The art of unclouded" is in Freeman to Fairburn, 21 May 1993, 7/21, F/UCSD; Freeman, interview by Tuzin, transcript 2, p. 2.

42. Quoted in Clark, *History, Theory, Text*, 215, also 31.

43. Freeman's sensibilities seemed to narrow as he got older: he could never understand why more people visited the home of Beatrix Potter, the children's books author, than that of Charles Darwin—"truth" should rule people's lives: see Freeman to Tuzin, 27 March 2000, 160/1, F/UCSD; "the world" is in Freeman to Stocking, 22 August 1990, 22/2, F/UCSD.

44. Stocking, *Ethnographer's Magic*, 360.

45. For interpretations of postmodernism's effects on anthropology, see Keesing, "Anthropology as Interpretive Quest"; Strathern, "The Persuasive Fictions"; see also Shankman, "The Thick and the Thin"; Gitlin, "Hip-Deep"; and A. Kuper, *Anthropology and Anthropologists*, 186–87.

46. Firth's view is in Parkin, "An Interview with Raymond Firth," 340; see Friedman, "Interview with Eric Wolf," 113; Clifford and Marcus, *Writing Culture*, 103; see also A. Kuper, *Anthropology and Anthropologists*, 36–56.

47. Freeman to *Newsletter* editor, 19 May 1995, F/UCSD; see Geertz, *The Interpretation of Cultures*, 50; "word monger" is in Williams, "Professing Culture," 286.

48. TS, 6 July 1989. Interestingly, Marcus and Freeman conjured up a friendly relationship late in Freeman's life.

49. Strathern to Freeman, 29 January 1996, 22/5, F/UCSD; Freeman to I. M. Lewis, 10 July 1986, 13/6, F/UCSD.

50. "Holistic" is in Freeman to Appell, 5 July 1989, 152/10, F/UCSD; see Caton, *Samoa Reader*, 326–31, original at 184/1, F/UCSD.

51. "Conspicuously" is in Freeman, "Paradigms in Collision," 32; Caton to Freeman, 18 August 1991, 5/13, F/UCSD.

52. Freeman's discovery of Diamond and the thymus are discussed in a letter to Macfarlane Burnet, 21 November 1979, 5/1, F/UCSD; Freeman's diary entries chronicle various tests conscientiously through the 1990s.

53. Freeman, *"The Question of Questions,"* 1–24.

54. Freeman on Buddhism is in TS, 1 January 1980.

55. Freeman told Tuzin that when dealing with Lowell Holmes he kept a *vajra* in his pocket. He could reach in and hold onto it as a way of feeling secure. See Freeman, interview by Tuzin, transcript 5, p. 37; "useful" is in Tuzin note in TS, 19 May 1980.

56. TS, 1 January 1980; see also TS, 3–7 June 1989.

57. "He is mine" is in TS, 6 February 1990.

58. Freeman, interview by Tuzin, transcript 3, p. 32.

59. Ibid., transcript 3, p. 69. Transcripts 3 and 4 of the interview are important for all these views. Freeman was not the first anthropologist to arrive at such a moral conclusion: see H. Kuper, "Function, History, Biography."

60. "Have a crack" is in Freeman's last letter to Oliver, 4 March 2000, 141/31, F/UCSD; "as theory watchers" is in Shankman, "The Thick and the Thin," 270.

Conclusion

1. Quoted in Caton, "Exalted Self," 378.

2. Correspondence with the author, 13 November 2006.

3. Schoeffel, interview by the author, 8 December 2012. Oliver produced an acclaimed three-volume work, *Ancient Tahitian Society*.

4. Fortes to Freeman, 18 December 1953, 8/9, F/UCSD.

5. Monica Freeman, interview by the author, 9 October 2002. James Fox, Indonesia expert and Freeman's colleague in Canberra, believed that Freeman's Iban studies were his greatest work and that all students of Iban society stand on his shoulders: Fox, interview by the author, 28 November 2002.

6. Popper's support of Freeman included a curt dismissal of American anthropologists

who could submit to those with power and influence in their discipline by voting at a meeting to condemn Freeman's "truth"; see Popper to Freeman, 14 June 1988, 18/8, F/UCSD. For other evaluations, see Heider, "The Rashomon Effect," 73; A. Kuper, "Coming of Age," 454–55.

7. Heimans, "Recorded Interview," 75.

8. Schoeffel, interview by the author, 8 December 2012.

9. Monaghan, "Anthropologist Who Sparked Dispute," A5.

10. Freeman to Pinker, 17 October 1994, 18/5, F/UCSD; extract from Sassoon's "Limitations," 122.

11. Quotations from Holmes, "Margaret Mead's Samoa," 539–44.

12. Doctorow, *The March*, 352.

13. Karl Heider predicted in 1989 that "making a unilateral declaration of victory" was never going to end this debate; see "Rashomon Effect: Reply," 450.

14. Needham to Freeman, 17 June 1999, 157/22, F/UCSD. Needham was renowned for his restrained, syllogistic prose style. See also correspondence with Oliver, 16/12, F/UCSD.

15. Caton to Freeman, 17 February 1989, 184/1, F/UCSD.

16. Caton to Freeman, 15 April 1992, 5/14, F/UCSD.

17. Heimans, "Recorded Interview," 91.

18. Schoeffel, interview by the author, 8 December 2012.

19. Weiner, "Ethnographic Determinism," 918.

20. Côte's claim in *Adolescent Storm and Stress*, 10; private correspondence with Aiono Dr. Fanaafi Le Tagaloa, 11 September 2000, Freeman Family Papers.

21. Freeman to O'Meara, 29 March 1987, 16/14, F/UCSD.

22. Freeman took comfort in the definition of "truth" that Karl Popper provided him in their correspondence: "'truth' means correspondence to the facts, or a statement is true if, and only if, it is formulated unambiguously and corresponds to the facts it describes" (Popper to Freeman, 25 June 1988, 18/8, F/UCSD).

23. Freeman to Doug Lewis, 24 February 1990, 13/4, F/UCSD. Sunyata is a Mahayana Buddhism term that refers to the sense of emptiness in all things, the realization that the world does not exist as the human self supposes it does.

24. Peterson, interview by the author, 10 July 2003; Fox, interview by the author, 28 November 2002.

25. For neopositivism, see A. Kuper, *Among the Anthropologists*, 34; A. Kuper, "Ernest Gellner."

26. Heimans, "Recorded Interview," 53.

27. Chapple, "The Unbounded Reaches," 744; Lieberman, "A Discipline Divided," 677; Hicks and Leonard, "Developmental Systems and Inequality," including comments.

28. Freeman's expression in talk to Sydney Institute, 1996, reported in *Australian*, 10 July 1996. He adopted the phrase from the evolutionary biologist Theodosius Dobzhansky. *Dilthey's Dream* was the title of a series of Freeman's talks on human nature and culture published in 2001.

29. Zeldin, *Intimate History*, 344.

30. A reading of *Current Anthropology* from 1980s onward demonstrates the steadily growing discourse on these developments: Hicks and Leonard, "Developmental Systems and Inequality" is an example. A more popular summary is Ferry, "Beyond the Human Genome."

31. Tuzin to the author, 10 July 2006.

32. Caton on lack of heirs is in "The Mead/Freeman Controversy," 587; "the paradigm" is in Tuzin, "Miraculous Voices," 589. Responses from John Blacking, José De Carvalho, Deborah Gewertz, Jaan Kaplinski, Henry Kingsbury, Mahesh Pradhan, and Geoffrey Samuel were negative; Michael Young was more positive. See also Tuzin, "Base Notes."

33. "Dogged politics" is in A. Kuper, "Coming of Age," 455; see also Heider, "The Rashomon Effect," 73. "Anthropologists hardly" is in A. Kuper, "Anthropologists Unite!," 167.

34. On postcolonial anthropology, see Brown, "Can Culture Be Copyrighted?"; for Dennett, see *Darwin's Dangerous Idea*, 195; D'Andrade, "The Sad Story of Anthropology"; see also Spiro, "Cultural Relativism." Tuzin spoke often of "the babble of competing advocacies."

35. Freeman, interview by Tuzin, transcript 2, p. 45.

36. "Buccaneer" is in ibid., transcript 1, p. 39; see also Heimans, "Recorded Interview," 98–99.

37. Wynn Owen, "Edmund Halley, 1740," 119.

Bibliography

Archive Collections and Manuscripts

Archives of the Australian National University. Staff Files. 19-6.2.2.6, pts. 1–4, and 19-6.2.2.6C [confidential], pts. 1 and 3, ANU.

Davidson, J. W. Papers. Three sets of these were used, each with a different provenance.
- Davidson and Freeman correspondence, 1947–54. Originally in the Freeman Family Papers, since transferred to F/UCSD.
- Davidson Papers. MS 5105, NLA.
- Davidson Papers. 57-30: Chair of Anthropology; 57-58: Staff Appointments; 57-114: Samoa Research Correspondence, all in ANUA.

Firth, Raymond. Papers. File 8/1/33, pt. 1, 1945–64, pt. 2, 1991–92. London School of Economics.

Freeman, Derek. Papers, 1940–2001. 188 boxes, F/UCSD.

New Zealand. Island Territories. IT1. EX13/1, pt. 2, Education: Samoa General File, 1926–49; EX89/3, pt. 3; EX89/3, pt. 4. NA/NZ.

Reay, Marie. Papers. 440-892: Derek Freeman, and 440-893: copies of Freeman letters. ANUA.

Ross, Kathleen. Papers. Alexander Turnbull Library, Wellington, New Zealand.

Private Papers

Freeman Family Papers. Assorted documents and correspondence, Canberra, some now transferred to F/UCSD.
- "Free Discussions Club. Unofficial report on the meeting held on the 8th April 1937: Germany under Hitler." Victoria College, University of New Zealand, Wellington.

- Freeman, Derek. "Notes towards an Intellectual Biography," n.d. [1986?], 64 pp. Annotated draft for Appell and Madan, *Choice and Morality*.
- Freeman to Stephen Morris, 19 January 1981.
- Freeman to Côte, 10 September 1994.
- Freeman to Le Tagaloa Leota Pita Ala'ilima, 16 December 1985.
- Freeman to Le Tagaloa Leota Pita Ala 'ilima, 6 August 1986.
- Freeman to Aiono Dr. Fanaafi Le Tagaloa, 27 March 1988.
- Freeman to David Mackay, 21 November 1997.
- Freeman to Aiono Dr. Fanaafi Le Tagaloa, 11 September 2000.

Freeman, J. D. "Mr Tom Harrisson and Research in Sarawak by the Australian National University—a Revised Version of a Report to Sir John Crawford, Director, Research School of Pacific Studies, ANU." September 1962, 10–15. Copy in possession of George Appell.

———. "On Samoan Social Organization." 1947. Seminar paper, London School of Economics.

Harrison, Wayne. "Derek and Monica." Harrison Productions, January 2012. MS on preparations for play *Heretic*, composed from diaries and workbooks in response to the author's queries. Copy in author's possession.

Low, Anthony. Correspondence regarding Freeman appointment to chair of anthropology, 11 July–27 October 1972. Temporary loan to author from Professor Low.

Ploeg, Anton. "The Culture of Fieldwork." Radboud University, Nijmegen, the Netherlands, undated. Copy in author's possession.

Tuzin, Don. "Margaret Mead and the Heretic: Anthropology's Great Clash." Paper presented to Friends of the UCSD Libraries, 3 October 2002. Copy in author's possession.

———. "Questions for Monica." Correspondence with Monica Freeman, 25 September 2006. Copy in author's possession.

———. Summaries and notes on Freeman diaries, 1963–90. Tuzin family archive. Copy in author's possession.

Audiovisual Materials

Margaret Mead and Samoa. Documentary directed by Frank Heimans, 1988. Produced by Cinetel Productions in association with the Science Unit of the Australian Broadcasting Corporation/Commission.

Interviews

Fox, James. Interview by the author. 28 November 2002.

Freeman, Derek. Interview by Doug Munro. 27 January 1999. Copy in author's possession.

———. Interview by Donald Tuzin. 25–30 June 2000. Five transcripts. Tuzin Papers, UCSD.

Freeman, Monica. Interviews by the author. 9 October 2002, 26 and 28 November 2002, 10 December 2003, 8 December 2005.

Gunson, W. N. Interview by the author. 11 November 2003.

Heimans, Frank. "Recorded Interview with Derek Freeman, 12 February 2001." Transcript TRC 4660, Oral History Section, National Library of Australia.

Low, Anthony. Interview by the author. 27 July 2006.

McCall, Grant. Interview by the author. 1 November 2016.

Passmore, John. "Interview with Emeritus Prof John Passmore 17 May 1991." Transcript 44-42, Oral History Collection, Australian National University Archives.

Peterson, Nicolas. Interview by the author. 10 July 2003.

Robbins, Joel. Interview by the author. 29 June 2011.

Rosenberg, Wolfgang, and Ann Rosenberg. Interview by the author. 31 January 2002.

Schoeffel, Penelope. Interview by the author. 8 December 2012.

Tcherkézoff, Serge. Interview by the author. 5 February 2004.

Tuzin, Donald. Interviews by the author. 29 June 2004, 30 June 2004, 8 August 2006, 29 August 2006.

Williamson, David. Interview by the author. 21 February 2012.

Print and Online Materials

Ala'ilima, Fay. "Derek Freeman, *Margaret Mead and Samoa: The Making and Unmaking of an Anthropological Myth.*" *Pacific Studies* 7, no. 2 (1984): 91–92.

Allen, Bryant. "Seriously but Not Solemnly." In Lal and Leys, *The Coombs*, 79–86.

Allport, Gordon. *Becoming: Basic Considerations for a Psychology of Personality.* New Haven, Conn.: Yale University Press, 1955.

Appell, G. N. "Freeman's Refutation of Mead's *Coming of Age in Samoa*: The Implications for Anthropological Inquiry." *Eastern Anthropologist* 37 (1984): 183–214. Citations are to the revised version available at http://www.gnappell.org/articles/freeman.htm.

Appell, G. N., and T. N. Madan, eds. *Choice and Morality in Anthropological Perspective: Essays in Honor of Derek Freeman.* Albany: State University of New York Press, 1988.

———. "Derek Freeman: Notes toward an Intellectual Biography." In Appell and Madan, *Choice and Morality in Anthropological Perspective*, 3–30.

Appell-Warren, Laura P., ed. *The Iban Diaries of Monica Freeman, 1949–1951.* Phillips, Maine: Borneo Research Council, 2009.

Barker, Sarah. *The Alexander Technique.* New York: Bantam Books, 1978.

Barnes, John. *Humping My Drum: A Memoir.* Self-published, 2008. www.lulu.com.

Barrowclough, Nikki. "Sex, Lies and Anthropology." *Good Weekend: The Sydney Morning Herald Magazine*, 9 March 1996, 30–39.

Barrowman, Rachel. *Victoria University of Wellington, 1899–1999: A History.* Wellington: Victoria University Press, 1999.

Bateson, Mary Catherine. "Using and Abusing the Works of the Ancestors: Margaret Mead." *Pacific Studies* 28, nos. 3–4 (2005): 162–75.

Beaglehole, Ernest. "Polynesian Anthropology Today." *American Anthropologist* 39, no. 2 (1937): 213–21.

Beaglehole, Tim. *A Life of J. C. Beaglehole: New Zealand Scholar*. Wellington: Victoria University Press, 2006.

Beeby, C. E. *The Biography of an Idea: Beeby on Education*. Wellington: New Zealand Council for Educational Research, 1992.

Belich, James. *Paradise Reforged: A History of the New Zealanders from the 1880s to the Year 2000*. Auckland: Penguin, 2001.

Bentall, Richard. *Madness Explained: Psychosis and Human Nature*. London: Penguin, 2003.

Book Review Forum. *Pacific Studies* 7, no. 2 (1984): 91–146.

Brady, Ivan. "Introduction: Speaking in the Name of the Real." *American Anthropologist* 85, no. 4 (1984): 908–9.

———. "*The Samoa Reader*: Last Word or Lost Horizon?" *Current Anthropology* 32, no. 4 (1991): 497–500.

Brown, Donald. Review of *Fateful Hoaxing*, by Derek Freeman. *Evolution and Human Behavior* 20 (1999): 290.

Brown, Michael F. "Can Culture Be Copyrighted?" *Current Anthropology* 39, no. 2 (1998): 195–204.

Byatt, A. S. *The Game*. London: Vintage, 1992.

Campbell, I. C. "Resistance and Colonial Government: A Comparative Study of Samoa." *Journal of Pacific History* 40, no. 1 (2005): 45–69.

Caton, Hiram. "Conversion in Sarawak: Derek Freeman's Awakening to a New Anthropology." *AnthroGlobe Journal*, 19 January 2006. http://www.anthroglobe.org/docs/conversion_sarawak.htm.

———. "The Exalted Self: Derek Freeman's Quest for the Perfect Identity." *Identity: An International Journal of Theory and Research* 5, no. 4 (2005): 359–84.

———. "The Mead/Freeman Controversy Is Over: A Retrospect." *Journal of Youth and Adolescence* 29, no. 5 (2000): 587–605.

———. Review of *Fateful Hoaxing*, by Derek Freeman. *Politics and the Life Sciences* 18, no. 1 (1999): 151–54.

———, ed. *The Samoa Reader: Anthropologists Take Stock*. New York: University Press of America, 1990.

———, ed. "Talking to a Heretic: Interviews with John Derek Freeman." 2002. MS, School of Humanities, Griffith University, Brisbane, Australia.

Chapple, Eliot. "The Unbounded Reaches of Anthropology as a Research Science, and Some Working Hypotheses." *American Anthropologist* 82, no. 4 (1980): 741–58.

Clark, Elizabeth. *History, Theory, Text: Historians and the Linguistic Turn*. Cambridge, Mass.: Harvard University Press, 2004.

Clifford, James. *Person and Myth: Maurice Leenhardt in the Melanesian World*. Berkeley: University of California Press, 1982.

Clifford, James, and George Marcus, eds. *Writing Culture: The Poetics and Politics of Ethnography*. Berkeley: University of California Press, 1986.

Colman, Andrew M., ed. *Oxford Dictionary of Psychology*. 2001. Repr., Oxford: Oxford University Press, 2009.

Colvin, S., ed. *The Letters of Robert Louis Stevenson*. Volume 4, 1890–1894. London: Methuen, 1911.

Conklin, Harold. Review of *Iban Agriculture*, by J. D. Freeman. *American Anthropologist* 59, no. 1 (1957): 179–80.

Cookson, J. E. "Appeal Boards and Conscientious Objectors." In *Kia Kaha: New Zealand in the Second World War*, edited by John Crawford, 173–95. Auckland: Oxford University Press, 2002.

Cornell, S. D. "The Reader Replies." *American Scholar* 56, no.1 (1987): 159.

Côte, James. *Adolescent Storm and Stress: An Evaluation of the Mead-Freeman Controversy*. Hillsdale: Lawrence Erlbaum Associates, 1994.

———. "The Correspondence Associated with Margaret Mead's Samoa Research: What Does It Really Tell Us?" *Pacific Studies* 28, nos. 3–4 (2005): 60–73.

———. "Correspondence Concerning the Review of *The Fateful Hoaxing of Margaret Mead*, by Derek Freeman." *Pacific Affairs* 73, no. 2 (2000): 263–67.

———. Review of *The Fateful Hoaxing of Margaret Mead*, by Derek Freeman. *Pacific Affairs* 72, no. 2 (1999): 308–10.

———. "Was Mead Wrong about Coming of Age in Samoa? An Analysis of the Mead/Freeman Controversy for Scholars of Adolescence and Human Development." *Journal of Youth and Adolescence* 21, no. 5 (1992): 499–527.

D'Andrade, Roy. "The Sad Story of Anthropology, 1950–99." *Cross Cultural Research*, February 2000. Copy consulted in 120/13, F/UCSD.

Davidson, J. W. *Samoa mo Samoa: The Emergence of the Independent State of Western Samoa*. Melbourne: Oxford University Press, 1967.

Dawkins, Richard. *The Selfish Gene*. Oxford: Oxford University Press, 1976.

Degler, Carl. *In Search of Human Nature: The Decline and Revival of Darwinism in American Social Thought*. New York: Oxford University Press, 1991.

De Masi, Franco. *Vulnerability to Psychosis: A Psychoanalytic Study of the Nature and Therapy of the Psychotic State*. London: Karnac Books, 2009.

de Moore, Greg, and Ann Westmore. *Finding Sanity: John Cade, Lithium and the Taming of Bipolar Disorder*. Sydney: Allen & Unwin, 2016.

Dennerley, Peter. "The Royal New Zealand Navy." In *Kia Kaha: New Zealand in the Second World War*, edited by John Crawford, 107–19. Auckland: Oxford University Press, 2002.

Dennett, Daniel. *Darwin's Dangerous Idea: Evolution and the Meanings of Life*. New York: Simon & Schuster, 1995.

Devore, Irven. "An Interview with Sherwood Washburn." *Current Anthropology* 33, no. 4 (1992): 411–23.

Diamond, John. *Your Body Doesn't Lie*. Sydney: Harper & Row, 1979.

Dobzhansky, Theodosius. "Does Natural Selection Continue to Operate in Modern Mankind?" *American Anthropologist* 58, no.4 (1956): 591–604.

Doctorow, E. L. *The March*. London: Little, Brown, 2006.

Eghigian, Greg, ed. *From Madness to Mental Health: Psychiatric Disorder and Its Treatment in Western Civilization*. New Brunswick, N.J.: Rutgers University Press, 2010.

Ember, Melvin. "Reply to Freeman: A Rejoinder." *American Anthropologist* 66, no. 3 (1964): 620–22.

———. "Samoan Kinship and Political Structure: An Archaeological Test to Decide between the Two Alternative Reconstructions." *American Anthropologist* 68, no. 1 (1966): 163–68.

Endicott, Kirk, and Robert Welsch, eds. *Taking Sides: Clashing Views in Anthropology.* 2001. Repr., Boston: McGraw Hill, 2009.

Eriksen, Thomas Hylland. *Small Places, Large Issues.* London: Pluto Press, 2001.

Eriksen, Thomas Hylland, and Finn Sivert Nielsen. *A History of Anthropology.* London: Pluto Press, 2001.

Ferry, Georgina. "Beyond the Human Genome." *Oxford Today* 28, no. 1 (2015): 28–32.

Field, Michael. *Mau: Samoa's Struggle for Freedom.* Auckland: Polynesian Press, 1991.

Firth, Raymond. "Siegfried Frederick Nadel, 1903–1956." *American Anthropologist* 59, no. 1 (1957): 117–24.

Foster, S. G., and Margaret Varghese. *The Making of the Australian National University, 1946–1996.* St. Leonard's: Allen & Unwin, 1996.

Freeman, Derek. "Aggression: Instinct or Symptom?" *Australian and New Zealand Journal of Psychiatry* 5 (1971): 66–73.

———. "'A Happening Frightening to Both Ghosts and Men': A Case Study from Western Samoa." In *The Changing Pacific: Essays in Honour of H. E. Maude,* edited by Niel Gunson, 163–73. Melbourne: Oxford University Press, 1978.

———. "'All Made of Fantasy . . .': A Rejoinder to Paul Shankman." *American Anthropologist* 100, no. 4 (1998): 972–77.

———. "Anthropological Theorizing and Historical Scholarship: A Reply to M. Ember." *American Anthropologist* 68, no. 1 (1966): 168–71.

———. *Anthropology in the South Seas: Essays Presented to H. D. Skinner.* Edited by J. D. Freeman and W. R. Geddes. New Plymouth: Thomas Avery, 1959.

———. "The Anthropology of Choice." *Canberra Anthropology* 4, no. 1 (1981): 82–100. Reprinted in Freeman, *Dilthey's Dream,* 21–39.

———. "Anthropology, Psychiatry and the Doctrine of Cultural Relativism." *Man* 65, no. 59 (1965): 64–67.

———. "The Burthen of a Mystery." *Oceania* 54, no. 3 (1984): 247–60.

———. "Clarification on Sociobiology." In Caton, *Samoa Reader,* 326–31.

———. "Controversy: Derek Freeman Replies to Paul Shankman." *Skeptic,* Autumn 2001, 64–66.

———. *Dilthey's Dream: Essays on Human Nature and Culture.* Research School of Pacific and Asian Studies, Canberra: Pandanus Books, 2001.

———. "Fa'apua 'a Fa'amu and Margaret Mead." *American Anthropologist* 91, no. 4 (1989): 1017–22.

———. "The Falemaunga Caves." *Journal of the Polynesian Society* 53, no. 3 (1944): 86–104.

———. "Family and Kin among the Iban of Sarawak." PhD diss., University of Cambridge, 1953.

————. *The Fateful Hoaxing of Margaret Mead: A Historical Analysis of Her Historical Research*. Boulder, Colo.: Westview Press, 1999.

————. "Heretic Draws on 50 Years of Research." *Australian*, 9 April 1996, 13.

————. "Human Aggression in Anthropological Perspective," Unpublished manuscript, 1963. Location unknown.

————. "Human Nature and Culture." In *Man and the New Biology*, edited by R. O. Slatyer et al., 50–75. Canberra: ANU Press, 1970. Reprinted in Freeman, *Dilthey's Dream*, 1–19.

————. *Iban Agriculture: A Report on the Shifting Cultivation of Hill Rice by the Iban of Sarawak*. London: HMSO, 1955.

————. "Inductivism and the Test of Truth: A Rejoinder to Lowell D. Holmes and Others." *Canberra Anthropology* 6, no. 2 (1983): 101–82.

————. "In Praise of Heresy." In *Dilthey's Dream: Essays on Human Nature and Culture*, 79–92. Canberra: Pandanus Books, 2001.

————. "The Joe Gimlet or Siovili Cult: An Episode in the Religious History of Early Samoa." In Freeman and Geddes, *Anthropology in the South Seas*, 185–200.

————. "(love)ution." *Spike* 36, no. 65 (1937): 45.

————. *Margaret Mead and Samoa: The Making and Unmaking of an Anthropological Myth*. Cambridge, Mass.: Harvard University Press, 1983.

————. "Margaret Mead, Martin Orans and Samoa." *Journal of the Polynesian Society* 106, no. 2 (1997): 209–11.

————. "Margaret Mead's Coming of Age in Samoa and Boasian Culturalism." *Australian Anthropological Society Newsletter* 79/80 (March/June 2000): 35–36. Also in *Politics and the Life Sciences* 19, no. 1 (2000): 101–3; and *Skeptic* 20, no. 1 (2000): 11.

————. "Nursery Rhyme." *Spike* 35, no. 64 (1936): 36.

————. "O le Fele o le Fe'e." *Journal of the Polynesian Society* 53, no. 4 (1944): 121–44.

————. "On Franz Boas and the Samoan Researches of Margaret Mead." *Current Anthropology* 32, no. 3 (1991): 322–29.

————. "On the Believing of as Many as Six Impossible Things before Breakfast." Unpublished manuscript, 1968. Copy in 112/7, F/UCSD.

————. "On the Concept of the Kindred." *Journal of the Royal Anthropological Institute* 91, no. 2 (1961): 192–220.

————. "Paradigms in Collision." *Academic Questions*, Summer 1992, 24–33. Reprinted as a pamphlet, *Paradigms in Collision: The Far-Reaching Controversy over the Samoan Researches of Margaret Mead and Its Significance for the Human Sciences*. Canberra: Research School of Pacific Studies, 1992.

————. "Poem for a Friend Killed on Mt. Evans." *Spike* 37, no. 66 (1938): 22.

————. *"The Question of Questions": T. H. Huxley, Evolution by Natural Selection and Buddhism*. Pamphlet, Research School of Pacific and Asian Studies, ANU, 1996. Reprinted in Freeman, *Dilthey's Dream*, 61–78.

————. "The Reader Replies." *American Scholar* 56, no.1 (1987): 157–59.

————. "The Reader Replies." *American Scholar* 56, no.2 (1987): 303–4.

———. *Report on the Iban*. LSE Monographs on Social Anthropology 41, University of London. London: Athlone Press, 1970.

———. "Response: Derek Freeman." *Pacific Studies* 7, no. 2 (1984): 140–96.

———. "Samoa: A Matter of Emphasis." *American Anthropologist* 67, no. 6 (1965): 1534–37.

———. "The Science of Heresy." *Skeptic* 16, no. 4 (1996): 16–19.

———. "The Seuao Cave." *Journal of the Polynesian Society* 52, no. 3 (1943): 101–9.

———. "Shaman and Incubus." *Psychoanalytic Study of Society* 4 (1967): 315–43.

———. "Siegfried Frederick Nadel, 1903–1956." *Oceania* 27, no. 1 (1956): 1–11.

———. "Social Anthropology and the Scientific Study of Human Behavior." *Man*, n.s., 1, no. 3 (1966): 330–42.

———. "Social Anthropology as a Form of Nomothetic Enquiry." Unpublished manuscript, 1959. Location unknown.

———. "*Social Organization of Manuʻa*: Some Errata." *Journal of the Polynesian Society* 81, no. 1 (1972): 70–78.

———. *The Social Structure of a Samoan Village Community*. Edited with an introduction by Peter Hempenstall. Canberra: Target Oceania, 2006.

———. "Sociobiology: The 'Antidiscipline' of Anthropology." In *Sociobiology Examined*, edited by Ashley Montagu, 198–219. New York: Oxford University Press, 1980.

———. "Some Observations on Kinship and Political Authority in Samoa." *American Anthropologist*, n.s., 66, no. 3 (1964): 553–68.

———. "'There's Tricks i' th' World': An Historical Analysis of the Samoan Researches of Margaret Mead." *Visual Anthropology Review* 7, no. 1 (1991): 103–27.

———. "Thunder, Blood and the Nicknaming of God's Creatures." *Psychoanalytic Quarterly* 37 (1968): 353–99.

———. "Totem and Taboo: A Reappraisal." *Psychoanalytic Study of Society* 4 (1967): 9–33.

———. "Towards an Anthropology Both Scientific and Humanistic." *Canberra Anthropology* 1, no. 3 (1978): 44–69.

———. "The Vailele Earthmounds." *Journal of the Polynesian Society* 53, no. 4 (1944): 145–62.

———. "Was Margaret Mead Misled or Did She Mislead on Samoa?" *Current Anthropology* 41, no. 4 (2000): 609–22. CA Forum on Theory in Anthropology: Sex and Hoax in Samoa.

———. "'Words Have No Words for Words That Are Not True': A Rejoinder to Serge Tcherkézoff." *Journal of the Polynesian Society* 110, no. 3 (2001): 301–11.

Friedman, Jonathan. "Interview with Eric Wolf." *Current Anthropology* 28, no. 1 (1987): 107–18.

Funder, David C. *The Personality Puzzle*. New York: W. W. Norton, 1997.

"Geddes, William Robert (Bill) (1916–1989)." In *Australian Dictionary of Biography*, vol. 17, edited by Diane Langmore. Parkville: Melbourne University Press, 2007. http://adb.anu.edu.au/.

Geertz, Clifford. *The Interpretation of Cultures: Selected Essays*. New York: Basic Books, 1973.

Gerrand, James. Review of *Fateful Hoaxing*, by Derek Freeman. *Skeptic* 19, no. 1 (1999): 47–48.

Gibbings, Robert. *Over the Reefs*. London: J. M. Dent, 1948.

Gitlin, Todd. "Hip-Deep in Post-modernism." *New York Times Book Review*, 6 November 1988, 35.

Gosse, Edmund. *Father and Son: A Study of Two Temperaments*. London: Evergreen Books, 1941.

Gray, Geoffrey. *A Cautious Silence: The Politics of Australian Anthropology*. Canberra: Aboriginal Studies Press, 2007.

———. "W. E. H. Stanner: Wasted War Years." In *Scholars at War: Australasian Social Scientists, 1939–1945*, edited by Geoffrey Gray, Doug Munro, Christine Winter, 95–116. Canberra: ANU EPress, 2012.

Gray, Geoffrey, and Doug Munro. "Australian Aboriginal Anthropology at the Crossroads: Finding a Successor to A. P. Elkin 1955." *Australian Journal of Anthropology* 22, no. 3 (2011): 351–69.

———. "'The Department Was in Some Disarray': The Politics of Choosing a Successor to S. F. Nadel, 1957." In *Anthropologists and Their Traditions across National Borders*, Histories of Anthropology Annual, 8, edited by Regna Darnell and F. W. Gleach, 141–71. Lincoln: University of Nebraska Press, 2014.

———. "'Leach Would Be First Rate—If You Could Get Him': Edmund Leach and the ANU, 1956." *Compass* 10, no. 5 (2012): 802–11. doi:10.1111/hic3.l2003.

Handy, E. S. Craighill. *The Native Culture in the Marquesas*. Honolulu: Bernice P. Bishop Museum, Bulletin 9, 1923.

Heider, Karl G. "Rashomon Effect: Reply to Freeman." *American Anthropologist* 91, no. 2 (1989): 450.

———. "The Rashomon Effect: When Ethnographers Disagree." *American Anthropologist* 90, no. 1 (1988): 73–81.

Heimann, Judith. *The Most Offending Soul Alive*. Honolulu: University of Hawai'i Press, 1997.

Hempenstall, Peter. *The Meddlesome Priest: A Life of Ernest Burgmann*. St. Leonard's: Allen & Unwin, 1993.

Hempenstall, Peter, and Noel Rutherford. *Protest and Dissent in the Colonial Pacific*. Suva: Institute of Pacific Studies Press, 1984.

Hicks, Kathryn, and William R. Leonard. "Developmental Systems and Inequality: Linking Evolutionary and Political-Economic Theory in Biological Anthropology." *Current Anthropology* 55, no. 5 (2014): 323–50.

Holmes, Lowell D. "Margaret Mead's Samoa: Views and Reviews." *Quarterly Review of Biology* 58, no. 4 (1983): 539–44.

———. "On the Questioning of as Many as Six Impossible Things about Freeman's Samoan Study before Breakfast." *Canberra Anthropology* 6, no. 1 (1983): 1–16.

———. *Quest for the Real Samoa: The Mead Freeman Controversy and Beyond*. South Hadley, Mass.: Bergin & Garvey, 1987.

————. "A Tale of Two Studies." *American Anthropologist* 85, no. 4 (1983): 929–35.

Hooper, Anthony. Review of *Margaret Mead and Samoa*, by Derek Freeman. *Oceania* 55, no. 3 (1985): 224–25.

Horgan, John. "Hearts of Darkness." *New York Times Book Review*, 12 November 2000, 2012–14.

Ings, Simon. Review of *Fateful Hoaxing*, by Derek Freeman. *New Scientist*, 15 May 1999, 47.

Jamison, Kay Redfield. *An Unquiet Mind: A Memoir of Moods and Madness*. London: Picador, 1995.

Jarvie, I. C. "Freeman on Mead." *Canberra Anthropology* 6, no. 1 (1983): 80–97.

"Judgments, 1937." *Spike* 36, no. 65 (1937): 49.

Keesing, Roger. "Anthropology as Interpretive Quest." *Current Anthropology* 28, no. 2 (1987): 161–67.

Kiernan, Brian. *David Williamson: A Writer's Career*. Melbourne: Heinemann, 1990.

Kuper, Adam. *Among the Anthropologists: History and Context in Anthropology*. London: Athlone Press, 1999.

————. "Anthropologists Unite!" *Nature*, 10 February 2011, 166–68.

————. *Anthropology and Anthropologists: The Modern British School*. London: Routledge, 1996.

————. "Coming of Age in Anthropology." *Nature*, 6 April 1989, 453–55.

————. "Ernest Gellner: Two Notes." In *Among the Anthropologists*, 138–44.

Kuper, Hilda. "Function, History, Biography: Reflections on Fifty Years in the British Anthropological Tradition." In *Functionalism Historicized: Essays on British Social Anthropology*, edited by George Stocking, 192–212. Madison: University of Wisconsin Press, 1984.

Lal, Brij V., and Allison Leys, eds. *The Coombs: A House of Memories*. Canberra: ANU EPress, 2006.

Lawrence, Peter. "The Ethnographic Revolution." *Oceania* 45, no. 4 (1975): 253–71.

Leacock, Eleanor. "Anthropologists in Search of a Culture: Margaret Mead." *Central Issues in Anthropology* 8 (1988): 3–23.

Leader, Darian. *What Is Madness?* London: Penguin, 2011.

Leo, John. "Bursting the South Sea Bubble." *Time*, 14 February 1983, 50–52.

Lepore, Jill. "Historians Who Love Too Much: Reflections on Microhistory and Biography." *Journal of American History* 88, no. 1 (2001): 129–44.

LeVine, Robert. "Cutting a Controversy Down to Size." *Science* 328, no. 5,982 (2010): 1108.

Levy, Robert. "Mead, Freeman and Samoa: The Problem of Seeing Things as They Are." *Ethos* 12, no. 1 (1984): 85–92.

Lewis, Herbert S. "Boas, Darwin, Science and Anthropology." *Current Anthropology* 42, no. 3 (2001): 381–406.

Lieberman, Leonard. "A Discipline Divided: Acceptance of Human Sociobiological Concepts in Anthropology." *Current Anthropology* 30, no. 5 (1989): 676–82.

Lindstrom, Lamont. "*Trumpet* and *Road*: Two Classic Cargo Texts." In *Texts and Contexts:*

Reflections in Pacific Islands Historiography, edited by Doug Munro and Brij V. Lal, 178–88. Honolulu: University of Hawai'i Press, 2006.

Lipset, David, and Paul Roscoe, eds. *Echoes of the Tambaran*. Canberra: ANU EPress, 2011.

Lorenz, Konrad. *On Aggression*. London: Methuen, 1963.

Mageo, Jeanette Marie. "Mālosi: A Psychological Exploration of Mead's and Freeman's Work and of Samoan Aggression." *Pacific Studies* 11, no. 2 (1988): 25–65. Abridged in Caton, *Samoa Reader*, 84–98.

———. "Aga, Amio and Loto: Perspectives on the Structure of the Self in Samoa." *Oceania* 59, no. 3 (1989): 181–99.

Malcolm, Janet. *The Silent Woman: Sylvia Plath and Ted Hughes*. London: Picador, 1994.

Mansfield, Katherine. *Collected Stories of Katherine Mansfield*. London: Constable, 1945.

Marcus, George. "One Man's Mead." *New York Times Book Review*, 27 March 1983, 3, 22, 24.

"Margaret Mead." *New World Encyclopedia*. http://www.newworldencyclopedia.org/entry/Margaret Mead.

McDowell, Edwin. "New Samoa Book Challenges Margaret Mead's Conclusions." In Caton, *Samoa Reader*, 211–16.

McDowell, Nancy. "Derek Freeman, *Margaret Mead and Samoa: The Making and Unmaking of an Anthropological Myth*." *Pacific Studies* 7 no. 2 (1984): 99–140.

———. "Introduction: The Essentialization of Margaret Mead." *Pacific Studies* 28, nos. 3–4 (2005): 4–18.

McGillick, Paul. "Heresy." *Meanjin* 55, no. 2 (1996): 258–66.

McKay, C. G. A. *Samoana: A Personal Story of the Samoan Islands*. Wellington: A. H. & A. W. Reed, 1968.

Mead, Margaret. "Anthropology among the Sciences." *American Anthropologist* 63, no. 3 (1961): 479–82.

———. *Coming of Age in Samoa: A Study of Adolescence and Sex in Primitive Societies*. 1928. Repr., Melbourne: Penguin, 1943.

———. "Life as a Samoan Girl." In *All True! The Record of Actual Adventures That Have Happened to Ten Women of Today*, 94–118. New York: Brewer, Warren and Putnam, 1931.

———. *Social Organization of Manu'a*. Bulletin 76. 1930. Repr., Honolulu: Bernice P. Bishop Museum, 1969.

Medawar, P. B. *The Future of Man: The BBC Reith Lectures, 1959*. New York: Basic Books, 1960.

Mehta, Rohit. *The Nameless Experience: A Comprehensive Discussion of J. Krishnamurti's Approach to Life*. Delhi: Motilal Banarsidass, 1976.

Mein Smith, Philippa, Peter Hempenstall, and Shaun Goldfinch. *Remaking the Tasman World*. Christchurch: University of Canterbury Press, 2008.

Mills, David. *Difficult Folk? A Political History of Social Anthropology*. New York: Berghahn Books, 2008.

Molloy, Maureen. *On Creating a Usable Culture: Margaret Mead and the Emergence of American Cosmopolitanism*. Honolulu: University of Hawai'i Press, 2008.

Monaghan, Peter. "Anthropologist Who Sparked Dispute . . ." *Chronicle of Higher Education*, 2 August 1989, A4–A6.

———. "An Australian Historian Puts Margaret Mead's Biggest Detractor on the Psychoanalytic Sofa." *Chronicle of Higher Education*, 13 January 2006, A14.

———. "The Battle of Samoa Revisited." *Chronicle of Higher Education*, 17 January 2010, B15–16.

———. "Boffins Behaving Badly." *Australian*, 30 June 2010.

Montagu, Ashley, ed. *Sociobiology Examined*. New York: Oxford University Press, 1980.

Mulgan, John. *Man Alone*. 1939. Repr., Auckland: Longman Paul, 1972.

Munro, Doug. *J. C. Beaglehole: Public Intellectual, Critical Conscience*. Wellington: Steele Roberts, 2012.

———. "J. W. Davidson: The Making of a Participant Historian." In *Pacific Lives, Pacific Places: Bursting Boundaries in Pacific History*, edited by Brij V. Lal and Peter Hempenstall, 98–116. Canberra: Journal of Pacific History Monographs, 2001.

———. "The Prehistory of J. W. Davidson." In *The Ivory Tower and Beyond: Participant Historians of the Pacific*, 77–121. Newcastle upon Tyne: Cambridge Scholars, 2009.

Murdoch, Iris. *The Good Apprentice*. London: Chatto & Windus, 1985.

Murray, Stephen O. "On Boasians and Margaret Mead: Reply to Freeman." *Current Anthropology* 32, no. 4 (1991): 448–52.

———. "Problematic Aspects of Freeman's Account of Boasian Culture." *Current Anthropology* 31, no. 4 (1990): 401–7.

Nardi, Bonnie A. "The Height of Her Powers: Margaret Mead's Samoa." *Feminist Studies* 10, no. 2 (1984): 323–37.

Openshaw, Roger, and Teresa Ball. "New Zealand Teacher Education: Progression or Prescription?" *Education Research and Perspectives* 33, no. 2 (2006): 102–23.

Orans, Martin. Review of *Fateful Hoaxing*, by Derek Freeman. *Science* 283, no. 5,408 (1999): 1649–50.

———. *Not Even Wrong: Margaret Mead, Derek Freeman and the Samoans*. Novato: Chandler & Sharp, 1996.

"Our Plunket Babes Wah and Blah." *Salient* 1, no. 15 (13 July 1938): 1.

Parkin, David. "An Interview with Raymond Firth." *Current Anthropology* 29, no. 2 (1988): 327–40.

Partner, Nancy. "Historicity in an Age of Reality-Fictions." In *A New Philosophy of History*, edited by Frank Ankersmit and Hans Kellner, 21–39. London: Reaktion Books, 1995.

Patterson, Thomas C. *A Social History of Anthropology in the United States*. Oxford: Berg, 2001.

Popper, Karl. *Conjectures and Refutations: The Growth of Scientific Knowledge*. London: Routledge & Kegan Paul, 1963.

Rappaport, Roy A. "Desecrating the Holy Woman: Derek Freeman's Attack on Margaret Mead." *American Scholar* 55, no. 3 (1986): 313–47.

———. "The Reader Replies." *American Scholar* 56, no. 1 (1987): 159–60.

———. "The Reader Replies." *American Scholar* 56, no. 2 (1987): 304.

Reay, Marie. "An Innocent in the Garden of Eden." In *Ethnographic Presents: Pioneering Anthropologists in the Papua New Guinea Highlands*, edited by Terence E. Hays, 137–66. Berkeley: University of California Press, 1992.

Robinson, Kathryn. "We, the Ethnographers." In Lal and Leys, *The Coombs*, 117–24.

Roscoe, Paul. "Margaret Mead, Reo Fortune and Mountain Arapesh Warfare." *American Anthropologist* 105, no. 3 (2003): 581–91.

Rousseau, Jérôme. "Iban Inequality." *Bijdragen tot de Taal-, Land- en Volkenkunde* 136, no. 1 (1980): 52–63.

Sachs, Oliver. *Awakenings.* 1973; London: Picador, 1991.

Sahlins, Marshall. Review of *Iban Agriculture*, by J. D. Freeman. *Journal of the Polynesian Society* 67, no. 3 (1958): 311–13.

———. *What Kinship Is—And Is Not.* Chicago: University of Chicago Press, 2013.

Sargant, William. *Battle for the Mind: A Physiology of Conversion and Brain-Washing.* London: Pan, 1959.

Sassoon, Siegfried, "Limitations." In *Collected Poems 1908–1956*, 121–22. London: Faber & Faber, 1961.

Scheper-Hughes, Nancy. "The Margaret Mead Controversy: Culture, Biology and Anthropological Inquiry." *Human Organization* 43, no. 1 (1984): 85–93.

Schneider, David M. "The Coming of a Sage to Samoa." In Caton, *Samoa Reader*, 223–24.

Schoeffel, Penelope, and Malama Meleisea. "Margaret Mead, Derek Freeman and Samoa: The Making, Unmaking and Remaking of an Anthropological Myth." *Canberra Anthropology* 6, no. 1 (1983): 58–69.

Schwartz, Theodore. "Anthropology: A Quaint Science." *American Anthropologist* 85, no. 4 (1983): 919–29.

Scott, Jonathan. *Harry's Absence: Looking for My Father on the Mountain.* Wellington: Victoria University Press, 1997.

Seymour-Smith, Charlotte, ed. *Macmillan Dictionary of Anthropology.* London: Macmillan, 1986.

Shankman, Paul. "Derek Freeman and Margaret Mead: What Did He Know and When Did He Know It." *Pacific Studies* 32, nos. 2–3 (2009): 202–21.

———. "The 'Fateful Hoaxing' of Margaret Mead: A Cautionary Tale." *Current Anthropology* 54, no. 1 (2013): 51–70.

———. "Margaret Mead, Derek Freeman, and the Issue of Evolution." *Skeptical Inquirer* 22, no. 6 (1998): 35–39.

———. "Margaret Mead's Other Samoa: Rereading *Social Organization of Manu'a.*" *Pacific Studies* 28, nos. 3–4 (2005): 46–59.

———. "The Samoan Conundrum." *Canberra Anthropology* 6, no. 1 (1983): 38–57.

———. "The Thick and the Thin: On the Interpretive Theoretical Program of Clifford Geertz." *Current Anthropology* 25, no. 3 (1984): 261–80.

———. *The Trashing of Margaret Mead: Anatomy of an Anthropological Controversy.* Madison: University of Wisconsin Press, 2009.

Shore, Bradd. "Paradox Regained: Freeman's *Margaret Mead and Samoa.*" *American*

Anthropologist 85, no. 4 (1983): 935–44. Reprinted with amplification in *Canberra Anthropology* 6, no. 1 (1983): 17–37.

———. "Reply to Freeman." *Oceania* 54, no. 3 (1984): 254–60.

———. "Reply to Freeman." *Oceania* 55, no. 3 (1985): 218–23.

———. *Sala'ilua: A Samoan Mystery.* New York: Columbia University Press, 1982.

Silverman, Martin G. "Our Great Deception, or, Anthropology Defiled." *American Anthropologist* 85, no. 4 (1983): 944–47.

Sinclair, Keith. *Halfway round the Harbour: An Autobiography.* Auckland: Penguin Books, 1993.

Smart, Christopher. "A Song to David." In *Selected Poems,* by Christopher Smart, edited by Karina Williamson and Marcus Walsh, 198–215. London: Penguin, 1990.

Smith, Roger. *Between Mind and Nature: A History of Psychology.* London: Reaktion Books, 2013.

"Special Section: Speaking in the Name of the Real: Freeman and Mead on Samoa." *American Anthropologist* 85, no. 4 (1983): 908–47.

Spiro, Mel. "Cultural Relativism and the Future of Anthropology." *Cultural Anthropology* 1, no. 3 (August 1986): 259–86.

Stanner, W. E. H. *After the Dreaming: Black and White Australians—An Anthropologist's View.* Sydney: Australian Broadcasting Commission, 1969.

———. *The South Seas in Transition: A Study of Post-war Rehabilitation and Reconstruction in Three British Pacific Dependencies.* Sydney: Australasian Publishing Company, 1953.

Stephen, Michele. "Klein in Bali and Ilahita: A Reflection on Cultural Fantasy and the Deep Unconscious." In *Echoes of the Tambaran,* edited by David Lipset and Paul Roscoe, 197–224. Canberra: ANU EPress, 2011.

Stocking, George, ed. *After Tylor: British Social Anthropology 1881–1951.* Madison: University of Wisconsin Press, 1996.

———. *The Ethnographer's Magic and Other Essays in the History of Anthropology.* Madison: University of Wisconsin Press, 1992.

———. *Functionalism Historicized: Essays on British Social Anthropology.* Madison: University of Wisconsin Press, 1984.

Strathern, Marilyn. "The Persuasive Fictions of Anthropology." *Current Anthropology* 28, no. 3 (1987): 251–81.

———. "The Punishment of Margaret Mead." *Canberra Anthropology* 6, no. 1 (1983): 70–79. Reprinted from *London Review of Books* 5, no. 8 (5–18 May 1983).

Tambiah, Stanley J. *Edmund Leach: An Anthropological Life.* Cambridge: Cambridge University Press, 2002.

Tarrow, Sidney. "Polarization and Convergence in Academic Controversies." *Theory and Society* 37 (2008): 514, 524.

Tcherkézoff, Serge. "Correspondence: Samoa Again: On Durkheimian Bees, Freemanian Passion and Fa'amu (Fa'apua'a)'s 'Confession.'" *Journal of the Polynesian Society* 110, no. 4 (2001): 431–36.

———. "Is Anthropology about Individual Agency or Culture? Or Why 'Old Derek' Is Doubly Wrong." *Journal of the Polynesian Society* 110, no. 1 (2001): 59–78.

———. *Le mythe occidental de la sexualité polynésienne 1928–1999: Margaret Mead, Derek Freeman et Samoa.* Paris: Presses Universitaires de France, 2001.

Thieme, F. P. Review of *The Future of Man*, by P. B. Medawar. *American Anthropologist* 63, no. 5 (1961): 1156–57.

Thomas, Caroline. *The Sorcerers' Apprentice: A Life of Reo Franklin Fortune, Anthropologist.* Hamilton: University of Waikato, 2011.

Tiffany, Sharon W., ed. "Reflections on Pacific Ethnography in the Margaret Mead Centennial 2001." Special issue, *Pacific Studies* 28, nos. 3–4 (2005).

Torgovnik, Marianna. *Gone Primitive: Savage Intellects, Modern Lives.* Chicago: University of Chicago Press, 1990.

Turner, Victor. "Symbols in Ndembu Ritual." In *Closed Systems and Open Minds: The Limits of Naivety in Social Anthropology*, edited by Max Gluckman, 20–51. Chicago: Aldine, 1964.

Tuzin, Donald. "Base Notes: Odor, Breath and Moral Contagion in Ilahita." In *The Smell Culture Reader*, edited by James Drobnick, 59–67. Oxford: Berg, 2006.

———. *The Cassowary's Revenge.* Chicago: University of Chicago Press, 1997.

———. "Derek Freeman (1916–2001)." *American Anthropologist* 104, no. 3 (2002): 1013–15.

———. "Miraculous Voices: The Auditory Experience of Numinous Objects." *Current Anthropology* 25, no. 5 (1984): 579–96.

———. *The Voice of the Tambaran.* Berkeley: University of California Press, 1980.

Wallace, David Rains. "The Left Hand of Darkness." *Los Angeles Times Book Review*, 12 November 2000, 1, 6–7.

Walter, Michael. Review of *Fateful Hoaxing*, by Derek Freeman. *ANU Reporter* 31, no. 15 (2000): 1.

Waterford, Jack. "Capital Times." *Canberra Times*, July/August 2001.

Weiner, Annette. "Ethnographic Determinism: Samoa and the Margaret Mead Controversy." *American Anthropologist* 85, no. 4 (1983): 909–19.

Wendt, Tuaopepe Felix S. "Derek Freeman, *Margaret Mead and Samoa: The Making and Unmaking of an Anthropological Myth.*" *Pacific Studies* 7, no. 2 (1984): 92–99.

Williams, Sarah. "Professing Culture: Anthropology among Anthropologists." PhD diss., University of California, Santa Cruz, 1991.

Williamson, David. *Dead White Males.* Sydney: Currency Press, 1995.

———. *Heretic: Based on the Life of Derek Freeman.* Melbourne: Penguin Books Australia, 1996.

Wilson, A. N. *Hilaire Belloc.* 1984; Harmondsworth: Penguin, 1986.

Wilson, E. O. *On Human Nature.* Cambridge, Mass.: Harvard University Press, 1978.

———. "Science and Ideology." *Academic Questions*, 1994–95, 73–81.

———. *Sociobiology.* Cambridge, Mass.: Harvard University Press, 1976.

Wise, Tigger. *The Self-Made Anthropologist: A Life of A. P. Elkin.* North Sydney: George Allen & Unwin, 1985.

Wood, F. L. W. *The New Zealand People at War: Political and External Affairs.* Wellington: Department of Internal Affairs, 1958.

Wynn Owen, Andrew. "Edmund Halley, 1740." *Magdalen College Record,* 2015, 117–19.

Young, R. E., and S. Juan. "Freeman's Margaret Mead Myth: The Ideological Virginity of Anthropologists." *Australian and New Zealand Journal of Sociology* 21, no. 1 (1985): 64–81.

Zeldin, Theodore. *An Intimate History of Humanity.* 1994; London: Vintage, 1998.

Zuber-Skerritt, Ortrun, ed. *David Williamson: Australian Playwrights.* Amsterdam: Rodopi BV, 1988.

Index

Page numbers in italics indicate illustrations.

Aboriginal affairs, 113–14, 115–16, 124

Academic Questions, 204, 284n13

Adair, Elsie May ("Did," Freeman's mother), 17–18, 23, 24, 90–91, 92–93; classical literature, boon bequeathed by, 139; death of, 54–5; family, *143*; relationship with, Derek's mental condition and, 135

Adair, George, 17

African Genesis (Ardrey), 94

Alexander, Frederick Mathias (and Alexander technique), 139–40

Allen, Bryant, 124

Allport, Gordon, 79–80

American Anthropological Association (AAA), 101, 179

American Anthropologist, 25, 61, 184, 196, 199, 201, 219, 231, 238

American anthropology: anger and sadness in relationship with Freeman, Shore's view, 191–92; conflict to come from, omens for Freeman of, 102–3; defense of (following "recreational lying" attack from Freeman), 200–201, 203–4; desecration of "totemic" Mead, accusation against Freeman, 192–93; divisiveness and crisis within, 230–31; four fields approach in, 183, 227, 229, 237, 238; Freeman's war over Mead with, 6–7, 8, 197, 200, 204, 215, 217, 224–25, 249–50, 253, 255–56; identity crisis for, 193; nature and nurture, interplay between as cornerstone of, 226

American Association for the Advancement of Science, 237

American Scholar, 187

Anglo-Celtic settler societies, 9

Appell, George, 13, 17, 39, 166, 229

Ardrey, Robert, 94

Areopagitica (Milton), 85

Arieti, Silvano, 138

Aristophanes, 234

Association of Social Anthropologists (ASA), 82, 93, 106, 265n36

Association for Social Anthropology in Oceania (ASAO), 106, 265n36

Auden, W. H., 22

Australasian Science Congress in New Zealand (1968), 109

Australian and New Zealand Association for the Advancement of Science (ANZAAS), 169, 229; ethology and human behavior, symposium on (1972), 236; presidential address in Auckland (1979), Freeman's "Sweet Analytics" in, 169, 239–40

Australian and New Zealand College of Psychiatrists, 96

Australian Association for Social Anthropology, 118, 161–62

Australian Institute of Aboriginal Studies (AIAS), 115–16

Australian National University (ANU), 4, 10, 56, 57, 74, 84, 86–87, 103, 104, 105, 110; anthropology at, lack of coherence in, 120; archives of, 11–12; Aztec stone, presentation to (and farce surrounding), 121–23, 132, 136, 169; designed to be different, 59–60; graduate student's perspective on Freeman's behavior toward students and staff at, 126–27; histories of, wariness of Freeman in, 111; intellectual surroundings at, Freeman's comfort with, 111; *The Making of the Australian National University, 1946–1996* (Foster and Varghese), 111; "Man and the New Biology" lecture series, 234–35; power games at, 120–21; recruitment policies, 64–65; *Reporter*, 115; retirement of Freeman from, 127; Sarawak incidents, Freeman and, 77–78

Australian Society of Psychoanalysts, 97–98

Ayers Rock (Uluru), 57

Aztec imagery, 6, 121–22, 132, 136, 169

Bargatzky, Thomas, 194

Barnes, John, 64–65, 68, 70, 75, 77, 88, 91, 94, 109, 110, 113, 117, 125, 126, 128, 132; confrontation (and reconciliation) with Freeman, 82–86; dereliction of intellectual duty, Freeman's charge of, 119; welcome from Freeman for, monumental misstatement of, 65–66

Barnicott, Nigel, 41

Barrowclough, Nikki, 221

Barunga, Albert, 115, 118

Basham, Richard, 177, 178

Bateson, Mary Catherine, 177, 178, 198, 220; sex and violence, bizarre suggestion on Freeman and, 238

Battle for the Mind (Sargant), 79

Bayatt, A. S., 7

Beaglehole, Ernest, 19, 20, 24, 25, 28, 33, 35, 41, 53, 80, 81, 87, 165, 229

Beaglehole, John, 20, 21

Beattie, John, 93; death of, 128

Becoming (Allport), 79–80

Benedict, Ruth, 172, 198, 214

Bentall, Richard, 141, 142

Berman, Shelley, 82

Berndt, Ronald, 82, 116, 132; death of, 128

Bishop Museum in Hawai'i, 20, 39, 202, 214, 265n42

Boas, Franz, 4, 5, 105, 110, 160, 161–62, 172, 198, 214, 227, 230, 235, 238, 242, 255; bankruptcy of Boasian culturalism, Freeman's belief in, 245; role of, Freeman's interpretation of, 182–83

Bonhoeffer, Dietrich, 138–39

Bonner, John, 171

Borneo, 4, 7, 37, 108, 113, 125, 128–31, 133–34, 166–67, 229, 231, 234, 248. *See also* Iban people; Kuching; Sarawak

Bowlby, John, 87, 88, 161

Brady, Ivan, 201, 212, 238

British Museum of Natural History, 87–88

Brooke, Rupert, 29

Brown, Donald, 215

Brown, John Macmillan, 29

Brunei, 37, 166

Buck, Peter, 20, *39*, 171, 173

Bühler, Karl, 41

Burnet, Frank Macfarlane, 114, 236, 243

Burridge, Kenelm, 124

Cambridge University, 53–55, 85

Canberra: Deakin, Freeman home in, 61, 85, 129; transformation into city, 112

Canberra Anthropology, 185

Canberra Times, 8, 122, 123, 206

Caton, Hiram, 8, 12, 72, 75, 78, 83, 106, 140–42, 176, 194, 235, 242, 244, 256; biological explanations for human behavior, visibility of, 239; faltering of relationship with Freeman and "devil take reputation," 201; Freeman as "Wise Elder" message from, 200–201; Janus-faced attitudes of, 215, 217, 224; language of Freeman, observations on, 253–54; "marvelous" letter to Freeman during Great Debate, 196–97; "political psychologist," 69–71; *Samoa Reader*, 197, 200–201, 203, 212, 242, 244, 269n29; sideline champion of Freeman, 197; views of others on Freeman, telling of, 131–33, 135; "visceral" nature of Holmes's criticisms of Freeman, 184

Chagnon, Napoleon, 219, 226

Chapple, Eliot, 257

Childe, V. Gordon, 41

Chowning, Ann, 179

Churchward, William, 109

Clark, Charles Manning, 60

Clifford, James, 109, 188, 212, 241, 253

Cohn, Norman, 94

Cole, Douglas, 205

Colonial Social Science Research Council (CSSRC), 36, 43–44, 52, 53, 54

Columbia University, 61

Coming of Age in Samoa (Mead), 3, 9, 95, 101–2, 105–7, 157–59, 160–61, 165–66, 203–4, 215; adolescence in Samoa, study aim of, 158; Boas's influence on, 160; "classic ethnology," celebration as, 159; cultural assumptions in America, goal of rethink on, 159–60; cultural conditioning, nurture before nature and, 160; cultural determinism, Mead's pursuit of, 166, 172, 175, 180, 186–87; "A Day in Samoa," opening vignette, 157–58, 173; detail and complexity in, 160; Goodman's dissenting views on, 179–80; influences on writing of, 172–73; moetotolo ("sleep crawling" phenomenon), 159; Orans and Côte's defense in light of new evidence, 216; "perpetual admonitions," simple discipline of, 158; popular success of, 157; precocity, punishment of, 158; psychological integrity in social organization, 159; psychological study based on small sample, 158; refutation by Freeman of, colleagues attitudes on, 165–66; sexual adventure, 158; social communities, boys in, 159; taupo ceremonial princess, 158–59; virginity, attitude toward, 159; "written to order," Freeman's accusation, 160

Conklin, Harold, 61

Cook, Captain James, 20, 39

Cornford, John, 22

Côte, James, 209, 211–12, 215–16, 220–21, 250–51

Crawford, John, 70, 72, 78, 79, 83–84, 85, 86, 87, 91, 103, 114, 119, 128; death of, 128

Cressman, Luther, 178

Crick, Francis, 11, 205, 231

Crocombe, Ron, 163

Culter, Roden, 70

cultural determinism: American adherence to, 164, 283n66; "antiquated doctrine" of, 238; Boas and foundations of, 182–83, 281n34

Current Anthropology, 203, 212, 234, 288n24

Daily Mirror, 94–95

Damien, Father, 138

D'Andrade, Roy, 260

Dante Alighieri, 234

Darwin, Charles, 22, 23, 81, 94, 163, 183, 234, 235, 244–45, 257, 260

Davidson, James "Jim" Wightman, 45, 54, 55, 56, 58, 60–61, 63, 65, 103, 105; death of, 128

Davis, Stan, 23

Dawkins, Richard, 206, 239

Dead Poets Society (Weir film), 139

Dead White Males (Williamson play), 206–7

Degler, Carl, 239

Dennett, Daniel, 259–60

Denoon, Donald, 34

Denver Post, 178–79

deoxyrobonucleic acid (DNA), 11, 231

Dhammapada, 138, 163

Diagnostic and Statistical Manual of Mental Disorders, 71, 97, 133–34

Diamond, John, 139, 243

Dilthey, Wilhelm, 257

Dobzhansky, Theodosius, 231, 235

Doctorow, E. L., 252–53

Donahue, Phil, 177

Donne, John, 85

Dowling, Norman, 23

Dryden, John, 136

Durkheim, Émile, 232, 255; sociology of, 87

Eccles, John, 138, 161

Edinburgh University, 67, 113

Eibl-Eibesfeldt, Irenäus, 89, 94, 176, 228

Elkin, Peter, 59, 112–13, 114, 115

Elton, Geoffrey, 210–11

Ember, Melvin, 100–101, 102, 105, 252

Epstein, A. L., 113, 114

Erikson, Erik, 161

Evans-Prtichard, E. E., 41

Evolution and Modification of Behavior (Lorenz), 104

The Expression of the Emotions in Man and Animals (Darwin), 94

Eysenck, Hans, 161

Faʻalolo, Leaʻana (Saʻanapu informant), 104

Faʻamu Tagia ("Faʻapuaʻa"), 197, 199–200, 201–2, 204, 205, 209, 211, 214–15, 218, 219

The Fateful Hoaxing of Margaret Mead (Freeman), 4, 204, 205–6, 215, 217, 223–24, 227, 239, 242, 252–53; publication of (1999), 213–14

Felise Vaʻa, Leulu, 199

Fellow Traveller, 20

Fenner, F. J., 114

Field, Michael, 194

Firth, Raymond, 13, 74, 82, 104, 164, 194, 212, 229, 248; Freeman and, early years, 36, 37, 38, 39–41, 43, 50, 53, 54, 55, 60–61, 63, 65

Fitzgerald, C. P., 60

Flew, Anthony, 184

Fofoa (friend of Faʻamu in Siʻufaga and a Mead informant), 199, 205, 211, 214

Fortes, Meyer, 13, 80, 93, 110, 113, 114, 194, 230, 233, 235, 248; death of, 128; Freeman and, early years, 40, 41, 43, 51, 52–3, 54, 57, 65; praise (and advice) for Freeman from, 165–6

Fortune, Barter, 24

Fortune, Reo, 10, 24, 194

Foster, Stephen, 111

Foucault, Michel, 140

The Foundations of Social Anthropology (Nadel), 63

Fox, James, 118, 124, 200

Fox, Robin, 198

Franco, Francisco, 22

Freedman, Maurice, 40

Freeman, Derek: Aboriginal affairs, interest in, 113–14, 115–16, 124; Academy of the Social Sciences in Australia, fellowship of, 118; admiration for Mead, enhancement of, 205–6; adolescent girls, criticism of Mead's "anecdotal" information on, 214–15; advocacy of cultural determinism, 20; alienation, sense of, 23; America, triumphant procession through (1981), 171; American anthropology, war over Mead with, 6–7, 8, 197, 200, 204, 215, 217, 224–25, 249–50, 253–54, 255–56; "Anatomy of Mind" article for *Salient* student magazine, 24–25; anthropological disillusionment, 5; anthropological interests, beginnings of, 19–20, 28; anthropological roots, 19–20; anthropological training, 4; Anthropology and Sociology at ANU, new home for, 59–61; "anthropology of choice," early ideas on road to, 233–35, 239; antipodean anthropologists' feelings about, 194; anxiety, depression, and, 167–68; arrival in Apia, 27; attachment behavior in children, studies of (Samoa, 1966–67), 173–74, 228–29, 233; attack on iconic Mead, publisher's concerns about, 164; Australia, preparations for academic life in, 57, 58–59; Australian Association for Social Anthropology, chair of, 118; Aztec stone presentation to ANU (and farce surrounding), 121–23, 132, 136, 169; Bad Homberg symposium (1977), 268; battles and reckonings of dark years (1970s) for, 118–19, 123, 136–37, 166–67, 212–13, 228–29, 235–41, 248; behavioral sciences and anthropological disagreements, 93–5; Big Ideas and inspirational achievements of, 258–59; biological determinism, attitudes to, 175, 183, 184, 193, 238; biological interests, 5, 7–8, 24, 41, 81, 96, 111–12, 120, 125, 130, 160, 162, 163, 183, 187, 192–93, 209, 226–27, 233–34, 235–36, 237–38, 239–40, 242–43, 258–59; biological sciences, social sciences, and advances in, 195, 197, 226, 227, 230, 235; bipolar condition (and effects of), 77, 134–35, 141, 213, 243; birth in Wellington, NZ, 4; Boas's background, work on, 161; Boas-Mead correspondence, "priceless boon" from Cole of, 205–6; body and mind, interest in physical workings of, 243;

Cambridge, academic life in, 53–55; campaign against Mead's work in Samoa, first serious salvo (May 1968), 161–62; campaigning styles, 251–52; Canada and California (1977), 268; Canada (and US West coast) for Simon Fraser University lectures, 205; caption on *Ulysses and the Sirens*, *151*; ceremonial abasement (*ifoga*), witness to, 31; chair of anthropology at ANU for, 113–14, 115; childhood family, *143*; choice behavior, perspective on, 175, 227, 229, 236, 238, 239–40; clarification and synthesis, brilliant work on, 256; "cognitive abreaction," 69–70, 79, 90, 94, 107, 228, 255–56; consummate ethnographer, 43–44; contradictions and confusions, display of, 70–71; Coombs building encounter with Margaret Mead, 98–100; correspondences with Mead (and ideas about), 161, 167–68, 168–9, 179–80; correspondents, immense circle of, 13; Côte's aggressive attack on (and response to), 209–10; criticism, conviction about scientific enquiry and, 124; critique of Freud's *Totem and Taboo* (and reaction to), 97–98; cross-disciplinary explorations, 231–33; cultural determinism and relativism, passionate rejection of, 5, 227, 238, 248; cultural relativism, abandonment of, 228; Curl Bequest Prize of the Royal Anthropological Institute (1960), 62; Deakin, Canberra home in, 61, 85, 129; death of, 3, 130; death of, premature announcement of (1988), 129; defense of Mead against Orans, 210–11; devotees of cultural determinism, defiance of, 186; diabetes, 129, 205; diary, Mead's appearances in, 105; diary, practice of keeping, 84–85; diary, psychiatric symptoms recorded in, 107–8; diary, quotes about courage and fighting back in, 186; diary, self-recording in, 12, 163; diary collection, Tuzin's access to, 140; "Dilthey's Dream" for, 257–58; diploma thesis "The Social Structure of a Samoan Village Community," 41–42; disciple of Indian divine Krishnamurti, 23–24; "Dragon of Canberra," 131; Durkheimianism in work of, 87, 109, 218, 219, 228, 270n9;

early teaching career, 4; ecological approaches, importance for, 228–29; eightieth birthday ascent of Mount Ainslie, 129–30; emotionalism of, strength of, 108; energy and ambition, 38–39; ethological laboratory initiative, 161; extreme emotionalism of, recognition of, 135–36; false assertions and misrepresentations in criticisms of, 184; fieldwork, approach to, 125; "finis coronat opus" on Samoa struggle for, 216; fluctuation in attitude toward Mead, 165; Free Discussions Club, encounter with Nazism at, 21–22; Freeman–Mead controversy, 70–71, 259; Freeman–Mead controversy, beginnings of, 13, 28–29, 30–31, 109, 110; Freeman–Mead controversy, classic refutation exercise, 100–101; Freeman–Mead controversy, coda concerning, 219–25; Freeman–Mead controversy, reignition of, 102–3; Freeman–Mead controversy, Shankman's musings on, 221–24, 225; graduate student's perspective on behavior toward students and staff at ANU, 126–27; Grand Inquisition of "Pensacola Crackpots" against, 211–12, 216, 221; "great hierarchical personality," possession of, 25; Great Mission, launch on, 20; growing up in Depression Wellington, 19; health of, deterioration of, 129–30; heart trouble, 129, 205; Hempenstall and, personal involvement, 9; histories of ANU, wariness of, 111–12; horseback in Western Samoa, *145*; hubris, exhibitions of, 72, 163; "Human Aggression in Anthropological Perspective," 232; "Human Nature and Culture," 230–31, 235; Iban, first contact with, 37; Iban, importance of place in life story of, 248–49; Iban, work on and with, 4, 7, 12, 43–57, 61–63, 67, 69–70, 71–73, 75, 76, 77, 80–81, 89, 97, 108, 118, 129, 141, 166–67, 170, 195, 206, 228–29, 233–34, 248, 256; Iban family, *148*; Indonesian research, supervision of, 62–63; "inductivist" accusation against Shore, 190–91; inner torments and outer "betrayals," 118–20; intellectual life, complex interplay of doubt and deliberation in, 166; intellectual

Index

Freeman, Derek (*continued*)

life, power and dark charisma of, 125–26; intellectual life, reflections on, 166; "interactionist paradigm," 5, 128, 189, 195–96, 201–2, 204, 226, 229, 234, 242, 243, 257, 287n68; juggling work on several fronts, 168; Karachi interlude, 67–68, 70, 76, 77; Keesing, misplaced faith in, 117–18, 119–20; "Kierkegaardian earthquake" for, Harrisson and, 66–69, 229, 269n28; "On the Concept of the Kindred," Curl Bequest Prize essay (1960), 62; Kuching work, 37, 66–67, 69, 71, 74, 75, 76, 77, 79, 81, 86, 132, 167; language of, Caton's observations on, 253–54; in later life, *151, 153, 154*; legal action against denunciation, threats of, 188; Leifiifi school in Apia, teaching appointment at, 26; London, academic life in, 36, 38–42, 52, 88–93, 93–95; Lorenzian turn, 94; man-most-likely-to, 25; master story, Wellington lecture (1998) on (and comfort with), 216–17; materialist musing at end of long life, 260; Mead book, scholarly exertions on (1977–81), 168–70; Mead project, slow-growing monster, 165; Mead's "culture-is-environmentally-determined" claims, case against, 110; Mead's "Life as a Samoan Girl," evidence clincher for, 215–16; Mead's *Social Organization of Manu'a*, target for, 164–65; meditative "Zenning," 129; mental state of, reflections on, 108–9, 131–32, 135–36, 208; Monty Python's Black Knight, identification with, 212; "mood prompts," 244; moral empathy with downtrodden, 166; moral universe, strength of, 72; morale boosts from Tuzin, Salk, and Popper, 168; mountaineering trauma, 23; National Press Club, address to, 206; nature/nurture debate, Tuzin's reflection on Freeman and, 258; New Zealand administration in Samoa, relationship with, 31; nightmares and "heavy heart," 118–19; obsession with Mead, widespread impression of, 170; Oedipal neurosis, thoughts about, 233; "On the Believing of as Many as Six Impossible Things before Breakfast," 162, 235–36; opposition,

intellectual invigoration by, 163, 164; over-identification with Aboriginal people, 116–17; "overwrought state" in Sa'anapu, 104–5; Oxford pilgrimage (1977), 268; Oxford seminar (1947), first inkling of disciplinary dissonances at, 40–41; pacifism, 21, 32; pacifism, abandonment of, 33; "Paradigms in Collision" (1991), 204–5, 207, 242; "paranoid schizophrenia," ignoble accusations of, 126–27, 133, 135, 177; personal obloquy against detractors, 185; personality of, colleague's perspectives on, 131–34, 140–42; personality of, singularity of, 66; perspectives of, variability of, 17; poetry, 21, 22–23; polarizing figure, 5; "pornographic carvings" controversy, 67, 68–69, 71–72; power games, deeply held convictions and, 120–21; "A Precursory View of the Anthropology of Choice," 236; Presbyterian upbringing (and rejection of), 17, 23, 32, 72, 84, 243; primordial brain impulses, link between culture and emotions, 234; pseudo-psychiatric descriptions of enemies, 136; "Psychiatry, Anthropology and the Doctrine of Cultural Relativism," test paper for ANZCP (1964), 96–97; psychoanalysis with Klein, "intellectual game" of, 92; psycho-analytical interests, 25, 53, 71, 80–81, 85–87, 88–93, 97–100, 106–7, 228, 233–34, 240, 249, 256, 271n22; psychology, member of Beaglehole's graduate seminar in, 19–20; publication of Mead book, final arrangements, 171; published name change, "J.D." to "Derek," 88; reading, formidable immersion in, 106, 161, 163, 169; record keeping of, inveterate nature of, 11; "recreational lying" accusation about Mead informants from, 199, 202–3; "red-letter" day of discovery of Alexander technique with Monica, 139; Rehabilitation Board in New Zealand, support for overseas studies, 36, 38; relations with Samoa, disputes about, 255–56; relentless logic and forensic dissection of arguments, 123; remaking himself, 79–95; remembered in Dunedin, *150*; Research School of Pacific Studies (RSPacS), 59, 60,

87, 111–12, 274n2; resolutions, introspective diary entries containing, 137–38; restless curiosity, 29–30; restlessness, 25–26; restrictive notion of anthropology from Stanner, rejection of, 102–3; retirement from ANU in 1981 (but not from academic life), 127–28; righting colonial injustices, commitment to, 117; Royal New Zealand Naval Volunteer Reserve, 33; Sa'anapu, 30–31, 33, 37–8, 41–42, 45, 56, 99, 102–5, 107, 109, 151, 161, 210, 233, 255, 264n10; Samoa, return to (1980), 170; Samoan islands, ethological observation in, 103–9; Samoan islands, focus of attention for, 37–38; Samoan islands, love for, 29; Samoan words and symbols, criticism of Mead's use of, 164–65; Sarawak incidents, 66, 69, 77–78, 85, 97, 119, 131, 186, 249, 252; scholarly morality of, 210–11; scientism, prosecution of, 256–57; self-analysis, Sarawak and beginnings of, 228; self-confidence, displays of, 38, 65, 141; self-recrimination, family and, 136–37; self-scrutiny, inspirations for, 138–39; sexual behavior in Samoa, perspective on, 180–81; sexual desire in Samoa, Mead's "romantic bilge" about, 203; sexual mores in Coming of Age, perspective on, 174; "Shaman and Incubus," 233–34, 248; shared missions and obligations with Mead, 170; Skeptic of the Year, 206; social anthropology, criticisms of, 82, 83; social anthropology, "eating away" cathedral of, 110; social anthropology and, 7–8, 39–40, 52–53, 57, 61–64, 80–83, 87, 92, 96, 102–3, 117–18, 120–21, 164, 193–94, 230–35, 248, 257; "Social Anthropology and the Scientific Study of Human Behavior," 232; social behavior, determination of course of, 232; Spanish Civil War, effects on, 22–23; stock market crash (1987) and retirement prospects, 205; structural functionalism, rejection of, 227–28; student activities, 21; subtexts in work of, conspiracy theories about, 250; "Sweet Analytics" paper, 168, 169, 176, 279n28; Ta'u, mea culpa state in, 106–8; Tcherkézoff and, criticism and compliments, 217–19; "theology"

for, 244–45; "There's Tricks i' th' World" essay (1991), 202–4, 214; thinking of, watershed in development of, 228–30; "Thunder, Blood and the Nicknaming of God's Creatures," 234, 259; title of logona-i-taga (heard at tree felling) conferred by Samoan chiefs on, 30; treatment in battles over Mead (and his treatment of critics in response), 212–13; trench warfare with critics of Iban studies, 167; truth, passion for (cartoon sketch), 144; truth, zeal for, 170, 236, 242, 256; truth for, purity of, 197; "Truth's Fool," self-chosen appellation (and truth about), 6, 247–48; Victoria University College, undergraduate at, 19, 20–26; views of others on, Caton's telling of, 131–33, 135; volatility and extravagance, reputation for, 123; "wacky" tendencies, 139–40; war-time escapades, stories of, 33–35, 36–37; wartime readiness, 147; Wellington Teachers' Training College (1936–37), 19, 24; words, language, and, 250–54; work pace, relentless nature of, 106; working among Iban (cartoon sketch), 148; youthful (1939) portrait, 144

Freeman, Hilary (daughter), 61, 129, 136, 171

Freeman, Jennifer (daughter), 61, 109, 115, 129, 171, 196

Freeman, John Henry (father), 18, 20, 23, 24, 90, 93; death of, 106; family, 143; relationship with, Derek's mental condition and, 135

Freeman, Margaret (sister), 18–19, 90–91, 98; death of, 129; family, 143

Freeman, Monica (née Maitland), 4, 9, 12, 58–59, 60, 89, 92–93, 98, 103, 108, 116, 120, 130, 170–71, 243, 244; Deakin, Canberra home in, 61, 85; Derek's state of mind, worries about, 118; dramaturgical adjustments on Heretic, witness to, 208; family life in Sa'anapu, 104, 109; holistic healing and Buddhism in later life, 129; home in Canberra, haven for family and friends, 129; Iban family, 148; life with the Iban for, 45, 46–52, 53–54, 55–7; metaphysics with Derek, 169; patience, soul of, 135, 136; struggles and self-recrimination of Derek, family bearing

Freeman, Monica (*continued*)
brunt of,136–37; verbal "work-outs" from
Derek, in receipt of, 93; working among
Iban (cartoon sketch), *148*
Freud, Anna, 41, 87, 89, 90, 93; death of, 128
Freud, Lucien, 45
Freud, Sigmund, 25, 71, 81, 93, 97, 98, 228, 233
Fromm, Erich, 87
The Future of Man (Medawar), 231

Galileo, 186
Geddes, W. R. ("Bill"), 51; death of, 128
Geertz, Clifford, 105, 212, 241–42, 245
Geisel, Theodor, 11
Gellner, Ernest, 94
Gering (Iban housekeeper at Rumah Nyala),
47, 50
Gibbings, Robert, 38
Gilbert and Ellice Islands, 36
Ginsburg, Morris, 20
Glick, Paula Brown, 178, 183, 252
Gluckman, Max, 41, 42, 50, 64, 65, 80–81, 228,
232
Goethe, Johann Wolfgang von, 63
The Good Apprentice (Murdoch), 210–11
Good Morning America, 177
Goodall, Jane, 93
Goodman, Richard, 179–80
Gorer, Geoffrey, 53
Gosse, Edmund, 88
Gregory, Herbert, 202
Griffin, Marion Mahony, 58
Griffin, Merv, 177
Griffin, Walter Burley, 58
Griffith University, 8, 12, 69, 196

Haddon, A. C., 39
Halley, Edmund, 260
Hamlet (Shakespeare), 234
Handy, Edward Craighill, 202, 214, 216
Harlow, Harry, 232
Harris, Marvin, 178, 183
Harrison, Graham, 118
Harrison, Wayne, 207
Harrisson, Tom, 52, 81, 108, 128, 136, 166,
253; animosity toward Freeman, 66–67;

compassion for, 167; death of, 166–67;
Freeman and "evil genius" of, 73, 74, 75–
76, 77, 78; "Kierkegaardian earthquake"
for Freeman and, 66–69, 229, 269n28; "pornographic carvings" controversy, 67, 68–69,
71–72
Harvard University, 62, 64, 87, 114, 178, 213, 237
Harvard University Press, 127, 171, 175–76, 177,
184, 215, 237, 250; reviews on *Margaret
Mead* by anthropologists from, 178
Heimann, Judith, 66–68, 72, 75, 229, 252, 253
Heimans, Frank, 12, 17, 18, 33, 40, 54, 98–99, 132,
139, 214, 255; Mead controversy, approach
to Freeman with proposition of film about
(1986), 197. See also *Margaret Mead and
Samoa* (Heimans film), 198–99, 202, 203
Hellenthal, Walter, 21–22
Heppell, Michael, 166, 248
Herdt, Gil, 238
Heretic (Williamson play), 5, 98, 106, 207–9
Hitler, Adolf, 22
Hocart, A. M., 39
Holmes, Lowell, 106–7, 109, 164, 175, 180, 183,
194, 198, 209, 211, 238, 252; tenacity of criti-
cism of Freeman (and personal animosity
toward), 188–89; triumphant taunting by
Freeman of, 190; "visceral" nature of criti-
cisms of Freeman, 184
Hong Kong, 37
Hopkins, Gerard Manley, 250
Howard, Jane, 171
Hunter, Sir Thomas, 24
Husserl, Edmund, 81
Huxley, Aldous, 138
Huxley, Francis, 93
Huxley, Julian, 87, 230, 232
Huxley, Thomas Henry, 23, 243, 256

Iban Agriculture (Freeman), 45–46, 48, 61
Iban people: dry rice cultivation, 45–46, 47, 48;
Freeman's work with, 4, 7, 12, 43–57, 61–
63, 67, 69–70, 71–73, 75, 76, 77, 80–81, 89,
97, 108, 118, 129, 141, 166–67, 170, 195, 206,
228–29, 233–34, 248, 256; headhunting rituals, 80; kinship structure, 54, 62; language,
44; long-house, 46; religious rituals, 63, 73,

80, 85, 89, 167; rites and festivals, 48, 80; Rumah Nyala, 45, 46, 47; shamanistic rituals, 89; social structure, 63, 73; traditional beliefs and values, 73; *tuai rumah* (longhouse headman), 48
Ilahita Arapesh of Papua New Guinea, 259
Institute of Anthropology at Oxford, 93, 94
Isherwood, Christopher, 138

Jakeway, Derek, 75, 76, 77
Jamison, Kay Redfield, 135
Jensen, Erik, 167
Journal of the Polynesian Society, 25, 29, 218
Judd, Ellen R., 173

Kaberry, Phyllis, 10
Kaye, Danny, 49
Keesing, Felix, 117
Keesing, Roger, 117–18, 119–20, 124, 164
Kepler, Johannes, 186
Klein, Harry S., 90–93
Klein, Melanie, 90, 93, 234
Krämer, Augustin, 105
Krishnamurti, Jiddu, 23–24, 25, 32, 40, 84, 129, 243, 244
Kroeber, Alfred, 162, 172, 230, 235
Kuching, 37, 66–67, 69, 71, 74, 75, 76, 77, 79, 81, 86, 132, 167
Kuper, Adam, 183, 200, 203–4, 212, 244, 254, 256, 259

Lawrence, Peter, 128
Leach, Edmund, 13, 82, 84, 86, 93, 118, 167, 194, 229, 248; death of, 128; Freeman and, early years, 44, 51, 52, 53, 54, 57, 63, 64, 74
Leacock, Eleanor, 188, 189, 238–39
Leader, Darian, 71–72, 77, 78, 108, 140, 141
League of Nations, 27
Leenhardt, Maurice, 109
Left Book Club, 20
Leibniz, Gottfried Wilhelm, 169
Lelaulu, Lelei, 194
Lévi-Strauss, Claude, 44, 130
Levy, Robert, 178, 192, 194, 195
Lieberman, Leonard, 257
London Institute of Psychoanalysis, 88

London School of Economics (LSE), 36, 37, 39–40, 41, 44, 54
Lorenz, Konrad, 89, 92, 94, 104, 114, 115, 228, 230, 236
Los Angeles Times, 178
Low, Anthony, 114, 121–22, 126–27, 128, 175
Lowie, Robert, 172, 180
lysergic acid diethylamide (LSD), 97

McDowell, Edwin, 176
McDowell, Nancy, 178, 185, 188, 220, 238
Madan, T. N., 13, 17, 39, 229
Mageo, Jeanette, 188
Maitland, Gwen, 45, 51
The Making of Man: An Outline of Anthropology (Calverton), 24
Male and Female (Mead), 56
Malinowski, Bronisław, 36, 39–40, 41, 44, 52, 63, 118, 164, 194
Man Alone (Mulgan), 32
Manchester University, 50, 64, 80–81
The March (Doctorow, E. L.), 252–53
Marcus, George, 183, 241, 242, 252
Marcus Aurelius, 139
Margaret Mead and Samoa (Heimans film), 198–99, 202, 203
Margaret Mead and Samoa (Freeman), 3, 4, 111, 162, 203, 214, 236; aftermath of publication and Great Debate, reflections on, 195–96; attack without compromise, Freeman's defense method, 186–92; "badly written and deeply destructive," Weiner's view, 183; balance and purpose in, 195; "Beyond Determinism" as last chapter in, 195; biological and ethnological endorsements for, 239; Boas's role, attacks on Freeman's interpretation of, 182–83; book tour, mixed experience for Freeman, 178; dark quality, intensity, and passion in, worries about, 184; detonation day (January 31, 1983), 176, 250; female attitudes to, 181–2; force of reaction against, effect on Freeman of, 186; integrative approach to anthropology, call for, 175, 185; interactive argument in, 239; language of, fair-minded assessments of, 184–85; language of, restrained nature of, 162–63;

Margaret Mead and Samoa (*continued*)
media blitz about, 176–77, 223; methodology of, attacks on, 182–83; missed opportunity in, 238; negative elements of Samoan character in, 182; negative reviews, bombardment of, 186; onslaughts against, 178–84; opponents vanquished, hopes at various points (1980s), 196–97; radio and television interviews about, 177; reissue in paperback as *Margaret Mead and the Heretic*, 206; respect for Mead, expression of, 174–75; Samoan commentators on, 194; "shockwave of publicity" about, 180; support for Freeman in "banquet of consequences" on publication of, 179–80, 192–96; two distinct messages from, 172–76

Marquesas Islands, 202

Martinoir, Brian de, 67, 68, 74–77, 86–87, 125, 126

Masing, James, 166, 170, 206, 248

Mass Observation, 20

Mataʻafa, Fetaui, 105, 194

Matterhorn, 45

Matthews, L. Harrison, 89

Maude, Harry, 38

Max Planck Institute for Behavioral Physiology, 89, 94

Mayer, Maria, 11

Mayr, Ernst, 171, 239

Mead, Margaret, 33, 36, 38, 42, 56–57, 68, 72, 74, 83, 95, 96, 105–8, 117, 127, 131, 167–68, 259–60; achievements, Freeman's respect for, 165; adolescence in Samoa, criticism of "anecdotal" information on, 214–15; adolescence in Samoa, study aim of, 99–100, 158; anthropology, public face of, 3–4; authoritativeness of, 160; banishment of, 224–25; centenary of birth of, celebrations of (2001), 220; Coombs building encounter with Derek, 98–100; "culture-is-environmentally-determined" claims, 110; death of, 169; disapproval by Freeman of acceptance of *taupou* titles by, 202–3; exaggerated stories told by girls in Siʻufaga to, 197, 199–200, 204; Freeman–Mead controversy, 66, 70–71, 259; Freeman–

Mead controversy, beginnings of, 13, 28–29, 30–31, 109, 110; Freeman–Mead controversy, classic refutation exercise by Freeman, 100–101; Freeman–Mead controversy, coda concerning, 219–25; Freeman–Mead controversy, reignition of, 102–3; Freeman–Mead controversy, Shankman's musings on, 221–24, 225; Freeman's books on, effects of, 5; iconic status of, 160–61; ideas of, Freeman's education in, 24–25; interdisciplinary failure of anthropology, identification of, 231; Library of Congress exhibition of treasures from Mead archive, 220; "Life as a Samoan Girl," 216; *Macmillan Dictionary of Anthropology* entry for, 227; *New World Encyclopedia*'s online entry on, 7; New Zealand intellectual influences on, 165; preconceptions imported by, evidence of, 216; "probative" significance of Faʻamu's revelations for, 201–2; public advocacy of, 160; recognition of Freeman's critical works, 164–65; rehabilitation of, 224–25; response to correspondence from Freeman, 161; reversal of Freeman's strictures against, ever-continuing nature of, 6; "romantic and erroneous" picture of Samoa, Freeman's view, 88; Samoan culture, absorption of ideas on, 19–20; sexual behavior in Samoa, positive depiction of, 162; sexual behavior stories told by girls in Siʻufaga to, 197, 199–200, 204; shared missions and obligations with Freeman, 170; totemic figure in American anthropology of, 192–93; Tuzin as student for Freeman, recommendation by, 10; "unscientific maneuvering," accusation of, 185

Medawar, Peter, 231

Meggitt, Mervyn, 179, 186

Meleisea, Malama, 181–82, 185

Mendel, Gregor Johann, 230

Merleau-Ponty, Maurice, 81

Métraux, Rhoda, 170

Milton, John, 85

Minkowski, Eugène, 81

Money-Kyrle, Roger, 87

Montagu, Ashley, 168, 236

Morris, Desmond, 89

Morris, Stephen, 78
Morrison, Heather, 24
The Most Offending Soul Alive (Heimann), 66
Mount Ainslie, 129–30
Mount Evans: illustration of, *143*; trauma for Freeman on, 23
Mount Kinabalu, 167
Mulgan, John, 32
Mulinuʻu II, Mataʻafa Fiamē Faumuina, 103–4
Munro, Doug, 12
Murdoch, Iris, 210–11
Murray, Stephen, 180; "bumbling, purblind scholarship," accusation against, 187

Nadel, Siegfried, 4, 41, 53, 56–57, 59–60, 72–73, 80, 83–84, 87, 89, 111, 112–13, 243; sudden death of, 63–64
Nader, Laura, 178, 183, 198, 252
National Library of Australia, 12
Nature, 200
Naval Intelligence, 36
Needham, Rodney, 69, 73, 74, 75, 82, 167, 229, 234, 253
Neumann, Hans, 31; death of, 128
New Scientist, 206
New World Encyclopedia, 7
New York Times, 176, 239
Newsweek, 177
Nietzsche, Friedrich, 169
Not Even Wrong (Orans), 211

Oceania, 217
Oceania (journal), 182
Oliver, Douglas, 62, 64, 179, 212, 213, 237, 248, 253
O'Meara, Tim, 193, 256
On Human Nature (Wilson), 237
Orans, Martin, 210–12, 215–16
Orwell, George, 37
Otago Museum, 4, 39, 55, 264n23
Otago University, 55, 56–57, 58
Oxford University, 44, 50–51, 52

Pacific Defense Conference (Wellington, April 1939), 32
Pacific Islands Monthly, 194

Pacific Science Congress, Thailand (1957), 73
Pacific Studies, 185, 189, 220
Pago Pago, 103; hospitalization of Freeman in, 107–8; Japanese shelling of, 32
Papua New Guinea, 10, 60, 112–13, 125, 128, 165, 176, 181, 259
Passmore, John, 58
Pasteur, Louis, 112
Patrick (Iban interpreter at Rumah Nyala), 47
Pearl Harbor, Japanese attack on, 32
Peranio, Roger, 73–74, 99, 125
Peterson, Nicholas, 117, 124
Pfeiffer, John, 171, 239
The Phil Donahue Show, 177
physical anthropology, 52, 183, 227, 231
Pinker, Steven, 250–51
Ploeg, Anton, 86, 124, 125
Popper, Karl, 13, 40, 84, 118, 163, 168, 172, 175, 228, 240–41, 249; Popperian principles, 98
Popular Front, 20
postmodernism, 200, 203, 207, 241, 242, 249, 289n45
Poto (Saʻanapu housekeeper), 104
Poumele, Galeaʻi, 199
Pratt, George, 38

Quadrant, 196–97
Quest for the Real Samoa (Holmes), 188–89, 194

Radcliffe-Brown, Alfred R., 39, 41, 42, 52, 59, 82, 164, 194, 231
Radin, Paul, 180
Rappaport, Roy, 177, 187, 193, 215, 242; "intellectual deviousness," accusation against, 187
Reay, Marie, 124
Redfield, Robert, 180
reflexive anthropology, 200, 220, 241, 259
Report on the Iban (Freeman), 46, 53, 248
Research School of Pacific Studies (RSPacS), 59, 60, 87, 274n2; memoirs of life in, Freeman in, 111–12
Roheim, Géza, 161
Rosenberg, Wolfgang, 25
Rousseau, Jerome, 167, 169–70
Russell, Bertrand, 45, 139, 169

Saʻanapu: Freeman and, 30–31, 33, 37–8, 41–42, 45, 56, 99, 102–5, 107, 109, *151*, 161, 210, 233, 255, 264n10; villagers in, *149*

Sahlins, Marshall, 61–62, 74, 100, 102, 206

Saint Anselm, 138

Saint Augustine's College in Canterbury, 44

Salaʻilua: A Samoan Mystery (Shore), 190–91

Saler, Benson, 248

Salient, 21, 24–25

Salk, Jonas, 13, 168, 205, 242

Salk Institute in San Diego, 168, 201, 205, 242

Samoan islands, 9, 103, *152*; assault on a chief by a *tauleʻaleʻa* (untitled man), 104; British officialdom in, 51–52; ceremonial abasement (*ifoga*) in, 31; expulsion of a chief (*aliʻi*) from Saʻanapu, 104; Falemaunga Caves, 29; Freeman's love for, 29; genealogical knowledge of, closely guarded domain of, 101; Mau, Samoan resistance movement, 27, 194; Nelson Memorial Library in Apia, 104; New Zealand administration in, 28, 31; Pago Pago, Japanese shelling of, 32; ritual submission (*ifoga*), 104; Seuao Cave in Safata, 30; social structures in, 42; titled chiefs (*matai*) in, dominance behavior of, 31, 42, 104–5, 159, 233, 234; village councils (*fono*) meetings, 30, 42, 104, 109; Western Samoa, independence negotiations with New Zealand, 56; World War II, Western Samoa in, 27–28, 32–33. *See also* Saʻanapu

Sandall, Philippa, 213–14

Sandin, Benedict, 167

Sapir, Edward, 20

Sarawak, 37, 45–46, 50–54, 61–62, 66–74, 76–79, 81–87, 90, 97, 106, 108, 131–32, 141–42, 166, 178, 203, 208, 228; Dayaks of, 4, 44, 51

Sarawak incident, 66, 69, 77–78, 85, 97, 119, 131, 186, 249, 252

Sargant, William, 79

Sassoon, Siegfried, 251

Sather, Clifford, 167, 248

Savaiʻi, Western Samoa, 27, 28, 32, *145*, 191

Scheper-Hughes, Nancy, 238–39

Schneider, David, 176–77, 183, 230, 252

Schoeffel, Penelope, 181–82, 185, 248, 255

School of Oriental and African Studies (SOAS), 36, 55, 94

Schwartz, Theodore, 176, 181, 183, 195

Science, 178

Semang people of Malaya, 234

Seneca, 186

Sepik area of Papua New Guinea, 10

Shakespeare, William, 186, 234

Shankman, Paul, 40, 98, 99, 100, 106, 108, 123, 185, 211, 226, 245; chronology of Freeman's critique of Mead, probe on, 221–22; Freeman–Mead controversy, musings on, 221–24, 225; freeman's statistics on "forceful rape," downplay of, 181; "Pensacola Crackpot" and one of "Four Horsemen of the Apocalypse," 221; rehabilitation attempt for Mead's Samoa findings, 162

Shipton, Eric, 40

Shore, Bradd, 177, 179, 180, 182, 184–85, 201; critic of Freeman, frequently targeted in rebuttal, 188; review of *Margaret Mead*, disabling dualism in, 190; self-promotion accusation against Freeman, 192; sexual behavior, perspective on *moetotole* and, 190

Silverman, Martin, 184, 238

Sinclair, Keith, 34–6

Sisi (Samoan nurse), 31, 35, 103

Skeptical Inquirer, 221

Skinner, H. D. ("Harry"), 39, 55, 62, 165

Smythies, John R., 75

Snelus, Alan, 77

Social Behavior in Animals (Tinbergen), 94

Social Change in Tikopia (Firth), 104

Social Organization of Manuʻa (Mead), 38, 164, 221

Sociobiology Examined (Montagu), 236

Sociobiology (Wilson), 236, 237

Soloi, pastor of Fitiuta (originally from Saʻanapu), 105, 107–8

Spate, Oscar, 60, 114, 117, 163

Spike, 21, 22–23

Stanner, Bill, 33, 60, 63, 64–65, 82–83, 96, 113, 114, 115, 124, 128, 132–33, 232–33; restrictive notion of anthropology from, Freeman's rejection of, 102–3, 119

Stevenson, Robert Louis, 29, 171, 225

Stocking, George, 175, 180, 194, 231, 240–41, 252
Strathern, Andrew, 242
Strathern, Marilyn, 124, 182, 184
Swain, Grant, 207
Switzerland, 45
Sydney Theatre Company, 207–8
Sydney University, 59, 64, 112, 114, 128, 186, 267n20

Tavistock Institute of Human Relations, 87
Tcherkézoff, Serge, 211, 226–27, 264n10; "Is Anthropology about Individual Agency or Culture? Or Why 'Old Derek' Is Doubly Wrong," 217–19
Terkel, Studs, 177
Thomas, Dylan, 234
Thomas Aquinas, 186
Time magazine, 157, 179
Tinbergen, Nikolaas, 13, 87, 89, 94, 114, 139, 228, 230, 232, 235, 236, 239
Torgovnik, Marianna, 159
Totem and Taboo (Freud), 97
The Trashing of Margaret Mead (Shankman), 98, 222–23, 224, 226
Trethowan, W. H., 78, 83, 132
Trinity College, Dublin, 39
Tristes tropiques (Lévi-Strauss), 130
Tuiteleleapaga, Napoleone, 170, 194
Turnbull, A. C., 31
Turnbull, Colin, 183, 252
Turnbull Library, Wellington, 38, 39
Turner, Victor, 81, 228
Tuzin, Don, 6, 9–10, 17, 22, 30, 37, 90, 94, 107, 108, 116, 117, 124, 129–30, 136, 170, 195, 196, 212, 213–14, 229, 239, 244–45, 260; death of, 10–11; doctoral research in Papua New Guinea, 165; engagement with Freeman, uplifting nature of, 125–26; extreme emotionalism, Derek's personal view to, 235–36; Freeman and nature/nurture, reflection on, 258; Freeman papers and, 11–12; Freeman's original biographer, 12–13; "grotesque" nature of AAA criticism of *Margaret Mead* in Chicago, 179; illness and death of, 10–11; "Miraculous Voices" essay (1984), 258–59, 288n24; monumental diary collection

of Freeman, access to, 140; recommendation to Freeman as student by, 10; reunion in San Diego with, 168

University of California at San Diego (UCSD), 75, 80, 130, 168, 176, 205, 216, 248; Mandeville Special Collections of Geisel Library at, 11; Melanesian Archive at, 12
University of London regulations, 36
Upolu, Western Samoa, 28, 29, 30, 32, 103, 145
Upon That Mountain (Shipton), 40

Vainu'u, Fa'imoto ("Loani"), 30
Vainu'u, Lauvī, 30, *146*
Van Gogh, Vincent, 138
Van Stavaren, Miss (primary teacher), 20, 91

Walters, Barbara, 177
Wanner, Eric, 176
Washburn, Sherwood, 138, 231, 235
Watson, James, 231
Weil, Simone, 138
Weiner, Annette, 180–81, 183
Wellington Cooperative Book Society, 24
Wendt, Albert, 170
Wilde, Oscar, 11
Williamson, David, 5, 98, 99, 106, 133, 135, 206–9, 221, 226
Wilson, E.O., 13, 118, 178, 236, 237–38, 239, 243, 257
Wittgenstein, Ludwig, 169
Wolf, Eric, 241
World War II: Freeman's war-time experiences, 33–35, 36–37; Japanese surrender, 37; Western Samoa in, 27–28, 32–33
Worsley, Peter, 59–60
Writing Culture (Clifford and Marcus), 241
Wu, David, 124

Yanomamö controversy, 219
Young, Michael, 39, 118

Zeldin, Theodore, 258
Zen Buddhism (and Buddhist symbolism), 129, 197, 241, 243–44, 260, 270n45
Zoological Society, 87, 89